CONTENTS

Acknowledgments

I want to acknowledge and express my gratitude and warm appreciation to:

Babson College for its generous offer to publish this book on the occasion of the Centennial Celebration of its founding in 1919 and for granting me the privilege of serving as Babson's seventh president. In particular, I would like to thank the following individuals at the college who were personally helpful in the publishing process: President Kerry Healey, Mark Rice, Ed Chiu, Andy Tiedemann, Cheryl Robock, and Lacy Garcia.

My talented editor and friend, Frank White, who made many helpful suggestions, additions, and corrections to my manuscript.

Nader Darehshori, retired CEO of Houghton Mifflin Company, who not only thoughtfully critiqued my manuscript but also put me in contact with several other individuals who were helpful in the publishing process.

The following friends and professionals who generously read or reviewed various versions of my text and who provided me with helpful feedback: Irv Rockwell, Barry Wanger, Mark Fuller, Steve Smith, Amanda Strong, John McArthur, and John Mackey.

The team at Strategic Communications Inc., who shepherded the manuscript through the final publishing process.

Finally, I want to acknowledge the help, encouragement, patience, and love of Charlotte, Kristin, Katrina, and Eric, all of whom played a key role in helping to bring this book to life.

INTRODUCTION

I seem to have been born with a well-developed sense of curiosity about the great mysteries of life. One summer evening in 1937, when I was four, my father and I were outside in the big back yard of our house, looking up at the stars in the sky. According to my father, who later described the incident in writing, the following conversation ensued:

"Daddy—what are stars?"

"That is a little hard to explain to a little fellow like you. There they are way off in the sky—and they are like other worlds. They appear to be pretty small for they are so far away. But they are really very big and some of them may have people living on them, just as we do on this world."

"Don't tell me! Don't tell me! I know! I learned about them in nursery school. If we lived on a star and looked at our world—it would look just like a star."

"That's right son—you have the idea perfectly."

After a long pause—"Dad, who made the stars?"

"I guess God made them."

"Did he make everything? The stars, and the world, and the trees, and the animals, and all the people?"

"That's right, son. I guess he made them all."

After a very long pause—to think it through—"Who gave him the idea?"

Evidently, my father was stumped for an answer. And many, many years later, so, too, am I.

The foregoing incident must have made an impact on my father, for he apparently gave it further thought. Following his description of the conversation, he put the following musings into writing:

> "So, there we have exemplified the difference between most of us who are adults and the small boy, thirsty for knowledge, who is learning new things at a tremendous rate. We adults know what we know. It is our tendency to close our minds and stop learning.
>
> 'Who gave HIM the idea?' was a logical question. Our adult minds would have instantly considered it final when told that God, the Alpha and Omega, had created everything. But to the child, to whom God was a very personal being, it was very logical to think one step further. His was truly the inquiring type of mind.
>
> If we who are adults could always maintain this same freshness of thinking when we tackle our problems—thinking one step beyond what we consider to be the accepted facts—how far might we progress? Newton saw the apple fall—he and everyone else knew that an apple always fell—but he wondered why it fell.
>
> The sum total of our accumulated knowledge exists today only because along the way, there has always been some person who thought one step beyond the known facts."

Now I am in my eighties and I am still searching for the answer to the question: "Who gave HIM the idea?"

. . . . .

On balance, I have lived a blessed existence. To be sure, my life hasn't all been a garden of delights. But I have had a very special wife, a great family, reasonable intelligence, a loving upbringing, a fine education, a (mostly) fulfilling professional life, many friends, excellent health, myriad adventures, and lots of laughter. But most of all, I continue to have a zest for living and a still-active curiosity about all things large and small.

Then there are my shortcomings. I don't take criticism well and I can get very defensive. I am often impatient. I lose my temper from time to time (especially when dealing with call-center operators). I am intermittently deficient in right-brain creativity. I am a lifelong penny pincher. I can be selective in my generosity and in my sense of compassion. I am, at times, quite selfish. I talk too much and listen too little. And there are myriad other character traits that I possess and acts I have committed about which I am not proud. In short, I am heavily indebted to other peoples' willingness to forgive.

As I proceed through my ninth decade, I've concluded that now is as good a time as any to engage in a bit of self-reflection. I think of this as "rummaging in the attic of my mind." Hence, this memoir. Or should I call it an autobiography, or perhaps just "a collection of recollections?" Take your pick.

My dear wife, Charlotte, keeps asking: "For what audience are you writing these recollections?" My reply is: "I'm writing them for you and for our kids and grandkids, and their kids and grandkids, so that future generations in the family will have a better understanding of their heritage." But perhaps a more honest answer would be that I am writing them for myself. I am finding it fulfilling to have a second go at reliving my life. I am enjoying the good parts, suffering once again through the bad parts, skimming quickly over the boring parts, and trying my best to avoid obsessing about my personal shortcomings.

CHAPTER ONE

FAMILY HERITAGE

"As the twig is bent, so grows the tree."
Roman Poet Virgil, 70 BC – 19 BC

My twig grew from Midwestern soil and was bent by loving parents with Midwestern values. Those values, for the most part, have stood me in good stead for eight decades:

"Get a good education"
"Work hard and you'll get ahead"
"Think of others"
"Whatever you do, do it to the best of your ability and make something
 beautiful of it"
"If at first you don't succeed, try, try again"
"The mind, like steel, is kept bright through use"
"Be frugal . . . rub every nickel twice before you spend it"
"Eat your Brussels sprouts; vegetables are good for you"
"Drink lots of milk and take your ABDG vitamins every day"
"Clean your plate, there are children starving in India"
"Keep your room tidy"
"Sticks and stones can break your bones, but words can never hurt you"
"Roosevelt with his 'New Deal' is ruining the country"
"Don't think dirty thoughts"

                                                    . . . and so on

I was born on September 20, 1933, at the Evanston Hospital in Evanston, Illinois. It was the height of the Great Depression in America and the year in which fewer babies were born per capita than in any other year of the 20th century. On reflection more than eight decades later, I have come to believe that being a "child of the Depression" from the Midwest has had, for better or worse, a profound impact on the subsequent trajectory of my life.

I was the second of two children born into my family. My sister, Mary Nancy Sorenson, was two years older than me. For some reason they never fully explained to me, my parents decided to name me Ralph Zellar Sorenson II, after my father.

The story goes that while Mother and I were still in the hospital, my Uncle Ky and Uncle Jim came to visit. Uncle Ky reportedly said, "Why do you want to call him Ralph Zellar Sorenson the Second? That's a terrible moniker for a little kid and besides there is already one Ralph in the family." Uncle Jim then chimed in, "I agree . . . but he sure is a cute little buddy." And so I unofficially became "Buddy," which later morphed into "Bud."

As for me, I grew up not much liking either Ralph or Bud, but I learned to live with both. Oddly enough, to this day I am never sure how to respond when asked my name. Ralph still sounds stiff and Bud sounds like I belong to a gang. C'est la vie!

My father, the original Ralph Zellar Sorenson, was born in Eau Claire, Wisconsin, on May 28, 1898. My mother, Verna Mary Koenig Sorenson, was born a couple of months later on August 8, 1898, in Chippewa Falls, a little town about 10 miles away. Despite the proximity of their birthplaces, they didn't meet each other until they were both about 30 and living in Chicago, Illinois.

My father's father, Anton Sorenson, and grandfather, Lars, emigrated from the tiny village of Tvedestrand, Norway, to Wisconsin in 1882, hence my surname Sorenson. My father's mother was Jane Aurandt and her heritage was a mixture of German and Pennsylvania Dutch. Anton and Jane were married in the mid-1880s and had four sons (Clarence, Sid, Harry, Ralph) and a daughter (Cecile). Anton, who worked first as a lumberjack and later for the local gas utility company in Eau Claire, died when my father was about four. His mother later married James Curtis and had another son (James) in the early 1900s. Despite the fact that he lost his father at such an early age, my father always identified strongly with his Norwegian heritage. I subsequently inherited this sense of identification.

On my mother's side of the family, the heritage was German. Her father, William Koenig, was a Methodist minister in Minnesota and Wisconsin. He traveled from parish to parish by horse and buggy every Sunday and preached each sermon in both English and German. Her mother, Pauline, was a twin and was born in Germany. She immigrated to the United States at an early age and later met and married William. Together they had six children: Arthur, Rose, Esther, Irene,

Jeannette, and my mother, Verna, who was the youngest, the prettiest, the most mischievous, and the most rebellious.

Both my father and mother apparently had relatively happy childhoods as they grew up in their respective hometowns in northern Wisconsin. As long as he lived, my dad regaled my sister and me with tales of all of the shenanigans he and his many boyhood friends were involved in. Half the fun was hearing my dad recite the wacky nicknames of these friends. He himself was Gug, and his two oldest brothers were Ky and Ig. Then there were Soggy, Toursie, Tuffy, Crutchy, Hecky, Nippy, CaCa, and, finally, Billy Ding Dong.

One of our favorite stories was how my dad and his pals delighted in playing tricks on "Old Bill Wetzel," the erstwhile and ever-vigilant town cop in Eau Claire. For example, he would tell how he and his buddies stole Old Bill's policeman's hat and hoisted it to the top of a lamppost. Whereupon they laughed with glee as Old Bill, red-faced and furious upon discovering their prank, chased them down to Half Moon Lake and into their favorite cave where there was a small hole in the roof through which their lithe bodies wriggled but Old Bill's rotund body could not.

Then there were the tales about log rolling contests down at the lumber mill on the lake and about overturned outhouses on Halloween. Another of my favorites was about how, one snowy winter day, my dad, on a bet, successfully guided his Flexible Flyer sled down the hill and through the front and back runners of a moving horse drawn sleigh that was gliding down the road. Apparently, it was a miracle of perfect timing.

More tragic was the account of how my dad, around the age of four (the same year he lost his father) saw his brother Harry, aged six, get run over by a trolley car and killed. This happened just after my dad, his two oldest brothers (Ky, aka Clarence, and Ig, aka Sidney), and Harry had jumped off the tailgate of a hay wagon on which they had been hitching a ride to town and Harry turned the wrong way into the path of the trolley. Also sobering was the story of how some never-identified kid heaved a brick over a high wooden fence as my dad was walking home from school on the other side. The brick hit my dad on the head and he had to have a metal plate implanted into the bone of his skull. The plate remained there until he died at age 91.

Evidently my dad, as a teenager, was smart, articulate, and popular. In high school, he was valedictorian of his class, won first prize in the annual statewide debate contest, and was elected president of his class. Though he never went to college, he was extremely well read. Later in his life, his hobby was collecting rare books, particularly those in the category of Americana.

More important to me, as his son, was that my dad was also a lovely human being. He was the kindest, most considerate, most humble and most compassionate man I have had the privilege to know. He also had a wonderful sense of humor. He was my hero and a great role model; I never could understand why he wasn't elected president of the United States!

My father's first job after graduating from high school in 1916 was as the manager of the local electric power company in a nearby Wisconsin town. For a young man of 19, this position carried with it considerable responsibility. In the summer of 1918, during the final year of World War I, his early career was interrupted when he volunteered to serve in the U.S. Army Tank Corps. In November 1918, after he had been trained and just as his tank unit was scheduled to sail to Europe, the Armistice was declared. He was discharged in January 1919 and returned to the Wisconsin, Minnesota Light and Power Company as operating manager of their branch in Menomonie, Wisconsin.

Although my father didn't see WWI military action in Europe, his brother Sid did. Upon returning to the U.S. after the Armistice, Sid, a taciturn man, spoke little about what had happened to him in Europe. However, when I was growing up, my father told Nancy and me about how, many years after the war, he had a chance meeting with a man at a convention in Detroit who had served with Sid in France. Having established that Sid and he had seen wartime action together, the man said to my dad, "Wasn't that the damnedest thing that happened to Sid in the Battle of the Marne?" My dad replied, "Why, what do you mean?" The fellow said, "About how he died and came back to life." Dad said, "I don't know anything about that, tell me."

The fellow then described how one afternoon a cannon shell had exploded near Sid in a foxhole and appeared to have killed him. Believing that he was dead, the medics took him to a nearby farmhouse that was being used as a makeshift morgue. They covered his corpse with a blanket and put it in an unheated room with other dead soldiers awaiting burial. Then they locked the door. At about three o'clock the following morning, Sid apparently regained consciousness and came back to life. He threw off the blanket, looked around in the dark and wondered where the hell he was. It no doubt scared the bejesus out of him to see the corpses around him. He arose and pounded on the inside of the door and shouted to be let out. When a medic opened the door, he was unnerved to see a ghost emerge. After the Armistice, Sid returned home to Eau Claire and quietly resumed his life there. Apparently, he subsequently never said a word to anyone about his having "risen from the dead." Of course, this story became part of our family lore. Nancy and I never tired of asking Dad to recount it around the dinner table.

Meanwhile, my mother, Verna, experienced all the advantages and disadvantages of growing up the youngest of five siblings. Pretty and precocious, she was most likely her parents' favorite child. However, I suspect that, at times, she found it difficult to grow up in a pre-suffrage, straight-laced, religious, Methodist home where drinking, smoking, dancing, flirting, and card playing were all "verboten." Naturally, when she got into her teens, she did all of these things. She apparently had lots of friends and a fair number of beaux. She was quite bright and had considerable creative talent. She painted watercolors and delicate designs on fine china. Following high school, she worked as a bank teller at the First National Bank of Chippewa Falls.

Both my mother and father left Wisconsin in their twenties to seek their fortunes and both ended up in Chicago. The Roaring Twenties were a heady time to be in the Windy City. It was home to oceans of bootleg booze, countless speakeasies, the "Gold Coast," flappers dancing the Charleston, Al Capone, and a rogues' gallery of other odd and assorted gangsters. It was also home to Colonel McCormick's notoriously conservative Chicago Tribune newspaper. By the mid-twenties, business was booming and the stock market was soaring. My mother and dad saw opportunity there.

My mom got a job at the Household Finance Company and enrolled in some accounting courses at the University of Chicago, where she earned a semester or two of credit but never completed a degree. It was rare for women to go to college in that era. Mother also seemed to have dated a lot. By all accounts she loved her life in Chicago!

Meanwhile, in 1926 my dad became Chicago branch manager of the Eureka Vacuum Cleaner Company. Apparently, he was pretty good at it because he rose steadily to become the overall sales manager for the western half of the United States. It was during the last half of the twenties that he began collecting rare books and investing in the stock market. He bought a car. He was a young man on the rise. Later in life, he told me stories about this period in his life. The only one that now sticks in my mind is about how his car was parked in the same garage on the same day that the infamous Chicago Valentine's Day gang murders took place.

My dad was introduced by a mutual friend to my mom sometime in 1929. I recall that Mom told Nancy and me that she was engaged to someone else at the time. In any case, some strong chemistry must have been at work during that first meeting because my mother broke off her other engagement and subsequently married my dad on June 14, 1930. The newlyweds initially lived in an apartment on the south side of Evanston, a suburb of Chicago, where just over a year later, on July 7, 1931, my sister Nancy was born.

Shortly before my parents' wedding, the huge stock market crash occurred on Black Friday in late October 1929, presaging the beginning of the Great Depression of the 1930s. At the time, my father had the not-inconsiderable sum of $50,000 invested in the market. He lost it all in the months after the crash.

Many years later, I came to realize what an enormously negative impact this loss and the subsequent Great Depression had on my father's psyche and perhaps that of my mother as well. From riding high and having a feeling of growing prosperity, overnight the young couple suddenly found themselves in a position where, of necessity, they had to be vigilant about the money they spent. In sum, it made them more cautious and conservative in their attitude toward life. It was during this era that they began their lifelong habit of "living frugally and rubbing every nickel twice before they spent it." This was the atmosphere in which I grew up and I am sure some of that mentality influenced me. To this day, I have the habit of watching my pennies and nickels.

This episode also contributed to my father's policy during the rest of his life of always choosing the security of a steady job or a conservative course of action rather than striking out toward some endeavor that entailed more risk and uncertainty. In other words, my father lost some of his entrepreneurial spirit. I hasten to add that, in retrospect, my father and mother were much more fortunate in the Great Depression than the majority of Americans, many of whom suffered greatly by losing their jobs, becoming destitute, or worse. By contrast, my father kept his job with the Eureka Vacuum Company during the early thirties and, in fact, continued to make his way up the career ladder in that firm. And there was always enough money to keep the Sorenson family housed, clothed, fed, and solidly middle class.

One result of the Depression within the Sorenson household was that my father and mother became staunch lifelong Republicans. This was because neither of my parents could stand President Franklin Delano Roosevelt and what they considered his New Deal nonsense. They felt the president was flailing about ineffectually and inconsistently with his New Deal public works programs like the National Recovery Administration (NRA), Works Progress Administration (WPA), Civilian Conservation Corps (CCC), Agricultural Adjustment Act (AAA), and the Public Works Administration (PWA). They also decried many of Roosevelt's political machinations, such as his efforts in his second term to "stack" the Supreme Court with Democrats. As a result, my parents felt the Depression lasted far longer than it should have and that, in the end, it was only the unfortunate advent of World War II that eventually turned the country's economy around.

CHAPTER TWO

EARLY MEMORIES

My own first memories date back to when I was about three years old. In 1932, my parents and Nancy had moved from their apartment to 2705 Ridge Avenue, a big four-bedroom rented brick house directly across from the Evanston hospital. It was the depths of the Depression and, fortunately, the rent was affordable for my parents.

I recall this house as a wonderful place in which to grow up. It had two screened-in sleeping porches on the second floor; one off of Nancy's room and one big one that had doors onto it from both my parents' room and what subsequently became my room. On returning from the hospital in early October 1933, just after my birth, my parents put my crib out onto this screened porch and had me sleep outdoors in the cool autumn air. Evidently, they subscribed to the theory that this would "toughen up my immune system right from the beginning." During the entire 10 years I lived in this house, I spent half of each year sleeping outside in the fresh air. I think it must have worked, because I have been blessed with good health most of my life.

One of my earliest recollections relates to how I lost my front baby teeth. One day when I was about four, my mother was taking me to nursery school at the local Presbyterian church. Like most churches, it had concrete steps leading to the front door. I distinctly remember tripping on one step and taking a bite out of the corner of the concrete step above. Goodbye, baby front teeth! It's amazing how a traumatic moment like this can make an indelible impact on one's memory even after 80 years.

Another early memory was of my first pet, Oscar the duck. How or why Oscar joined our family, I have no idea. He was white and had a long neck and we kept him in a fenced-in area in our large back yard. One day, when no one was looking,

I plucked Oscar out of his pen. Then, carrying him under my arm, I crossed the busy street in front of the house, walked down the diagonal path that bisected the large vacant lot next to the Evanston hospital to make my way to Clancy Martin's drugstore. I really don't know why I thought this was a good idea; just exploring, I suppose. Anyway, Clancy was startled to see a little four-year-old boy with a duck wandering alone into his drugstore. Apparently, he recognized me, though, because he telephoned my mother to inquire whether she was missing a son and a duck. My frantic mother must have heaved a sigh of relief. She quickly recovered Oscar and me and brought us home. To the best of my recollection, that was the first and last time that I went on a wandering expedition with Oscar.

When I was about five, Daniel the Spaniel joined our household. A tan and white cocker spaniel puppy, Danny became one of the major loves of my life. To this day, I remember going for runs with him around the block at least a couple of times a day. I vividly recall asking myself why anyone would ever want to walk if they could have the marvelous feeling of running. Having a delightful running companion like Danny compounded the joy!

Danny turned out to be a wonderful addition to the family. All of us doted on him, and he lived to be 16 years old. He died after being hit by a car on his way home from across town where he had been visiting one of his female friends. By the time of his death, both Nancy and I had finished college and left home permanently. So, for the last five or six years of his life, Danny filled an important void for my mom and dad.

Our house in Evanston was only about a block-and-a-half away from a small public beach on the shore of Lake Michigan. By the time we were three or four, my mother, who loved swimming, had taught Nancy and me to swim. We both developed a lifelong love of the water. On most nice summer days, we would play on the beach and swim in the lake, where there was always a lifeguard. On weekends, my parents would often join us.

One Saturday, I remember playing with my parents in the shallow water when a heavy-set teenage neighbor kid started shouting for help about a hundred yards out in the lake. Evidently, the lifeguard on duty was either AWOL or not paying attention because no one seemed to be swimming to the young man's assistance. So my dad rose to the occasion and swam out to perform the rescue. I recall seeing the drowning boy grab my father around his neck. Dad, swimming for all he was worth and occasionally disappearing himself below the surface of the water, began hauling the boy toward shore. I was terrified that neither one of them was going to make it. But by sheer determination Dad *did* make it back to shore with his burden and saved the young man's life. I remember that he never received any thanks from the boy or his family, which seemed very unfair to me at the time. However, I don't think my father, in his modest way, expected any recognition. But in my young eyes, my dad, by his selfless act of courage that day, became a larger-than-life hero to me and an example I have never forgotten.

Entrepreneurial Insight #1: Raising Hamsters for Fun and Profit

Like a lot of kids our age, Nancy and I went through a range of pets, including the rather odd combination of snakes and hamsters. We learned a lot from all of our creatures, but some of them also provided valuable entrepreneurial experience. The hamsters stood out in this regard. We started with a pair and ended up with 82, more than we wanted or needed for pets. However, it turned out that hamsters were sought after for laboratory experiments. We ended up selling 50 or so of them to Northwestern University's biology lab, located about six blocks from our house. The rest we eventually sold for medical research to the Evanston hospital.

The hamsters gave Nancy and me our first exposure not only to being entrepreneurs but also to the miracle of reproduction. Hamsters, we discovered, love to produce baby hamsters. Nancy and I witnessed the entire cycle. I vividly recall rushing home from school one day to watch the birthing process.

Owning snakes and hamsters also taught us a lesson in discipline, which is very important when you are in business. The only way our parents would allow the animals into our house was if Nancy and I agreed to take full responsibility for ensuring that they were fed and watered and that their cages were kept clean. If we slipped up or failed to do our daily tasks, the snakes and hamsters would die! Of course, we also had to keep the two species separated, for obvious reasons.

Early on, some of them did pass away as a result of our negligence. Our consciences were pricked and our finances suffered, so thereafter we became more conscientious and the death rate dropped to near zero. Of course, nothing is ever perfect and there was the day that I forgot to close the doors of the cages. The result was mayhem in our basement with snakes chasing hamsters and us chasing snakes and hamsters around for days until we could round them up!

Lesson Learned: It's never too early to embark on an entrepreneurial journey, but if you want to be an entrepreneur, you have to stay focused!

The silkworms offered a more benign pastime. We somehow acquired a starter batch of seven- or eight-day-old worms, fed them leaves from a mulberry bush from across the street, and watched them grow. After about 20 days they began weaving the cocoons with which they covered themselves. Then something miraculous happened inside the cocoon: The worms transformed themselves into moths that eventually emerged from the cocoons and flew away! Ah, how glorious and mysterious is nature!

When I was five, I started kindergarten and later studied through fourth grade at Orrington Elementary School in Evanston. An excellent school, it was a block from our house and was also attended by the gifted children of a lot of faculty members from nearby Northwestern University. I give the teachers and other students there much credit for the strong educational start that served as the foundation for my subsequent academic career.

At the time, however, what I enjoyed most about kindergarten was being read wonderful stories by our teacher, taking daily naps on 3'x4' rectangular sheets of brown wrapping paper spread on the wooden floor, and having the job of keeping the clay in the clay crock moist so it could be easily molded by me and my classmates into marvelous shapes and figures.

In first grade, I was confronted by my first major ethical dilemma. Walking home through an alley one wintry afternoon with Nancy and our neighborhood pals, Howie Vaughn and Jacky O'Keiffe, one of them managed to smash in the cellar windows of a neighborhood house with the blades of the ice skates that were slung over his shoulder. Thinking that no one had seen us, we ran back to our respective homes. However, the next day an announcement was made over the school P.A. system saying that if any students had knowledge of a neighborhood window-breaking incident the previous afternoon, they should report immediately to office of Miss Todd, the principal.

Upon hearing that announcement, I instantly experienced a shiver of fear. I was the youngest of the four co-conspirators and the only one isolated in the first grade. What were the other perpetrators going to do? What should I do? Should I keep my trap shut or trot down the hall to Miss Todd's office and tell all? Not being familiar with the old concept of "honor among thieves" and being scared to death, I promptly made my way to the principal's office. Confronted by the stern eye of the formidable Miss Todd, I immediately spilled the beans and ratted out myself and my other three partners in crime! They, meanwhile, had all exercised omerta and observed the age-old code of silence. The punishment: Each of us had to pay 10 dollars in damages and apologize in person to the neighborhood homeowner. Nancy and I each paid our reparations out of our respective collections of silver dollars. This reduced my precious collection from 19 dollars down to 9! That was bad enough. But an even worse punishment was being ostracized and banished for several weeks from membership in the neighborhood gang. Would I do it again? It would be a tough decision!

Other memories of my five years as a student at Orrington Elementary School include secretly falling in love with Joan Blackburn in third grade and once, unbeknownst to her, kissing her on the back of her head while standing behind her in a lineup. Alas, at the time it was a case of unrequited love, since she paid no attention to me. Imagine my surprise, years later, to receive a call from her when she was a student at Vassar College and I was at Amherst College, asking me to go to her prom with her. Since I hadn't seen or heard from her for more than a dozen years, I decided not to risk it and took a pass on her invitation. Maybe she knew who I was, after all!

While at Orrington School, I also remember fierce games of kickball and "battle-royales" on the jungle gym in the school playground. In the winter, the school playing field was flooded and turned into an ice skating pond that made for an excellent place to learn to skate.

My one moment of glory at Orrington was playing the title role in the student production of the play *Rumpelstiltskin*. The play began with me being covered in the middle of the stage by an immense pile of hay. Five minutes into the first act, to the accompaniment of music and loud applause, I popped up out of the hay to confront the princess. It was a heady experience that gained me some notoriety as a budding actor.

Finally, I remember that when I was in third grade my mother made me go to Miss Peacock's Saturday dancing classes at the school. I hated going to those things. We had to wear neckties and white gloves. And occasionally we had to foxtrot with the imperious Miss Peacock herself, who wore such a tight girdle that it felt through my gloved hand like she must be made of steel!

On December 7, 1941, when I was eight, Pearl Harbor occurred and America entered World War II. As a family, our life didn't change too much. My father, who had served in World War I and was then 43, was too old for military service, although I believe that he gave it some thought. However, his younger half-brother, Jim, did serve in the Corps of Engineers and fought for several years against the Japanese in multiple island campaigns in the South Pacific. In addition, I had five older male cousins who served overseas in various branches of the military. All of them came home alive, although one was wounded, one contracted leukemia, and Uncle Jim suffered from a serious case of malaria in the South Pacific that forced him to spend a whole year after the war recovering in a military hospital.

My early memories of WWII are hazy. I remember my parents avidly following the course of the war in the daily *Chicago Tribune* and on nightly radio newscasts. My father also served in Evanston as a volunteer neighborhood air raid warden. I, meanwhile, bought bubble gum and collected the airplane cards that came along with my purchases. I became adept at identifying both American and enemy aircraft. My favorite airplane was the American P-38 Lightning twin fuselage fighter plane that I thought was really cool. But I also learned to identify Japanese Zeroes and Nazi Messerschmitts just in case I might look up one day and see them launching an attack over the shores of Lake Michigan.

I also learned patriotic ditties, although I'm not sure I fully understood their full meaning. For example, one that I still remember went like this:

> "Hitler had only one big ball,
> Goering had two, but they were small.
> Himmler had something similar,
> But Goebbels had no balls at all."

I believe this ditty came courtesy of creative G.I. composers serving in Europe. It was sung to the tune of what later became the theme song of the movie, *The Bridge on the River Kwai*. Others included "Der Fuhrer's Mustache," a parody of Hitler, and "The Russian Winter," about the folly of Hitler opening a second front to the east.

Influenced by wartime propaganda, my friends and I also learned how to make a verb out of the word "Jap," as in, "to Jap someone." This meant to betray or screw someone. It was a racist term, just as was the expression "to Jew someone" that was also still in use at the time. Racism was widespread in America in the 1940s. Today, more than 70 years later, these terms are rightly considered to be politically incorrect, even though the underlying racist sentiments may still exist.

Apart from gas rationing and growing a victory garden, however, my young life didn't change very much. Nancy and I loved going with our mother to Marshall Field's department store where we learned how to run up the down escalator and down the up escalator. We also found it fun and fascinating to stick our feet for minutes on end into the foot X-ray machines in the shoe department and study the bone structure of our feet. Of course, that was before the potentially harmful effects of X-rays were widely known.

One of my best memories of that time in my life was going alone with Nancy, at ages eight and ten respectively, on the elevated train (the "EL") from Evanston to Wrigley Field in Chicago to see the Chicago Cubs vanquish other National League baseball teams. We always brought our autograph books along in the hopes of getting yet another player's signature. Bill Nicholson and Phil Rizzuto were real catches. In the fall, we would also sneak into the Northwestern Wildcats football games at Dyche Stadium, about six blocks from our house. My prize autograph from those excursions was that of Otto Graham, the All-American quarterback and later pro football star.

In today's scarier post-millennial world, it would be unthinkable for suburban parents to allow their eight- and ten-year-old unaccompanied kids to take public transportation into the big city to see a baseball game or attend a college football game on their own. But in the 1930s and '40s it was a commonplace occurrence. Alas, change happens . . . and not always for the better.

A much scarier memory of my early years in Evanston was the afternoon when Nancy and I, aged nine and seven, were playing in the attic of our house and found a stash of Japanese paper lanterns. We also found some candles and matches and decided it would be fun to use the lanterns to light up the attic. Instead, we nearly burned down the house!

When the lantern paper caught on fire, Nancy and I took off at high speed down the stairs and out the front door, where we watched smoke seeping out of the vents at either end of the roof. Fortunately for us, my Uncle Jim was just coming up the front walk as we were tearing out the front door. He instantly bounded up the stairs, fetched some water from a second-floor bathroom and doused the flames in the attic. Having nearly burned down the house, Nancy and I learned the hard way that little kids should not play with matches.

Entrepreneurial Insight #2: Door-to-Door Sales

When I was eight, my father launched me on my first solo adventure as an entrepreneur in the world of business. He suggested I apply to the local Curtis Publishing Company representative for a magazine route, selling and delivering the *Saturday Evening Post* and *Ladies Home Journal* door-to-door. This I did for two years until we moved away from Evanston. I learned to ring doorbells within a six-block radius and give my pitch to whoever answered the door as to why a subscription to either or both of the magazines would be very beneficial to their household. Once I signed them up, I faithfully delivered the magazines on a weekly basis. On the whole, I was quite successful and earned what seemed at the time like a fair amount of money, which I used to underwrite my baseball games and bubble gum indulgences. I also was able to put some cash in my savings account so that I could occasionally buy a $25.00 10-year War Savings Bond for $18.75. Thanks to the foresight of my father, I still have the uncashed check from the Curtis Publishing Company for the first dollar that I ever earned on my own as an entrepreneur!

Lesson Learned: If you want to be an entrepreneur, always accept the help and advice of older, wiser mentors.

With the exception of the attic-burning incident, I have almost nothing but good memories of my first 10 years of growing up in Evanston.

CHAPTER THREE

OHIO

Life for the Sorenson family changed significantly in 1943. Two or three years earlier, my father had left the Eureka Vacuum Cleaner Company and joined the Westinghouse Electric Company. His new job was to help the company plan for the eventual postwar re-conversion of their facilities from manufacturing military products back to making household appliances. Initially, his responsibilities were based in Chicago. As an additional duty, he was temporarily loaned to the U.S. government as a consultant to the federal Office of Price Administration (OPM) that had been set up as an agency to set prices in the wartime economy. However, in 1943 Westinghouse asked him to transfer to Mansfield, Ohio, the location of the company's appliance division headquarters and the site of its manufacturing facilities.

My father evidently thought this was an offer that he couldn't, or shouldn't, refuse. My mother, on the other hand, was decidedly less than excited about the idea of moving away from her beloved Evanston—a community that she adored and where she and my father had many close friends. Nevertheless, loving my dad and being a dutiful wife, she reluctantly acquiesced to the transfer. As for Nancy and me, we were too young to have much of an opinion about the matter. Even though we, too, had loved our life and friends in Evanston, we looked at the proposed move as a new adventure.

Thus, in September 1943, one week before my 10th birthday, the moving van arrived, and we immigrated to the small (population 40,000) industrial town of Mansfield. My father had served as the family advance man and had already spent three or four months on-site in his new job. He had also rented a nice house with a big yard for us at 451 Park Avenue West, about 10 blocks from the center of town.

From the very beginning, I liked Mansfield. There, I spent seven of my most formative years having adventures, learning new things, making good friends, and trying to live up to the then popular Midwestern ideal of becoming an "all-American boy." Later, as an adult, I became fond of saying that "Mansfield, Ohio was a great place to be from." By that, I meant that, from a boy's perspective, Mansfield was a good place in which to grow up. It was only after I had left it to go away to college that I began to realize how narrow and circumscribed life was for most people in small-town Midwestern America. Later, as an adult, I never considered going back to live or have a career there.

The week after we settled in Mansfield, I was enrolled in the fifth grade at Brinkerhoff Elementary School. Fall classes had begun a few days before my arrival. My initial memory of the school occurred my first day there when Mr. Sechrist, the principal, showed me into Miss Smith's fifth grade classroom about 10 minutes after the start of the morning class. The other kids were already seated, and I had to walk across the front of the room to find an empty desk on the far side. All eyes were on the new kid who, halfway across the room, promptly dropped his armful of books and paper onto the floor with a loud crash. Mortified, I gathered up my belongings and slunk into a seat, sure that from that moment on I would be labeled as a total loser.

However, things quickly began to get better. From an academic point of view, I found that even though I was the youngest in my class, I was already significantly ahead of most of the other kids, thanks to the solid educational head start provided me by Orrington School in Evanston. I was also reasonably well coordinated and, though only medium-sized, I soon won a spot playing end on the school football team. I was also adept at playground games such as marbles and tag, despite the fact that on one occasion I left the lower half of one of my adult front teeth in Billy Rinker's skull as a result of a collision during a particularly vicious chase.

I guess I made friends fairly easily because it was not long before I found myself accepted as "one of the gang." Soon my neighborhood and school friends included Johnny Fox, Bobby George, Malcolm Erich, Dick Eliot, Junior Brobst, Skip and David Carse, Billy Reale, John Fighter, Jack Pierce, Loyal Bemiller, and a number of others.

At that point there weren't too many girls in my coterie of pals, with the exception of Patsy Weamer, who lived across the street. She became my sister's best friend and my friend as well.

Skip and David Carse, one a year older and the other a year younger than me, became two of my best friends. At the time, their father and my father were colleagues at Westinghouse. Skip and David were funny, smart, and very athletic.

I thought they were both great. Much later in life we continued to be friends even though we didn't see one another very often. Both had successful careers, Skip as a professor of religion at NYU and David as head of marketing for the Evinrude motorboat engine company. In the late 1950s their father, who suffered from depression, committed suicide, an event that made a deep impression on me. Up until that time, I had never known anyone who had committed suicide. It raised questions that I found unanswerable and that I still have difficulty understanding. The impact on Skip and David was no doubt infinitely more profound. Searching for the "why" of that event was probably one of the main reasons why Skip decided to pursue a career teaching religion. David, a superb athlete all his life (he served as a frogman in the Navy) dropped dead in his late thirties while out doing his daily training run.

In sixth grade at Brinkerhoff School my one claim to fame was that I became the class spelling champion. On spelling tests I only missed one word all year. I still remember the word. I left out the letter "c" in spelling excellent. Actually, credit for my spelling prowess goes to my mother. Since our house was only a half-block from school, every day I went home for lunch. Lunch, as was the case of all the meals at our house, was almost always a well-balanced affair with a healthy dose of protein, veggies, salad, and fruit. And lunch was always study time as well, particularly on spelling test days. My mother, with the patience of Job, would indefatigably drill me in advance on my spelling words by having me spell them in the air with my forefinger. I doubt that any of my classmates had secret learning weapons to compare with my mother. And not only would she drill me on my spelling but she would also quiz me on my other school subjects as well. I also owe a huge debt of gratitude to both of my parents for instilling in me a great love of reading by constantly reading aloud to Nancy and me from the time we were two until we were able to read fluently by ourselves. Learning in the Sorenson household was a family affair.

Shortly after the move to Ohio in 1943, my father got me launched on my second entrepreneurial venture: selling Argosheen cleaning compound door-to-door. This was a magical substance that seemed able to clean almost anything. To this day, I have no idea what was in it. It sold for $1.00 per jar. My cost was $.50 per jar, so I made a pretty good profit. Here was my marketing approach: I would ring a neighborhood doorbell and ask the lady of the house if I could demonstrate a fantastic new product. If she said yes, I would reach into my shoulder bag and take out my homemade 10"x4" demonstration board that had painted white woodwork on one side and linoleum on the other. Next, I would whip out a detached shoe heel made of synthetic rubber (the only kind available in that wartime era). With the heel, I would make great black marks on both the woodwork and the linoleum. Then I would dip a small cloth into a jar of Argosheen and rub the cleaning compound on both sides of the board. Presto! The black marks completely and instantly disappeared! Sale made, I would then proceed on to the next house. Truth be told, in about three-fourths of the cases, the lady of the house would say "No thanks," or else just slam the door in my face. This was my first real lesson in learning how to take rejection with equanimity.

Entrepreneurial Insight #3: Argosheen and Mrs. Brown

My most memorable experience while selling Argosheen involved Mrs. Brown, who lived several blocks away. As was my routine, I rang her doorbell and went through my demonstration. Impressed, Mrs. Brown asked me if it would work on wallpaper. Ever confident, I said, "Most certainly." So she invited me into her living room to prove it. Never daunted, I set to work on a 2'x2' patch of wallpaper. Unfortunately, the harder I rubbed, the darker the patch of wallpaper became. It was a disaster, there for all to see, right on the wall of her beloved living room! Mrs. Brown definitely was not very happy. Offering my abject apologies, I got out of there as quickly as possible.

That evening, while our family was having dinner together, the telephone rang. My father answered and after listening a moment handed me the phone saying, "It's a Mrs. Brown for you." Wanting to sink through the floor, I reluctantly took the receiver, sure that Mrs. Brown was going to insist that I come back and pay her a lot of money in damages so that she could re-paper her living room. Instead she said, "Buddy, would you be kind enough to stop by my house tomorrow to drop off two jars of that Argosheen cleaner? The patch of wallpaper that you experimented on has now dried and it looks totally clean and beautiful. Now I need enough Argosheen to do the whole living room and I might even want to do the dining room as well."

Lesson Learned: Sometimes boldness pays off . . . but be careful not to push your luck too far.

My first year in Mansfield brought with it another lesson . . . this one not so pleasant. As I recall it, one afternoon in the spring of 1944, when I was still 10, three older neighborhood boys took me into a tent they had pitched in a nearby vacant lot and forced me to do some things sexually that made me feel instantly degraded and that filled me with self-loathing. It was a totally traumatic experience. And it became the dirty little secret that I was unable to say anything about at the time and that I carried with me for more than 30 years before being able to mention it to another human being. However, like so many other coming-of-age experiences, I survived this incident and eventually went on to develop what I believe has been a healthy attitude toward, and appreciation of, sex.

In the 1940s, the existing social mores in America attached a huge stigma to homosexuality. Just as there still was widespread prejudice against Jews, blacks, "Japs," and women, there was perhaps an even greater antipathy toward homosexual men and women. And the concept of "transgender" people simply didn't exist . . . at least not in Mansfield, Ohio. Today, in our America of the 21st century, my sense is that, although we have made considerable progress in addressing and reducing racial, religious, and sexual prejudice, much still remains to be accomplished in this regard. Indeed, judging from current media accounts, incidents such as those I experienced in the tent and even more serious incidents of sexual abuse of young boys and girls are still widely prevalent in America. The only difference is that today these incidents are increasingly being brought into the open. This has led to a growing number of criminal prosecutions that have resulted in jail sentences for the perpetrators. In any case, based on my personal experience as a 10-year-old, I can attest to the fact that such sexual abuse at an early age can cause serious psychological trauma and memories that can last well into adulthood.

After sixth grade at Brinkerhoff School, I spent two years at John Simpson Junior High School followed by four years at Mansfield Senior High. Mansfield schools, while not great, were also pretty good. Along the way, I had a few excellent teachers who took an interest in me and encouraged me to work hard and do well. I also became involved in a number of extracurricular activities. In junior high, I was the features editor of the school newspaper and sang in the glee club. I joined the Boy Scouts and eventually became an Eagle Scout.

In terms of my religious education, I learned my catechism and joined the Methodist church along with the rest of the family. However, I was never a very faithful churchgoer and I later switched to the Presbyterian church so that I could play on their basketball team. (It turned out that the Presbyterians were better basketball players than the Methodists.) Piety, at least with respect to my involvement with organized religions, would never be a hallmark of my life.

When I was about 12, I began working summers as a caddy at the Westbrook Country Club, where my parents were members. On Mondays, the caddies were allowed to play golf, so I took up the sport and grew to love it. I never became very good, but by the time I was 14, I was able to shoot in the 90s. Then I discovered tennis. After my freshman year at high school, I was hired by Tom Bloor, manager of the Woodland Tennis and Swimming Club, as a lifeguard and caretaker of the club's three tennis courts. Tom, who became an early mentor to me, was at the time a student at Amherst College and an outstanding tennis player. He taught me to play the game and, with him as a coach, I quickly shifted my sports allegiance from golf to tennis. Ultimately, I became good enough to play varsity tennis both in high school, and, later, at college. Tennis opened the door to the formation of good friendships with other tennis players on the Mansfield High School team, including Billy Reale, Fritz Herring, Malcolm Erich, and Hal Schaus.

Summers working at the Woodland Tennis Club were glorious. Not only was I able to play all the tennis I wanted but I also had a chance to get a great tan while sitting beside the swimming pool in the lifeguard chair making sure no one drowned and watching all the teenaged girls in the bikinis that were just beginning to come into fashion.

Entrepreneurial Insight #4: Entrepreneurs Work Long Hours

In order to earn extra money during my teenage years, I launched two other entrepreneurial ventures. The first was a joint venture with my best friend, Johnny Fox. In the fall, winter, and early spring, the two of us ran a trap line for muskrats. We would rise before dawn and bike to a stream west of town to don our wading boots and check whether we had caught anything in the 20 or so traps that we had set the previous day. Sometimes we got nothing, but often we would catch two or three muskrats. In those instances, we would take our catch to the hunting shop in town where we would sell the muskrats for four to five dollars each, depending on the size and condition of the pelts.

The second venture was that of earning money mowing lawns. I lined up a half-dozen or so clients around town and spent most weekends and some afternoons making sure their grass lawns and grounds were kept neat and tidy. This, of course, was before power mowers were in wide use and all the lawn mowing was with an old-fashioned push mower. It was hard work. But I tried to be conscientious about making sure I didn't let my clients down. And my earnings from mowing lawns helped me save enough money so that I was eventually able to buy a Whizzer motorbike.

Lesson Learned: Being a successful entrepreneur involves hard work, long hours, and making sure you are conscientious on behalf of your clients.

During my teenage years I also found myself engaged in a number of other activities that were popular in small Midwestern towns at the time. For example, I also learned how to hunt with the 12-gauge, 7-shot, pump shotgun that I had inherited from my maternal grandfather. Having mastered the fundamentals, I sometimes went with other Mansfield kids and their fathers on Saturday morning foxhunts and nighttime coon hunts with dogs. In the former, 30 or 40 stalwart Mansfield hunters would form a giant mile square ring around the acreage of a local farmer's woods or fields. Then we would all slowly close the circle hoping to scare up a fox or two. Once a fox was spotted, we would all bang away with our shotguns. In addition to killing the occasional fox (for whom the county paid a bounty since farmers saw foxes as predators), we also considered crows to be fair game. My most memorable foxhunt was the morning when the father of one of the other kids got a bare butt full of buckshot while squatting under a tree to have a bowel movement! I vowed that would never happen to me!

As for coon hunting, on a number of occasions, I went into some local woods at nine or ten o'clock at night with two or three other kids and their dads, along with powerful flashlights and half a dozen hunting dogs. We would set the dogs loose and they would comb the forest for raccoons. Once they caught the scent of one, the hounds would all converge in full-throated pursuit. Most often, they would tree the coon, at which point hunters would surround the tree and raise our shotguns to finish things off. Occasionally, however, the dogs would chase the frightened raccoon down into a hole in the ground. Whereupon, there would ensue frantic digging on the part of the hounds, resulting in a few scratched dog snouts and yelps of pain. The saga typically ended with a blast from the executioner's shotgun. Sometimes entire raccoon families were wiped out.

The day came, however, when I lost my appetite for shooting animals after using my BB gun to kill a mourning dove while doing target practice from my bedroom window. When I saw that I had scored a hit, I ran downstairs and out the door to where the beautiful little bird lay near death but still quivering on the ground. I remember thinking to myself, "Oh no, how could I have taken the life of this little innocent creature?" This episode cured me of any desire to do further killing and ended my teenaged hunting expeditions.

Scouting was another activity that engaged my interest and energy during my teenage years and shaped me as an adult. First, there was the Boy Scout oath:

A Boy Scout Is:
Trustworthy, loyal, helpful;
Friendly, courteous, kind;
Cheerful, obedient, thrifty;
Brave, clean, and reverent.

Subconsciously, if not consciously, I believe I've tried to live up to these qualities throughout my life.

Second, there were the skills and attitudes I learned in the process of earning the 21 merit badges required to become an Eagle Scout: skills like camping and survival, map reading, cooking, leadership, fishing, swimming, and first aid. Then there was knowledge of nutrition, a love of nature, wilderness knowledge/ appreciation, and bird/animal identification.

Becoming an Eagle Scout also brought with it the privilege of spending two weeks of the summer at an isolated Canadian fishing and wildlife camp located in the wilderness a couple of hours' drive north of Ottawa. I went there two successive summers and loved every minute of those trips.

Then there was the fun provided by the motorbike that I bought with the money I had earned from my entrepreneurial ventures and various other jobs. The bike had a Whizzer two-stroke gasoline motor attached to the frame of a Schwinn bicycle. It supplanted the boy-powered bicycle that I had used until then for all of my small-town transportation needs . . . only it took less energy and went twice or three times as fast. Several of my other friends also had Whizzers and we buzzed around town like kings of the road. It was a blast!

Unfortunately, after a couple years, my Whizzer career ended when, in a moment of inattention, I crashed it into the rear bumper of a parked car. I was tossed over the top of the car and landed on its front hood. The bike was totaled, and I was bruised, saddened, and humiliated. As my friends delighted in pointing out, only a nitwit would be capable of crashing into the rear bumper of a parked car on a dry surface in broad daylight. However, it turned out there was a side benefit to owning the Whizzer. Namely, before it met its demise, I had totally disassembled and reassembled its motor and in the process learned a good deal about the workings of an internal combustion engine.

My high school experience in Mansfield was, for the most part, positive. I continued to do well academically and ultimately graduated fourth in my class of 370 students. Along the way I was involved in a whole raft of extracurricular activities. I was co-editor of the yearbook, president of the Society of Prospective

Collegians, a member of the Debate Club, and was elected Attorney General of Buckeye Boys State (an annual weeklong simulation of state government functions for high school juniors from around the state).

In my junior year, I had a starring role in Varsity Varieties, a song and dance show based on a "Roaring Twenties" theme. With Chloe Snyder (on whom I had a crush) as my partner, we danced a wicked Charleston routine. Chloe was dressed as a flapper and I was duded up in a straw hat, saddle shoes, and a black-and-white checkered suit. Our performance won a standing ovation from the audience of about a thousand spectators. I only wished at the time that Chloe enjoyed my company as much off-stage as she did on-stage!

The nadir of my high school public appearances occurred when I participated as a member of the Debate Club in a public speaking competition sponsored by the Daughters of the American Revolution. My topic was John Marshall, the second, and some would say, greatest chief justice of the U.S. Supreme Court. I had prepared and memorized a barn burner of a speech. When I got to the very climax of the speech, with my arms outstretched in the process of singing the praises of Chief Justice Marshall, I opened my mouth, and nothing came out! Suddenly, I was only aware of the 250 pairs of eyes staring at me, waiting for the punch line. Still nothing. My brain had stopped working and my vocal chords were mute. I flushed and broke out into an instant sweat. Finally, I babbled out some lame non sequitur that made no sense and slunk back to my seat, mortified and humiliated. Needless to say, I didn't win the competition. However, I did learn a lesson: When speaking in public it's usually best to have a written script or at least a few reminder notes jotted down in the event your brain draws a blank in the middle of following a train of thought. This practice has stood me in good stead through the years.

While in high school, I also spent two years as a Junior Rotarian. In this latter capacity, I attended all of the monthly lunch meetings of the local Rotary Club and got to know a number of the town's leading businessmen and government officials. It also exposed me to some of the issues facing the town leaders.

At the time, Mansfield was thriving as a small manufacturing hub in the booming postwar economy. At one point in mid-century, it was featured in *Life Magazine* as the quintessential American small town.

In addition to being the headquarters of Westinghouse's appliance division, Mansfield was the site of a number of successful locally owned unionized companies. These included the Ohio Brass Company, Tappan Stove Co., Mansfield Tire and Rubber Company, Empire Steel Co., Thermo Disc, Mansfield Plating Company, Gorman-Rupp, and others. Sadly, over the ensuing 70 or so years almost all of these firms have disappeared or are struggling financially. Some failed completely, some were acquired and subsequently closed down, with the local jobs shipped abroad, and some found themselves unable to keep up with technological changes in their respective industries. Today Mansfield is an exemplification of a struggling Midwestern Rust Belt community.

However, when I was a Junior Rotarian in 1950 and '51, Mansfield business was still booming, and the town fathers were discussing ambitious plans for the community's future growth and expansion. At the monthly Rotarian luncheons, I was privy to these discussions and then was charged with the responsibility of serving as liaison to the high school student body and administration.

A troubling and confusing event occurred during my high school junior year. My mother, then in her early fifties, was going through a difficult menopause and began suffering periodic bouts of depression. In addition to menopause, I suspect some of this depression stemmed from the fact that she had never quite reconciled herself to small town life in Mansfield. Mansfield was truly a "company town" that embodied all of the social pettiness that characterized such towns during that era. My dear mother, having had many close friends in Evanston and having lived an active and fulfilling social life full of variety and excitement in cosmopolitan Chicago, had suddenly found herself transplanted into the cliquish closed society of Mansfield. With her heart left behind in Evanston, she apparently felt herself to be isolated in Mansfield, trapped between the elitist social strata of the town's wealthy owner-class and the less inspiring company of the local middle and lower-class strata. Probably as a result of these combined factors, Mother suffered from what, at the time, was called a "nervous breakdown." My concerned father, who loved her dearly, searched urgently for a way to get her help and subsequently, with her consent, got her accepted at a private clinic on the North Shore of Chicago that dealt with such problems. There she stayed for about two months.

During that period, Nancy was a freshman at Northwestern University and my dad and I were alone at home in Mansfield. While at the clinic, Mother received psychotherapy and electric shock treatments that were the norm at the time. Very worried about my mom, I wrote to her once or twice a week to tell her about my activities and reassure her that Dad and I were managing fine at home and that I loved her. But the house seemed pretty quiet and lonely without her and Nancy. Meanwhile, Nancy was able to visit Mom in the clinic on a weekly basis from nearby Evanston.

As for my father, I remember him during my mother's absence as being a totally supportive husband who was rooting for my mother to get better and who wrote to her almost daily. He did his best to keep a sense of normalcy for me at home. In retrospect, I think he suffered feelings of guilt that he had contributed to her depression by uprooting her from Evanston and taking her to a place to live that held little for her. I will never know the full story behind the cause of my mother's breakdown. I have often wondered about the real causes of it and whether she might have received better treatment—no electric shock, for example—in more recent times. In subsequent years, we never talked about it either within the family or with outsiders. To our family's great relief, she returned home from the clinic in a much better frame of mind.

As a postscript, I should note that in subsequent years the Mansfield families that had previously snubbed my mother and father increasingly accepted them. While widening their circle of friends, my mother also spent more time perfecting her skills as an artist, working on paintings in oils and acrylics, as well as in watercolors. Both she and my father became active in the local art scene, my mother as an award-winning painter and my father on the board of trustees of the local art museum. Meanwhile, my father continued to work as an executive at Westinghouse. For many years he was manager of the Small Appliance Division and subsequently he served as liaison between Westinghouse and the country's electric utility companies. He retired in 1963 at age 65, much loved and respected by his colleagues.

Both my mother and father increasingly became active and well-liked citizens in the town. In 1948, they moved out of the house that they had rented when they first came to town and, for $15,000, bought a nice house in an old, tree-lined neighborhood at 391 Third Street. They continued to live together in this comfortable house for another 40 years until my mother died at age 90 and my father at 91. After their deaths, when Mansfield was well into its decline, my sister and I sold their house for $35,000, an amount that represented less than one half of one percent annual appreciation over a 40-year period. During a period when real estate values had skyrocketed in most of the rest of America, the meager proceeds from the sale of their house was testimony to the fact that, in buying their one and only home, my parents had picked the wrong neighborhood in the wrong town!

When working at the Woodland Club the summer after my junior year in high school, I became better acquainted with a bunch of kids who lived in the "fashionable" Woodland neighborhood where the club was located. Some of these included Frank Black, Ben Bissman, Frannie Draffan, Betty Brown, Susie, Sally, and Tom Hout, Priscilla Slaybaugh, Joan Bruce, Sally Ritzenthaler, and my first real girlfriend, Susie Cummins. Susie was a year behind me in high school and was the daughter of Otis and Portia Cummins, who also had two younger children, Sally and Cokie. That summer, Susie and I decided to "go steady" and continued to do so during my senior year and until the end of my freshman year in college. (I might point out that "going steady" was completely the norm for high school kids during that era. If you weren't going steady with someone, you were somewhat of a social outcast). Susie was an attractive, petite brunette who was smart and caring and had lots of friends. We were very fond of one another and had much in common. Like me, she loved to read and dance and go to the movies. No doubt, hormones also played a role in our relationship. I liked her family a lot as well. Her father, in particular, took a shine to me. He was a successful entrepreneur who had founded the Mansfield Plating Company, which did metal plating of industrial products. He had a good sense of humor and became something of a mentor for me.

Senior year in high school brought with it the challenge of deciding where to apply for college. Though neither of my parents had graduated from college, there was never any question that I was college-bound. That idea had been instilled in Nancy and me since the first day we entered kindergarten. Nancy, who had graduated from high school two years ahead of me, had decided on Northwestern University in Evanston where she currently was a sophomore. I thought I, too, might be interested in Northwestern. At the same time, Tom Bloor, my friend and mentor, was encouraging me to consider Amherst College in Massachusetts, where he currently was a senior. I knew nothing about Amherst apart from the fact that it was a small, all-male, liberal arts college and that Tom thought it was great. I had also heard of Yale University and that it had a good reputation as an eastern Ivy League college. Meanwhile, almost all of the other college-bound seniors at Mansfield High (about 20 percent of the class) were only looking at Midwestern institutions, mostly in Ohio and surrounding states.

In the end, I applied to Northwestern, Amherst, and Yale, though I had never visited the latter two. Money still being tight in the Sorenson household, I also applied for scholarships at each place. In the spring, I received acceptance letters from all three. Yale offered me a tuition-only scholarship, Northwestern offered me an "honorary scholarship" (whatever that meant) and the promise of providing me part-time work on the campus, and Amherst offered full tuition, room, and board. They had made the choice easy for me. I chose Amherst sight-unseen.

Later that spring, I drove to Amherst for a look-see with Tom Bloor, who was returning from spring break. Over a long weekend, Tom showed me the campus and introduced me to some of his friends. I thought I would like the place. Tom also took me to Rahar's Tavern in nearby Northampton where I met some Smith College girls and had my first-ever drink of alcohol! Following my short visit, I hitchhiked the 680 miles back to Mansfield, which took me two days. Along the way, I was picked up by an odd assortment of drivers. This was the first of several times over the ensuing four years that I depended on my thumb for transportation from Amherst back to Mansfield.

CHAPTER FOUR

AMHERST

In September of 1951, having graduated from high school and worked a final summer at the Woodland Club, I said goodbye to family, friends, and Susie and headed via train to Amherst.

Amherst College, founded in 1821, is noted for its beautiful campus. Built on a hill in the lovely little town of the same name, its chapel, library, dining hall, classrooms, dormitories, and fraternity houses were outstanding examples of the handsome Georgian architectural-style buildings that graced a number of other New England college campuses. Rolling green lawns and lovely hilltop vistas overlooking the broad playing fields and hills to the south further enhanced the setting. I loved the feeling of the place.

On arrival, I was issued a class schedule, plus a green "beanie cap" that all freshmen were required to wear for the first semester. I was assigned to a two-room second-floor "suite" in North Hall with four other roommates, all total strangers to one another. The other four were Peter Scott, Hoke Noble, Jan Farr, and Bob Spencer. While I quickly became friends with all four, I developed a particularly close friendship with Peter. He and I subsequently roomed together our sophomore year in another dormitory.

The very first night at Amherst brought a bit of unintended drama. My new roommates and I had lined up our beds next to another, barracks style, in one of our two rooms. My bed was the one up against the only window in the room; outside of it was an iron fire escape. At about 11:30 p.m., just as we were all falling asleep, there suddenly was a terrifying shriek followed by a loud "thump" right outside the open window. It turned out that a sophomore, Curley Price, had been up to some mischief on the fourth-floor platform of the fire escape and had lost his footing. He fell and bounced two stories down the open ladder holes to the second-floor platform and landed just inches from my head. On the way down, he had raked his ribs on the exposed edges of the iron floor bars. He immediately began to bleed profusely. We dragged him into the room through the window and managed to get him to the infirmary. In the morning, our bedroom was still covered by Curley's blood. Welcome to Amherst! The next day, a thoroughly chastened Curley, freshly released from the infirmary with several broken ribs, apologized for making mischief and causing such a ruckus. Later, he became a friend.

I was somewhat overwhelmed the first week or two at Amherst. I felt myself to be an unsophisticated, largely ignorant, public school bumpkin from the Midwest. Half of our class of about 300 men had attended elite eastern boarding schools or private day schools. While there were a number of scholarship students like me, a majority of the others seemed to come from well-to-do families or were "legacies" whose relatives had attended Amherst before them. It all seemed a bit intimidating.

At the time, Amherst had a required core curriculum for the first two years. The courses in freshman year were English I and II, physics, calculus, world history, literature, and a language (for me it was German, which I had taken along with Latin in high school). Twice a week we were also required to go to non-denominational chapel services.

Of the required courses, the most famous and demanding was English I. It was designed to help students unlearn all the bad writing habits they had acquired in high school and, instead, to develop the ability to articulate their thoughts in crystal-clear declarative sentences, each with a subject, verb, and object. Every week, students were required to write and submit three original papers, one each on Monday, Wednesday, and Friday. In turn, at the beginning of each class, the professor would give back to each student a written critique of the paper that had been handed in during the previous class.

I attribute much of my subsequent academic success at Amherst to an incident that occurred during my freshman year in the first week of English. In the very first class on Monday morning, Professor Waidlich gave us the following assignment: "Write an essay describing how you got to Amherst." Most of the students then wrote about how they were a legacy following in their fathers' footsteps, or how their SAT scores and high school academic records were strong, or the fact that they were good at sports as well as in the classroom. Country bumpkin that I was, I answered the question quite literally. In class on Wednesday I handed in an essay in which I had written something along the following lines:

"At 11:00 a.m. on the morning of Wednesday, September 8th, I walked out the front door of my house at 390 West Third Street in Mansfield, Ohio, and proceeded ten meters down the front walk to my parents' Buick car. I climbed into the passenger seat. My father then drove me about a mile to the local train station. I got out of the car and at approximately 11:30 a.m. I boarded a train bound for Northampton, Massachusetts, via Cleveland, Ohio . . . etc., etc."

After comparing notes with other students who had also turned in their essays, I was sure I had totally blown the assignment. I came to class Wednesday morning filled with apprehension, particularly when Professor Waidlich opened the class by saying that, in general, he was disappointed in the essays we had written. He went on to say that there was only one student in the class who had truly listened to the assignment and written a literal response. He proceeded to read my essay out loud.

Wow! I had totally scored. I wasn't such a Midwestern hayseed after all. To this day, I am convinced that it was the academic confidence engendered in me by that single experience in the first week of classes that launched me on what turned out to be a successful academic career at Amherst.

The moral of this story: Early success and encouragement lays the foundation for later success and achievements. I am certain that Professor Waidlich never knew what a seminal role he played in my educational development, but I am grateful to him to this day. I am only sorry that I never thanked him in person. In my later career as a teacher, I would like to think that I, in turn, might have played a confidence-building role similar to Professor Waidlich's in the lives of a few of *my* students.

My subsequent experience at Amherst opened my eyes to a whole new world of knowledge and had a profound, life-changing impact on me. Amherst had the great benefit of being small. In total, there were only 300 students in the entire class of 1955. Amherst was also, first and foremost, a teaching-oriented college. Professors, all of whom were male, put the students ahead of their research. While there were a few large lecture courses, most classes tended to be limited in size. There were many seminar courses with only 10 to 15 students. In these, there tended to be a lot of give-and-take discussion between students and professors and among the students as well. Students were challenged to think for themselves.

While at Amherst, I began to understand the meaning and value of a "liberal arts" education. Until I went there, I had little or no understanding of literature, history, music, art, religion, politics, philosophy, economics, evolution, or the sciences.

Amherst's core curriculum required, in my freshman and sophomore years, that I take a wide variety of courses in the liberal arts, humanities, and sciences. This opened my eyes to the lessons of history, the charm of literature, the beauty of art and music, the utility of the scientific approach to thinking and experimentation, the necessity of economics, the usefulness of learning foreign languages, the fascination of politics, the complexity of philosophic thought, the eternal questions posed by a study of comparative religions, and the importance of being able to articulate clearly one's thoughts verbally and in writing.

In retrospect these many years later, I realize how fortunate I was to have landed at Amherst, where I was able to have my perspective on life broadened so greatly.

My experience at Amherst convinced me that the best foundation for living one's life fully and productively is the study of the liberal arts at the undergraduate level, followed, if desired, by graduate study to prepare for whatever career or profession one subsequently chooses to pursue. Of course, for economic or other reasons, this approach to education is not yet available to every young person. But in my view, it represents an ideal toward which societies should strive.

I believe that in America, too many students view an undergraduate education simply as a means to prepare themselves to get a job after graduation. But there is more to life than a job or career. It is important to keep one's priorities straight. I favor the saying that "one should not just live to work, rather one should work to live life fully."

Technically, while at Amherst, I majored in economics, thinking at the time that it might give me the broadest career options after I graduated. Actually, however, I took the minimum number of economics courses required to qualify for the major. Instead, I grazed through Amherst's diverse smorgasbord of courses and enrolled in as many different electives as possible. I was like a kid in a delicatessen! Of course, there were some offerings that disappointed. My philosophy and German professors were pretty boring, and I found I didn't develop a great love of the math and science courses that I took. But, on balance, Amherst was a great academic feast for me.

In a nutshell, Amherst greatly broadened my horizons and, in the process, taught me how to think, learn, write, and speak. Hence, I owe a tremendous debt to Amherst and the role it played in preparing me subsequently to live my life.

Lest the foregoing sound entirely idyllic, in the interest of honesty, I should at this point make a confession. While at Amherst, I became a "grade-grubber" and thus, in retrospect, I think I shortchanged myself. I often came across a subject or idea that fascinated me and that I would have liked to have researched or pursued further. But most often I didn't make the time or have the strength of character to do so. Instead my mantra too often became: "gotta get the grades; gotta get the grades." And so I got the grades. (I graduated magna cum laude and Phi Beta Kappa). In retrospect, I have wished from time to time that I had been less of a conformist at college and more of an independent thinker and maverick. Had I chosen that path, no doubt my life would have unfolded differently. However, life isn't made for regrets and I doubt that being more of a nonconformist would have led to a better life than the one I have today.

Amherst certainly wasn't all study and no play. In addition to its academic side, it was also a great place to spend four years making friends, playing sports, dating, partying, and maturing.

Toward the end of my freshman year, there was fraternity "rushing" and I joined the Alpha Delta Phi (aka A.D.) social fraternity. Prior to the year I came to Amherst, the rushing process, in which upper-class fraternity members "tapped" freshmen to join their respective houses, was often a source of heartache for those who weren't "tapped" by any fraternity. In my freshman year, however, for the first time there was "100 percent rushing." This meant that every freshman who wanted to join a fraternity was guaranteed a place, albeit not necessarily in the fraternity that was his first choice. Though the new system wasn't perfect and there were still some hurt feelings, it was an improvement over the previous approach, which smacked of blatant elitism and resulted in much damaged self-esteem throughout the campus.

At the time, I didn't give much thought to the rightness or wrongness of the fraternity system. I was just happy that I was asked to join A.D., which was my first choice. It probably helped that Tom Bloor, my friend and mentor from Mansfield, was an Alpha Delt and had introduced me to some of the "brothers" when I visited Amherst with him the previous spring. Tom, no doubt, also put in a good word for me, although he had already graduated the year before. It was only in later years that I began to have second thoughts about the "clubbiness" of the fraternity system. In any case, Amherst has since abolished fraternities on its campus.

Like all fraternities at the time, A.D. had a secret handshake and a certain amount of ritual accompanied by a bit of mumbo jumbo. Once a week, the brothers met in what was called the "Goat Room" to discuss matters of little import. I never took any of that protocol very seriously and, in fact, found it rather silly.

A.D. had the reputation on campus of being a fraternity made up of "scholar-athletes." We A.D.s did nothing to discourage that impression. And it was true that we had some pretty outstanding scholars and athletes among our brothers . . . present company excluded. In any case, we were a close-knit group not given to the partying excesses of some of the other fraternities. Not that we didn't party. Friday and Saturday nights typically saw a number of kegs of beer consumed in the basement barroom accompanied by lots of singing and laughter. Apart from an occasional macho incident and drunken reveler, it was all fairly harmless.

On the weekends, there were also lots of women dates from nearby Smith and Mount Holyoke colleges at the parties, together with a weekly smattering of visiting male freeloaders from Dartmouth, Harvard, Yale, and Williams who were drawn by Amherst's proximity to the Smithies and the Holyoke girls.

By convention, if one of the brothers wanted to "make out" with his date in the course of the evening, he would drape his necktie over the doorknob to his room. It was tantamount to a "Do Not Disturb" sign. The only inconvenience was that both Smith and Holyoke enforced parietal hours that required the girls to be back in their dorms by midnight . . . on pain of expulsion or worse. In that pre-pill and pre-women's liberation era, "going all the way" was a good deal less prevalent than on today's campuses. Terrified of getting their date pregnant, most of the guys engaged mainly in so-called "heavy petting." Viewed from the perspective of today's mores, it was tame. And while there was a good deal of alcohol consumption on campus, I never heard of any incident involving drugs while I was at Amherst.

I broke up with Susie, my high school girlfriend, at the end of my freshman year. During the three years that followed, I had a fair number of dates, mostly with Smith women, during my time at Amherst. However, none of these flirtations was very serious. The mythology at the time was that Amherst men dated Smithies, but married Mount Holyoke women. I did the former, but as shall be seen, not the latter.

A lot of the learning at Amherst took place outside the classroom. Frequent bull sessions were the order of the day. It was in these sessions that all the really important things were discussed. In addition to women, sex, sports, and the news of the day, we often discussed and debated weightier matters: What is life all about? Do you believe in God? How would you deal with this or that moral dilemma? What career or professions are you thinking of pursuing? Why? Do you plan to go to graduate school? How important is money? Who are your heroes? Ralph Waldo Emerson once said: "I pay the schoolmaster, but it is the schoolboys who educate my son." In large measure, this was true in my case.

When I entered Amherst in 1951 the Korean War was still being fought and a nationwide military draft system was in force. All males were required to register on reaching age 18. While I had a fairly high draft number, I decided that I would join the Air Force R.O.T.C. unit at Amherst. Once I joined, I was given a student deferment and I also received a modest monthly stipend that, being a scholarship student, I greatly appreciated.

As an R.O.T.C. student I attended courses on military strategy and tactics and on military protocol. Once a week, we were also required to report to the playing fields in our newly issued Air Force uniforms and learn from our drill sergeant how to salute, march, and obey orders. In the summer between our sophomore and junior years we also attended a month-long summer camp at Rome Air Force Base near the Finger Lakes in upper New York State. While I was never gung-ho about being an R.O.T.C. cadet, I tried to be a conscientious cadet.

By the start of my junior year, the Korean War was beginning to wind down and all of us cadets were told that the Amherst R.O.T.C. unit was going to undergo a "RIF," i.e., a reduction in force. Only those of us who were physically qualified to fly and willing to train as pilots would be retained in the program. Going to flight training school entailed agreeing to three years of full-time military service immediately following college. Non-flying cadets only had to agree to a two-year commitment. For me, this posed a dilemma. I was already thinking that I might want to go to graduate school after college and I wasn't excited about putting that off for three years after graduation rather than for two years. My dilemma was resolved when an obligatory Air Force-sponsored physical exam revealed that I was partially color blind and thus unqualified to be a pilot.

This might have ended the matter. But, in the end, a funny thing happened. Most of the other student cadets who couldn't pass the flying physical or who didn't want to sign up for the three-year post-college commitment voluntarily resigned from the R.O.T.C. program. I decided not to resign and, instead, to let them throw me out of the program if they no longer wanted me. Lo and behold, the Air Force powers-that-be modified their edict and ordained that two non-flying cadets would be retained in the Amherst program. And so another student, Charlie Kopp, and I were chosen to fill those two spots. Thus, I remained in the R.O.T.C. program, which led to a two-year adventure as an Air Force lieutenant following graduation.

Sports also played a major role in my college life. Having played varsity tennis in high school, I tried out for the freshman team at Amherst and was asked to join it. I played number two or three in both singles and doubles. While not winning any prizes as an all-star, I was good enough join the varsity. It was great fun and over the years we had rousing matches against other small New England colleges such as Williams, Wesleyan, Trinity, Bowdoin, and Bates.

I learned to play squash at Amherst. While never good enough to entertain the idea of trying out for the varsity team, I came to appreciate the game and enjoyed playing it in inclement weather when it wasn't possible to get out on the outdoor tennis courts.

My other varsity sport was swimming. Under the tutelage of grizzled old "Tug" Kennedy, our very successful and beloved veteran coach, Amherst was considered a powerhouse in the New England small college league. Having always loved swimming and been a lifeguard, I tried out for the team and made it. In my freshman year, I swam the 50- and 100-yard dashes and some relay races. But then, Coach Kennedy converted me into a diver. I competed on the varsity team in that capacity until, during a swim meet in my junior year, I ingloriously ended my diving career doing a one-and-a-half backward flip off the high board. As I opened up for my entry into the water I managed to hit the diving board and crush the knuckle of my right hand's forefinger. Fortunately, it was toward the end of the season and I only missed one or two more meets. But for the rest of that spring I wore a strange-looking cast with a kind of hook that put my forefinger in traction.

This incident had an unintended, but in the end, happy consequence. Because I still had to wear my cast and was right-handed, that spring I was unable to write my exams. As a result, all of my professors agreed to let me take my exams orally. I guess I was a better talker than a writer, because that semester of my junior year, I received the best grades of my entire college career!

My reminiscence of Amherst wouldn't be complete without mentioning that in the 60-some years since my graduation, I have attended several of the class reunions that are held every five years. These have, for me, typically tended to be bittersweet affairs.

The bitter part has been the realization that, try as I might, I can never recapture the halcyon days of my four years at the college. Often, I find that, when encountering certain returning classmates who were among my closest college friends, we very quickly run out of things to say to each other after three or four minutes. In other cases, I find it sad to see how some of my classmates have deteriorated either physically or mentally. Some seem to have reached the stage where, for one reason or another, they have lost interest in life and are simply "waiting for Godot." Of course, I realize they may think the same of me! And at each successive reunion, the list of deceased classmates grows longer.

The sweet part is that I have often encountered returning classmates whom I had known only in passing while at college, but who have since led fascinating lives and who now make interesting conversation-mates. They have kept their curiosity and mental vitality and are eager to enter into lively exchanges of ideas and opinions. I find there is much I can learn from them. They have been the source of a number of new friendships.

Amherst

May 2010 brought the 55th reunion for the Class of '55 at Amherst. I was asked to serve as program chairman for the event. The topics we chose to discuss were as follows:

1. "Waiting for Godot ... Gracefully:" An exploration into the challenges, opportunities, and possibilities offered by the final third of one's life.

2. An exploration of "Conscious Capitalism:" Is *laissez faire* capitalism *à la* Milton Friedman that focuses single-mindedly on maximizing shareholder value still a valid model for healthy economic and social progress? Or is "Conscious Capitalism," which focuses on *optimizing* returns to all stakeholders (customers, employees, supply chain partners, shareholders, communities, and the environment) perhaps a better model for ensuring positive economic and social progress in the future?

3. Whatever happened to the concept of "bipartisanship" and civility in our American political system?

4. Whither goes American health care and how will future changes impact Americans in general and Amherst graduates of our vintage in particular?

5. What has been the history of "diversity" at Amherst over the past 55 years?

6. Glimpses into the life and poetry of former Amherst faculty member Robert Frost with particular focus on Frost as an early American proponent of environmental conservation.

7. Showcasing the artistic, literary, and musical talents of classmates. An exhibition of the paintings, sculptures, writings, and musical contributions of the members of the Amherst class of 1955.

It turns out that, 55 years after graduation, the class of '55 still had many thoughtful and articulate members willing to serve on panels to discuss the first six topics and still other creative and artistic classmates who contributed to an exhibition of their work. The program sessions were well done and led to many stimulating and, at times, heated discussions among classmates. The consensus among the classmates who attended was that the event had been a great success. For me, that reunion was much more sweet than bitter!

CHAPTER FIVE

COLLEGE SUMMERS

Following my freshman year at Amherst, I obtained a job back in Mansfield shoveling asphalt for the Mansfield Asphalt Paving Company. I wanted to make some money and, at $1 per hour, the pay was good for a 17-year-old kid. The work, however, was backbreaking. I was part of a crew that paved roads all over Richland County, Ohio. Trucks bearing steaming hot asphalt would drop their loads on the roadbeds. It was then the task of our shoveling crew to spread the asphalt evenly over the foundation surface so that the huge engine-driven rollers could smooth and compress the blacktop into a finished driving surface. Summers in Mansfield were hot, and we often found ourselves shoveling 150-degree hot asphalt in air temperatures ranging from 80 to 100 degrees. I came home each day totally exhausted and dehydrated. Then it was up at six the next morning to report for work at 7:30 and begin the daily routine all over again.

My crew included five workers, four of whom were black. I, the youngest, was the only white person on the crew. The others were Jimmy, Tommy, A.C., and Ryan. We became good friends and I learned a lot about life from them that summer. During our rest breaks, they would try their best to educate me about booze, women, money, and the pluses and minuses of domestic life. Every Monday morning, I heard all the lurid details about their weekend late-night adventures, which included drinking, fighting, fornicating, and gambling in Mansfield's red-light district. I was all ears!

The summer after my sophomore year became a repeat of the summer before, but this time I earned $1.25 per hour. I joked that I was vice president in charge of shoveling asphalt on a road paving crew. In fact, I was the least senior person out there. In retrospect, I am very grateful for those two summers shoveling asphalt. I ended each summer in great physical shape and I became more worldly-wise in terms of practical street smarts. In an era when racial prejudice was prevalent in Midwest America, the experience gave me an opportunity to make new friends from the black community and to better understand life from their point of view. That lesson has remained with me for the rest of my life. Among other lessons, I learned that people from different ethnic groups and classes can be friends if they can look beyond the differences that seem to be so important to so many people.

The summer after my junior year took me far from the road crew. The director of alumni relations at Amherst was an alumnus from the class of 1934 named Al Guest. He and his family had a summer home on Martha's Vineyard and he was chairman of the board of directors of the island's East Chop Tennis Club. By tradition, each summer he hired a member of the Amherst varsity tennis team to be the tennis "pro" at the club. That summer, he hired me.

What a cushy job! For the most part, I taught teenage boys and girls how to develop good serves and ground strokes, plus a bit about court tactics. My clientele also included a goodly share of "summer widows" who enjoyed life on the Vineyard while their husbands pursued their careers on Wall Street or in industry. They tended to be good tippers.

As it turned out, I also became the teaching pro at the West Chop Tennis Club on the Island. The fellow who had originally been lined up for the job had to cancel at the last minute and I was asked to fill in for him. West Chop was about a 10-minute drive around the Vineyard Haven harbor from East Chop and I alternated mornings and afternoons between the two. The families of my West Chop clients tended to be wealthier, more aristocratic, and snobbier than those on East Chop. Many of them were from old-line Boston Brahmin families. Others were academics, writers, or artists. The East Choppers were by and large from more middle-class families that had been "summering" on the Island for generations. I got along with all of them. Though still somewhat of a naïve Midwesterner, it helped that I was studying at Amherst, which, along with Williams and Wesleyan, comprised the "little three" of the Ivy League.

I charged $7.50 an hour for tennis lessons and my lesson book was pretty full every day. Instead of making about $60 a week shoveling hot asphalt, I was earning $150 to $200 a week teaching tennis, something I enjoyed doing! In addition, I had the franchise to sell Spaulding tennis rackets and balls at both tennis clubs. That added another $40 to $50 per week to my wallet. I felt like I was rolling in dough!

But the best part of that summer was my life on the Island away from the tennis courts. Again, by tradition, the East Chop tennis teacher lived with Pippy Hand and Niven Wall, two elderly sisters who had a fantastic summer home next door to the East Chop lighthouse on a bluff overlooking the ocean. Pippy and Niven were great. They had well-developed senses of humor and were wonderfully hospitable. We totally hit it off. Every afternoon when the sun "went over the yardarm" they would break out the gin bottle and have their daily round of very, very dry martinis while sitting on their lovely front porch overlooking the water. I typically joined them for a bottle of beer or a gin and tonic before going out to join my Island friends, mostly other college students, to experience the Vineyard's nightlife . . . such as it was.

There were dances to be crashed at the Edgartown Yacht Club, parties on the beach, more parties at various Island summer homes, even more pizza parties, and movies. Sometimes the talk was deep and philosophical (what is the meaning of life); more often it was not (among us guys, it was beer, babes, sports, and bombast). Sometimes, there was heavy drinking, although I was never into much imbibing. A couple of beers or G&Ts were my limit. Fortunately, I have never had addictive tendencies. If I had, that summer might have been a disaster! There were plenty of college girls on the Vineyard that summer who were waitressing, bartending, or babysitting, and I dated around without serious infatuations.

Some days I would take time off to go clamming up-Island or swimming on South Beach with one or another of my buddies, most of whom were college students. Among those I still remember were Sam Eells (who was studying at Williams), John Hill Wilson (Princeton), Danny Fracas (University of Virginia), Mark Hanschka (Amherst), and George Morgan (also from Amherst). George was the son of Professor Charlie Morgan, who had taught me art history at Amherst. The Morgans had a wonderful up-Island house in Tisbury and they often included me for dinners, beach parties, and clam-digging expeditions. Several other Amherst faculty members also had places on the Vineyard, including history professor Bucky Salmon, who, six years later, lent my bride and me his Island retreat for part of our honeymoon.

I also spent lots of time that summer just reading and daydreaming. My major reading project was Tolstoy's *War and Peace*, which I devoured from cover to cover. I loved its scope and grandeur.

I was not aware of it at the time, but I was experiencing what is known as "social mobility." Though I was middle-class myself, through hard work and a bit of luck, I was being accepted into the upper classes. It was a subtle and nuanced process, but one that is repeated throughout our society on a daily basis. Though I have not studied the matter at length, I am informed that this is by no means the norm globally—and my travels abroad confirm it.

Perhaps the most indelible memory of that 1954 summer was my encounter with "Carol." One Sunday morning, I had slept in late after attending a party in

Edgartown the night before. Pippy and Niven were off-Island, so I had the house to myself. A bit the worse for wear, I wandered into the kitchen and made myself a cup of coffee and poured a bowl of cereal. It was a gray morning with a bit of a breeze. It looked like rain was in the offing. (And it was!)

As I sat at the table eating breakfast, the wind began to pick up. Then, with my cup halfway to my lips, hurricane-force winds suddenly struck and blew out several of the kitchen windows, sending glass shattering all over the floor and counters. I was so startled that I dumped the scalding cup of hot coffee all over myself! I didn't have a lot of time to worry about that, though!

With the wind howling and blowing even harder, I sprang up and ran through the living room to the door that opened onto the covered front porch and the broad expanse of lawn beyond. I arrived just in time to witness all the porch furniture blowing off the porch and being sent swirling across the lawn, over the bluff into the sea. Going from room to room to try to close all the wooden shutters, I next looked out the window just in time to see the entire rear wing of the house across the road being blown off its foundation. It clattered away, furnishings and all, into the air. Petrified, I realized I was in the midst of a full-blown hurricane!

For about 15 or 20 minutes, I huddled on the floor behind what I hoped was a sturdy wall, listening as the gale-force winds continued to howl outside. Then, suddenly, the wind completely stopped. I cautiously opened the door and made my way outside. The silence was eerie.

I walked slowly down the road bordering the bluff in the direction of the small village of Oak Bluffs. Devastation was everywhere. A couple of hundred yards along the road, a car was teetering on the edge of the cliff. As I approached, the earth under it gave way and it toppled over, dropping about 30 feet into the water below. Porches and walls had become detached from houses. Debris was strewn everywhere.

Suddenly, the silence felt ominous. Fortunately, my intuition told me to turn around and head back to the house. I did so just in time. When I had covered about half the distance back, those gale-force winds struck again. Almost too late, I realized that I had been in the legendary "eye of the hurricane" where everything seemed deceptively calm and quiet. With my head into the wind and my body at about a 45-degree angle to the ground, I battled my way back to home base and managed to reenter the house, where I huddled again on the floor. The hurricane, with redoubled ferocity, continued its deafening rampage outside for what seemed an eternity, but in reality was probably about 10 or 15 minutes. Then everything finally fell silent again, this time for good.

After waiting for a time to make sure that the hurricane had really blown over, I again ventured outside. After first ascertaining that, apart from losing its kitchen windows and all its porch furniture, Pippy and Niven's house had survived relatively unscathed, I walked the entire half-mile into Oak Bluffs. There was devastation on all sides. Everywhere I looked, there were uprooted trees, badly damaged houses, broken furniture, and scattered trash. In the little Oak Bluffs marina, many of the boats had been torn loose from their moorings or anchors and tossed high and dry, dozens of feet up on shore. Some were missing masts or had had their bows staved in. The most ludicrous sight was a 30-foot sloop that had evidently been lifted by a huge storm wave and neatly deposited perfectly upright on four pilings of the marina's main pier.

I only learned afterward that the hurricane had been named Carol. It became famous as the most powerful ever to hit the coastal area around Martha's Vineyard and Cape Cod.

What happened in its aftermath was a lesson for me in the full range of human behavior. On the side of the angels was the outpouring of Good Samaritan activities on the part of the vast majority of Islanders. Almost everyone turned out to help their neighbors repair property damage and to provide medical assistance, physical nourishment, or spiritual comfort. On the side of the devil was the fact that the Vineyard was also the site of a significant amount of post-hurricane looting and vandalism. Apparently, natural disasters, just like manmade disasters, bring out both the best and worst instincts in our fellow humans.

The summer of 1955, following my graduation from Amherst, found me waiting for my orders from the Air Force, assigning me to the two years of required active duty that I owed the country as a result of having been in R.O.T.C. in college. I spent most of the summer back on the Vineyard teaching tennis again and generally having a good time. This summer, however, I stayed in Vineyard Haven as a guest of my friend Sam Eells and his family. The Eells had a wonderful property right on the water that included a small lighthouse that had been converted into guest quarters. That was where I stayed, and I loved it. My hosts were a warm and generous family from Cleveland. They said, "stay as long as you would like" and I did. Sam had become my closest friend on the Island and that summer of '55 was the manager of the East Chop Tennis club where I was again the tennis instructor.

Toward the middle of the summer I became nervous because I had not yet received my orders to report for active military duty. I had tried to make clear to the Air Force that I would like to commence active duty by the end of the summer. This was so that I could fulfill my two-year obligation and still be discharged in time to start graduate school studies in September 1957.

However, the summer came and went without any orders. Toward the end of August, I headed home to Mansfield, where my parents were happy to catch a glimpse of me before I headed off in uniform to defend the country. To fill the time and earn a little money while waiting for my orders to arrive, I went back to work for a couple of months at the Mansfield Asphalt Paving Company. This time I was assigned to work on the assembly of a huge asphalt mixing machine. It was more interesting and less backbreaking than shoveling hot asphalt out on the road. And this time I was paid the princely sum of $1.50 per hour!

CHAPTER SIX

MY LIFE IN THE AIR FORCE

September of 1955 came and went. Still no orders! Finally, on the 26th of October a letter arrived from the Air Force. I was to report five days later to Manhattan Beach Air Force Station for further processing to a permanent post at APO 81, NY, NY. I had no idea what that meant.

"APO 81" was Air Force-speak for an overseas airbase, the location of which was designated only by an Air Force Post Office number. It turned out that these Post Office numbers were considered classified information. Since I was still a civilian, I wasn't entitled to know the location of APO 81, even though I was being sent there. What to do? Should I pack a swimming suit and suntan lotion? Or should I pack long underwear and warm gloves?

I finally drove out to the Mansfield Airport where an Air National Guard station was headquartered. After first refusing to let me see the classified list of APO locations, the officer in charge finally took pity on me and showed me the list. As I read down it, I spotted bases in places like France, Germany, or the Azores. They all sounded pretty good to me. Then I got to APO 81: Iceland! It was to be long underwear and warm gloves. A freezing Arctic climate was not what I had bargained for.

Nevertheless, two days later, I boarded a commercial flight in Cleveland and flew to New York. It was my first-ever airplane ride, and as such, an exhilarating experience. I reported for duty at Manhattan Base Air Force station in Brooklyn where I was given a physical and a couple of Air Force uniforms with a gold bar on each shoulder signifying I was now officially a second lieutenant.

The next day, I flew on a Military Air Transport plane to the Air Force base in the tiny village of Keflavik, Iceland. Apart from a one-day visit to Canada, it was my first trip to a location outside the U.S.

On my arrival in Iceland, I was told to see Colonel Wisnewski, the officer in charge of base personnel. When I reported to him, he asked to see my orders. After studying them for a few moments he looked up and said there seemed to be some mistake. The base in Iceland was considered to be a "sensitive hardship post" inasmuch as there had recently been some Communist agitation on the island. As a result, Air Force protocol called for only assigning fully qualified and experienced airmen and officers to the base. Since I was neither, Col. Wisnewski informed me that orders should never have been issued posting me there. My heart leaped! Maybe I would end up being reassigned to one of those interesting places in Germany, France, or the Azores after all!

The colonel thereupon began shuffling through a bunch of papers on his desk and asking me some questions about my background and education. He finally looked at me with what I thought was a bit of a gleam in his eye and said, "I'll tell you what, Lieutenant Sorenson, now that you are here, we might as well see if we can find a way for you to stay. It turns out that we have a Lieutenant Nelson on the base who has just been granted a compassionate reassignment back to the U.S. to deal with a serious family problem. Until today, he has been serving as adjutant and personnel officer in the 1400th Field Maintenance Squadron. I'm going to assign you to take his place. You go report to Major Robert Morrison, the commanding officer, and tell him you are Lieutenant Nelson's replacement."

Hiding my disappointment, I saluted, said, "Yes sir," and exited.

Next, I made my way to a cavernous hanger with a small Quonset hut attached to one of its sides that contained the squadron's orderly room and Major Morrison's office. When I walked into the orderly room, Sergeant Bowen, a large, friendly-looking man in his late thirties, greeted me. He asked, "Yes, Lieutenant, what can we do for you?"

"I'm here to see Major Morrison," I replied.

He looked at me a bit quizzically and said, "He's busy doing paperwork right now, but have a seat and I'll see if I can fit you into his schedule."

After cooling my heels for about 15 minutes and observing the 10 or so airmen who were manning desks in the open plan orderly room, I was told by Sgt. Bowen that Maj. Morrison would see me now. Entering the commanding officer's cubicle, I noticed that its five-foot-high walls offered little privacy. All the airmen in the outer office could probably hear anything said within its confines.

Maj. Morrison sat behind his desk with his head down writing on a piece of paper. He didn't look up when I entered and just continued his scribbling. Sitting there, he appeared to be a bit chubby with a round face, glasses, and dark hair. I fetched up in front of his desk and stood rigidly at attention in front of him.

After about a minute or so he finally looked up and said, "Yes, Lieutenant, what do you want?"

I replied, "I'm Lieutenant Sorenson, sir, reporting for duty as your new adjutant and personnel officer."

"What the hell do you mean? I already have a perfectly good officer, Lieutenant Nelson, filling those posts," he sputtered.

"Sir, Colonel Wisnewski just told me that Lieutenant Nelson has been granted a compassionate reassignment back to the U.S. for family reasons and that I am to report to you for duty as his replacement."

Growing physically agitated, he asked, "How long have you been in the Air Force?"

"One day, sir."

"How old are you?"

"I turned 22 a little more than a month ago."

"Jesus Christ! What's your AFSC?" he asked.

Having no idea what that meant, I replied, "I don't know, sir, I'm R.O.T.C."

At that, he blew up. "Holy Mother of God, don't you even know that AFSC means your Air Force Specialty Code? Or that only fully qualified and experienced officers are to be assigned to this base?"

Still standing at rigid attention, I didn't know what to say, so I just remained mute.

Then he ranted on, "That goddammed Wisnewski has done it to me again! For God's sake, sending me a one-day wonder who doesn't even know his AFSC from a hole in the ground."

He seized the telephone and dialed Col. Wisnewski's number. Wisnewski answered; Morrison roared into the phone. "I've got this young kid standing in front of me who has only been on active duty for one day, who doesn't even know his AFSC classification, and whose only qualification seems to be that he is one of those smart-ass college students who attended a few R.O.T.C. classes. How the hell do you expect me to run the administrative and personnel end of this squadron with a dumbass like that?" . . . or words to that effect.

Mortified, I just stood there.

Wisnewski, at the other end of the line, evidently said something to the effect of, "Calm down. Nelson is leaving for sure today and there is no other officer on the base that I can reassign to take his place. So it is Sorenson or nobody. Take your choice. It's up to you."

Still fuming, Maj. Morrison banged down the phone, looked up at me, and said, "Goddammit, I guess I'm stuck with you. Go see Sergeant Bowen and tell him to teach you something. And you better be a fast learner!"

Red-faced and shamed, I slunk out of his office into the open orderly room. All the airmen sitting there, who obviously had heard every word of the conversation, were casting knowing glances at one another and seemed barely able to contain their smirks and laughter. Eventually, all of these men would be under my supervision and I was not off to an auspicious start.

Fortunately, Sgt. Bowen, wise old hand that he was, suggested we take a walk to get a cup of coffee. On the way he said, "Don't take it personally, Lieutenant. It's not your fault. You'll see. It's gonna be okay. Major Morrison is really a good guy and a very effective commander. He's just upset because Colonel Wisnewski didn't consult with him about Lieutenant Nelson's being sent back to the States. So he was taken by surprise, but he'll get over it. Meanwhile, let me tell you a bit about the 1400th Field Maintenance Squadron."

He went on to say that the squadron comprised about 150 airmen, most of them trained aircraft maintenance mechanics and specialists, plus six officers. The six were Maj. Morrison (the commander), three maintenance officers, a supply officer, and me (the future adjutant and personnel officer). The mission of the squadron was to do major repairs and maintenance on base and transient aircraft.

The base, which had a total of about 1,500 military personnel and perhaps 500 civilians, was under the overall control of the Air Force's Military Air Transport Service (MATS) but also housed contingents from the Army, Navy, and Marine Corps. At the time, it was the only base to house units from all four of these services. Since almost all aircraft at the time made a refueling stop in Iceland on their way to or from the U.S. and Europe, Keflavik was considered to be an extremely important base from a strategic point of view. The Korean War had recently been declared over, but the Cold War versus the Russians was in full swing. And, as mentioned earlier, in 1955 there had been recent signs of Communist agitation on the part of some Icelanders. Hence, Keflavik had been declared a sensitive base and was in a state of constant alert. This was why there was a policy of not assigning inexperienced officers or airmen to the base. It was also why a posting to Iceland was considered a hardship assignment and why tours of duty there were limited to one year.

Sgt. Bowen assured me that, as first sergeant, he was the senior non-commissioned officer in the squadron and that he knew its workings inside and out. He also indicated, in a kind tone of voice, that he would do his best to teach me the ropes. He subsequently proved to be as good as his word. As any young officer will tell you, experienced sergeants are vital to your success!

After my little talk with Sgt. Bowen, I checked out my living quarters. The Bachelor Officer Quarters (or BOQs) were all located in a series of Quonset huts that lined both sides of one street on the base. Each hut housed about 16 officers, two to a cubicle bedroom measuring about 10'x12'. My roommate was First Lieutenant Bill Plummer, a pilot in the fighter squadron located on the base. Bill was from Arkansas and was married with two kids who were back home in the States. We hit it off from the beginning. Having served on active duty for about six years, he was wise to the ways of the Air Force and subsequently became one of my mentors on the base. We had dinner together that night in the officer's mess, after which I fell into an exhausted sleep on my new bed.

Thus ended day one of my active military service. Little did I know what was in store for me on day two.

After waking and breakfasting on day two, I reported to the squadron's hangar, where Sgt. Bowen showed me my cubicle office and introduced me to the orderly room personnel who were to be under my overall supervision and to the supply officer and three maintenance officers in the squadron. I met two of the four, the supply officer and one maintenance officer, just as they were preparing to take off as pilot and co-pilot in a C-47 transport plane for a routine two-hour maintenance check and training flight. The rest of the morning I spent being briefed by Sgt. Bowen on my various new responsibilities.

Shortly after lunch, there was a call to Maj. Morrison from the base's control tower saying that the air controllers had lost radar contact with the squadron's C-47 aircraft toward the end of its scheduled flight. It was 30 minutes overdue for meeting its ETA (estimated time of arrival) back at the base. The weather was cloudy and overcast and several search planes were immediately dispatched to see if they could locate the missing aircraft.

For a couple of hours, a sense of anxiety permeated not only everyone in the 1400th Squadron but personnel all over the base as well. Then, about three o'clock in the afternoon, came the terrible news that one of the search planes had spotted the debris of a plane crash on the side of a small mountain not far from the base. There was no apparent sign of life at the crash site.

Further investigation confirmed it was indeed the plane from the 1400th Squadron piloted by the two officers that I had just met for the first time that morning. Neither of the pilots survived the crash.

Since it was November and darkness descended on Iceland at an early hour that time of year, it was too late to send a search party to the site of the crash that evening. But early the next morning a ground party was dispatched. Little remained of the bodies of the two officers.

Everyone on the base was devastated, especially the members of the 1400th Squadron. Though I had just met the two men, I was shaken up and greatly saddened by the whole affair. The cause of the crash was never definitely determined. It most probably was weather related and/or a failure of the plane's radar system.

In any event, the tragedy affected me personally in two ways. First, I was assigned the duty of supply officer for the squadron in addition to being adjutant and personnel officer.

Second, Maj. Morrison approached me the day after the crash and said, "Lieutenant, you apparently are a well-educated college graduate. I never learned to write that well and I would appreciate it if you would do me a favor and write drafts of condolence letters to the widows and families of the two pilots who died in the crash. I'll try to add my personal sentiments to the letters before they are sent out over my signature."

This dose of reality was my military equivalent of total "baptism under fire." I did the best I could composing those letters and then gave them to Maj. Morrison for his edits and additions. I never saw the final versions that he sent off. But it was one of the hardest assignments that I had confronted up to that time in my life. Maj. Morrison seemed to appreciate my effort and he thanked me warmly. Moreover, from that time forward he began treating me as a seasoned officer and contributing member of his team.

Over the ensuing months, I learned quickly and was able to master most of my various military responsibilities. Essentially, they boiled down to overseeing the administrative aspects of the squadron, handling personnel assignments and problems, and making sure that the supply room, with its inventory of tools and spare aircraft parts, ran smoothly. Sgt. Bowen, true to his word, took me under his wing and taught me the Air Force way of handling these matters.

The Air Force had a set way of doing everything. These protocols were all captured in thick manuals of Standard Operating Procedures or "SOPs" in Air Force-speak. There was a regulation covering almost every aspect of life on the base. The only factor that led to occasional conflicts and confusion was that the Army, Navy, and Marine Corps each had their own manuals of SOPs that didn't always agree with one another. However, these interservice conflicts didn't arise very often and for the most part things proceeded smoothly on the base. After a while, my job became pretty routine and, frankly, a bit boring.

My major feeling of accomplishment was that, in time, Sgt. Bowen and the airmen who were under my command came, I believe, to respect me and enjoy working for me. As a result of trial and error, I learned some basic leadership skills that served me well in my later professional life.

Some excitement was introduced into my professional life on the base when, on one occasion, I was asked to serve on a Courts-Martial Board panel of judges and, on another, to serve as defense attorney in several cases defending airmen who were accused of committing various offenses or infractions under the UCMJ (Uniform Code of Military Justice). The most interesting legal situation I encountered was as a judge in the case of an airman who was being court-martialed for striking a superior, in this case a sergeant in charge of an aircraft maintenance crew.

The circumstances of the case were as follows: The airman in question was a young mechanic's assistant who had just arrived on the base a few days prior to the date of the alleged infraction. His rank was that of an Airman Third Class, the lowest possible in the Air Force. He had gone through basic training in the States and this was his first field assignment.

The morning in question, the crew sergeant, as a practical joke and in the spirit of initiating the newcomer, had sent the green airman over to another squadron's hangar to ask a particular maintenance crew sergeant there if he could borrow a fallopian tube that was needed in the repair of a C-54 transport plane. The airman dutifully set off on his search and found the sergeant in question. When asked by the airman, that sergeant said he didn't happen to have a spare fallopian tube in inventory, but he did have a spare skyhook. The airman said, no, he had been sent to find a fallopian tube and had been told not to come back without one. Whereupon, this second sergeant suggested that the airman go over to the Navy hangar on the base and ask its maintenance crew chief if he had a spare fallopian tube. The airman received the same answer from the Navy man but was told that there was a good chance that the crew chief at the Army's helicopter hangar might have one. The Army crew chief finally took pity on the naive young airman and told him that a fallopian tube was part of a woman's private anatomy and that he had been sent off on a wild goose chase.

The airman, feeling that he had been played for an ignorant fool, lost his cool. He returned to his home hangar and decked his sergeant in the mouth and nose. The sergeant, whose nose was broken, brought charges.

After hearing the evidence by both the prosecution and defense attorneys, our three-officer judicial panel retired to consider the evidence. The prosecution "lawyer" had argued that it was an open-and-shut case. The airman had clearly struck his superior NCO in front of several witnesses and was guilty of a serious crime as defined in the Uniform Code. The "lawyer" for the defense retorted that the airman had been provoked beyond a reasonable limit by his sergeant and that the circumstances were sufficiently extenuating that a not-guilty finding should be returned.

The three of us on the panel of judges had had difficulty keeping a straight face during the presentation of the case. After all, sending someone off to chase spare fallopian tubes was a pretty innovative practical joke. On the other hand, it was a form of bullying that provoked the airman and that, in turn, landed him in court. Still, in the military, physically striking a superior NCO for any reason is defined as a serious offense and there was no question that the airman in question had done so . . . provoked or not.

After deliberating for less than a half-hour, we returned our unanimous decision: guilty with extenuating circumstances. The sentence: 30 days' confinement in the base prison and a permanent notation in the airman's personnel records.

Most of the cases in which I served as defense lawyer involved minor infractions. None was as intriguing as the "great fallopian tube chase." But they exposed me to how the military justice system worked and gave me practice analyzing evidence and speaking on my feet.

The most enjoyable and interesting aspects of my posting in Iceland were my off-duty experiences. I found Iceland itself to be fascinating. With only about 300,000 inhabitants, its form of government dates back to 1000 A.D. and is the oldest continuous democracy in the world. Its language, Old Norse, has also remained relatively unchanged for almost a millennium. Its name, Iceland, is a misnomer. Few people realize that its mean average temperature is actually warmer than that of New York City. Greenland, by contrast, truly has an arctic climate. (From a descriptive point of view, their names should probably be reversed.) The capital of Iceland is Reykjavik, which with a population of about 150,000 is also far and away its largest city.

Iceland's scenery is dramatic, starting with the fact that there are almost no trees. By contrast, there are hundreds of miles of rugged coastline, dramatic glaciers, huge rock outcroppings, extensive grasslands, many inland lakes and streams, and an impressive number of waterfalls that almost rival Niagara Falls. During the year I was there, the wind seemed to blow constantly . . . around the clock and in all seasons. On the airbase, I remember the constant salt-water smell of fish borne by the on-shore breeze coming from the little nearby fishing village of Keflavik and its neighboring whaling station.

I found the Icelanders, as a whole, to be admirable people. They are purportedly the most literate nation in the world, with virtually no one unable to read and write. Moreover, they read and write more books per capita than any other country. Descended from Nordic stock, they tend to be intelligent, hardy, and attractive. There is virtually no poverty on the island. At the time I was stationed there, the mainstays of the island's economy were fishing, sheep farming, harnessing geothermal power, and aluminum smelting.

Not long after arriving in Iceland, by chance I met Val, who was working at the airbase's telephone exchange. A year older than me, she lived in nearby Keflavik where she rented a two-room apartment in a snug little village house. She had dark curly hair, a ready smile, and a vivacious personality. She was very pretty. I asked her out for a dinner date or two at the base officers' club. Soon she became my regular date on weekends. Sometimes we would go to an officer's club dance or to a movie on the base or in the tiny movie theater in Keflavik near the apartment where she lived.

There was a strict limit on the number of passes granted to U.S. military personnel wanting to go off the base to visit Reykjavik or explore other parts of Iceland. The 1400th, with about 160 personnel, had a total allocation of about a dozen passes that could be issued at any one time. This sometimes made it difficult to get off-base. However, I had a secret weapon. Namely, as adjutant, I issued the passes for our squadron and, in that capacity was able to leave the base any time I wanted!

Moreover, the first month I was in Iceland, I negotiated with Lieutenant Page, a fellow officer who was returning to Syracuse, New York, on a two-week leave, to buy a second-hand car for me while in the U.S. and deliver it to a military dock near New York City for shipment to me in Iceland. I gave him $250 for the purchase of the car and told him that he could use it for his own transportation while on leave prior to delivering it to the port. He was happy to do the deal and subsequently bought an old wooden-sided Ford station wagon that arrived in Iceland in mid-December.

So, with off-base pass in hand and a car to drive, Val and I drove the 30 miles or so into Reykjavik to spend two days over Christmas at the home of a couple who were friends of hers. In addition, I somehow had managed to get us invited to a Christmas party hosted by the American ambassador to Iceland. As a result, we met almost everyone assigned to the U.S. diplomatic corps in the country. Several of these people subsequently became friends.

Christmas itself was a warm affair celebrated at the home of the couple who were our hosts in Reykjavik. They had also invited three or four other friends over for a roast lamb dinner. (Given Iceland's sheep population, Icelanders eat a lot of lamb when they are not eating fish). Potatoes, root vegetables, and plenty of Aquavit for libations accompanied the lamb.

This was the first Christmas that I had spent away from home, so I was a bit homesick. But I had received a big care package from Mansfield that helped my spirits considerably.

The following week, it was back to Reykjavik for a New Year's bash at some other friends of Val's. This was my first real glimpse of Icelanders as world-class drinkers. Because of the country's high northern latitude, from October until March there is little daylight. In December and January, the sun goes down about 2:30 p.m. and doesn't rise until about 10 a.m. There isn't a lot to do outside. Consequently, Icelanders spend a lot of their time in winter staying inside and drinking, partying, making love, and reading . . . more or less in that order.

At the New Year's Eve party that we attended, the drinking started early and continued in earnest well into the wee hours of the morning. This was truly serious drinking, believe me. One hundred twenty proof Aquavit flowed as if from a waterfall. There must have been 40 or 50 toasts in the course of the evening. Someone would raise his glass, say "SKOL!" And take a drink. All the other partiers, in turn, would raise their glasses, say "SKOL!" and take a drink. Then the original proposer of the toast, getting right into the spirit of the moment, would raise his glass again and say "SKOL-Y-BOT!", meaning "bottoms up" and drain his glass. Whereupon, the rest of the revelers would be expected to "SKOL-Y-BOT" each other and drain their glasses as well. The only non-alcoholic nourishment that evening was pickled herring and smoked salmon canapés followed, late in the evening, by pastries and cake. In the America of today, the drinking of that New Year's Eve would clearly be classified as binge drinking. By the end of the evening, half of the revelers had passed out, a quarter had become morose, and the rest were still going strong, laughing, singing, and shouting at one another. As I said, drinking is a serious affair in Iceland. Or at least it was that winter of 1955-56.

When I wasn't dating Val that winter, I was spending most of my off-duty hours playing poker with my fellow hut mates in our Quonset quarters. We would play "dealer's choice" hands for hours on end. We played for money, but the stakes were relatively small. By late spring, I was pretty "pokered" out and declined to join in most of the subsequent games. From a monetary point of view, I ended up slightly on the plus side, with net winnings of about $300. It was enough to pay for my car, with a little left over.

As the days lengthened into summer, my off-duty passion became fishing. Iceland is legendary for having some of the best trout and salmon fishing in the world. So, throughout the summer, I would take off every available weekend that I didn't have duty-officer responsibilities and head out to a renowned stream or lake to try my luck with a spinning rod. On several weekends I took Val, who also loved to fish, with me.

We would typically drive off late Friday afternoon after work and return on Sunday afternoon. In late June, the sun didn't set until 1:00 or 2:00 a.m. So, in the evenings we would fish until midnight, and then bed down in Air Force-issue sleeping bags in some abandoned stone sheep enclosure and breakfast on the fish we had caught the night before. Sizzling fried fish cooked over an open fire, with bacon, toast, and coffee for accompaniment, leisurely consumed in an incomparably beautiful setting: What could be more glorious! Mostly, we caught German Brown or Dolly Varden trout or Arctic Char. Occasionally, if we were stream fishing, we would dine on freshly caught salmon.

On weekends when Val didn't accompany me, I was often joined on my fishing expeditions by two or three other fisherman friends from the base. As one of the few officers with a car—a station wagon no less—I was mighty popular on the weekends.

Apart from fishing, the major highlight of my summer was the three-week leave that I took to visit Europe. Together with a friend of mine, Lieutenant Bill Connors, we took off for Germany in mid-August. We landed at Rein-Main Air Force Base near Frankfurt. I was thrilled to set foot for the first time on mainland Europe. It was something I had dreamed of doing for a long time. Bill was equally excited, since it was his first visit to Europe as well. His background was similar to mine. He, too, had been a liberal arts student in college and was a graduate of an R.O.T.C. program. We made good traveling companions.

Having arrived around midday, we spent our first afternoon renting a Volkswagen Beetle and driving around Frankfurt. The first thing that struck us was that much of Frankfurt was still filled with rubble and debris caused by the Allied bombings more than 10 years earlier. Whole blocks still lay in ruins. Many buildings had only one or two walls still standing. At the same time, much repair and rebuilding activity was in evidence. Construction scaffolding was everywhere. The whole scene was a grim reminder of the extended trauma European civilization had endured a few years earlier in World War II.

We were glad to head south out of Frankfurt late that afternoon. We drove until we saw the sign for what appeared to be a charming little Gasthaus under some trees in a beautiful rustic setting. We asked if they had a room. "Ya, wir haben ein zimmer frei heute abend," the innkeeper's daughter assured us. She then showed us to a delightful room overlooking a pastoral scene complete with grazing sheep and cattle. After a hearty dinner of sausages and sauerbraten washed down by a couple of tankards of good German draft bier, we climbed under our eiderdown comforters, laid our heads on incredibly soft feather pillows and dreamed the dreams of the innocent.

The following morning, we were treated to a delicious breakfast of freshly baked croissants, newly churned butter, Hero strawberry jam, perfectly cooked four-minute soft boiled eggs, hand-squeezed orange juice, and steaming hot mugs of brewed coffee. To this day, more than a half-century later, I still remember that breakfast in the wonderful little countryside inn in Germany. Parenthetically, I might mention that this was the first time I had ever tasted a croissant. It was love at first bite!

The next day we drove further south on the fabled German autobahn and over the next couple of days made brief stops in Wiesbaden, the Black Forest, Munich, and, finally, in the mountain village of Garmisch-Partenkirchen, near the spot where Hitler had the "Eagle's Nest," his famous retreat. I don't remember much about these stops apart from the fact that in Garmisch we were treated to fabulous views from the top of a gondola ski-lift ride.

Next it was on to Italy, with stops in Venice, Florence, Tuscany, and in Rome. In each place we sampled the typical tourist attractions. We took a gondola ride and visited St. Mark's in Venice. We spent an afternoon at Florence's Uffizi Museum, where I was blown away by seeing paintings and other famous works of art that I had studied at Amherst. Michelangelo's statue of David, and Ghiberti's intricately wrought cathedral doors further enchanted me. Tuscany beguiled us with its tiny villages and beautiful vistas overlooking vineyards, valleys, and hillsides dotted with tall, slim cypress trees, all standing at attention.

Finally, we reached the southernmost point of our travels: Rome. We stayed at a lovely little inn, named the Buona Stella, or Beautiful Star, located on one of the Seven Hills of Rome. High above the city with breathtaking nighttime views, it fully lived up to its name. In later years, I tried on several occasions to rediscover the Buona Stella, but alas, to no avail. Rome, of course, was its own charming self. We were awed by the Vatican and the ceiling of the Sistine Chapel. We were delighted by the water music of the city's fountains and our taste buds were captivated by the city's Italian cuisine.

Then, all too soon, it was time to head north again toward France. Along the way, we stopped for a brief look at the Leaning Tower of Pisa. Then, after an overnight stay near Nice on the Côte d'Azur, we drove straight through to Paris.

Ah, Paris! I remember it as the pinnacle of our trip. Untouched by World War II bombing, it was totally intact and cast its unique magical spell on two young 22-year-olds visiting Europe for the first time. We sampled all the city's delights, from the Louvre and the Jeu de Palme Impressionist museum to the Eiffel Tower, the Arc de Triomphe, the Avenue Champs Elysees, Montmartre, and the Left Bank cafés where Hemingway and his writer and artist friends had hung out. We even spent an evening at the Folies Bergere, where we witnessed, for the first time in our lives, a bevy of bare-breasted beauties strutting their stuff to the musical rhythms of Edith Piaf-type show tunes.

From Paris it was on to London, our last stop. While it was good to be back in an English-speaking country, I remember London as being a bit of a letdown after Paris. We visited all the usual tourist sites and were generally underwhelmed by English cooking. The excursion that most sticks out in my mind 60-some years later is our visit to London's Silver Vaults. Located underground in a large building, the Vaults comprised the world's largest silver-trading market. There were seemingly hundreds of small stalls filled with every imaginable product made of silver: flatware, platters, teapots, candlesticks, cigarette boxes, soup tureens, and gravy bowls. I learned how to tell the difference between sterling silver and silver plate: Sterling carried the tiny imprint of a lion. I took advantage of our visit to the vaults to purchase a spectacular pair of sterling candlesticks for my parents and a cream and sugar set as a wedding present for my old Mansfield friend, Tom Bloor, who was getting married that September.

Military life back in Iceland seemed tame after having completely fallen under the spell of Europe. Thinking back on the experience all these many years later, I now understand why Midwestern rural families in America asked the question of their doughboy sons returning from European duty after World War I: "How do we keep them down on the farm, after they've seen gay Par-ee?"

Shortly after my return to Iceland in August, I broke up with Val. She was interested in marriage or a long-term relationship and I didn't feel I could offer her that. I concluded that it was probably best to make a clean break and not string her along until my one-year Icelandic tour of duty ended on November 1st. I have to admit, however, that after having done what I thought was the honorable thing, I felt a pang of jealousy when Val began to date another officer about a month after we split up.

In September, I was asked to state my preferences in terms of a base assignment back in the U.S. for my second year of military service. I was able to list three choices. I was mainly interested in sunshine and warmth, so I put down two Air Force bases in Florida and one near San Francisco in California.

On September 30th, my reassignment orders came through. I was posted to Edwards Air Force Base in the Mojave Desert of Southern California! I had wanted sunshine and warmth but not necessarily desert duty in one of America's hottest climate zones. Talk about jumping from the refrigerator into the fire! On the other hand, I learned that Edwards was the Air Force's premier flight test center where all of the hot new aircraft were being developed and flight-tested. This sounded exciting. In any case, I would find out soon enough whether I had drawn the short straw or the long straw.

Once I received my orders spelling out my next assignment, I officially went FIGMO. In official Air Force parlance this stood for: "F . . . 'em I've Got My Orders." It also meant that officers and airmen alike typically slacked off and became a bit blasé about their duties in the last month before shipping out. I probably was no exception.

At the end of my tour of duty, Maj. Morrison, who had become a mentor to me, wrote a glowing end-of-tour "Fitness Report" evaluation. Shortly before I left Iceland, he tried very hard to convince me to become a "career officer." He said he thought I would have a bright long-term future in the Air Force. I told him I was very flattered, but there was one very good reason why I wasn't likely to take him up on his suggestion.

"What is that?" he asked.

In reply, I merely pointed at the chest of his uniform on which was pinned a set of silver wings and said, "I've observed that all of the Air Force generals seem to be flying officers. Having been rejected for flight training because of color blindness, I'm not a pilot and I don't think I want to be in a career where the top posts would never be open to me."

He expressed disappointment at my reply, but didn't dispute my reasoning. In the Air Force of the 1950s this was the equivalent of the career "glass ceiling" of later years.

On November 1, 1956, after I had sold my car for as much as I had originally paid for it, I bid farewell to my friends and colleagues in Iceland and flew back to the United States.

On arrival, I traveled to Mansfield for a reunion with my mother and dad. I was glad to see them, and they, me. After a year's absence, we had much to talk about. As usual, they welcomed me with open arms. Also, as usual, my mom, having decided that I was looking too thin, tried her best to fatten me up on her delicious home cooking.

By this time, they had been empty nesters for more than five years, ever since Nancy and I had gone off to college. Nancy, having graduated from Northwestern University in 1953, was now teaching physical education at New Trier High School in Winnetka, Illinois, so she wasn't in Mansfield when I visited there on my way to California. I did, however, reconnect with a few of my other old friends who were still in town.

Mansfield seemed pretty dull to me on that visit. I was almost certain that I never would return there to live on a permanent basis. I'm sure my parents sensed this and were disappointed. At the same time, I am also sure that they weren't surprised. In any case, their feelings toward Nancy and me had always been those of unconditional love. So, I knew that whatever I decided to do with my life, they would be there to support me. At the same time, I also knew that they would always miss me if I ended up living away from Mansfield. Of course, as it turned out, I never did return to live there and indeed, as long as they lived, my parents did miss me. In subsequent years, this thought gave me more than a few twinges of guilt. I tried to assuage these feelings by convincing myself that each of us has to live his or her own life and follow one's own destiny, no matter where the path leads. I still believe this is true, though it does cause heartache for parents around the world.

While in Mansfield, I bought an old, used Chevrolet to drive from Ohio to California. En route, I stopped in Evanston for a visit with Nancy. She was in good spirits and seemed to be enjoying her teaching job at New Trier. I then set off on my first-ever drive west through the Great Plains and over the mountains to California's Mojave Desert. I loved the scenery and the grandeur of the West, but didn't tarry along the way, as I was to report for duty by the middle of November 1956.

On arrival at Edwards Air Force Base, I was assigned to duties similar to those I had had in Iceland as adjutant, personnel officer, and supply officer. This time, however, my home was to be the 1300th Flight Line Maintenance Squadron. Whereas Field Maintenance Squadrons did major repairs and maintenance jobs on aircraft, Flight Line Maintenance Squadrons did routine aircraft maintenance, repairs, and service.

Compared with Keflavik Base in Iceland, Edwards constituted a cushy assignment. The Bachelor Officer Quarters were in charming little palm-shaded three-bedroom casitas. I was assigned to one where my two roommates were Lieutenant Dick Christianson, who, by coincidence, was a friend who had served with me in Iceland and had simultaneously been reassigned with me to Edwards, and Lieutenant Bill Townsend, from Jackson, Mississippi, who was a fighter pilot and flight instructor. As for other amenities, the base had an elegant Officer's Club, a beautiful 18-hole golf course, a swimming pool, and excellent tennis courts. In short, Edwards was no hardship post.

Of course, there was the climate to contend with. During the summer, the daytime temperatures routinely got up into the 100s. The base mythology was that at noontime, one could fry eggs merely by cracking them on the concrete runways! I never personally ascertained whether this was true . . . but there were days when I could easily believe that this was possible. The only blessing was that the air was dry and, thus, I didn't feel the heat as acutely as I would have in a humid climate. It was important to keep hydrated, however. Beers at the Officers' Club served this purpose admirably!

What made my experience at Edwards fascinating was the fact that it was the Air Force's only flight test center where newly designed military and civilian experimental aircraft were tested and put through their paces. The undisputed stars of the base were the elite corps of hotshot test pilots stationed there. Most famous of these was Chuck Yeager. But there were many others as well, including a number of future astronauts. Gus Grissom, of later astronaut fame, was one of these. Several new fighter, bomber, and transport planes were being developed at the time and it was exciting to be part of the process of testing and maintaining them.

Bill Townsend, my casita mate, was a flight instructor. He occasionally took me up for flights in a T-33 single jet engine fighter trainer. It had tandem seats and, once in the air, Bill would let me pilot the plane from my seat in the front cockpit. What a rush it gave me! He would then take the controls for the fancier maneuvers such as loop-the-loops or Immelmanns.

On a couple of weekends, we flew down to a base near San Diego where we overnighted until Sunday and I visited with my childhood friend, David Carse, who was doing military service as a Navy frogman at the base on Coronado Island. I say visited, but perhaps I should have used the word caroused. David loved to party and had a whole bevy of women admirers and fellow frogmen who liked to party with him. I didn't get much sleep during those weekends. Apart from the two weekends when I flew to San Diego, there were several other occasions when I drove down to visit David.

On one of those weekend trips, he told me that the previous week he had gotten himself into a bit of disciplinary hot water. Apparently, when returning home to his small villa quarters after a rowdy party where he had had too much to drink, he wandered into the wrong villa by mistake. Going straight to the bedroom, he undressed and got into bed, only to discover that there was already a woman in the bed. It wouldn't have been so bad if the woman hadn't been the wife of his commanding officer. In the subsequent inquiry, David testified it had all been an honest mistake, that it was easy to confuse one villa for another since, in the dark, they all looked alike. Having a silver tongue, he ultimately was able to talk his way out of the situation. It helped that the commander's wife reportedly corroborated the fact that it had all been a mistake. Knowing David, I was never sure whether it really had been an error or whether it was one of those "accidentally-on-purpose" situations where, in fact, David and the commander's wife were actually having an affair. On those weekends with David, there was never a dull moment.

On a couple of other occasions while I was at Edwards, a bunch of us were able to commandeer a C-47 Air Force transport plane for weekend "training" jaunts. One weekend we flew to Seattle and on another to Minneapolis. In each case, we visited and partied with some hometown buddies of one or another of my traveling companions.

A scary incident occurred during our return flight from Seattle. Midway in the flight, the officer who was piloting the plane informed the five of us who were riding on benches in the cargo compartment behind the cockpit that we were experiencing some serious icing on the wings of the plane. It was a white-knuckle moment. The mood wasn't lightened when the pilot went on to inform us that we had better all strap on parachutes since he wasn't sure he could control the situation. And, indeed, we could sense the plane beginning to skew about in an unnatural manner. In the end, the pilot got permission to make an emergency landing at the civilian airport in Portland, Oregon. After having our wings de-iced, much relieved, we continued safely back to Edwards.

In June of 1957, I applied for an early release from the Air Force so that I could attend the graduate MBA program at the Harvard Business School beginning in September. Technically, my two-year active-duty obligation wasn't up until the end of October, but the Air Force powers-that-be granted my request.

Even before heading off for active duty, I had planned to do graduate studies. While a senior at Amherst I had sat for both the Graduate Management Admission Test (GMAT) and for the Law School Admission Test (LSAT). I had done well and scored in the upper 95th percentile on both tests.

As an undergraduate and in the Air Force, I had thought a good deal about the profession I wanted to pursue as a career. At one time or another I had considered medicine, the ministry, law, and business. Medicine sounded good, but I never really felt a genuine calling. As a sophomore, I did feel a real pull to go into the ministry . . . but it was short-lived. I concluded that I was too imperfect as a human being to go down that path. Besides, I had also begun to believe that organized religions all too often were more of a hindrance than help in my personal spiritual journey.

That left law and business. (I never gave much thought to teaching, writing, engineering, acting, becoming an artist or architect, or to any of the many other professions that might have been options. It either was a case of no aptitude or little interest.) Law, on the other hand, seemed potentially a fit. However, I discarded that profession after spending a day shadowing a successful lawyer friend of my family in Mansfield in the fall of 1955 while waiting for my Air Force orders to report for duty. My reaction to that day could be summed up in one word: boring. Spending my future poring over contracts and arcane statutes and helping clients look for loopholes in the law seemed to me neither promising nor fulfilling as a career. In retrospect, I probably chose the wrong lawyer to shadow or the wrong day on which to shadow him. Had I chosen a skillful litigator and experienced the drama of seeing him or her in action in a courtroom, I might have come to a different conclusion.

Thus, by process of elimination, I chose to go to business school to earn a graduate degree in business administration: an MBA. I reasoned that business was a huge tent, offering myriad opportunities and maximum flexibility. Besides, I reasoned that if I were successful in business I could always hire lawyers to do the necessary, boring legal stuff!

So it was that during my second year on active duty in the Air Force I had applied for admission to Harvard Business School and had been accepted.

In late August 1957 I said goodbye to my friends at Edwards Air Force Base and, with discharge papers and a commendation letter in hand, I set off in my car for the cross-country drive to Boston. As luck would have it, none other than David Carse had finagled leave from the Navy and had agreed to share the adventure and driving duties with me. It was a carefree trip. We first headed north to San Francisco where we sampled some nightlife in the course of which David scored a one-punch knockout on an aggressive drunk who tried to pick a fight with him. David struck second and hard, to the applause of the barroom onlookers who were entertained by the brief flurry of excitement.

At Lake Tahoe we paused for a day of nonstop water-skiing and sunbathing, hosted by a couple of attractive and hospitable 20-something young women who supplied the motorboat. Then, it was onward and eastward across the Rocky Mountains and the Great Plains for a nonstop driving stint to Evanston, Illinois, where David's family was living at the time. After a hearty meal with lively conversation, I had a good night's sleep, bid David and his folks goodbye and drove on alone back to Mansfield. There, I spent a week visiting with my family and catching up with my friends before driving on to Cambridge, Massachusetts, in early September in time to start classes at Harvard.

CHAPTER SEVEN

HARVARD BUSINESS SCHOOL

On arrival at Harvard Business School, I was assigned a room in Gallatin Hall with a roommate named Bill Richards (not his real name), from a little town in Arkansas. Quiet, shy, studious, and friendly, Bill was an ideal companion with whom to share a room. His family more or less owned his hometown, where his father was CEO of both a local manufacturing company and the local bank. According to Bill, Mr. Richards, Senior, was affectionately referred to around town as "Big Boss" and Bill himself was referred to as "Little Boss," a sobriquet he hated.

My first year at Harvard Business School came as a rude awakening. I felt I had landed in terra incognita that should have been marked on the map with the warning "There Be Dragons!" High school, college, and the Air Force had not prepared me for this experience!

To begin with, the workload was horrendous. Every evening, we were required to read and dissect three separate "case studies," each posing one or more management problems that we were expected to identify, analyze, and decide how best to handle as a manager. Courses were labeled: Marketing, Production, Finance, Control, Organizational Behavior (OB), Business Responsibilities in American Society (BRAS), and most notorious of all, Written Analysis of Cases (WAC).

Cases varied in complexity and ranged in length from a few pages to 30 or 40 pages. Many contained masses of tricky quantitative data that had to be painstakingly dissected, which required extensive computation. I typically staggered away from my desk and into bed at midnight, having clocked five or six hours preparing my cases for the next day.

Then it was up at seven in the morning for breakfast, followed by attending three one-hour-and-twenty-minute classes every day. We first-year students were divided into eight "sections," each comprising 90 students. I was assigned to Section C. All of my classes were held with my same fellow Section C classmates. We sat in an amphitheater-type classroom with the eager-beaver students typically filling up the front rows. The more laid-back or just plain scared students arrayed themselves in the back row, affectionately dubbed the "peanut gallery." It was as far away from the professor as possible.

Initially, I was filled with apprehension each time I walked into the classroom. I was not alone in this regard. Most of us were terrified of the dreaded "cold call." For example, Professor John "Black Jack" Matthews, our marketing professor, would typically walk into the class, swivel his head surveying his 90 potential victims, and then without warning, he would strike. "Mr. Hicks," he would say, "would you care to share your analysis of this management situation with all of your 89 fellow students." It was not a question. It was a command. "And by the way," he would add, "why don't you begin by telling all of us just exactly what is the *real* problem here."

Whereupon Mr. Hicks, who may or may not have come to class prepared, and who as often as not was instantly paralyzed with stage fright, would stammer out his theory of the case, lamebrained as it might be. When he had finished, Black Jack might stroke his chin and bark, "Hmm, so is that all?" Then he would swivel to the opposite side of the room, zero in on another student, and demand, "Well, Mr. Nelson, what do *you* think of Mr. Hicks' analysis?" And so it would go. And woe be it to he who was unprepared. That person would be torn apart either by Black Jack himself or by one of his traitorous fellow students.

I say "he," because in 1957, the Harvard Business School, like Amherst, was a single-sex institution. All of the students were men. All students were addressed as "Mister." And all students were expected to wear coats and ties to class. Unlike today, six decades later, academic formality still ruled the day.

By 9 p.m. every Saturday night, as part of the infamous Written Analysis of Cases (WAC) course, we were required to have deposited in a chute outside Baker Library a complete in-depth written analysis of the management issues contained in a particular case study. The chute was locked shut at precisely nine o'clock. At 9:01 p.m., the scrum of students who had gathered around the chute to participate in, or watch, the mad dash of the last-minute-Charlies trying to beat the deadline, would typically repair to the nearest watering hole across the Charles River to hoist a few beers. Some drank for the sheer relief of having finished the assignment on time. Others drank to drown their sorrows at having missed the deadline or done a lousy job in their written analysis.

For much of the first semester, I was in over my head and felt there was a chance that I might flunk out of the MBA program. Little by little, however, I regained my confidence and even began to understand and appreciate the power of the case study method of learning. It was quite different from Amherst, where much of the teaching was based on the lecture method, wherein the professor would do most of the talking, laying out a concept or theory, and the students would dutifully spend their time in class taking notes, memorizing facts, or daydreaming.

Instead, the case study method was based on an inductive approach to learning. The whole idea was to help students learn how to think originally and independently, analyze information and data in depth, and reach decisions under conditions of uncertainty, i.e., when not all of the facts bearing on a situation were known. It was further aimed at helping students hone their ability to express themselves and their ideas in a clear, articulate, persuasive manner, both in front of an audience and in writing. Fifty percent of one's course grade was based on classroom participation, so there was a strong incentive to develop one's communication skills. Very often, there was no "right" or "wrong" solution as to how to manage the management situation in question. As in real life, there were only "more effective" or "less effective" approaches to managing.

The opening chapter in a book entitled *The Case Study at the Harvard Business School* is entitled "Because Wisdom Can't be Told." It begins with a quote from the French novel *Le Pere Goriot* by Honoré de Balzac. The quote is as follows: "And so, as he grew older, he sought to pass along to his only son all the wisdom he had accumulated in his long life . . . a last noble illusion of age!"

Much of our educational system in America is still based on Pere Goriot's premise that by lecturing to students in the classroom it is possible to pass along to them knowledge and wisdom while they sit passively listening, taking notes, and memorizing. In my experience, life in the "real world" doesn't work that way. For one thing, most of the facts and theories passed along to students in those lectures have a very short half-life. For another, listening to lectures and memorizing information doesn't help students learn how to think independently or develop originality of thought.

If my own life is at all typical, true learning is a much more active, experiential affair. The poet James Russell Lowell is reputed to have said, "One thorn of experience is worth a whole thicket of advice." I believe he had it right. We learn best by doing, by working things out ourselves or cooperatively with colleagues. Except in the rare case of true geniuses and prodigies, wisdom and originality of thought comes for most of us through trial and error, through being confronted by problems and conundrums that we have to think through on our own.

The case method approach to learning is an attempt to simulate what happens in the "real world" by posing to students real problems confronted by managers in actual organizations and by encouraging students to think independently about how *they* would handle the problem. Then, once the student has decided on an approach, to give him or her practice at publicly articulating his or her ideas to classroom peers in a clear, logical, persuasive fashion.

It is important to point out what a case study is not. It is not just a story of how one company or another, or one manager or another, handled a particular management situation. Rather, a case study, as used at Harvard Business School, is first and foremost a means of posing an actual management problem that some real-life manager or entrepreneur has actually faced. It also typically includes enough data and information to enable the student to come to an intelligent decision as to how he or she would handle the problem. However, it stops short of providing a "correct answer" to resolving the issue.

It is true that the simulated reality of case studies is no long-term substitute for actual real-world work experience. However, I am convinced that the simulated reality of independently studying and analyzing cases based on actual management situations drawn from many different organizations and industries can give MBA students a significant head start in their evolution into seasoned and successful management leaders in their subsequent careers.

For Harvard Business School students in the late 1950s, the important point was that each of us, by the time we graduated from the two-year MBA program, had analyzed upwards of 500 case studies drawn from myriad industries and involving countless managers and management problems in both large and small, public and private enterprises. And not only had we analyzed these situations, we had gained considerable experience publicly expressing and debating our ideas in a classroom setting with 89 other bright students. I found it a very powerful and useful learning experience.

Today, more than a half-century later, the case method is still practiced at most business schools around the world, but it is increasingly being supplemented by real-life team learning. Under this approach, small groups of students work together to draw up entrepreneurial business plans to start enterprises that they then actually launch. In other instances, they team up to work directly with real companies or organizations on real problems. It is all about learning by doing.

But enough of discussing educational philosophy. What about the non-academic aspects of my first-year HBS experience? Here, there is little to tell. My life as a student was basically a nose-to-the-grindstone daily routine that varied very little from week to week. That is, it was, until a life-changing event happened to me in the spring semester of 1958, a moment that I will describe in the next chapter.

Entrepreneurial Insight #5: Always Time for Snacks!

When I returned to Boston after spending Christmas break with my family in Mansfield, I found myself running short of money. So I decided to start an entrepreneurial venture. I petitioned the administration of the school to grant me permission to start an evening sandwich concession. After some negotiation, they said yes, provided I use the school's dining hall to make the sandwiches. And so, each evening at about nine o'clock, I set off with brown paper shopping bags filled with a variety of sandwiches and made the rounds of the dorms on campus, selling these and other snacks to satisfy the evening hunger of studying students.

It was a good business. It was so good that after a couple of weeks I had to hire two classmates to cover some of the dorms. I continued to run the sandwich concession during my second year at HBS. It was lucrative enough that after a year and a half I actually experienced an opportunity-loss in income when I graduated with my MBA degree! It was my first adult experience as an entrepreneur. I was also able to generate additional capital when I sold the concession to a student in the class behind me.

Lesson Learned: You can be an entrepreneur anywhere—including business school!

One other non-academic incident that occurred during the second semester had sad consequences for Bill Richards, my HBS roommate. On a weekend in late February, several of my HBS friends and I went skiing in Maine. We had invited Bill to join us, but he opted to spend the weekend on his own in Boston. Bill almost never partied or went out on the weekends. While the rest of us were skiing, however, he decided to explore Boston. Evidently, after a Saturday evening dinner at a downtown restaurant, he stopped by a bar on Charles Street and met a young woman over drinks. One thing led to another and they found themselves spending much of the night together.

On my return from skiing Sunday night, Bill said nothing to me about his weekend escapade. Fast-forward a couple of months to exam time near the end of the spring semester. One afternoon, I returned to our room to find Bill looking white as a sheet and stricken. Evidently, Bill's young lady partner in his Saturday night dalliance had shown up in the HBS dean's office looking for Bill and saying that she was pregnant with his child. Having been told where Bill lived by the dean's assistant, she had shown up at our room shortly before my arrival and confronted Bill with the claim that she was pregnant, and he was going to be the father unless he paid her to do something about the situation.

The young lady proposed that Bill meet her the next morning at the International House of Pancakes with $1,000 in cash to underwrite an abortion. By the time I returned to our room, the young lady had left. Bill, shaken to the core, agonized about what he should do. At the time, it turned out that by an unhappy coincidence of timing, Bill's father, Bill Richards, Sr., was also on the HBS campus attending the 13-week Advanced Management Program (AMP) for senior executives. Bill was mortified that his father might hear about the pickle he was in. To avoid that happening, he made the decision to go to the bank that afternoon to withdraw $1,000 in cash to "take care of the matter." (In those days, $1,000 was a lot of money.) The next morning, he dutifully went to the International House of Pancakes where the young lady was waiting with her male "cousin." With a minimum of conversation with either the young lady or the "cousin," Bill paid her the money, wished her well, and left without a receipt, thinking he had resolved the situation.

A week went by, during which Bill, much relieved, took three or four of his final exams. Then, one Friday night, the same woman returned again to the administration building and started walking up and down the halls saying to any and all that she had to see Bill Richards and that she was carrying his baby. This time, she was directed to Mellon Hall, where his father, Bill Richards, Sr., was at the time attending the traditional Friday evening cocktail hour with his fellow AMP participants. Evidently, the distressed young lady showed up in the Mellon lounge and announced to the crowd in a loud voice that she was looking for Bill Richards. Young Bill's father made his way through the crowd and said to the young lady, "Yes, I'm Bill Richards. What can I do for you?" She took one look and replied, "No, you're not the one." Then she turned on her heels and left. Mr. Richards Senior was left scratching his head. It wasn't long, though, before Bill Senior's fellow happy hour companions began ribbing him. "We didn't know you had a girlfriend, Bill!" "You've been holding out on us." "Does she have any friends with whom you could fix us up?" And so forth.

Meanwhile, the young lady had made her way back to Bill Junior's room, found him there, and confronted him once again. "You know you made me pregnant and you need to pay me to have an abortion," she said. "It will cost you $1,000." Furious, he replied, "But I already paid you $1,000." She: "What $1,000? You didn't pay me anything and you have to meet me tomorrow morning at the International House of Pancakes to pay me the $1,000. And you'd better be there."

By this time, Bill had concluded, rightly or wrongly, that the woman was a scam artist who was trying to extort money from him. He certainly wasn't going to pay her another $1,000. However, not wanting to take any chances and fearing that she would continue to haunt him and his father in Cambridge, he packed all of his belongings that same evening, carried them to his car and drove off back to Arkansas without finishing the last of his exams. He reasoned that there was no way the person in question could come after him across state lines.

Regrettably, that turned out to be the last day of Bill's attendance at Harvard Business School. He used the summer to take a trip to Europe, during which he wrote me a letter that he was considering a return to Harvard in the fall but had not yet made up his mind. Ultimately, however, because the spring episode had left such a bad taste in his mouth, he never came back to Cambridge. Instead, after a year had passed during which he worked in the family businesses in Arkansas, he finished up his MBA degree at the University of Texas. I later learned that he subsequently returned to his hometown where he followed in his father's footsteps and ultimately became president of the local bank.

I often thought about how ironic it was that Bill, who was one of the nicest, most straitlaced people I have ever met, should have had his life so drastically impacted by a single night's out-of-character indiscretion. By contrast, I have also had a number of other acquaintances who, not nearly as innocent as Bill, have committed one much more serious indiscretion after another without ever having to pay the piper. Such is life!

CHAPTER EIGHT

A LIFE-CHANGING ENCOUNTER

One Sunday afternoon in April of 1958, during my second semester at HBS, I was studying at my desk when three of my friends barged into the room and invited me to join them on an afternoon expedition to nearby Wellesley College. At first, I demurred, saying that I had to catch up on a lot of homework. They, however, persisted.

"Quit playing the martyr," they said. "Give yourself a break. You have to come up for air once in a while." . . . or words to that effect. Not having been to Wellesley and being somewhat curious, I succumbed to their importuning.

So the four of us drove out to the Wellesley campus. On arrival, my three companions hopped out of the car, announced they would meet me again in a couple of hours, and scattered in various directions. It turned out that they all had Wellesley girlfriends that they were off to visit. I, in turn, knew no one on campus. What to do? There was nothing for it but to start exploring the campus. It was a beautiful spring day and the campus was in full bloom. I randomly wandered into a quadrangle of buildings comprising four student dormitories built around a lovely inner courtyard. Once in the courtyard, the only person I saw was an attractive woman student sitting on the sill of an open ground floor window, sunning herself and reading a book.

Carefully tiptoeing through the flowers in the planted garden under her window, I approached her with some brilliant opening salutation along the lines of, "Hi. Lovely afternoon, isn't it?" Soon we were engaged in conversation. It turned out she was Dutch, and her name was Talitha Boone. She was the daughter of the Dutch ambassador to the United States. After a few minutes of idle chitchat, another woman student carrying a tennis racket strolled up the walkway to a door located next to Talitha's window. Finding that the door was locked, the new student turned to Talitha and asked if she would be kind enough to go out into the hall and open the door from the inside. Talitha said, "Sure," and disappeared for about 45 seconds, during which time I turned to see who had made the request. It was 45 seconds that changed my life! To begin with, I took one look at the newcomer and instantly lost my heart to her. Not only was she beautiful but she also had a mischievous smile and a somehow beguiling manner. About 5'6" tall, she had dark curly hair, laughing eyes, and radiating charisma.

"Oh, do you play tennis?" was my clever opening query, observing that she was dressed in tennis whites and carrying a tennis racquet. Quick as a flash, she replied, "Yes. Do you?" I admitted that I did. Thereupon, my pulse began to quicken when, by way of invitation, she queried, "Would you like to play?" Instantly, I answered in the affirmative. By this time, Talitha was at the door. As she opened it, the new girl said, "Great. I'll go up to my room and get you a racket." "YES!" I thought to myself. After a few minutes of additional chatter with Talitha, the new girl returned, with tennis balls and a second racket in hand.

Abruptly and somewhat impolitely leaving poor Talitha to return to her open window and her book, my new friend and I set off toward the tennis courts.

"What's your name?" she asked.

"Bud Sorenson. What's yours?"

"Charlotte Ripley," she responded.

Charlotte turned out to be a worthy opponent on the tennis court. She also turned out to be smart, witty, and charming as well. I was in bliss.

One thing led to another and soon a full-blown romance bloomed. The following weekend, we drove to Crane Beach, north of Boston near Gloucester, and walked on the sand with the sun in our faces and the wind blowing our hair. Charlotte, a nymph of nature, was barefoot. I, for some reason, took my shoes off but kept my socks on to walk on the sand. Charlotte found this quite amusing and kidded me mercilessly about my strange sartorial lack of abandon. When she wasn't poking fun at me, we traded stories about ourselves.

I learned that Charlotte was 18 (I was 24 at the time) and a freshman at Wellesley. She had been born in Cambridge, lived in Lexington and Andover, Massachusetts, and Allentown, Pennsylvania, and now resided with her parents in the town of Stockbridge in western Massachusetts. Her father, George, was a banker and she had two younger brothers and two sisters, one older and one younger. Mr. Ripley was a scion of an old and distinguished, though by then somewhat impoverished, New England family. Her mother, Ruth, whose maiden name had been Bergeson, was of Norwegian/English heritage and, like Charlotte, had also graduated from Wellesley College. Ruth's father had been an ear, eye, nose, and throat physician in downtown Boston. He had died of lead poisoning when Ruth was 14.

The Ripley house in Stockbridge had been built in 1798 as an inn located halfway between Pittsfield and Great Barrington, Massachusetts. Charlotte's mother and father had moved there in 1949 and had renovated the house and reopened it as a bed and breakfast inn. They had renamed it Pilgrim's Inn. It was only open from June through August to cater to visitors to the area who came to enjoy Stockbridge's summer musical, theatrical, and artistic offerings. The Stockbridge area hosted Tanglewood (the Boston Symphony's summer home) as well as the Berkshire Summer Theater, Jacob's Pillow Dance Festival, and in later years, Shakespeare & Company, located on the Edith Wharton estate. Running the inn was a family affair under the direction of her delightful and whimsical mother. Charlotte and her sisters, Ginny and Anne, made the breakfasts in the mornings, served tea in the afternoons, and made up the guest rooms on a daily basis. It was more of a family project than a way to make money.

Charlotte finished elementary school and the first two years of high school in Stockbridge. Her parents then sent her away for her final two years of high school to Saint-Mary's-in-the-Mountains, an isolated girls boarding school in Littleton, New Hampshire. Charlotte claimed that her parents rusticated her to St. Mary's because they wanted to get her away from the boys in Stockbridge. Moreover, they thought she might enjoy St. Mary's because she was a good skier and the school was close to several New Hampshire ski resorts. St. Mary's was tiny. There were only about 20 girls in Charlotte's class. Charlotte was a good student and she particularly loved her art history and French language courses. She also served as editor of the school newspaper. Following a family tradition, in her senior year she applied to Wellesley College, which her mother had attended and where her sister, Ginny, was currently a student. Charlotte had no trouble being accepted.

Charlotte, it turned out, was not only very intelligent; she also had considerable artistic and creative flair. At Wellesley, she intended to major in art history. While she initially found Wellesley to be challenging, by the spring semester of her freshman year she was doing fine academically.

However, her life in the dormitory was not so smooth. In Shafer Hall, she had been assigned a hyperactive roommate with whom she was not terribly compatible. The roommate, who was a straight-A math whiz, evidently spent most of every day smoking, playing bridge, and tinkering with everything in sight. The straw that broke the camel's back occurred one day when the roommate climbed up on a dresser and fiddled with the automatic sprinkler head in their room.

Unfortunately, it turned on and sprayed the room with filthy, oily water that had been in the pipes for years. The sirens began screaming and four fire engines from the Wellesley Fire Department roared up to the dormitory. By the time the firemen had turned off the sprinkler head, it had thoroughly soaked the entire room and ruined most of Charlotte's possessions. Charlotte was crushed. Her room rendered unlivable, she was reassigned away from her roommate to a small single room in another dormitory, Munger Hall.

Having shared life stories with each other on the sands of Crane Beach, the following weekend Charlotte and I attended Wellesley Night at the Boston Pops with Arthur Fiedler conducting. We sat at a table with three or four other Wellesley women. While the music wasn't memorable, a little incident that occurred in the course of the evening was. During the intermission, I bought a pitcher of sangria for the table, a gesture that evidently made a great impression on Charlotte. In later years she told me it was that inadvertent generous gesture that went a long way toward endearing me to her. One never knows what small gestures will end up being important in a relationship.

The rest of that spring, Charlotte and I lightened up on our studies to spend almost every weekend together. The wooing process was well under way and it seemed to be casting a spell over both of us.

When the school year ended, I managed to obtain a summer position in Watertown, Massachusetts, at a division of the Raytheon Company. While fairly well paid, it was the most tedious job I have ever had both before and since. My job was to calculate, by hand, maximum/minimum reordering quantities for hundreds of different shop supply items that were used on a daily basis in the division's factory. Think nuts and bolts, screws and screwdrivers. The work was boring, boring, boring. With today's computers and automated software programs, what took me an entire summer of individual slide-rule computations could probably be done in one or two afternoons.

That summer, I shared an apartment at 1056 Beacon Street in Brookline with two of my old classmates from Amherst, Van Seasholes and Mark Hanschka, both of whom were doing graduate studies at Harvard. Van was in the School of Education and Mark was in the Law School. Over the course of the summer, Mark, who was brilliant, decided he didn't like law school and so he switched to the Harvard Medical School beginning the following fall. We also had a fourth graduate student apartment mate, Herb Benson, who in later years became the founder and director of Harvard's Mind/Body Institute. However, Herb and I evidently didn't have much interaction with each other that summer. I say that because some 45 years later, when we met each other once again, it took us both about 15 minutes of intense conversation before we suddenly recognized each other and remembered we had shared an apartment together for a whole summer.

On a few weekends that summer, I drove up to Gloucester to go lobstering with the father of my old Amherst roommate, Bobby Jedrey, or tuna harpooning with Dr. Fred Breed, who had been Bobby's mentor and benefactor while at Amherst. Fred had a great life. From September through May he was a prominent North Shore ophthalmologist who also had a teaching appointment at Harvard Medical School. From June through August, he was renowned as one of the most successful tuna fishermen off the New England coast. He was one of the few remaining tuna fishermen who used a hand-thrown lance to spear the fish. Some of the tuna he speared weighed in at five or six hundred pounds. Once hit, the tuna would often give us a merry chase before they gradually lost their strength and were hauled aboard. I found the whole process fascinating and exhilarating. I doubt the unfortunate tuna shared my feelings, although in that pre-Rachel Carson era I am sure that thought never crossed my mind.

On several other weekends that summer, I drove out to Stockbridge to be with Charlotte. My first visit there sticks out in my mind as the most memorable. I had arranged by phone with Charlotte to meet her at her home at about 2:00 p.m. one Saturday afternoon in late June. She gave me driving directions to Pilgrim's Inn that were clear and easy to follow. I had no problem finding the house, which was no longer being run as a small inn. On my arrival at two o'clock, however, there was no Charlotte. In her place I met her 14-year-old sister, Anne, who told me that Charlotte had decided to do some volunteer work that afternoon handing out programs at the matinee performance of the Boston Symphony Orchestra at nearby Tanglewood. Anne had been briefed to tell me to just go on up to Tanglewood, where sooner or later I should be able to find Charlotte.

It turned out to be later rather than sooner, since I had to comb through two or three thousand milling Tanglewood patrons before finally spotting Charlotte. All the while, I was thinking that this wasn't a very nice way to welcome me on this much-anticipated visit to see my true love for the first time in her home setting. Things improved, however, and we had a great time over the weekend. The entire Ripley family was welcoming then and evermore over the years to come.

Our romance continued until late in the fall of the following school year when both of us suffered a dose of cold feet. So, we decided to declare a "mutual independence campaign" in our relationship. However, absence seems to have made both our hearts beat fonder, and a couple of months later we decided to start dating again. After that, as the following letter written in January 1959 suggests, I was head over heels in love.

January 29, 1959

My Dear Char,

Just felt I had to try to put on paper some of the things I feel so strongly and yet haven't really been able to tell you. It's peculiar how difficult it sometimes is for two people who mean very, very much to each other to communicate completely their innermost thoughts and emotions. When I'm with you, Char, I often feel my heart crying out a hundred different messages, yet at times it's tough for me to get these messages from my heart to yours.

What I have to say is quite simple. I love you, my darling, far more than I ever dreamed it was possible to love. I love you because you're warm and wonderful and because to me you're the most beautiful person I'll ever know. When you smile, or laugh, or look at me I feel almost like bursting.

Even more, though, I love you because of what you are inside. I love you because you are tender and smart and kind and sensitive and because you try so very hard to understand why life is what it is. You're not afraid to ask questions and struggle with yourself, Char, and whether you know it or not, this kind of struggling is what makes living really worthwhile.

So, dearest Char, I just want you to know that, in spite of the "little walls" that sometimes seem to unexplainably appear, I love you more and more as each day passes and only pray that you can find it in your heart to love me.

Bud

. . . . .

From about that time on, my heart never faltered, although as shall be seen as this tale continues, Charlotte had a hiccup or two before we finally ended up walking down the aisle together. But more about that later.

CHAPTER NINE

A CAREER DECISION

In my final semester in the MBA program at Harvard in early 1959, I was confronted with the challenge of deciding what I should do following graduation. My frame of mind at the time is best described in an essay I wrote in December 1958 that I discovered while sorting through some papers in a trunk full of old memories. Here is what I wrote:

"As I sit here at my desk about to start writing this paper, the thought occurs to me that mapping my future is probably the most important assignment I shall have in my two years at the Business School. It is also one of the most difficult; for the first time I find myself having to formally 'commit' myself on paper in areas where formerly I've always been able to 'hedge' . . . even when thinking to myself. Even as it promises to be both important and difficult, writing a paper of this kind is probably one of the most valuable things I could do right at this point in time.

As an approach, I shall initially try to sneak away to a neutral vantage point and attempt to take a fairly objective look at my good and bad points.

The first time that I tried to objectively list my strengths and weaknesses was in February 1957, when I was in the process of applying for admission to Harvard. At that time, I made the following statement:

'My most valuable assets are a logical mind, an adaptable personality, ambition, and good health. Sound judgment and systematic thinking help me to make decisions. I get along well with almost everyone and can adapt easily to practically any environment. I can make and hold loyal friends and am a loyal friend. In accomplishing a job, I am usually enthusiastic, resourceful, and self-reliant. I like hard work, but I must have a definite goal. I have a natural determination to do well in any job that I attempt. I'm willing to take risks, but only when the odds suit me. My tastes are simple; my interests are diverse. Essentially an optimist, I expect a full, rich life.

On the liability side of the ledger, I'm inclined to worry excessively when striving toward difficult goals. At such times I am impatient and disagreeable. I am capable of serious errors of tactlessness and am often inconsiderate of others. Thoroughness in accomplishing a job is not yet a habit with me. My memory is unpredictable, but improving. I have many other faults; at present, however, I feel that these I have listed are the ones I need most to overcome.'

Today, in December 1958, I feel that I still have essentially the same set of personal assets and liabilities. Some changes have, of course, occurred. On the plus side, I feel considerably more mature. I feel far better prepared, because of my work at Harvard, to enter the business world. I think I am better able to make decisions, and I've made some progress toward becoming more considerate and tactful as a person. On the minus side, I don't feel as creative as I would like to be. I am tremendously restless right at this time. I seem to be going through a period of stifling reflection that takes up too much time and does not seem particularly constructive, and I've become somewhat of a procrastinator.

Finally, one change has occurred that I shall put in the middle area merely because I'm honestly not sure whether it is good or bad. I am not as great an idealist as I once was; things that I once saw arrayed in Technicolor, I now see in black and white.

These, then, are the strong and weak points that I shall take with me when I leave school and enter a career. With these strengths and weaknesses in mind, I'd like to go on to develop my long-term objectives.

Perhaps the best way to state those objectives is to group them under two general categories: non-career objectives and career objectives.

As <u>non-career objectives</u> I shall seek the following:

1. A marriage that grows stronger with time and that is full of love, sharing, humor, freshness, sympathy, and understanding.

2. A fairly large family—whose future will be secured both by the personal abilities of its members and financial holdings.

3. A life that is full of laughter and tears, pleasure and sorrow, gaiety and concern; a life that is characterized by simplicity, humility, tolerance, and generosity.

4. An active, inquiring mind that never stops learning.

5. A healthy, well-kept body.

6. A greater than average degree of personal independence.

7. Some time to spend on family, hobbies, community affairs, and outside interests.

Accomplishing these non-career objectives will require tremendous effort, hard work, courage, and luck; nevertheless, I have faith that they can be accomplished.

My long-range career objectives . . . as of this writing . . . are as follows:

1. The operation of a successful personal business or a share in the ownership and an effective voice in the management of a small to medium sized business. In either case, however, I want . . . somewhere along the line . . . to have a go at operating my own business.

2. A career whose primary attractions are that it is interesting, challenging, offers responsibility and a chance to be creative, and is well suited to my capabilities.

3. Enough money to be a little more than comfortable.

4. Location: Basically, I believe that one can be happy in almost any location. However, I feel that some places are much more conducive to happiness than others. With this in mind I think I'd probably like to work in New England, near one of the Great Lakes, or on the West Coast (in that order of preference). I'd also like to live in or near a cultural community, but not in a big city. Insofar as changing locations is concerned, I shall expect to move occasionally during the early part of my career; ultimately, however, I'd like to settle in one place.

While location preference and money will be very important in future career decisions, I do not feel they are basically as important a consideration as that of interest. Just how important location will be can only be answered in light of specific job opportunities.

Finally, I'd like to discuss my short-range plans for achieving the above career objectives.

Immediately after graduation I plan to get a job that will give me an opportunity to get some grass roots selling experience. I want to do this for several reasons. First, I feel that my interests and capabilities best suit me for a sales-oriented career. Second, I think that actual selling experience is a necessary and very valuable first step for anyone interested in marketing.

This selling job will probably be with a medium to large sized firm selling industrial or semi-industrial products. I tentatively plan to stay with this company for 2 to 5 years depending on the experience I'm getting, how well I am doing, and the nature of other opportunities that arise.

(As of the date of this writing, I am considering a possible alternative first step: working as a research assistant at the IMEDE International Management Development Institute, in Lausanne, Switzerland. Were I to do this, it would be for a one-year period, at the end of which I would still plan to go into selling here in America).

A possible second step will be to explore the opportunity to get a few years' experience with a management-consulting firm. I feel this could be a fascinating and very broadening experience. I also think that with some prior business experience I could be competent in this field and could be a valuable asset to some consulting firm. Finally, and very important, I feel that this business offers an excellent opportunity to get a first-hand look at the operations of a variety of businesses.

I consider this experience in management consulting to be desirable in many ways, but not absolutely necessary.

As a next step, I want, within the next seven years, either to start a personal business or to join a small nucleus of others in setting up a new, entrepreneurial enterprise. I feel that this is something I must do while I'm still young. To take this step will take courage, particularly if, by that time, I have a family and other responsibilities. Nevertheless, I feel that, with the right opportunity the potential rewards will more than offset the temporary loss of personal financial security. I shall enter any such enterprise determined to succeed but prepared for failure.

One possible type of business that I may look into is that of becoming an independent manufacturer's agent; another is to set up some type of service organization, perhaps to do consulting work; still a third would be to join a few other individuals in setting up a manufacturing enterprise.

These, then, are possible paths that I may pursue in an effort to achieve my long-term career objectives."

Entrepreneurial Insight #6: Applying Entrepreneurial Thinking to a Career Decision

The near-term career decision I finally made was influenced more by my entrepreneurial instincts than by conventional job-search thinking. In short, I was inspired by Robert Frost's encouragement to "take the road less traveled by" as described in one of my favorite poems, Frost's *The Road Not Taken*. I opted for a life of entrepreneurial adventure rather than a life of traveling the better-worn paths typically taken by recently minted Harvard MBA graduates who were headed for high-paying jobs on Wall Street, in consulting, or in manufacturing firms.

In short, I accepted the offer to work as a research associate in Switzerland at the IMEDE International Management Development Institute. At the time, Europe was still emerging from the chaos of World War II and was destined to become a much stronger economic region in the future. This, I thought, might open up many opportunities to create new entrepreneurial ventures. I reasoned that knowledge of how business worked in Europe would be a valuable building block in my future career. I was trying to apply entrepreneurial thinking to my career decision. However, another reason underlying my decision was that I was also captivated by the romantic allure of living abroad in beautiful Switzerland, with its mountains and valleys and (to me) foreignness. This reflects how enchanted I had been by my brief visit to Europe while on leave during my earlier military service in Iceland.

Lesson Learned: Entrepreneurship isn't just about starting new businesses; it is also a way of thinking about new opportunities and then translating those opportunities into action.

IMEDE was a three-year-old European business school that had been founded by faculty members from HBS and initially underwritten financially by Nestlé Alimentana, the Swiss-based food company. Its mission was to provide a one-year management course for European midlevel managers who were deemed by their companies to have the potential to become senior-level executives.

As a research associate at IMEDE, my assignment was to travel around Europe gathering information on management problems confronting various companies. Then I was charged with writing case studies on these problems that could be used for teaching purposes at IMEDE as well as in business schools back in the United States. I was to work under the supervision of Professor Burt Dunn, a marketing professor who had, like me, done his undergraduate work at Amherst and his doctoral studies at Harvard.

CHAPTER TEN

SWITZERLAND

This job decision having been made in March of 1959, my final weeks at Harvard passed in a happy blur. Commencement came and went, and I managed to graduate with magna cum laude honors. In love with Charlotte and feeling on top of my game academically, I felt as though I was at a crossroads in my life. And I was.

Meanwhile, Charlotte and her sister Ginny were given a marvelous gift by their Aunt Helen that enabled them to spend the summer between Charlotte's undergraduate sophomore and junior years studying art history in Italy as part of a Wellesley study abroad program. They, along with a dozen or so other Wellesley students, were slated to sail to Europe in late June 1959 on the *S.S. Arcadia*, a Greek student ship. Since I was also scheduled to go to Europe that summer to start my new job at IMEDE, I naturally seized the opportunity to get myself booked on the same *Arcadia* passage as Charlotte and her fellow students.

In early June, I paid a brief visit to my family in Ohio. If my mother and father weren't especially thrilled about the prospect of my working halfway around the world in Switzerland, they did their best not to show it. Their attitude had always been to trust my judgment and to go along with whatever life decisions that I might make. Deep down, however, I am sure they were disappointed that I wasn't going to be working closer to home.

Following this visit, I duly showed up on the appointed day in Montreal, Canada, the *Arcadia's* port of departure. Waving goodbye to Charlotte's family on the dock, I embarked for new adventures and a new life on a new continent. The fact that Charlotte was also on the *Arcadia* made that initial ocean crossing all the sweeter.

While Charlotte bunked in with her sister Ginny, I was assigned to an inner cabin deep in the bowels of the ship. I shared the cabin with a young pre-hippie vagabond from California named Rudi and his equally bohemian girlfriend. They had hitchhiked across the country from the West Coast and were planning to hitchhike across Europe to Greece where they hoped to "settle down." They had a total of $300 to their name and all of their worldly belongings were stuffed into their two backpacks.

The first thing Rudi asked me when we met was whether I would mind signing up for the second sitting at mealtimes and then whether I could make it a practice to linger awhile in the ship's common areas after dining before returning to the sleeping cabin. It turned out that he and his honey liked to eat early and immediately return to the cabin for extended bouts of vigorous lovemaking after each lunch and dinner.

After most meals, they also tended to bring generous quantities of fruits, bread, crackers, nuts, and other semi-nonperishable foods to the cabin from the bountiful buffet tables in the dining room. They intended to squirrel away this food to sustain them later, during their hitchhiking journey to Greece. Rudi was determined to stock enough edible provisions to ensure that they wouldn't have to buy any meals at least until they crossed into Italy from France. When we docked in Le Havre, France, I was amused to watch Rudi pack his knapsack before disembarking. When he got to the top of the sack, it was evident that he didn't have enough room to pack his only pair of lace-up shoes and the remaining food that he and his girlfriend had filched for their land journey. He looked at his shoes in his left hand and the food in his right and then walked across the hall, opened a porthole, and threw the shoes overboard. "I only need my sandals," said he. I often wondered in later years whatever happened to Rudi and his girlfriend.

Meanwhile, for me the voyage to Europe passed pleasantly enough. Making the crossing with Charlotte clearly enhanced the experience. Shared lunches and dinners, frequent heart-to-heart conversations, shuffleboard games, and various other shipboard diversions made the time pass quickly. The only minor discordant note during the ocean crossing was when Charlotte felt that I was perhaps spending a bit too much time at the ship's railing having conversations with a Norwegian girl who was one of her Wellesley classmates. I, of course, did my best to convince my love that these conversations were entirely innocent and platonic. Which they were! But this little episode taught me a thing or two about being sensitive to other people's perceptions when it comes to relationships.

After seven or eight days, we spotted land, docked at Le Havre, disembarked, and proceeded to Paris by train. There, I booked in for nights at the same hotel as the Wellesley contingent. Wellesley professor Curtis Shell, the program leader, was kind enough to let me join the group on their visits to the Louvre, the Jeu de

Switzerland

Paume impressionist museum, Notre Dame Cathedral, and other Paris sites of artistic interest. On day two, I also made a trip with them to Chartres Cathedral. It was a blissful interlude for me.

Then the time came for the Wellesley group to depart for Italy and for me to take the train to Switzerland. But before Charlotte and I went our separate ways, we plotted for her to come from Italy to visit me in Lausanne for two or three days during the course of the summer.

Sure enough, a couple of weeks later I received the following letter from Charlotte:

Florence, July 11, 1959

My darling!

The secret inside my heart says, "I love you" and "I miss you".

So, my darling, here is my idea. On Friday, the 17th of July may I please get up at 6 a.m., cross the street and get on the train for Lausanne arriving at 3:11 p.m. I could see so much new countryside on the way that it would really be time gained. And it would be fine with Herr Shell. Besides. Florence is our longest stay and it is the nearest to Lausanne. Also, I could help you unpack and we could take an Alpine picnic, and we could go for a swim, and I could see your little car, and meet your little French maid, and I could pick you some flowers. Could you call me, please, please, or send me a wire. I will bring you an olive if the answer is yes.

I think of you constantly, my love. You are my "Wise Man".

Char

. . . . .

I immediately replied by postcard:

My Darling,

YES! YES! YES! See you at 3:11 p.m. Friday with your olive. Your idea is magnifique! I'll arrange for a place for you to stay. Au revoir till Friday.

xo Bud

. . . . .

And so, Charlotte came, and it turned out to be a magical weekend! We did all of the things Char mentioned in her letter and more.

But the weekend was also not without its humorous aspects. For one thing, I was temporarily staying in a borrowed one-room studio apartment in downtown Lausanne. The studio had a balcony overlooking train tracks and some other apartment buildings. The first evening, the moment came when we had to figure out our sleeping arrangements. Remember, this was the decade of the fifties where "going steady" with someone didn't necessarily mean sleeping with each other. To make a long story short, we decided to observe proper pre-marital New England decorum. This meant I ended up on the balcony in a sleeping bag while Charlotte slept inside in the studio's comfortable bed. To add insult to injury, just to make sure her virtue remained intact, Charlotte locked the balcony door from the inside and fully lowered the roll-down wooden shutters!

If the nights were a misery for me, the days were glorious. With me at the wheel of my new blue Volkswagen Bug car with a sunroof, I proudly showed Charlotte all of the sights in and around Lausanne and introduced her to my new colleagues at IMEDE. We picnicked to the sound of cowbells in an Alpine meadow beside a beautiful mountain lake. We drank wine and ate cheese and picked wildflowers.

We also talked about our hopes and dreams. We sailed on, and swam in, Lac Leman (Lake Geneva). In between our perambulations, we had more long and heartfelt talks over leisurely lunches and dinners at some of Lausanne's many charming restaurants and bistros. By the end of the weekend, both of us were even more smitten with each other and captivated by the romance and adventure of an exciting new life in Europe.

Before we knew it, it was time for Charlotte to catch the train to rejoin her classmates in Florence. Three weeks later, I sent Charlotte the following letter plotting a final rendezvous in Venice at the end of her summer study abroad session.

Lausanne, August 9, 1959

Dearest Char,

I've got an idea! What would you think if I were to come to Venice for the weekend? Here's the plan: I think I can get Friday afternoon off without too much trouble. Therefore, I shall leave here at noon by car and arrive in Venice very late Friday night and be with you for the weekend. We can see Venice by gondola at midnight by moonlight. And I can talk with you and plan with you. And we can feed the pigeons in Piazza St. Mark . . . and we can laugh and dream, if only for two short days. So, what do you think of my idea. I hope you like it, because I'm coming! Oh, Char, you must have known that I couldn't let you leave without seeing you again!

Now, if you think that my plan is a good one, don't do anything, but just wait until you see me late Friday night. I'll meet you at your hotel. If, on the other hand there are any complications on your end, just wire or call me at IMEDE anytime up until noon on Friday.

Barring catastrophes, Char, I'll see you in Venice Friday night, the 14th.

'Til then, my darling, all my love. My thoughts are always with you.

Bud

. . . . .

Thus, on August 14th, I drove my little VW Bug to the city of canals where we once again had the opportunity to enjoy one another's company.

I don't remember all the details of that weekend. But an incident does stick in my mind. One evening, Charlotte and I hired the obligatory gondola with its singing gondolier as helmsman. We snuggled together in the gondola's cushions and were poled in and out of some of Venice's colorful out-of-the-way canals. The ambiance was totally romantic. The temperature was perfect, the moon was bright overhead, and the gondolier was in good tune singing Italian ballads such as "O sole mio." It was a glorious moment. Suddenly, however, it seemed to be raining and our gondolier loudly increased the volume of his singing. Charlotte and I looked up, only to see that we were being peed upon by an Italian gentleman letting loose over the railing of his third-floor balcony! Although the gondolier had valiantly tried to cover up the splashing noise by singing louder, the magic of the moment was broken. So much for our romantic evening!

Alas, all good summer interludes must come to an end, and after a couple of days of exploring other nooks and corners of Venice, I drove Charlotte and her sister, Ginny, from Venice to Innsbruck where the poignant moment came for us to part . . . Charlotte to visit friends in Vienna and Sweden before returning to the States and her junior year at Wellesley and me to drive back to Lausanne and my new job. Parting was, indeed, sweet sorrow. We were not to see each other again for almost a year, until the middle of the following June.

Lausanne turned out to be all I had hoped for and more. The following are descriptive excerpts from the first letter I wrote to Charlotte upon my arrival (nota bene: in these letters I sometimes referred to Charlotte as "Za," which was the diminutive of "Za-Za," a nickname that her family had given her some years earlier).

An Entrepreneurial Journey Through Life

July 11, 1959

Hello my darling,

Lausanne is quite unbelievable! But before giving you a complete play-by-play description of my first impressions, my darling, darling, Za, I want to tell you just how wonderful it was to be with you on the fairy-tale journey across the Atlantic and for those two marvelous days in Paris. Two weeks ago, last night we arrived in Stockbridge just in time to devour a most fantastic peach shortcake. There must have been something mystical about that shortcake . . . or perhaps magical is a better word . . . for I haven't felt quite the same since. The grass seems greener, the sky bluer, the air clearer, the birds more musical (especially canaries), and the world much more joyous. In short, I'm quite intoxicated! Intoxicated with life in general . . . but even more so, intoxicated with you! With your warmth, with your beauty, with your laughter, with your love. Dear, dear Charlotte, I love you, love you, LOVE YOU!

And now, Za, for Lausanne:

Lausanne, itself, seems to fit all the proper adjectives and a few others besides. Quaint, picturesque, charming, slightly cosmopolitan, etc. etc. ad-infinitum. Besides all the standard adjectives I would add that Lausanne seems to be a wonderfully gentle town . . . delightfully easy-going with the atmosphere of an unspoiled resort town. Perhaps the most outstanding feature about the geography of the town is that it is almost entirely built on hills, so everything is up and down. I was met at the train by Derek Tweedly, a 'veddy, veddy' English young man who has been most kind to me since my arrival. He is also a research associate who has already spent one year here and who will spend next year also. After getting me situated temporarily at a hotel, Derek took me right down to the school. Char, I was completely flabbergasted. This is the most beautiful set-up I think I have ever seen. Chateau Bellerive is an absolutely beautiful estate. From my office on the third floor where I am now sitting I look right out over the front lawn and some trees on Lake Geneva and the breathtaking, snowcapped mountains on the other side. The Chateau, itself, has been beautifully equipped with everything that a school such as this should have.

Switzerland

Everyone whom I have met so far has been very warm and friendly and has done his best to make me feel at home. The first night I was here several of us went for a swim at five o'clock at a swimming place right across the road from the school. How good it felt! Afterwards we had a delightful and delicious dinner at an outdoor restaurant for 1.90 Swiss francs . . . the equivalent of less than 50 cents. And it was a three-course meal too! Later, Derek and I strolled through the streets of the town. Down by the lake there were two sidewalk cafés that had orchestras so there was much music and laughter. Many other people were also strolling around or sipping wine or beer at little tables. Most of them were quite young. The entire atmosphere was most gay and appealing.

Yesterday, I moved from my hotel into the studio apartment of one of the other research associates who is presently on vacation. It's very, very nice and I shall be able to stay there until I find something that I really like. Last night I again had a swim and later went sailing on Lake Geneva with a boy named Per Hedblom (Swedish) who also works at IMEDE. He has a little snipe sailboat for the summer. It was really a wonderful way to spend a warm summer evening.

This afternoon I go to pick up my Volkswagen at 4 o'clock. I'm quite excited about it. Barring complications I should be able to drive around the countryside and along the lake by this evening!

Well, darling this has been long and rambling and yet I still haven't been able to tell you half of what I would like to tell you. I guess it needs to be told or shown in person!

All my love, Za. Say hi and goodbye again for me to Ginny, Herr Shell, and all of the gals. Hope Florence has been doing a good job of providing you with a full measure of its charm and culture.

Goodbye for now, darling,

xo Bud
. . . . .

If I was euphoric about my introduction to Lausanne, I was also very positive about my initial reaction to the work I would be doing at IMEDE.

First, a little background about the school itself: The faculty and staff comprised six or seven professors, most of whom were on leave from the Harvard Business

School, and an equal number of research associates or case-writers. There also was a full complement of administrative staff members, gardeners, and dining room personnel. And, of course, there were the student participants, about 40 of them, who were scheduled to begin their one-year management course in August 1959 . . . about a month after my arrival. All were drawn from the middle management ranks of their sponsoring companies and all were considered to have the potential to take on senior-level responsibilities. Their average age was about 35.

The first day I arrived, I met Burt Dunn, the marketing professor under whose supervision I was to work, as well as the dean, Clark Myers, the other professors, and my fellow research associates. It turned out that two of the latter were friends who had been classmates and section mates of mine at the Harvard Business School. One was John McArthur, a Canadian, who many years later became dean of HBS. The other was an Australian, Jim Wolfensohn, who in his subsequent career became president of the World Bank. Another research associate was an Englishman, Peter Brooke, also an HBS graduate, who later capped his career by becoming Minister for Northern Ireland and a Life Peer in the House of Lords. Rounding out the crew of research associates were a wild Italian (Angelo Tagliavia), a Swede (Per Hedblom), another Canadian (Les Jonas), another Englishman, Derek Tweedly, and a couple of additional Americans (Bruce Scott and Norm Berg), both of whom later became HBS professors.

Choosing to work abroad at IMEDE turned out to be one of the best decisions I ever made. My subsequent experience there totally opened my eyes to the fact that there was a rich and varied life beyond the borders of the United States. It also gave me a much more balanced perspective with respect to understanding the culture of my own country, America.

Burt Dunn turned out to be a wonderful mentor. He taught me much of what I learned about the art of writing case studies. It turned out that writing excellent cases was, indeed, an art.

First, one had to decide what specific management issues or problems were to be posed by the case. This required knowledge of the overall design of the course in which the case was to be used and where the case in question would fit into that design. For example, in a marketing case, were the issues related to product line policy, pricing strategy, channels of distribution, advertising and promotion, or something else? Then one had to do research to identify a European company facing that particular type of issue. The next step was to establish a relationship with the management of that company and persuade them to cooperate in the development of the case. For competitive and other reasons, this was not always easy.

Then, you had to visit the company and spend a considerable amount of time interviewing the relevant executives and gathering as much information and data as possible about the issue in question.

Now came the hard part: sifting through all of the field notes to determine what was wheat and what was chaff. The challenge was to include in the case that which was relevant to making a management decision on the problem or issue at hand, while not committing the sin of letting the case study become too long or verbose.

Finally, there was the task of actually writing the case study in a manner that was both clear and succinct. The goal was to pose the management problem to the students together with sufficient background information and data for them to make a reasoned decision as to how they personally would handle the situation. Typically, the case study stopped short of describing to students the actual course of action that had been pursued by the real-life managers in the company being studied. This was to underscore the notion that usually there are no "right" or "wrong" answers to most management problems. There are only better or worse ways of handling various situations.

Under Burt Dunn's tutelage, I became a reasonably accomplished case writer. During my stay at IMEDE, I wrote somewhere in the neighborhood of 20 cases . . . each with an accompanying teaching guideline. A few of those cases became classics, with some being used at business schools 40 years later.

Moreover, I was particularly fortunate in that, unlike most other young case writers, I was given the opportunity by Burt to actually teach some of my cases to the IMEDE students.

This initial exposure to teaching changed the entire future course of my life. From the first moment I stepped in front of the classroom, I adored the teaching experience. I took to teaching like a bear to honey.

Never in my career ponderings had I ever thought of the teaching profession. But after my initial class in front of the IMEDE students, I was hooked on the idea of becoming a teacher. Isn't it intriguing the role that chance and serendipity can play in our lives! In this regard, I am sure I have been luckier than most.

In the course of my stay at IMEDE, I made a plan that would lead to becoming a university professor. Toward the end of my first year there, I decided to say yes to the dean's invitation for me to stay on at the school as a research associate for a second year. I convinced myself that the additional intimate interaction with the faculty, students, and other research associates would give me a solid foundation for later studies in a doctoral program back in America. Also, I rationalized that continued on-the-ground exposure to a wide variety of companies doing business in Europe would later make me more qualified to teach international management. However, the real reason that I agreed to a second year at IMEDE was simply that I had come to love life in Europe and had fantasies about marrying Charlotte and bringing her to Lausanne to share Europe's delights with her.

CHAPTER ELEVEN

A LONG-DISTANCE LOVE AFFAIR

While I was traveling all over Europe learning to be a journeyman case writer, Charlotte was back in America studying in her junior year at Wellesley. At the time, having an ocean between us seemed like cruel and unusual punishment. The old saying that "absence makes the heart grow fonder" was certainly accurate in our case . . . or at least in my case.

Soon, love letters written on flimsy airmail stationery were flying back and forth across the seas.

However, it was not as though I was living a totally cloistered existence as a monk during this time. On the contrary, I was taking full advantage of Lausanne's proximity to great ski resorts and beautiful Alpine hiking trails. With newly made friends, I was also becoming acquainted with the charms of Lausanne's myriad restaurants and bistros. In my spare moments I did as much sightseeing as possible, both throughout Switzerland and in neighboring France. On occasion, I also dated some of the local Lausanne ladies. But my heart remained with Charlotte.

To fill my weekends during the fall and spring, I joined the lakefront tennis club that was just down the street from IMEDE. There, I made a number of new acquaintances, most notably Joachim Lungarshausen, a young German who was studying at the University of Lausanne. Joachim and I were about equal in terms of tennis ability, which led to many titanic battles on the courts. Joachim also became my pal off the courts. Almost from the beginning, he and I bonded, and he later became one of my closest lifelong friends.

Then there was Madame Jean, my French teacher. From the outset, I made up my mind to learn French while I was at IMEDE. To that end, I, along with several other research associates, started taking group French lessons from Madame Jean. Although I had studied Latin and German during my high school and college days, I arrived in Lausanne not knowing a word of French. Madame Jean valiantly set out to remedy that shortcoming. Thanks to her teaching skills and patience, over the course of a few months, I gradually became sufficiently fluent to do field interviewing in French for the cases I was writing, as well as to carry on reasonably intelligent conversations with native French speakers. Once I learned to communicate in French, my whole European experience became infinitely richer.

During the period from the summer of 1959 to June of 1960, Charlotte and I enriched the postal services on both sides of the Atlantic with a constant deluge of letters. In those letters, we poured out our hearts to one another. We talked about everything: our daily activities, our hopes and fears and aspirations, world events, anecdotes about friends and funny incidents in our lives, and just about everything else. But most of all, they were good, old-fashioned love letters.

Apart from our written correspondence, the only other contact the two of us had with one another during our 10-month separation consisted of two three-minute trans-Atlantic telephone calls. Because international calls were so expensive in those days, Charlotte carefully timed each of those calls with an hourglass egg timer. Imagine that: hearing each other's voice for a total of just six minutes over the course of 10 months!

How our long-distance romance progressed during our period of separation is perhaps best captured by a sampling of excerpts selected from the dozens of letters that have survived from that era 50-some years ago:

Bud to Charlotte

> Lausanne July 24, 1959
>
> Hello my darling,
>
> Welcome to Rome! (And on your right, young ladies, is St. Peter's and the Vatican City, located in which is the Sistine Chapel which contains . . . etc., etc.,) Rome is a wonderful city, Za; here's hoping you enjoy your stay there as much as I did mine.
>
> Za, I can't possibly do justice to this past weekend in Lausanne with mere words. All I can say is that I just glow every time I think of it. I'll always remember it under the category of "Very Special Events". Thank you, my dearest, for the wonderful inspiration that brought you to me for those 2½ unforgettable days.
>
> Just in case you might be wondering, Za, I want to tell you that now, more than ever, I feel that our "blueprint for the future" is not only

wonderful, but wise as well. I love you, Charlotte, in every possible way that is good. Most simply, darling, I want to build and share a lifetime with you. I guess that, in one sense of the word, the lifetime has already begun; in fact, it started in the late afternoon of April 13, 1958—a red, white, and blue letter day! But let's plan to start our lifetime together in the _real_ sense of the word—in a giving and receiving, laughing and crying, understanding and compromising sense—next summer. It's something worth working for, planning for, and waiting for.

In the meantime, Za, we both can do some more growing and living and learning. And the best part of all is that, with faith in each other, we both can face this next year joyfully and without fear, and with each of us determined to get as much as we possibly can from the experiences to come.

I say all of this, darling, sure in my heart that I love you and that together we can build something that is very special and very lasting.

Bud

. . . . .

Charlotte to Bud

Rome, July 29, 1959

Bud, my darling, darling person,

You have so much love in your heart. Received your letter yesterday when we arrived in Rome and promptly burst into tears. Probably at the bigness of it all—love and marriage—and probably partly at the nearness of it all. You will be marrying a girl, Bud, whose head is always in the clouds and who lives in a very soft dream world. For this whole year, I realized yesterday, I have been partly in love with love. This is difficult to explain, because I think it is basically the difference between the love of a man and that of a woman. For a woman, it is more natural to be "in love" as a sort of abstract state of mind. I have floated blissfully along, never really considering what love really means—its totality. Strangely enough, my dearest Bud, it came as a bit of a shock to me when I really conceived of the whole thing. A lifetime! Starting next year! A _new_ life. A new set of goals, or one new goal decided on by two people.

Darling, I hope you understand what I mean. I want to love you—just as freely as the blowing wind. Maybe someday I will shake off all my selfish side whims and be to you just as generous and tolerant and gentle as you are to me.

It's very difficult, as I have mentioned, to realize that It has happened. We talked about it before, do you remember. How, when one is deciding, he argues and rationalizes and then decides. Then afterwards there comes a state of suspension until the decision is actualized. I think that sometimes we need more of the arguing and rationalizing and making sure, and then I think that we have done enough talking and wondering. The thing that keeps me from being afraid is you—that you are so honest and kind and true and everlasting. Maybe the fact that we are realizing so strongly the hard work of marriage and are ever treading so gingerly, will help us at first.

The fairy tale weekend in Lausanne, my darling you! I shall never forget your bunch of wildflowers and bottle of milk in the morning, the daisy chain and the emerald lake, the well, the beautiful picnic, and the cowbells!

One of the most provocative questions you have ever asked me was on the boat, when we were talking about the next year and you said, "Haven't you ever wanted to go out and create something of your own?" I really think I do now, darling, with you. You will make the most wonderful, loving husband in the world, and your children will all adore you because you will bring them treats and tell them stories and spend time with them. Oh, darling you—

Thank you for your beautiful letter. You express things so well. And I love you to tell me that you love me.

Wait till you see what I bought in Florence for next year!! You'll never guess! It's beautiful. Oh yes, I saw a monk in Florence who looked exactly like you. Tried to take a picture, but he was talking with a girl. We decided that all the handsomest, most eligible men in Italy are monks! Did I tell you about the woman who came running through the Uffizi crying, "But where is the Mona Lisa"? Your camera is superb. Of course, at first, I left the light meter shut and set it accordingly. You were so thoughtful to let me take it.

Bud shall I just tell people that I am going to be married next year? TO YOU!! Oh, Bud, it's too big, too wonderful.

My love to you, my darling,

Za

. . . . .

<u>Bud to Charlotte</u>

Lausanne, August 3rd, 1959

My dearest Za,

Za, just as with a good wine, a good idea mellows and improves with time. Thus it will be with our plans for marriage—for this is one of those rare and wonderful ideas that somehow has in it all of the basic ingredients which are needed to make it truly lasting. What I am trying to say is that I really feel thankful and humble every time I think that we are to be husband and wife.

Darling, of course you must tell people that you are to be married next year (to me!!)—but only when you feel completely ready to do so and only if it feels perfectly natural to say so. So, wait as little or as long as you would like, and one day you will probably find that it will pop right out and that is the day we will begin to share our secret with the rest of the world. (After all, it's an awfully good secret and one that, when the time is right, really should be shared, just like daisy chains should be shared).

Saturday was the Swiss National Holiday (August 1st). I celebrated by spending the whole afternoon at the beach with Les Jonas and a Dutch boy named Alex Dyjkemeister who is spending a few days in Lausanne. It was a beautiful day with a hot, bright sun. Afterwards the three of us went out to dinner at a restaurant located right on the water. We sat outside on a beautiful balcony. I had a very special dish called Fondue Bourguinogne. It consists of chunks of raw steak each of which is bite-sized and each of which one cooks to his own taste by dipping it on the end of a fork into a sizzling chaffing dish filled with boiling oil. There are also special sauces into which one dips each bite before wolfing it down. It was dee-licious!

Now, imagine this to top it all off: because it was the national holiday, there were all kinds of fireworks being shot off over the Lake from both Lausanne and Montreux. So there we were, sipping our wine, eating a fantastic meal, and at the same time watching a lovely fireworks display. Not bad, eh?

Sunday, Les, Alex and I drove up into the mountains to a little mountain village called Chateau d'Oex. There we saw, completely by chance, a perfectly charming village celebration complete with a parade. Seemingly almost everyone in the village participated in the parade, including cats, dogs, horses, and some cows with <u>huge</u> cow bells that went gong-gong instead of tinkle-tinkle. After the parade there were some most unusual native wrestling matches between some of the young boys and men of the village. Later in the afternoon we drove to a tiny little village in the mountains called Gruyeres, the home of the very famous Gruyere cheese. There we went to the very beautiful chateau that dominates the town and I was initiated into the pleasures of cheese fondue. A real taste treat!

Za, remind me to tell you the amazing story of a very large Rolls Royce automobile, a very old lady, and a very small Volkswagen (mine). However, the play is not over yet quite, so I shall wait until I can tell you the final result of the denouement before telling you the rest of the story.

Good night for now, my darling. It grows late (12:15 a.m.) and my eyelids are heavy—so I shall stop talking to you on paper so I can go to bed and start talking to you in my dreams.

Bud

. . . . .

<u>Charlotte to Bud</u>

Rome, August 1st, 1959

Darling Bud,

I am the luckiest girl in nine worlds to have you be in love with me! How I wish I could be with you so that we could talk. Everything always seems right when we are together. I find myself thinking constantly about next year—my "peacock in paradise". It will be hard, I'm sure, and very new and strange, but I am certain that it will work.

A Long-Distance Love Affair

Bud, I miss you so. Is there a way for me to see you before we sail, in Copenhagen perhaps or in Bremerhaven? Actually, that is even farther from Lausanne than Venice, although it might come at a more propitious time.

I find it hard to express myself on paper. I have all sorts of new thoughts about love and marriage and you, but they are nebulous and difficult to translate into writing. But my whole focus, darling, is being centered more and more firmly on our blueprint. I just hope that I can be the most perfect wife for you, help you with your plans and life, and always be there with you when you need me. I have such tremendous respect for you, for your "ambition" (although that is not an apt word) and for the straight-forward way you lead your life. I think this respect is the real "drawing in the sand" in any marriage.

Bud, I have seen the most beautiful things in Italy, inexpensive too! Thick Italian pottery with gay, peasant designs and linens and beautiful silver. Ginny and I in our thrifty Yankee way, however, go from store to store oh-ing and ah-ing and then leaving with regrets.

Am just about to leave for another concert in Domitian's Stadium. Ravel, Berlioz's March of the Witches, Wagner excerpts and some Strauss. I am so thrilled to know at least a small bit about music.

Your last letter was beautiful. I've read it many times. Wish I could talk with you. It seems like such a long year, such a long wait, and then such a momentous step to take. I always think of you though, in a year just as gentle and understanding as now. I think that is what makes me want to come.

Charlotte

. . . . .

Bud to Charlotte

August 19, 1959

Dear Za,

Za, I'm really glad we got to talk together this past weekend. I'm not sure whether we solved anything, all I know is that right this moment I feel stronger about you than ever before. Darling, we'll make a good team—good in every way. I know this is true because my mind tells that it is so and my heart sings that it is so. I miss you very, very much. Suddenly, as I left Innsbruck, I realized how much I wanted you to be with me. It's just something that I felt and feel very strongly. Now my prayer at night is for faith during any uncertainty that might arise in either of our minds during the next few months.

Goodnight, my darling,

Bud

. . . . .

<u>Bud to Charlotte</u>

August 30, 1959

Dear Charlotte,

Have just returned from a most marvelous weekend. Left early yesterday with Jim Wolfensohn and drove to Lucerne where we heard an excellent concert last night—Brahms' "Concerto for violin and Orchestra in D-Sharp" and also a Brucker symphony (Symphony #9 in D-Sharp) that, though quite unfamiliar to me, turned out to be a very pleasant surprise. The concert was part of the annual International Music Festival at Lucerne. When we arrived there the theater was completely sold out. By fortuitous circumstance, however, we happened to meet a couple of the girls who worked in the ticket office and, after making friends with them, managed to wrangle two tickets for the concert.

Afterwards, we drove south to the little village of Brienz (which is located very close to Interlaken on Lake Brienz) where we spent the night for a song in a most delightful chalet. This morning we tore ourselves away at a fairly early hour so that we could enjoy a truly breathtaking drive along Lake Brienz, through Interlaken, and finally to Gstaad. Later in the afternoon we drove back to Lausanne feeling most pleased about our enchanting little two-day excursion.

Last weekend, Les Jonas and I drove down to Grenoble, France to visit some friends of his who are studying there. I've many tales to tell about our trip. Remind me, someday, to relate a few of them to you.

Hope this reaches you in Copenhagen. Trust your trip since Innsbruck has been outstanding and that no mishaps have befallen you.

'Bon voyage' back to the States.

Love, Bud

. . . . .

Charlotte to Bud (after a phone call)

September 3, 1959

Dearest Bud,

Forgive me for not writing. It was inexcusable and I'm so sorry. You have every reason to be cross. It's strange to think of leaving so soon, of leaving without seeing you. Your life has become so new and exciting for you. To hear you talk on the phone about what you had done (although I'm afraid I monopolized the conversation) sounded so different. I suppose, as you say, there are certain to be changes in one's outlook and values during a period of time. I only hope they are not too big changes. Darling, darling, again I apologize. It was completely thoughtless of me not to write. I do think of you constantly, Bud. And just to remind you of my thoughts—they are that you are truly the most wonderful, warm-hearted, generous, understanding person I shall probably ever know, and I love you Bud darling, I really do.

I can't believe that I shall be sailing home in 4 days without seeing you. I do wish I could see you. America is so far and so different. Europe is really another life. I need you. I feel quite alone. This has taught me a lesson in thoughtfulness—its importance. I hope you didn't mind my calling. It might have been too unexpected.

My love to you,

Charlotte

. . . . .

Charlotte to Bud

1:30am, September 4, 1959

Darling, darling, darling Bud,

I feel miserable, still, as a result of my negligence in writing and also because I can't leave, I just can't, on the strength of that phone call and your letter. You were hurt first and then I was, realizing how I had let you down. Tears don't help, and I feel completely hollow inside. So <u>please</u> forgive me. I can almost feel it when there is no kind of inner communication at all. I love you, love you, darling Bud and I feel torn at the thought of leaving you on such a note. Even leaving at all.

It's past one, and I had been unable to sleep, so decided to write to you. You can't know how distressed I was after talking with you. Really, I couldn't believe that we could have both been so cool in our conversation. I was glad you prepared me in your letter. Oh Bud, Bud—I want to be with you more than anything. I love you.

I feel a tremendous need to get my thoughts in order. I have been no use to anyone since we left Goteborg. Bud - I am so sorry. Why did I have to hurt <u>you</u>?

I miss you terribly,

Za

. . . . .

<u>Bud to Charlotte</u>

Monday Night – 10:45 p.m.

November 2nd, 1959

My darling Charlotte,

I've a million things to tell you, the most important of which comes first. *TAKE ALL THE TIME YOU WANT, MY DARLING, AND DON'T SAY YES TO MARRIAGE UNTIL AND UNLESS YOU FEEL COMPLETELY READY!* As you say, Za, it is so very, very hard to communicate all of one's feelings in letters. However, my darling, I think I know what you have been trying to tell me each time you write. I sense that you feel a certain unreadiness for marriage. I sense too, that you may be trying too hard to force yourself into feeling a mature kind of love that will permit you to accept freely and willingly the responsibilities of being a wife. Char, as you know perhaps better than I, love is not the kind of thing that one can force. Rather it's something which simply bubbles spontaneously through a person.

So, dear Za, please don't even try to set a date as to when you will no longer feel a hesitancy toward marriage . . . not next spring, next summer, or even next year. Instead let's just say that perhaps someday you will suddenly feel able to say, "OH, BUD, YES, YES, YES . . . NOW I AM READY TO BE YOUR WIFE!" On that day, Char, and only on that day, I shall be ready to be your husband. Then we will be able to give ourselves to one another completely, and honestly, and joyfully. And if, for some reason, that day never comes, Char, I guess it will just be God's will . . . something that we will just have to accept and be thankful that we didn't make a mistake.

Just one more thing, Charlotte, in case you may be wondering. I feel for you, right at this moment, the deepest love that a man could ever feel for a woman. A deeper love than I've ever felt before. And for this reason, I've an overwhelming faith that the future will one day see us together as husband and wife in a truly meaningful marriage.

Good night, my darling

B-

. . . . .

Charlotte to Bud

Sunday, November 8, 1959

Dearest Bud,

Your tremendous gift of understanding makes me feel humble . . . and so grateful. When I received your letter, I cried and cried at the bigness of your love. I had hoped so much that you would say that, even though I knew it was beyond the call of duty.

B—. I wish you had been here today. It was one of those funny days . . . gray, damp, chilly weather, and a rather bleak view with all the leaves off the trees. I felt rather vague and empty about life and couldn't really concentrate on what I was doing. So about 11, I put on my coat and took a walk, up to the traffic light and then I walked across the lacrosse field to the tennis courts, and then just stood in the first one leaning on the net, letting the wind and moisture blow down all around me. I tried to remember how you looked that Sunday in April over a year and a half ago. I remembered how happy I was and how warm I felt toward you, and how kind you were to me.

After 10 minutes or so I continued on my walk, down by the lake to the spot where we talked about this year and where we ran around barefoot in the cold rain. I began to think about love, and how human love is, to a certain extent, limited. I think that the only love that can ever fill a person completely and give him a continual spiritual glow is the love of God. So, darling, when we are together, let's really try to pray and work on it until it becomes easy to do it together, and not a strained occasional thing.

The last thoughts I had as I was on my way back to the dorm. I suddenly felt a great sense of frustration, knowing that I have such a tremendous lot of energy and not having anything to use it for, except for myself, feeding knowledge into myself. I suppose it is a feeling somewhat akin to yours when you say that you want to get out and do something, create something yourself.

I got back to the dorm and "picked" a beautiful red-gold chrysanthemum from a vase in the hall outside of the Men's Room (which I do very naughtily once in a while!) They are one of my favorite flowers . . . so sturdy and yet fragile and with such rich, strong colors. Mother gave me a shell once, my "yield shell," because she wanted me to learn to give in to and not resist change. I filled it with water and put my flower in it and set it underneath my white Lausanne swan with a piece of white coral beside it. It looks so pretty.

Chet Gale came out this afternoon, but I wasn't really in the mood to be gay. I would much rather have had you here, just so that you could put one arm around me and I could have put my head on your shoulder and we could have just sat quietly. You are such a reassuring person, Bud, and today I wanted to be reassured.

Oh, my darling, darling, darling Bud. You are all men to me, as you once said. Friend, when you take such good care of Ginny; Father and brother when you encourage me and help me learn new things, strong and tender lover; and husband even now because of your great tolerance and your generous understanding. I love you, and my heart is yours.

Charlotte

. . . . .

Bud to Charlotte

November 8, 1959

Sunday Afternoon

My warm, wonderful, precious Za,

What a surprise! I arrived in Brussels twenty minutes ago and found three letters from you awaiting me at my hotel!! They had been forwarded to me here by Derek Tweedly when he arrived back in Lausanne from Frankfurt.

Darling, how can I tell you how much I love you? You are so gentle and understanding and tactful and loving! And Za, one day (in the not-too-far-distant-future) you will make the most perfect wife in the whole world; not "perfect" in the sense of a conventional "model" type wife who always does exactly the "right thing at the right time." Rather "perfect" in the sense that you will always inject a vibrancy into our marriage— through your ability to make even the simplest, every day experiences into gay and festive occasions—through your knack for doing the unexpected when the unexpected is most needed—through your desire to learn and grow—through your sensitiveness—through your laughter— but most of all, through your great capacity to give freely and generously and completely of your love.

What a lucky, lucky, lucky person I am! What an enriching and humbling experience to be your husband! Darling, our marriage, when it comes, will be like a rare and precious flower. And, Za, I shall always do my best to guard and cultivate and care for the soil in which it is planted. That's because I LOVE YOU!

Bud

. . . . .

From this sampling of letters, it should be evident to even the casual reader that Charlotte and I were (and still are, 50 years later) seriously in love!

The long and the short of it is that in December 1959, following the custom of that era, I wrote the following letter to Charlotte's father to ask if it would be all right if I proposed to his daughter:

December 3, 1959

Dear Mr. Ripley,

I am sure that it will not come as a surprise to you when I say that I love Charlotte with all my heart and would like very, very much to marry her in June. May I, therefore, have your permission to make Charlotte my wife.

Both Charlotte and I feel that the love we share for each other is something quite rare and special. With this love as a base and with faith, understanding, sharing, humor and hard work, we are both convinced that we can and will build a strong and lasting marriage. In short, we both feel very ready and very eager to become husband and wife.

You are no doubt interested in how I shall be able to provide for Charlotte. At present I have neither a lot of money nor many material belongings. I do, however, have confidence and ambition and a complete willingness to work hard to give Charlotte the kind of life and the kind of love that she deserves. Consequently, though we will live very simply and modestly and probably have some struggles at first, it shouldn't be long before we will be able to start building for our future and our children's future. Perhaps most important of all is that Charlotte and I both believe quite strongly that we will always be able to find happiness regardless of whether we have a "lot" or a "little" in the way of material goods.

There isn't much more to say except to tell you quite simply that I shall always care for and cherish Charlotte and do my very best to be the best husband in the world to her.

If you should consent to have me as your son-in-law, I would feel deeply and humbly honored.

Sincerely,

Bud

. . . . .

To my great joy and relief, Mr. Ripley replied that it would be fine with him and Charlotte's mother, Ruth, if I were to marry Charlotte. I then wrote to Charlotte and formally asked her to marry me. She replied that she was not quite sure she was ready. I wrote her that I understood, that I loved her, and that she should take all the time she needed to make up her mind. She replied that she appreciated my understanding and that she loved me too. I continued my airmail campaign. Later in December, she finally said YES, with all her heart. I inquired "When?" She suggested June 25, 1960 would be a good date. I said, "Wonderful." I then inquired how would she feel about spending the first year of married life in Switzerland since I was thinking about staying on a second year at IMEDE. She said she thought that would be fantastic.

Then came all the hard work of planning the wedding, a task that fell entirely on the shoulders of Charlotte and her family. My only role was to break the happy tidings to my family. This turned out to be slightly awkward because Charlotte's dad and mother beat me to the punch by promptly writing to my mom and dad telling them how pleased they were about the great news. The only problem was that their letter arrived before mine. Whereupon my dad wrote me asking: "Hey, hey, what gives??" But no harm, no foul. It turned out that both families were very happy that Charlotte and I were to be married.

The only slight fly in the ointment was that Charlotte had not yet met my mother and father. This was remedied in February when Charlotte and her parents flew to Ohio to meet my parents for the first time. This was an intimidating proposition for Charlotte, who had just turned 20 in December. Not only was it the first time she had flown on an airplane but she was also full of apprehensions about the visit. What if she didn't like my parents? What if they didn't like her?

The visit got off to a shaky start. My mom and dad drove to the Cleveland airport to meet all three Ripleys. The only glitch was that the Sorensons' normally trusty Buick had a total breakdown during the 70-mile drive back to Mansfield. This was awkward, in that it was difficult to engage in happy get-acquainted talk while standing outside on the shoulder of a superhighway. But the humor of the situation actually helped to break the ice and soon everyone began to feel comfortable with one another. Eventually, the car problem was fixed, and the little troupe made it back to Mansfield safely.

While the visit went reasonably well, Charlotte felt overwhelmed by the outpouring of Sorenson hospitality. My parents wanted her and her parents to meet everyone in town. Hence there was very formal bridal tea at the Women's Club, and several other lunch and dinner parties featuring the future bride.

The beautiful and charming bride-to-be was presented to dozens of new and unfamiliar faces without the presence of the bridegroom-to-be. To smooth over the latter's absence, Charlotte drew a likeness of me on a large easel-sized piece of cardboard that she used as a prop when asked to give a little introductory talk to all the proper Mansfield matrons who attended the bridal tea. Charlotte rose to the occasion and turned out to be a big hit with the hometowners. Everyone thought she was terrific, including her future parents-in-law.

Meanwhile, the future bridegroom was going merrily along his carefree way, traveling about Europe and sending encouragement to the wedding planners, who were doing all the heavy lifting. The one task he had to perform was to find a suitable diamond ring for his wonderful bride.

Shortly after proposing to Charlotte, I traveled to Brussels to do field research on a Belgian-based company. In the course of my discussions with the company's senior managers, I mentioned that I was recently engaged to be married and inquired whether they could recommend a reliable source from whom I could purchase a diamond for an engagement ring. This being Brussels, one of the diamond capitals of the world, I reasoned that this would be a good place to find the perfect stone. They gave me the name of Willy Badart, a diamond dealer whom they said was very knowledgeable and impeccably honest. That very afternoon, I visited him in his little shop. He was a small, rotund man of about 60 with a twinkle in his eye and a ready smile. We immediately hit it off with one another. He showed me his inventory of unmounted diamonds and guided me to the selection of a flawless white stone a little over a carat in size. I was delighted with my choice and was sure that Charlotte also would be. As it turned out, she was.

With the transaction complete, Willy invited me to dine that evening in his apartment. Willy turned out to be a gifted raconteur. One story he told made an indelible impression on me.

It emerged that Willy had been head of the Belgian underground movement in World War II. In that capacity he ran a spy operation throughout the war. He told me about one particular agent who had worked for him. An artist and illustrator by profession, this man did double duty as one of Willy's most effective spies. That is, he was until he was captured in 1942 by the Nazis and sent to Buchenwald, the concentration camp in central Germany.

There, Willy's agent was subjected to terrible privation, but he nevertheless survived until he was put to death in a gas chamber toward the end of the war. However, during the time that he was still a prisoner, he managed to get hold of a copy of a book written in French entitled *The Testament*, by Francois Villon. Villon was a French poet with criminal tendencies who spent a fair share of his life incarcerated. Written in verse in 1461, much of *The Testament* was a depiction of Villon's life in a French prison. Struck by the irony of reading Villon's verses while he, too, was incarcerated, Willy's artist/agent took it upon himself to illustrate the margins of Villon's book with ink-drawn cartoons of *his* everyday life in Buchenwald. Over a two-year period, he filled the margins of almost every page of the book. Somehow, shortly before his death, he managed to smuggle the illustrated book out of the concentration camp and had it ultimately delivered to Willy Badart.

It was this book that I was privileged to be shown by Willy during the evening I spent with him. This experience made a powerful impact on me. The illustrations made war-time life in a Nazi concentration camp come alive to me. The artist/agent was brutally graphic in his drawings. They depicted hangings, beatings, shootings, a gas chamber, starving emaciated prisoners with clothes hanging from their skeletal bodies, inadequate housing facilities, wives being separated from their husbands, children being separated from their mothers, and other equally gruesome scenes. A few showed acts of kindness among the prisoners in the camp. That evening spent scrutinizing every page of Willy's book is one that I have never forgotten. Years later, I had the opportunity to visit Buchenwald. On that occasion, the memories of my evening with Willy came flooding back to me. The somewhat sanitized modern-day version of Buchenwald somehow didn't communicate the horrors depicted in Willy's book.

The rest of my year of separation from Charlotte passed in a blur, marked by anticipation, apprehension, and excitement. I'm sure that, back in Wellesley, Charlotte was feeling those same sentiments.

The day in June 1960 came, however, when it was time to fly back to the United States to get married to a bride whom I had not seen for 10 months. My friend, Joachim Lungarshausen, drove me to the Geneva airport and sent me off with a wave and a hearty farewell shout of "Bon Voyage and Bon Marriage." Arriving at New York's Idlewild Airport some hours later, I emerged from the customs area and almost immediately spotted Charlotte waiting for me on a balcony.

Ah! How wonderful it was to see her again! Although if truth be told, at first both of us felt a bit awkward and shy with one another, after having been apart for so long and with our publicly announced marriage only 10 days away.

We were able to break the ice a bit on a four-hour bus ride to her family's house in Stockbridge, where a warm welcome awaited us. Of course, the place was abuzz with wedding plans and preparations and with the myriad details connected with arranging a ceremony to be attended by 300 guests. As with any wedding, the stress level was about 6 or 7 on the Richter scale. Both the long-distance bride and the long-absent groom had mild cases of pre-ceremony jitters.

Complicating matters still further was the fact that the process of becoming re-acquainted in person was interrupted by the fact that the gallivanting groom left Stockbridge after just a couple of days to visit his family in Ohio. He then stayed in Mansfield for the better part of a week before arriving back with his parents and sister on June 22nd, three days before the wedding. Thus, the two principals in the upcoming nuptial ceremony had practically no time to become re-acquainted before walking down the aisle together.

Finally, the afternoon of June 24th, the day before the wedding, Charlotte and I had a couple of hours to ourselves in which to take a long walk together down a country road. During our walk, the dam burst, and we started pouring our hearts out to one another. It seems the bride-to-be had some serious last-minute doubts about whether she was truly ready to go through with the ceremony scheduled for the next day!

She questioned whether we were really right for each other. We'd been away from one another for so long and despite all our letters and our six minutes of conversation, she felt that we hardly knew each other. She wondered whether she would be letting herself in for a boring bourgeois life as the wife of someone involved in the world of business. Her interests were creative, artistic, and whimsical and she was not the least interested in making a lot of money or living the high life. Besides, she was barely 20 and hadn't yet finished her undergraduate degree and perhaps she should wait awhile before marrying.

My heart sank, probably because I had some of the same doubts. However, I did my best to try to calm both her fears and mine. Since I was six years older than she, I was supposed to be the mature, reassuring voice of wisdom and reason. On the verge of panic myself, I tried to encourage Charlotte not to be afraid. Though not quite knowing whether it was true, I told her that what she was going through was all quite natural, that all brides have last-minute doubts, but that in our case everything would be okay because we were really meant for each other.

By the end of the walk, we had both calmed down enough to agree not to startle our two families by announcing that we were calling off the wedding. That night, however, was largely a sleepless one for Charlotte. At 4:00 a.m., wise old Captain Thorpe, a retired ship captain who was in his eighties and worked as a part-time handyman for the Ripleys, found her wandering around the house preparing to execute her mother's suggestion of painting the family tree on a picnic table. He sternly admonished her to go back to bed to get some sleep before the dawn of her wedding day.

The morning came, and the wedding went forward. At four o'clock on a beautiful afternoon, Charlotte walked down the aisle of little Trinity Church on

Main Street in Stockbridge. The pews were packed with family members and friends. The bride was radiant in a gorgeous ivory satin wedding gown that had been handed down from her grandmother. As I watched her approach the altar on the arm of her father my heart was bursting with love for her. She was the most beautiful woman I had ever seen. And she was to be my wife!

The ceremony itself went off without a hitch. Reverend Curry presided and, when it came time to make our vows, we each did so smoothly and without prompting, having memorized them in advance. However, when it came to the "love, honor, and obey" part, Charlotte omitted "obey." That was fine with me. Though I am sure that at the time we were both in a bit of a daze, to this day, more than 50 years later, I remember it as a wonderfully joyous occasion.

After the ceremony, a modest wedding reception was held in the beautiful garden behind the Ripleys' rambling 1798 house that had once served as the halfway inn between Great Barrington and Pittsfield. In typical Ripley style, the event was delightfully underorganized. The wedding cake that had been ordered had failed to show up, but the local innkeepers had stepped up and delivered a suitable substitute. This only added to the spontaneity and festive atmosphere of the occasion. It helped that, despite rain in the morning, the weather that afternoon was perfect. The wedding guests helped themselves to champagne, lemonade, and appetizers under a tent that had been erected at the last minute for the occasion. Charlotte and I, together with our parents and the other members of the bridal party, greeted all our guests in an informal reception line located in front of an arbor of roses on the lawn.

Members of the bridal party included Charlotte's sister Ginny, who was Maid of Honor, plus her sister Anne, her childhood friend Suzy d'Autremont, and my sister Nancy, who were bridesmaids. My best man was Tom Bloor, my friend and mentor from Mansfield. My groomsmen were Bob Jedrey, my Amherst roommate, and Harvard Business School roommates Jim Killough, Bob Stinson, and John Beard.

All too soon, after toasts, the cutting of the wedding cake with a civil war sword, the throwing of the bridal bouquet from the balcony, and much conviviality, it was all over and time for Charlotte and me to make our getaway. We changed into our traveling clothes and hopped into a Volkswagen Bug that we had borrowed from Nancy. It had been decorated with streamers, tin cans, and "Just Married" signs. Then off we drove to the cheers and waves of all of the wedding guests.

We spent our wedding night in familiar territory at the Lord Jeffery Amherst Inn in nearby Amherst. Then it was off the next morning to begin our wonderful two-island wedding trip. The first island was Martha's Vineyard. When we drove into Woods Hole, Massachusetts, we discovered that the normal ferry to the island was not running due to a ferry workers' strike. So we contracted with a local fisherman to take us to the Vineyard on his fishing boat. Since we had been unable to take our car with us due to the ferry strike, upon our arrival in Vineyard Haven we rented a motor scooter to serve as our mode of transportation while on the Island. Thanks to the generous hospitality of Bucky Salmon, my friend and former professor at Amherst, we had at our disposal his rustic "up-Island" cottage that fronted on the sand dunes of South Beach. It was a glorious spot to begin married life. We swam, we clammed, we ate lobsters, we sunned, we talked, we snuggled, and we explored. There were few outside distractions.

There was one incident, however, that occurred the first morning of our visit. Charlotte decided it would be a good idea if she learned how to drive the motor scooter. I thought I gave her good instructions. Evidently not. When it came time for her to solo, she somehow managed to gun the scooter straight into one of the Vineyard's picturesque stone walls. Fortunately, my precious new bride was none the worse for the experience. The scooter, however, had to be briefly returned to the shop for minor repairs. Henceforth, I was appointed the official driver of the vehicle.

The seven days we spent on the Vineyard spun by only too quickly. Soon it was time to depart for the next honeymoon island adventure. We made our way back to Stockbridge, said our goodbyes to the Ripleys and to the Sorensons, who had been touring New England during our absence, and headed back to Idlewild Airport. There, we boarded a plane for Madrid, Spain, where we caught a connecting flight to the island of Majorca in the Mediterranean. There, I had booked accommodations at the Bendinat, a charming little 10- or 12-room boutique hotel right on the coast. At the time, Majorca was almost totally undeveloped and had a wonderful sense of peace and quiet about it. It was the perfect setting for phase two of our honeymoon.

We were given an attractive room with a balcony and windows overlooking the water. The first afternoon, we unpacked, and Charlotte laid out on the bed an array of seven different nightgowns from her wedding trousseau. Each was more diaphanous than the next. That night after dinner we returned to the room and found that the sweet maid who turned down our bed had selected her favorite and left it on the pillow. The others she had hung in the closet. Thus began a tradition. Each afternoon Charlotte would leave all seven nightgowns on the bed, and each evening our amused maid would pick out her choice for the night. Of course, none of the nightgowns suffered much wear or tear during the course of our stay!

The days on Majorca passed magically and lazily. We did lots of reading, had long conversations, ate leisurely meals, swam both in the pool and in the

Mediterranean, worked on our tans and did a bit of sightseeing. It was idyllic. On a couple of days, we rented a car and explored the island from one end to the next.

Another day, while on the beach, we chanced to strike up a friendly conversation with a certain Guillaume Coll and his wife, Carmen. They had been married for a year. Guillaume was huge, and his slender wife kept kidding him about how he was too fat and he ate too much. They ended up inviting us to have dinner with them in the nearby town of Palma de Majorca. We accepted the invitation and they said that Guillaume would pick us up at our hotel about seven that evening. When Guillaume arrived, we discovered that the mode of transport into town was a rattletrap motorcycle. Guillaume genially invited the two of us to hop on behind him. Grasping onto Guillaume's gigantic bulk, Charlotte did so, and I hopped on behind her. Gunning the motor, Guillaume promptly roared off onto the narrow highway into town. A threesome on a motorcycle is scary at any time. But at high speeds on a narrow curvy road the ride can be absolutely terrifying. And thus it was. Hanging on for dear life, we were mightily relieved to arrive safely at Guillaume and Carmen's little apartment. The couple, though obviously of modest means, was wonderfully generous and hospitable. Carmen had worked hard to prepare a delicious dinner for us, served with ample quantities of local Majorcan wine. Though neither couple spoke the other's language very well, we were somehow able to carry on an interesting conversation. They were curious about life in America and we were curious about life in Majorca. The evening was a nice grace note during our island interlude. When it came time to leave, Carmen insisted we take the leftovers home with us to the Bendinat. Taking our departure, the only thing we dreaded was the return trip on the motorcycle, particularly since Guillaume had had several glasses of wine with dinner. However, in the end we made it back safely to the hotel with memories of an unexpectedly pleasant evening.

Also staying at the Bendinat were three older English ladies in their fifties who were extremely friendly and seemed fascinated with the young American honeymooners who were their neighbors. On several occasions they engaged us in conversation and at the end of their stay one of them invited us to come visit them at her home in England. A year or so later, on a trip to London, we did so and had dinner with them in their somewhat ostentatious "country manor" that reeked of new riches.

After about 10 days of Majorcan magic, we packed our bags and with a great sense of anticipation flew off to our new life as a married couple in Lausanne. On our arrival, there was an initial hitch in our halcyon plans. Before leaving for America, I had arranged for us to move into a pleasant apartment located close to IMEDE and Lake Geneva in the part of town called Ouchy (pronounced "Ooo-she"). The only problem was that the apartment was currently occupied by a departing IMEDE research associate and his wife who were not scheduled to vacate it until the end of August. This left several weeks during which we would have to find temporary housing. This I had not been able to line up prior to leaving for the States.

The first night following our arrival in Lausanne, we booked into a perfectly horrible hotel room overlooking the tracks next to the central train station. It was drab, dark, and noisy, and was absolutely devoid of any hint of beauty or grace. After the fairy-tale life of our honeymoon, we were suddenly hit in the face with a dose of dismal reality. Both of us suffered a total sense of let-down. It was particularly hard on Charlotte. Her fairy-tale fantasies of a glorious married life in charming Lausanne suddenly came crashing down. After a nearly sleepless night, punctuated by the periodic roar of passing trains, we woke to a gray, drizzly morning. Charlotte dissolved in tears, no doubt wondering what she had gotten herself into. It was the first crisis of our married life. I tried to comfort her and reassure her that everything would be all right. But she was disconsolate.

The only thing I could think to do was to go out and try to find us a decent place to stay for six weeks until our permanent apartment was ready. Leaving my new bride in our drab hotel room, I set out in my VW Bug in search of new lodgings. I checked "for rent" classified ads in the *Gazette de Lausanne*, made phone calls, and started driving around, looking at available short-term rentals.

Then a miracle occurred. The third or fourth place I looked at was an absolutely delightful studio apartment on the top floor of a charming Swiss chalet high up in the middle of some hillside vineyards overlooking Lac Leman. It was about a 10-minute drive east of Lausanne in the little hamlet of La Conversion. The studio included a light and airy south-facing living/bedroom, a kitchenette, and a balcony with a spectacular view of the vineyards, the lake, and the Dents du Midi mountains in the distance. It was perfect! I immediately signed a short-term lease with Monsieur Damazat, the one-legged retired vigneron who owned the chalet and lived with his wife on the first floor.

Then I raced back to our shabby hotel and told Charlotte the news. She perked up immediately. We packed, checked out, and returned to our new digs in the vineyard. We were both thrilled to have found the perfect temporary love nest in which to begin our life adventure in Switzerland. It wouldn't have happened, though, if I had accepted the status quo!

CHAPTER TWELVE

LAUSANNE

In the end, we lived the first three years of our married life in Lausanne. After several weeks, we moved to the IMEDE leased apartment on the fourth floor of 9 Avenue Floreal in the Ouchy neighborhood. While not so charming as our aerie in the vineyards, it was far more practical. Only three blocks away from IMEDE, it had a living room, two bedrooms, a kitchen, and a bath. Best of all, it was just above a corner boulangerie located on the ground floor of the apartment building. So, each morning we awoke to the wonderful smell of freshly baked bread. Typically, our day would begin with me going downstairs to purchase mouth-watering croissants or a piping hot loaf of "mi-blanc carre" bread straight out of the oven. Then, back upstairs I would go to our apartment where Charlotte would have already prepared the rest of a delicious, healthy breakfast.

As an aside, on occasion we were known to have picked up a freshly baked loaf of bread so hot that if we opened up a hole in it and stuffed some Gruyere or Emmental cheese inside, the cheese would melt of its own accord and become molten. The result was our own unique and tasty version of a traditional toasted cheese sandwich.

It took a while for Charlotte to acclimatize herself to life in Lausanne. While I had an active professional job that I would go off to do each day, she was left to fill her days on her own. It was lonely for her at first. Still only 20, with no "permis de travail" (work permit), no friends, and only rudimentary French language skills, she found daily life was a challenge. But, being Charlotte, she rose to the occasion.

She enrolled in French lessons at the "Ecole de Francais Moderne" at the University of Lausanne. She made friends with a few of our neighbors and with the wives of some of the faculty and participants at IMEDE. She took violin lessons. She taught English as a second language at the "Ecole Benedict" in Lausanne. She explored the city and the surrounding countryside. She wrote fantastic letters to her family providing vignettes of her impressions of the idiosyncrasies of Swiss mores and customs.

She did some contract work for the Lausanne Tourist Bureau translating their official tourist brochure from French into English. In short, little by little, she used her innate creative talents to build a life for herself during the time that I was occupied by my job at IMEDE.

Then there were the weekends and evenings when as newlyweds we could play together. I took pleasure in sharing with Charlotte all of the nooks and crannies of Lausanne and its surroundings that I had discovered during the year that I had spent there alone.

On evenings that were warm and pleasant, we would often dine at one of the little open-air restaurants that dotted the lakeside waterfront in Ouchy. Our favorite menu items typically featured "filet de perche" or "filet de fera," which were deliciously prepared fish freshly caught in Lac Leman. Or, when the weather was inclement, we would visit a candle-lit "carnotzet" to savor the signature Swiss dishes of "fondue de fromage" (cheese fondue) or "raclette," a special variety of savory Swiss cheese melted against a vertical grill and served molten on a plate along with boiled new potatoes and little cornichon pickles.

The best way to capture the tenor of our life in Lausanne is to read how we contemporaneously described our adventures in letters sent back to the United States. The following are some excerpts:

Bud to the Ripleys

> August 1960
>
> Lausanne, Suisse
>
> Dear Everyone,
>
> Sunday we moved from our charming but temporary apartment in the hills with the lovely balcony overlooking the lake and the mountains. Now we are living in our cozy and comfortable apartment in town with the spare bedroom for YOU when you come to visit us!
>
> Guess what! Before they left their temporary apartment, the Sorensons gave their first PARTY. It was a cocktail party for 14 people . . . a grand mélange including old friends who were leaving, new friends who were arriving, and a few others of various sizes and shapes. It was a rousing success! Your loving daughter and sister, who is the most wonderful wife

in the whole world, proved herself also to be a most clever and gracious hostess. You should have seen her! The Ripley tradition of hospitality has already begun to charm Lausanne. Starting practically from scratch an hour before the party.

Charlotte created a truly imaginative and delicious assortment of hors-d'oeuvres that turned out to be the hit of the party . . . as proven by the fact that they had completely disappeared by the time the last guests left. Moreover, between putting the final touches on the pre-party preparations and greeting the first guests to arrive, Char changed in a jiffy and reappeared looking radiant. Then during the party Char made everyone feel completely at ease and, in short, absolutely sparkled. Hooray!

One weekend we drove up to Villars and spent the night with some friends from Mansfield who have had a chalet in the mountains all during the past year. The air there was almost unbelievably crisp and clear, and we greedily gulped it in with every breath. On both Saturday and Sunday Char and I took long walks in the mountains. The scenery was magnificent!

Za and I are now both full-fledged members of the local tennis club. Consequently, we have been doing our best to play as often as possible. Last week, for example, we went to the club almost every noon (I have an hour and a half for lunch) and played. Afterwards we had picnics on the balcony of the little clubhouse. These were particularly fun since each day the picnic basket contained new and different surprises . . . grace à ma femme.

Love all of you very much,

Bud (& Charlotte)

. . . . .

Charlotte to the Ripleys

August 1960

Lausanne, Suisse

Dear, dearer, dearest ALL,

We are, at last, cozily and comfortably ensconced in our apartment. We had unusual luck in getting this particular one, since hot water is included in the rent, we have the use of a washing machine, and the location is so ideal. We are five minutes' walk from IMEDE, three minutes from the Metro that takes one up the hill to the major shopping center and banks, and three minutes to a small and charming park which is laced with woods and paths and has a lovely view of the lake and mountains. We stand in a group of apartment buildings, but are on the fourth floor, so that we aren't "watched" from above by rows of balcony observers and we have our own view of the mountains. We are also fortunate in having such clean and modern furnishings . . . some of the apartments we visited were "affreux".

Apartment living is a new concept to me: one day I ran to the window to see if the trees were twisting in the wind . . . but only to see geraniums nodding in their window boxes.

The Swiss don't wave, so we have exchanged nods ourselves with several neighbors. (Bud found that his barber lives directly across from us!) The kitchen and guest bedroom side look out on Avenue Floreal and catch the afternoon sun, while the living room, balcony, bedroom side face the east, the mountains and the barber.

We invited our former landlord and his wife plus a Swiss-German girl and a boy from East Berlin to our first dinner party. They came bearing flowers (traditional Swiss custom), raspberries, and their dog, Mickey, from whom they are never parted. Bud put two old candles into plastic yogurt containers (yogurt . . . flavored . . . is comparable in popularity to ice cream in the States) and we brought out our new pottery plates and had a gay, gay evening. Hilmar, the German boy, told us a little of life behind the Iron Curtain. He had left with only his clothes and probably will not risk returning.

We spent last weekend with some Canadian friends, John and Natty McArthur, and an Englishman named Peter Brooke. We left early Saturday morning with our stocks of cheese, ham, bread and chocolate and drove to a town called Brig, about three hours south of Lausanne in the "Vallee de la Rhone". There we left the car and took an aerial tramway partway up the foothills of the Eggishorn mountain. It was a glorious day. The air was clear and sparkling. From eleven in the morning until about seven in the evening, when we arrived at the Hotel Jungfrau, we hiked up and up, through Alpine meadows and pine forests and finally way above the tree line along the side of a glacier.

It was amazing to see the range and variety of people who come out to hike: from small children literally in diapers, to priests to real professionals carrying sheathed ice axes. The following day, Sunday, we made, as they say, the "final ascent".

It was an exhilarating feeling when we finally reached the summit. Our descent, however, was totally unconventional and perilous. For some crazy reason we chose to descend down the steep and unmarked "face of the mountain" that was <u>covered</u> with rock slides. The footing was very insecure, and we inched our way down for about three hours. It was extremely dangerous and on two or three occasions we set off minor rock slides, one of which dislodged a rock that hit Natty McArthur on the side of her head and caused considerable bleeding. We finally made it down safely, but I can assure you that we would think twice about doing that again! The final portion of the descent from the hotel to the valley, well over a thousand meters, we did in record time, running down a steep and winding goat path.

Bud takes his first trip on Monday to Amsterdam. Coincidentally, and just by chance, a Swiss friend of mine from Wellesley will be coming through Lausanne at the time and will spend a few days here. I am hoping that she will make some trips to the butcher shop with me and show me what to do with the ubiquitous sausages! Half of the boucherie is devoted to their display and I find it hard to know where to begin.

Bud and I have been extremely careful with our centimes. He drew up an elaborate chart with headings for every conceivable item. On food, we have been averaging about 9 francs a day (approximately $2.00) for both together. A short list of menus to keep you from worrying: the most popular dishes have been veal scaloppini, chicken with a mushroom-wine sauce, lamb curry, the inevitable tuna fish casserole, liver, and beef stew. We eat once or twice a week at the "foyer de l'universite", very inexpensive and a wonderful place to meet foreigners, many from the Middle-East, Scandinavia, Germany and France. We have been able to do quite well with our French, and happily enough, both of us have been told that we do not possess the obtrusive American accent.

We went to a fascinating party the other night, given by a German friend of Bud's. Many Dutch, a Pole, Germans, Scandinavians, Swiss, and Italians were there. We were the only English-speaking couple. Once again, we have been exceptionally fortunate in getting to know so many Europeans, because so often Americans here tend to lead very insular lives within their own group.

The days seem to melt into one another, so fast that it is hard to remember how we have spent them. We arise . . . ideally . . . at seven, breakfast, study French or read until eight-thirty, then Bud leaves for work. Sometimes I take my rope marketing bag and walk with him to school, returning via the boucherie, boulangerie, epicerie, and laiterie . . . every item seems to come from a different store. Bud returns for an hour and a half at noon or else we will take a picnic and go to the tennis courts or for a walk along the shore.

Love to you all,

Char (and Bud)

. . . . .

Charlotte to the Ripleys

September 15, 1960

Lausanne, Suisse

Greetings from the Love Nest to all Pilgrims!

A quick list of some things we have done recently: An organ concert in the Lausanne Cathedral, a fashion show for me, my first (which I found rather amusing), some tennis, dinner with one of the professors and his family, dinner here for a Swiss/French couple who are planning to move in next year after they are married, (made Specialité de la Maison #2: veal curry).

We spent an evening with a Sicilian friend who works at IMEDE. (Note: you must read "The Leopard" by the Italian author, Giuseppe di Lampedusa, if you haven't already. Pay particular attention to the fresh and original images. A beautiful book, truly). He, Angelo, is fiery and independent although very sensitive . . . a true Latin . . . twelve years older than his Canadian wife, Sheila, who is his antithesis . . . cool, rational and fair in coloring as opposed to his darkness. An extraordinary marriage, contrary to all the "Dates and Mates" books put out in the United States which stress marrying the boy next door. We have spent several evenings with them and Sheila and I have become good friends. She is refreshing and brilliant, and there is something about her that appeals to me. The electricity of human nature! We are planning a trip to Basel to study art in the museum there. Sheila has impeccable taste as far as interior decoration and dress are concerned, so I might be able to learn something from her.

Bud had a very successful stay in Amsterdam with the Albert Heijn Company and with the Heineken Brewery. Such a wonderful husband, he is. Never forgets to tell me all the intricacies of the problems he is studying. The result: daily I get more interested and feel a closer part of his work.

Bud and I continue to breakfast in the sunshine and dine by candlelight. Even the in-betweens are rosy . . . .

Love, love, love, love,

The Twain

. . . . .

Charlotte to the Ripleys

October 17, 1960

Lausanne, Suisse

Dear All

So much to tell you. We have been making a great deal of progress with our French. I just finished reading Anne Frank's diary in French and Bud is starting it now. We have been working diligently on our homework for our tutoring lessons, and most important, we have been going out more often with French speaking people to dinner and such. One Sunday we went on a "Rally" . . . a most unusual day! Thirty cars, about one hundred people (all members of the tennis club) all driving furiously through the rain from one "stop" to another, each hoping he had followed his directions correctly and had answered all the questions correctly. At one "stop" we were given an envelope containing a postcard picture of the center of a certain village. The postcard had been cut up into puzzle pieces and it was our job to piece it together and find the town. At another "stop," croissants and coffee greeted us. It took us four hours to reach the dinner-spot. Outside the restaurant, several large burners were set up to make raclette (melted cheese served with baked potatoes and little pickles). It was freezing cold and there was a magnificent radiantly white mountain peak which jutted up from nowhere into the sky. Wine, wine, wine and everyone was burbling with joy and lightly lusty good cheer. We met a number of attractive people . . . and what is more, found that we had come in 7th in the race and won a bottle of white Vermouth.

We have made friends with the elderly couple who live across Avenue Floreal and to whom we used to only nod and smile. They live very modestly with their cat; the husband does a lot of woodworking in the cellar; and Mme. embroiders and frames pictures. She claims to have been miraculously cured of a painful and long-lived illness by the evangelist Paul Osborne. She talks about it frequently and there is something unquestionably radiant about her face . . . and eyes. One day last week, I took her some cookies and we sat all afternoon in her kitchen sewing (she taught me some new stitches) and talking in French. Her daughter-in-law was there too, mourning her beloved cat that had just fallen off the fifth-floor balcony on the concrete! The second time! On the table in the kitchen were some charred curls of something or other. They turned out to be medicinal mushrooms that Mme. takes around to all the sick. She says she also does some faith healing.

My courses start at the university next week . . . French and some audited courses in political science. We are planning a trip to London in November. The days spin by. Our cleaning lady says that that is the way to grow old fast. But I don't mind.

Every day I am glad I was brought up in the Ripley family in Pilgrim's Inn. I work all the surfaces and think about philosophy and groups and people all day. You have helped me in a million ways. Especially in *realizing that people are just people after all. One shouldn't be afraid to give of one's self.*

Love, Charlotte

. . . . .

Bud to the Ripleys

November 22, 1960

Lausanne, Suisse

Dear All,

Bon jour, ma chere famille; c'est Bud qui parle. I have just wrested the typewriter away from my wonderful and beautiful wife so that I could say hello and personally tell you that your daughter (sister) grows more lovely each day. When in Lausanne, the days literally fly by. Neither of us can quite believe that we've actually been married for five months. Ah! La vie, c'est parfaite!

Much love,

Bud

. . . . .

Bud to the Ripleys

December 30, 1960

Dear Ripleys, one and all,

Here I am at last . . . writing to all of you. And what better way to spend the waning hours of 1960 . . . one of the most eventful and perhaps momentous years of my life. Not only did it bring marriage to your most extraordinary daughter, but we only four days ago celebrated her once-in-a-lifetime-coming-of-age 21st birthday!

Although Charlotte claims to be a "new person" since reaching "her majority", she really hasn't changed one whit. The fact of the matter is that, whether 20 or 21, she continues to grow more and more wonderful each day.

Meanwhile, my work at IMEDE continues to be stimulating. Having the opportunity to observe and participate in the development of a school such as IMEDE is an extremely interesting experience. In some ways, it is much as though I were watching the early development of a school such as the Harvard business school must have been some 50 years ago. For in many quarters of Europe the whole concept of formalized management training has yet to be accepted. In other quarters, the concept is accepted, but the American training methods are not. In an environment such as this, IMEDE, as one of the first European centers of management development, must necessarily find its way through trial and error.

The goal, of course, is to design an educational approach that recognizes the special needs of the European business community while, at the same time, retaining the most worthwhile features of educational methods used in U.S. business schools. As you can well imagine, this is not an easy task, particularly when one realizes that Europe is not yet a homogeneous nation such as the U.S., rather is still made up of many individual countries, cultures, languages, etc . . . each with its special needs, each with its own ideas. Nevertheless, in spite of the obstacles, IMEDE seems slowly but surely to be forging ahead in what is hopefully the right direction.

My own work this year is much the same as it was last year, with a few notable exceptions. For one thing, I am and will continue to teach more often, an activity that both thrills and fascinates me. Moreover, I am more deeply involved in the process of course planning and administration. On the other hand, I am doing considerably less traveling . . . a fact that, as you may be able to guess, does not particularly bother either Charlotte or me. All in all, I think that the experience that I am receiving is invaluable and will serve as an excellent basis for later work in the international field.

Char and I have spent considerable time talking and thinking about next year. As a result of our interests and my experience, it seems quite likely that I shall be in the market for a job next year that will enable me to stay either directly or indirectly in the field of international business. I think there is an excellent future in this area. In all probability, then, I shall attempt to locate something in the line of marketing or general administration with a U.S. consulting or manufacturing firm having international interests.

Lausanne

Meanwhile, our life together here in Lausanne continues to be quite remarkable . . . as I am sure you have been able to sense from Charlotte's many letters. How fortunate we are in every way!

Your sparkling eyed daughter-sister has just come in and is maintaining that it is growing late and time to go to bed. So . . .

My love to each and every one of you,

Bud

. . . . .

From the above excerpts, it should be evident that Charlotte and I quickly came to love living in Lausanne and that our life as a married couple was off to a strong and healthy start. We both came to realize that the bonding that occurred between us as a result of beginning our marriage five thousand miles and an ocean apart from our families and friends in America had been a true blessing. We were able to get to know each other in a profound and meaningful way that probably would not have been possible had we started out our journey together in our familiar American surroundings.

As a result of our personal experience, we have frequently recommended to other couples that they should start out their married life by putting an ocean between themselves and their families and friends if they want to end up having a successful marriage! It isn't always possible, but we can attest to its value!

CHAPTER THIRTEEN

A NEW JOB

In the fall of 1960, I had begun thinking about what I wanted to do professionally after I completed my second year as a research associate at IMEDE. When Charlotte and I had married, the original idea was that we would spend a "honeymoon year" in Europe and then return to the U.S.

Hence, in early 1961, I undertook the task of writing a resume and starting the hunt for a new job. In a letter I wrote to my parents at the time I described the process as follows:

April 9, 1961

Dear Mom and Dad,

You are no doubt curious to know whether there have been any recent developments in my job-hunting campaign. This is the way things stand now:

Though I applied to the Harvard Alumni Placement bureau some time ago, I have heard nothing from them as yet and do not expect to until the end of the month. One of the professors at IMEDE (Prof. Len Langer) has written personal friends of his who are with two companies in the Boston area to tell them about me and to pass along copies of my resume. The two companies are Baird Atomic (where Len's friend is the President) and General Radio Co. (where another friend heads up the International Division). So there is a chance I shall hear from either or both of these companies. Now, along more concrete lines: I have had two interviews with the McKinsey consulting company which has just set up a European branch in Geneva and I am going back for a third on Tuesday morning. As of this moment, I have no idea what the outcome of these talks will be. In any event, were the Geneva people to decide that I might be interesting from the firm's point of view and were I to decide that I wanted to look into the situation further, the chances are that I would continue negotiations with their New York office at such a time as I got back to the States. As far as the consulting firm Arthur D. Little is concerned, I think there is still very much an open door there. I have some good friends in the ADL Zurich office and have done a number of favors for them from time to time; consequently, I feel that, if and when I decide to talk with them after I get back to the U.S., I will have some fairly strong backing and this could well lead to something.

Now, for the most surprising development in the job-hunting campaign. About a week ago, I received a completely unexpected and somewhat astonishing offer to become the personal assistant to Dr. Max Gloor, the current head of Nestlé's German subsidiary, who is slated to become the overall Director of Marketing for the entire worldwide Nestlé Company as of May 1st. As such, he will probably be in line to become the next Managing Director (i.e. President) of Nestlé worldwide.

Just how and why he decided to offer me the job as his assistant I'm not sure I know . . . except that I have done some work with him and for him on several occasions during the past year and a half and have therefore had the opportunity to get to know him to a certain extent. He is one of the most impressive, if not the most impressive administrator, I have met since coming to Europe.

In any case, the offer is an extremely tempting one and one that, if I were in the States, I would not even think twice about before accepting. As Dr. Gloor described it to me, the job would involve working with him on a very intimate basis and doing a little bit of everything . . . from analyzing and making recommendations on specific problems and/or projects (for example, he indicated that one of my first projects would be to examine Nestlé's pricing policies in various markets around the world) to working with Nestlé's international product managers and to performing certain administrative functions for Dr. Gloor. As is the case with any new position, the job would probably define itself as time went on and become just about whatever I was able to make out of it.

As it is, I shall want to examine the offer extremely carefully and give thorough consideration to the various pros and cons before giving a final answer. The deadline for making a decision is the first week in May . . . however, as a matter of courtesy, I shall probably want to give an answer somewhat prior to that time.

The job would involve our staying in Europe (here in Lausanne, since the Nestlé Headquarters are in Vevey, a little village on the lake just 15 minutes down the road toward Montreux) at a salary to be negotiated but that would in all probability be somewhat lower than that for a comparable job in the U.S. On the other hand, the job, as I see it represents an extremely rare opportunity and one that I may decide is too good to pass up. What makes it so inviting is that Dr. Gloor himself is quite an outstanding individual, one for whom I have the highest respect, both as a person and as a businessman, and one from whom I think I could learn a tremendous amount. The job as his assistant would probably last for two or three years at the end of which time it could lead to any one of a number of interesting operating assignments either within Nestlé or without.

I am naturally interested to hear your reaction to the above and would welcome any ideas, advice or suggestions that you might have. I have always valued your opinions highly and thus will be looking forward to hearing any comments that you might like to make on the basis of what I realize is rather sketchy information.

With warmest love, Bud and Char

. . . . .

Although I no longer have a copy of this letter, evidently my father replied at some length to my request for advice. Two weeks later, I wrote my parents a follow-up to my letter of April 9th. It read as follows:

April 24, 1961

Dear Mom and Dad,

First of all, many thanks, Dad, for your long and thoughtful letter. I feel that your advice and suggestions are both sound and logical; they provide helpful perspective for my employment deliberations.

To date, there has been no radical change in my basic situation since my last letter. I have decided to take your advice and wait until pretty close to the deadline before giving a final reply to Dr. Gloor. The issues, as I see them are as follows.

In favor of the Nestlé offer are:

It would be a job that, in my opinion, would be both challenging and interesting.

It would involve working with and for a man whom I greatly respect and admire and while Dr. Gloor is an extremely forceful person, I feel that in my workings with him I would enjoy a fair degree of initiative provided I could prove that I was justified to exercise this initiative.

As I mentioned before, there is good reason to believe that Dr. Gloor is the heir-apparent insofar as the future managing directorship of Nestlé is concerned; if this were to occur, it could definitely be a "plus" for my career, provided I did a good job while working for him. This point, however, falls more in the category of an intangible, possible long run advantage and one that should not weigh too heavily in my present decision.

The job would give me an unprecedented opportunity to get a bird's-eye view of all phases of the marketing operations of one of the few companies that can truly be said to operate on a worldwide basis.

To supplement your research on the company: Nestlé, including all its subsidiaries, has total sales of about $1.5 billion; it operates 146 plants in 30 countries, with sales organizations in many more countries; in all, it employs about 70,000 people; the traditional mainstays of its product line have been chocolate, condensed and evaporated milk, infant feeding products, and Nescafe; recently, however, it has branched out into a number of different food lines (e.g. Maggi soups, Crosse and Blackwell specialty items: canned fruit and vegetables, condiments, jams, etc.); and the company is experimenting with new product lines all the time.

So, in view of the scope and nature of its operations, I believe I would have an excellent opportunity to get a feel for consumer goods marketing conditions in a wide variety of world markets. I feel this experience would be both valuable and salable . . . particularly if one believes, as I do, that the international side of U.S. business is going to become increasingly important as time goes on.

Examining the salability in specific terms, I am reasonably certain, following my discussion with McKinsey, that I would be able to negotiate an attractive offer with them in two or three years, assuming I took the Nestlé job now. They have given me a positive indication that this would be the case. In fact, they were most enthusiastic about the type of experience I could get in this particular job at Nestlé. I believe this reaction from McKinsey is typical of the consulting field in general.

In terms of your point, Dad, concerning companies being interested in hiring people "horizontally" would be true in this case, although I recognize that there are still some U.S. firms that might not feel that "foreign" experience was as good as U.S. experience. This would be one of the risks, though, to my way of thinking, not a really serious one.

On the other side of the ledger, I see the following disadvantages:

As you so aptly point out, if Char and I had our "druthers", we would most probably want to return to the U.S. rather than stay over here. In any case, we most certainly would prefer to be nearer to you and the Ripleys than would be possible if we were to stay over here. In this respect, however, whatever happens, we plan to come home to the U.S. this summer. Moreover, since everyone at Nestlé is entitled to a month of annual vacation, the chances are that we would be able to get home at least once a year were we to take the Nestlé offer. Finally, we would hope that you two would plan to spend some time with us over here. And don't say that this isn't possible for we would <u>insist</u> that you come!

If we were to stay over here, it would be more difficult for Char to complete her last year of college and, in any case, it would probably be delayed. There is a possibility that she might be able to get credit for some work done here at the University of Lausanne or the University of Geneva, but this is by no means a certainty.

The Nestlé job would get me started off in the food industry and might later make it difficult for me to switch into some other industry, electronics, for example. This, however, is a risk one runs no matter what industry one enters, and in this respect, I might add that I personally think the food industry is quite interesting.

Finally, there is the question of salary. Though, to date, nothing specifically has been said, I suspect the salary offer from Nestlé would, in absolute terms, be somewhat lower than the salary for a comparable job in the U.S. (In our discussion, Dr. Gloor said that, although he was not exactly sure yet what the Vevey headquarters' salary policy was, he thought that what I could expect would be about a 25-30% increase in my present salary ($5,600). In European terms, where the cost of living is considerably lower than in the U.S., this would be quite reasonable compensation. In U.S. terms, however, a salary of $7,000-$7,200 is not very high.

So the foregoing is pretty much how I see the situation at present. On the whole and as of this moment, I should say that the scales are tipped somewhat in favor of the Nestlé offer. This assessment, of course is dependent on a satisfactory negotiation of a specific arrangement with the company. I shall want to be certain that the job is exactly what I think it is and that the salary and fringe benefits are fair before I make a final decision.

In the event that I do finally decide to take the offer, I hope you will understand that the decision will represent what Char and I will feel to be the very best decision, based on a rational consideration of all factors involved and a good deal of soul-searching.

One final comment on this subject (for I fear I have been rather lengthy), if we do end up deciding to accept the Nestlé offer, it will be with the firm intention of re-examining our position at the end of a couple years with a view toward returning to the U.S. either through making a change and going with a U.S. firm, or through taking an assignment in Nestlé's U.S. operation. The point is that, at that time, I shall be operating with some solid business experience behind me and, thus, should be in a much stronger bargaining position.

Whew! I seem to have waxed long, if not eloquent! Our very best love to you both. We will keep you immediately posted as to any developments.

Love,

Bud & Char

. . . . .

A New Job

From this letter, it is clear that Char and I were giving a great deal of thought to the question of whether we should return to the U.S. (the alternative both Charlotte's and my families would clearly have preferred) or stay in Europe and accept the offer to go to work for the Nestlé Company. And the decision was . . .

Dear Mom and Dad,

Well, yesterday was the big day! I finally made the decision. I am going to take Dr. Gloor's offer to become his assistant at Nestlé! After much, much weighing of the various pros and cons, I have come to the conclusion that this represents an exceptional opportunity and one that I feel I must take.

Here's how it happened. On Monday of last week, I had a long discussion with Dr. Gloor in which we went very carefully over the nature of the job. This discussion served to re-affirm my earlier impressions concerning the kind of challenge that the position involved. We also talked in broad terms about my expectations vis à vis salary arrangements and the long-term future. Then, on Wednesday, we had a second conversation in which Dr. Gloor made a concrete offer: An annual salary of 32,000 Swiss Francs that is equivalent to slightly over U.S. $7,500. This, it seemed to me, was a most satisfactory and generous offer, particularly when one takes into account the lower income tax rate and lower cost of living here in Switzerland. With these two factors taken into consideration, the salary is the equivalent of somewhat over $9,500 in America. In addition, after the first of next year I shall become eligible for participation in an annual bonus arrangement. Moreover, according to Dr. Gloor, there is a possibility that I shall have occasion to visit the U.S. from time to time on business, in which case arrangements could probably be made for Char to accompany me and we could take some vacation at the same time. Yesterday, I had a final discussion with Dr. Gloor, at which time I accepted his offer.

So, you see . . . a new chapter is about to begin. As you can well imagine, both Char and I are very, very excited. Both of us firmly believe that we have made the right decision and that the experience of these next two or three years will be invaluable no matter where the path leads afterwards.

Char joins me in sending both of you our very best love,

Bud and Char

. . . . .

Having made the decision to stay in Switzerland, in early June of 1961, Char and I flew to America, where we spent a month visiting with both her family in Stockbridge and my family in Mansfield. At the end of June, I flew back to Lausanne while Char stayed on in the U.S. for an extra two weeks with her family.

Upon arriving back in Lausanne as a temporary bachelor, I had the pleasure of moving into the charming new apartment we had leased just before leaving for our trip to the U.S. Located high above Lac Leman in the Lausanne suburb of Pully, it had four rooms and a balcony, all with spectacular views of the lake and the Dents du Midi mountains on the far side. We were on the third floor of a rather strangely named building called Modern City A. Just below our balcony were two tennis courts and next to us was a posh girls boarding school called Ecole Montchoisi. Our landlord lived in a corner apartment next to us on the right. He was a handsome Swiss man in his late fifties and his considerably younger, blonde mistress was in her late thirties. They turned out to be a rather reclusive couple that was fond of nude sunbathing on their balcony! In the apartment on the other side of us lived a friendly English couple with three young children. He was a teacher at Ecole Montchoisi and she was a stay-at-home mom.

This apartment in Modern City A was to be our wonderfully warm and cozy nest for the next two years. Light and airy, it had a living room, master bedroom, eat-in kitchen, study/guest room, and bathroom. Living there proved to be a delightful experience. We loved it! Over the course of our sojourn, we hosted many lively parties there and welcomed a steady stream of family and friends who made good use of our guest room.

I started my new job at Nestlé on July 1, 1961. My assignment for the first three weeks was to attend a special indoctrination course at IMEDE that Nestlé sponsored each summer for a cross-section of their executives. It was an opportunity to study at first hand some of the problems and challenges facing the company on a worldwide basis. The course was a great introduction for me to the company and to some of my future middle-management colleagues. It gave me a running start to take on the challenges of my new position.

Toward the end of this indoctrination course, I received a letter from my dad that indicated that he was fully on board with my decision to stay in Europe and work for Nestlé. The following is an excerpt:

July 20, 1961

Dear Son,

A New Job

Very soon now the Nestlé seminar at IMEDE will have ended and you will start actively on your new job. I hope you will like it and that it will measure up to all of your expectations. Isn't it wonderful to have practically your whole future ahead of you, starting on your first really big opportunity. I am sure you cannot help but learn a great deal there that will be valuable in future years.

Recently Norman Straus, president of J. Walter Thompson said something like this to the Economic Club of Detroit: "The postwar economic growth of free-world nations has been so swift that the day is gone when a major American company can confine itself complacently to the domestic market. Just as major marketers moved in this country from local to regional and then to national distribution, many have recognized that they must now move out of the U.S. to other free-world markets if they are to realize their ultimate potential". So you apparently are sitting in a good spot where you can gain an excellent understanding of the marketing problems of many areas of the world.

Love to you & Char,

Dad

. . . . .

Given the respect and love that I had for my dad, his approbation and approval as expressed in these letters meant a lot to me at the time.

After I completed the Nestlé indoctrination program, I sent a letter to my parents containing the following comment:

Today marks the completion of my first full week of work! And I must say that it has been one of the most absorbing weeks of my life! The work itself is both fascinating and challenging. Approximately one-half hour after my arrival, I had enough to keep me busy for at least a month— which is the way I like things to be. The people I have met and associated with so far have been most accommodating and friendly. The association with Dr. Gloor, in particular, has thus far proved to be most stimulating. As a man, he has a tremendous capacity for effective work. So, all I can say is that to date things have been going very well.

Love, Bud

. . . . .

Charlotte added the following P.S. to this letter:

> *Bud has <u>never</u> looked better or happier! He clicks his heels every morning and dashes off to work with a rose and sunshine in his buttonhole!*
>
> *Char*

. . . . .

Evidently, life in all its aspects—new job, marriage to wonderful Charlotte, and the adventure of living in Europe—was fully agreeing with me as I started my new career.

The two years I spent working at Nestlé turned out to be a great success and a tremendous learning experience. I made many friends, had considerable responsibility, and was given many interesting assignments.

The assignment that stands out for me was that of designing a format that could be used by all of Nestlé's worldwide subsidiaries to articulate their annual marketing plans and objectives and to lay out a budget for achieving them. Until Dr. Gloor became the Worldwide Head of Marketing, this annual planning and budgeting process had been a helter-skelter affair with each subsidiary using its own approach.

My format included a model marketing plan and budget. It was intended not to be a straitjacket but rather a systematic approach that encouraged subsidiaries to make sure that they had carefully considered all the factors that might affect the subsequent accomplishment of their qualitative and quantitative goals.

Designing the model format involved several iterations, multiple drafts, and about six months of hard work. The process was not without both its amusing and tense moments.

Perhaps the moment of greatest tension occurred early in the drafting process when I received a call one afternoon from the secretary of Mr. Enrico Bignami, managing director and CEO of Nestlé, saying that Mr. Bignami wanted to see me right away. Since he had the reputation of being quite gruff and not suffering fools gladly, I was immediately apprehensive as to why he might want to see me.

I hurried to his secretary's desk and she promptly ushered me into a huge office where Mr. Bignami, a large and imposing man, was sitting behind his equally large and imposing desk, reading some papers. I halted in front of his desk and stood more or less at attention for what seemed like a minute or two, but what in reality was probably about 30 seconds. The following conversation then ensued.

Mr. Bignami, finally looking up from his papers: *"Ah, it's you, Sorenson. Sit down."*

Me: *"Good afternoon, Mr. Bignami. What is it you wanted to see me about?"*

Mr. Bignami, looking directly at me and fixing me with a stare: *"Sorenson, I've been reading a draft of your proposed Model Marketing Plan and Budget and I just wanted you to know something."*

Me: *"Yes sir. What is that?"*

Mr. Bignami: *"Sorenson, for many, many years now, we here at Nestlé have been making a lot of money using common sense. Now, after reading your draft, I think you are trying to teach us how to lose money scientifically."*

Me (completely stunned and devastated): *"I'm afraid I don't know what to say other than that I am very sorry you feel that way."*

Mr. Bignami (suddenly breaking into a big smile): *"Don't worry, I was just trying to get your full attention and it appears I have succeeded. Actually, I think your draft is pretty good and can potentially be useful to us. However, I do have a few ideas as to how your approach might be strengthened and be made more flexible."*

He then proceeded to go over the draft with me and to make some insightful comments and suggestions that I subsequently incorporated into my later drafts.

At last, he leaned back in his chair and relaxed. He said he had heard a bit about me from Max Gloor and welcomed the chance to get acquainted with me.

After inquiring about my background, he proceeded to tell me a bit of *his* life story. Italian by birth, both his father and mother were ardent members of the Fabian Society, the prominent British Socialist movement inspired by the writings of Sydney and Beatrice Webb, George Bernard Shaw, and others. As a teenager, Mr. Bignami said he had spent many evenings listening to his parents extol the virtues of socialism with other like-minded Fabians. However, the more he listened, the more he came to conclude that the concept of socialism was overly idealistic and would never work in the real world. Instead, his thinking took a 180-degree turn and he became a convert to capitalism as the most effective and practical approach to economic prosperity and social progress.

As a consequence, after he finished his high school baccalaureate, he searched for and found an entry-level job with the Swiss-based Nestlé Company, which had solid capitalist roots. After a brief training program, the company sent him off to Argentina to be a sales assistant. He recounted how, upon disembarking from the ship on which he had taken passage, he had walked barefoot down the gangplank with the only pair of shoes he owned tied around his neck by their shoelaces to save them from wear and tear. (Whether this part of his story was true or apocryphal, I never came to find out. It made for a good story, even though it sounded a bit far-fetched to me at the time.)

He then recounted how, over the years, he had been given assignments involving increasing responsibilities until he had finally ended up in his current position as CEO. His message was that Nestlé was a great company, and that if one had talent and worked hard, there was great opportunity there for long-term career advancement. He also pointed out the food industry was excellently positioned for future steady growth since, in good times and bad, people had to eat!

The meeting ended most amicably and from that time on I enjoyed a good relationship with Mr. Bignami.

If the foregoing was, momentarily, the tensest moment of my assignment to design a universal approach to marketing planning and budgeting, the funniest moments came when we finally sent out the approved Model Plan and Budget to all of Nestlé's worldwide markets. True to their respective cultural stereotypes, their individual reactions on receiving the new approach were truly amusing in their variety.

For example, the Germans almost immediately wrote back to say that they thought that the new standardized approach was "sehr gut" but didn't go far enough. They then spelled out a number of additional Teutonic bells and whistles that they thought would make the approach even more thorough and rigorous.

The French wrote back saying, in effect: "Zut Alors! There you go again, you know-it-alls at headquarters, trying once again to tell us how to run our business. We Frenchmen know our market better than you do, and while we will acquiesce to using the new format, it is with considerable reluctance."

The English, in most cultured terms said, in effect: "Jolly good show. The new uniform approach makes sense to us and should make our life easier."

The Americans said, "Well it's about time. We were beginning to wonder when you Europeans would finally begin to get up to date and understand all of the various aspects of a truly comprehensive approach to marketing planning and budgeting."

And the Italians just put the Model Plan and Budget in a bottom drawer and pretended they never received it!

At last I began to understand the intricacies and nuances of working at what was at the time the most truly multinational company in the world. When I was hired, I was one of only two Americans working in the company's Swiss headquarters. Since there were about 1,300 total headquarters employees comprising perhaps 50 different nationalities, that made the two of us genuine members of a minority group. The other American was my friend, Tom Wyman, who later in his career went on to be CEO of the Green Giant Company, Vice-Chairman of Pillsbury Corp., and CEO of CBS.

The two of us were the exception that proved the rule, the rule being that Nestlé had an unspoken policy at the time of avoiding hiring Americans to work at headquarters. The reason: They were considered to be too expensive, too outspoken, and too presumptuous. Perhaps because the two of us were exceptions, however, both of us ended up being given credit for having had more impact on the company than we actually deserved.

The marketing planning and budgeting format I designed enjoyed considerable success and came to be embraced and appreciated by headquarters and subsidiary personnel alike. I later learned that it became the cornerstone of Nestlé's annual marketing and planning process for at least a couple of decades after I left the company. It was an achievement that gave me a considerable sense of accomplishment and for which I was given more than generous recognition by my boss, Dr. Gloor, and by my colleagues in the company.

During the remainder of my two-year stay at Nestlé, I was given a number of other interesting assignments. One related to Nestlé's 1961 acquisition of Findus, the large Scandinavian-based frozen seafood company. Since I was of Norwegian heritage and had a Scandinavian-sounding name, I was delegated to fly to Stockholm to be in charge of introducing the Findus senior executive team to Nestlé and to indoctrinating them into the Nestlé culture and approach to management.

I was also assigned to attend most of the annual sessions when the managing directors and marketing teams from all of the major subsidiaries came to Vevey to present, in person, their marketing plans and budgets for the coming year. In addition to Dr. Gloor and me, these sessions were attended by a number of other headquarters executives, including the respective regional presidents, the various product group managers, the international head of advertising, the marketing research manager, and the company's chief financial officer. At these sessions, I was occasionally asked for my opinion and also asked to contribute any ideas that I might have to the dialogue. I learned a lot about the cultural similarities and differences that characterized various international markets from attending these sessions.

I believe that my opting to stay in Europe and work for Dr. Gloor at Nestlé was one of the best career decisions I could have made. It put me right at the forefront of the strong push toward the internationalization of business that was just beginning to gain momentum in the 1960s.

It also created a wonderful life adventure for Charlotte and me during the early years of our married life together. I was a lucky man to be in the right place at the right time. And I enjoyed every minute of it!

CHAPTER FOURTEEN

TRAVELS IN EUROPE

During our three years of married life in Switzerland, we had many marvelous travels and adventures. Determined to experience as much of Europe as possible, it seems we were constantly on the go, traveling to one country or another.

The following excerpts from letters we wrote at the time, together with some commentary, provide a sampling of some of our travels:

November 22, 1960

Dear, dear all,

Our trip to London was incredible. The flight from Geneva to London was exciting, as we tried to read and study everything about the royal city. We flew over Paris and then straight through the most glorious sunset that turned all the clouds a magic rosy-orange. We were to stay upon our arrival in London with the Brookes, the illustrious family of our good friend (and one of Bud's fellow research associates at IMEDE) Peter. I think I wrote to you that Mr. Brooke is Minister of Housing and Local Government (also of Wales) in Macmillan's cabinet and Dame Barbara (as I learned to call her) is vice-chairman of the Conservative Party.

On arriving in London, Bud and I put up our umbrellas, breathed in the fog, and took a taxi to Simpsons-on-the-Strand. How distinguished all the gentlemen appeared with their "bowlers" and tailored clothes, and how lovely to sit in front of a glowing fire and sip sherry before dining, and how elegant to be served roast beef with an English accent.

We took the whizzing, whining "tube" to the Brooke's home in Hampstead, a delightful quarter of brick houses (that reminded me of those in "The Three Little Pigs") and lanterns. Peter had drawn us a little map showing us the proximity of the graveyard, the church, and Hugh Gaitskill's house (in reverse order, if you will!) to their own. Mr. Brooke met us at the door and immediately led us to the living room on the second floor. "Tea?" he asked, and we knew that we were in England. Every morning during our stay, Dame Barbara, who was indefatigable, woke us with tea and shortbread and a fire. No one in London seems to have central heating, although it is just that everyone "is planning" to have it installed next week.

We had an "English" breakfast the following morning (every morning, in fact) of sausage, ham, eggs, marmalade, toast and tea. Then we packed the car and set off for Surrey and the Brooke's enchanting cottage that was straight out of a nineteenth century novel. It had weather-beaten tile on the roof and walls, plus flowers and vines growing in a tangle around the lattice windows. There were heavy wooden Dutch doors with iron bolts. The inside was full of books and old tattered chairs and "objects" gathered from all over the world. We had meals of kidney pie and gooseberry pies and huge teas.

We took long, long walks over the down, gathering heather and gorse and gleaming branches of ivy. It was all misty and moisty and perfect. Saturday evening, we went to a neighboring town to see a huge bonfire. Guy Fawkes was being burned in effigy. (On November 5th, 1605 Guy Fawkes tried to blow up the Parliament.)

Tuesday, while Bud was working, Dame Barbara invited me to her "club" for lunch, after which we could go together to Parliament. The club, called the "Naval and Military Club" happened to be one of those rather exclusive only-for-men, deep-re-leather-chairs clubs that, unfortunately (or vice-versa), opened its doors a crack only a few years ago to admit "a few" women. I was fascinated. As of now, women are admitted only to the dining quarters, and even there seemed to be an invisible, but tacitly understood, line, giving the men 3/4 and the women only 1/4 of the room.

The afternoon in the House of Commons was thrilling. Dame Barbara took me in through Westminster Hall, the entrance reserved for Members of Parliament (MPs), then down the hall to a circular atrium, where one waits to be admitted. Suddenly a cry of "hats off, strangers!" and a procession of buckle-shoed and bewigged men came into view: the Speaker, his scribes, and the mace-bearer. They entered their chamber, had a few moments of private prayer, then the public was admitted. Mr. Brooke was under attack from then on by the Labor Party on the subject of Conservative housing policies. I wanted to protect him, our host, as the Laborites jeered and sneered, but as he had warned us the night before, this is common parliamentary procedure. Prime Minister Macmillan spoke with him afterwards on the touchy subject of the establishment of the American Polaris submarine base off the coast of Scotland. Gaitskell, the leader of the Labour Party was also in attendance.

Dame Barbara Brooke and I were seated in the front row of the balcony. All of a sudden, everyone in the House of Commons rose, stamping the floor and cheering. A diminutive but hale Winston Churchill strode into the Commons, pounded his cane, smiled his famous smile and raised his arms. It was his last appearance in the House of Commons. How LUCKY I was to see him!

On another day, Mr. Brooke also gave Dame Barbara and me peers' seats to the House of Lords. There was a great difference between the participants of the H. of L. and the H. of C. The former were silver-haired and wearing carnations in their buttonholes; the latter were wearing heather-colored V-necks and looked more like pragmatists than aristocrats. The Lords' discussion that day concerned the changeover, apparently imminent, from shillings and pence to the metric system. I was startled to see that most of the Lords were fast asleep during this stimulating discussion.

Another morning we went to the "Old Bailey" criminal court and happened to sit next to a fascinating man who told us numerous details about English court procedure. The judge who was judging our particular case was the same who had tried the "Lady Chatterley" obscenity case and also a very highly publicized murder case that had been held the week before. Our neighbor informed us in advance that when the judge entered today he was expected to be carrying in his left hand a black hat and white gloves that he always donned when passing the death sentence.

We also spent hours in various bookstores in London and in the National Gallery and also walking down side streets and alleys and through the lovely parks. We saw the play "Passage to India" (extremely provocative, "The Mousetrap" (a mystery in a country inn), and the delightful musical "Irma La Douce" that was very Parisien and pixy-ish.

Love, love,
Charlotte & Bud

. . . . .

Bud to the Sorensons

April 9, 1961

Dear Mom and Dad,

As you probably gathered from our postcards, we thoroughly enjoyed our trip to the south of France. Altogether, we were gone nine days. The first four nights we stayed in hotels, the fifth night we stayed with a Frenchman named Yves Dusonchet, a neighbor of ours in Lausanne who was visiting his family in St. Tropez. The last three nights we camped out!

In the course of our wanderings we met a number of unusual and interesting people including:

Two Berbers from the Sahara Desert who had worked their way north to France via Spain and who were sunning their camel (KiKi) on a beach which we happened to pass.

Lenny Marshall, a young American writer who had just been released from jail after having spent six days there for having stabbed an Algerian in self-defense.

Our Lausanne neighbor, Yves Dusonchet, and his French family who had lived most of their lives in Egypt and another friend of theirs whose great-grandfather had once been prime minister of Egypt (in 1915).

Bernard, who had spent forty years as a fisherman and sailor and who now ran a harbor side restaurant in Toulon and his waitress, Mon-ee-ka, a blond bombshell who had seen her better days and who was extremely fond of American sailors.

Bernard's best customer, Baptiste, the dried-up proprietor of a liquor store, who ate raw garlic and who invited us to his store where he insisted that we drink whiskey out of a dirty cup that he tried to wipe clean with his filthy shirttail. Baptiste entertained us with stories of his manly exploits sleeping with women from all around the world during his days as a sailor on a merchant ship. However, his boastful manner vanished when his wife suddenly shrieked down the stairs at him from somewhere in their apartment above the shop crying out: "BAPTISTE, FERME TA GUEULE ET ARÊTE TOUS TES BLAGUES!" (Baptiste, shut up and stop telling all of your lies!). At the first sound of her voice, Baptiste instantly lost all his swagger and seemed to shrink inches in stature. Whereupon he quickly suggested to us in a whisper that it was probably a good time for us to leave.

Jean Lurcat, a well-known French artist and ceramicist who lived in the little French village of St. Cere and from whom we bought a large platter with the artistic image of a cock embedded in it.

Also, we saw countless changes in scenery, villages, and memorable works of art. Favored by lovely weather, we enjoyed ourselves thoroughly.

Bud & Char

. . . . .

Mention of Lenny Marshall, the young American writer mentioned above, deserves further elaboration, for therein lies a tale. It happened like this:

One afternoon, Charlotte and I were having *tea alfresco* at an outdoor waterfront restaurant in St. Tropez. Next to us was a nervous-looking, dark-haired young man who kept staring at us from the neighboring table. He was perhaps in his late twenties.

Suddenly he burst out, saying to us in English:

"Don't I know you?"

We replied, "We don't think so."

Young man, "Are you Americans?"

Us, "Yes."

Young man, "Well, will you talk to me? I've *got* to talk to someone. You see, they have just let me out of jail and I've no one to talk to."

We were hooked and agreed to listen to him. A torrent of words then spilled out from him.

"You see, my name is Lenny Marshall and I come from New Orleans. I'm trying to be a writer. But I was having difficulty in New Orleans coaxing my literary muse to jump from my mind onto the paper. So, several months ago, I moved to St. Tropez to see if the atmosphere here would stimulate my creativity. Shortly after my arrival, I met Rudi, a young German who had also decided to try out the ambiance here. We were both looking for a place to stay, so about two months ago we teamed up and jointly rented a charming little farmhouse on a hill overlooking St. Tropez about ten minutes' drive from here.

"The first month at the farmhouse was glorious. With my muse fully restored, I started writing a short story. Soon, words were pouring out onto the paper of their own accord. What started as a short story began to flesh itself out into a full-blown novel. Clearly, the farmhouse ambiance was working its literary magic on me.

"Then, about a month ago, Rudi decided to hitchhike to Paris to see his girlfriend. That was fine by me, since it allowed me even more time to concentrate on writing my novel. But then it happened!

"Late one rainy night a week ago, I heard a loud, insistent pounding on the kitchen door of the farmhouse. From the kitchen where I was sitting, I shouted out through the door, 'Qu'est-ce?' (Who is it?). The voice from the porch on the other side answered in accented French, 'C'est moi. Quelque chose est caissee dans ma moto. Voulez-vous m'aider?' (It's me. Something is broken in my motorcycle. Can you help me?)

"Since it was late and raining hard, I decided to take pity on whoever it was and opened the door. Outside was a brawny, young, rain-soaked Algerian man. He stepped boldly into the room and looked all around. Spotting a bed through the open door of the bedroom next to the kitchen, he demanded. 'Est que cet lit, ton lit?' (Is that bed, your bed?) Somewhat nervously I replied, 'Oui, mais pourquoi vous demander?' (Yes. But why do you ask?). He then began to advance on me and shouted at me, 'Parce que je veut coucher avec tu.' (Because I want to sleep with you.)

"At that point I really got scared and started backing up while he kept advancing. Suddenly, I was cornered between the sink and the kitchen table. He just kept coming toward me. So I did the only thing I felt I could do. Spotting a kitchen knife on the table, I picked it up and stabbed him in the shoulder. And then I stabbed him again, and then again and again.

"Finally, spurting blood, he fell away from me and slumped motionless onto the floor. Then I panicked, thinking for sure that I had killed the guy.

"What to do?! Since there was no telephone in the farmhouse, I ran out the door and up the road to the neighboring farmhouse where I pounded on the door. It was about midnight and there was no answer. Even more panicked, I began shouting 'Help! Help!' at the top of my voice toward the upstairs windows of the farmhouse.

"Finally, a light came on in one of the rooms. A window opened and the French farmer who was my neighbor stuck his head out and shouted back at me, 'Qui c'est-ce et quel est la probleme?' (Who is it and what's the problem?).

"I shouted, 'C'est moi, Lenny Marshall, ton voisin, et je viens de tuer un Algerien!' (It's me, Lenny Marshall, your neighbor, and I've just killed an Algerian!)

"He shouted back, 'Un Algerien! Ce ne fait rien.' (An Algerian! It doesn't matter.) Then he started to close the window.

"I then pleaded, 'Arretez, arretez, s'il te plais, telephoner les gendarmes.' (Stop, stop, please telephone the police.)

"Somewhat reluctantly, he grudgingly agreed to make the call and, leaving me standing outside in the rain, did so. A few minutes later he returned to the window and said that the police were on the way.

"With my heart in my throat, I walked slowly down the hill. Two gendarmes were arriving just as I got back to my farmhouse. Together, the three of us walked from the road to the house. But when we entered the kitchen, I was shocked to see that the corpse was no longer there on the floor!

"Instead there was a trail of blood leading out the door, across the porch and out toward the meadow beyond. We followed the bloodstains and about 50 meters from the house we found the Algerian, bleeding profusely, but still alive. The gendarmes administered first aid as best they could, and then carried him to their police van and told me to get in as well. Siren blaring, they drove to the St. Tropez hospital where they admitted the Algerian.

"Then they drove me to the police station, where they put me in a cell. They called this 'protective custody' and said they were doing this for my own safety. They explained that there was bad blood between the Europeans and immigrant Algerians. They said that the Algerians formed gangs that often sought retribution if they thought one of their fellow Algerians had been harmed.

"I think they also kept me in a cell because they didn't entirely believe my account of what had happened. In any case, I was five days in custody before a representative from the American Consulate in Nice arrived to negotiate with the gendarmes for my release. And they still kept me in my cell for another night before they released me just a couple of hours ago."

By this time in the account, Charlotte and I were sitting there with wide eyes and open mouths, both wondering if Lenny Marshall was for real or whether he was just spinning a tale for two gullible fellow Americans.

But then Lenny asked us if we had a car and if so, could we please drive him back to his farmhouse. Wondering what we were letting ourselves in for, we nevertheless said we would drive him there.

When we arrived, we observed that it was, indeed, a charming and picturesque setting. But when Lenny invited us into the house that he hadn't visited since the night of the knifing, we immediately saw that the front porch and the pillars supporting its roof were both covered with great smears of dried blood. Inside the kitchen, it was worse. Everything was in shambles and there was more dried blood all over the place. And parked right there in the corner of the kitchen was what had to be the Algerian's motorcycle.

As we surveyed the scene, we suddenly heard shouting from outside the open kitchen door. It turned out the shouts were coming from Lenny's housemate, Rudi, and his girlfriend who had just been dropped off by a trucker with whom they had hitchhiked for the last leg of their journey from Paris. After greetings and much hugging, Lenny launched into an even more elaborate account of what had happened to him during Rudi's absence. Thinking back, I suspect that the recounting of his ordeal for an audience was a therapeutic catharsis for Lenny.

In any case, our adventure ended that afternoon with Lenny, Rudi, and the girlfriend all piling into the back seat of our little VW Bug and us driving them back to St. Tropez. They explained that they couldn't bear to spend the night in the "charnel house" and that they would seek refuge with friends in town. We said our goodbyes and dropped them off on the quay in St. Tropez.

A week or so after returning to Lausanne, we encountered our friend and neighbor, Yves Dusonchet. Having told Lenny's story to Yves when we were staying with him in St. Tropez, we were eager to hear whether he had learned anything further following our departure from town. He said that, as a matter of fact, he had.

He recounted that he had been curious enough about the story that he had made further inquiries to a friend of his who worked in the police department. His police friend verified that everything Lenny told us was absolutely true . . . with one significant exception. It turned out that the Algerian at the door was not just some stranger in the night. Rather, he was Lenny's gay lover who had moved in with Lenny just after Rudi left for Paris. The whole altercation was the result of a lover's quarrel that had ended in violence.

The Algerian lover survived, but with more than 175 stitches as a result of his knife wounds. As far as Yves knew, no charges were ever filed against Lenny and the Algerian made a complete recovery. We never learned whether he and his Algerian friends ever sought retribution from Lenny.

Our life in Lausanne continued to be full of love, laughter, and many adventures. In addition to our trips to England and France, we also traveled extensively in Austria, Germany, Spain, and Norway.

In Austria, we spent two days viewing the famous Oberammergau Passion Play and then journeyed on to Salzburg, Innsbruck, and finally to Vienna, where we spent a week with the Guschlbauer family, who were old friends of the Ripleys. Their son, Dorli, who was musically inclined, later became Concert Master of the Salzburg Symphony Orchestra. Dorli took us to a performance of "The Silver Flute" opera and to see the extraordinary Lipizzaner Horses perform at Vienna's Spanish Riding School.

Spain also worked its charms on us as the following letter I wrote attests:

Dear Mom and Dad,

We've been home from Spain now almost two weeks after a most marvelous trip. Our route took us to Barcelona, Valencia, Granada, Malaga, Cordoba, Toledo, Madrid, Burgos, San Sebastian, Biarritz, France, Bordeaux and then back to Lausanne.

Spain is a country of marked contrasts. I kept thinking to myself driving through Southern Spain, "If only there were water." I am sure that the Spaniards could do wonderful things with their land if there were proper irrigation. As it is, in the regions where there are government-sponsored irrigation and conservation projects the land is green and flourishing. Private enterprise is also doing its part, though capital is still in short supply.

Our contacts with the Spaniards themselves were far too limited to draw many valid conclusions. Language plays such a tremendous difference when one goes to a new country, particularly when it comes to meeting the people. We found that our French was more useful than our English, since, as a romance language it is much closer to Spanish and is more widely spoken in Spain.

However, we did meet a few Spaniards, particularly, in Madrid where we had an introduction to an elderly couple who were genuine Castilian aristocrats. (They even had titles, Marquis and Marquise, though I am not sure they meant very much). I think they received their titles in return for having built a chapel or for some other philanthropic contribution. They were strong Catholics and more than a little to the right of center in their views. However, they were very nice to us and we spent an interesting afternoon with them during which they took us to El Escorial, the palace and monastery built by Philip II of Spain. We chuckled a bit, though, at the horrified expressions on the Marquis and Marquise's faces when we told them we had camped out a couple of nights along the way. Apparently upper-class Spaniards wouldn't think of doing something like that!

We also got together with a couple of ex-students from IMEDE, one of whom is Spanish (Basque by origin) and is general manager of the government-sponsored development bank. He is definitely of the easy-going "eat, drink, and be merry" school who thoroughly enjoys life on a sensory level.

Earlier, I mentioned the contrasts in Spain. At the bottom end of the scale we were very much touched by the abject poverty of the great majority of the Spaniards we saw. Still, they are a happy race by nature and most seemed to bear their lot with smiles and laughter. Another conclusion is that all Spaniards from 6 months to 60 are total night owls. The streets of every town are filled to overflowing with humanity at midnight, and not only with adults, but with children and babes-in-arms as well! Such gaiety!

Spain's history is a fascinating patchwork quilt of laminated civilizations. First, there were the Iberes (c.a. 5th century B.C.), then in rapid succession: Celts, Phoenicians, Carthaginians, Romans, Franks, Visigoths, Moors, and finally Christians! And each incursion left its own legacy. In fact, there are so many "legacies" that the "Spaniards", per se, don't seem to have developed a real culture of their own . . . but, then, perhaps this is an unfair conclusion.

As to the rest of our trip, we loved the Alhambra in Granada, the marvelous variety of architecture throughout the country, the Prado Museum in Madrid (a real standout) the mouth-watering seafood (that we ate twice a day, every day), the bullfight in Madrid (a mild disappointment), the thousands of mules (the primary means of transport, particularly in the South), swimming nude in the Mediterranean, and the beautiful blue, sunny skies that were with us from start to finish. So you see, to say the trip was a success is putting it mildly!

Much love,

Bud and Char

. . . . .

Christmas and New Year's of 1961 were spent in Norway. The following excerpts from a letter I wrote home at the time captures the essence of our Scandinavian holiday adventure:

> Christmas in Oslo is a festive occasion. Everyone starts making preparations weeks before . . . baking cookies (everyone must have at least 7 kinds), cooking pigs' heads, decorating (their Christmas trees are festooned with white lights and little Norwegian flags) etc. The actual celebration takes place on Christmas Eve and is usually a family affair. In our case we went to a very old Norwegian church in the late afternoon before coming back to the apartment that had been lent to Ginny (Charlotte's sister who was spending the academic year in Norway). In addition to Ginny, a very interesting Japanese-American girl joined us for the traditional Christmas feast. The menu was sumptuous and comprised roast pork, fish pudding, sauerkraut, boiled potatoes, various vegetables, aquavit, and beer. The grand finale was a sweet "Kronsakaker" cake primarily made of almond paste that had layers stacked up like a pyramid. Inside the cake a ring was hidden. Whoever found the ring in their helping was destined to have good luck during all of the following year. Following dinner we were all in good spirits and we sang around the Christmas tree and opened Christmas gifts.

> During the week following Xmas, we dined with the Wettre's (Norwegian friends from IMEDE) and traveled South to the shipping village of Tonsberg for a three day visit with Ginny's friends, Yngvar and Inky Hvistendahl. Yngvar's family owns ships on which various Ripley's have traveled back and forth across the Atlantic. It turned out that I knew Yngvar's wife, Inky, from when I was at Amherst and she was a student at Smith. It's a small world! We had a delightful time while there and did everything from going to a very elegant formal dance at the equivalent of the local yacht club to having a tasty cod dinner on board one of the Hvistendahl's seagoing ships that was in port for repair.

> After we returned to Oslo we spent the days leading up to New Year's exploring the Oslo area (Viking ships, Kon-Tiki Raft, folk village, etc.), going cross-country skiing with the Wettre's and generally visiting and having fun.

> Then, on New Year's Day, we set off for Tvedestrand! But Tvedestrand is certainly worth a chapter and since it is now almost Midnight I shall

plan to send you a full account in the next day or two so as to be able to do it full justice.

Love, Bud

. . . . .

To understand why I wrote that "Tvedestrand is worth a chapter," it is perhaps helpful to point out that Tvedestrand is the Sorenson family's ancestral village. It is a tiny seaside town located 110 miles south of Oslo on the Oslo Fjord. The previous summer, Nancy, who was traveling in Europe, had visited Tvedestrand to do a little sleuthing into our family history. I reference her findings in the following letter.

<u>Bud to the Sorensons</u>

January 15, 1962

Dear Mom and Dad,

On to Tvedestrand! Early on New Year's Day we set forth by train, heading south through beautiful snow-covered forests and fields. Occasionally, we would catch sight of a sparkling fjord. It was a lovely winter day with the sun shining brightly from its low position above the Southern horizon.

The train traveled very slowly and the trip took about 5 hours. We had a tasty lunch in the dining car, sitting across from a table of four jovial young men . . . all of them deaf and mute. They were a gay lot and after lunch one of them came over and "chatted" with us in sign and body language. Strangely, we were able to communicate with him better than we could with some other Norwegians who spoke English. It's amazing how expressive one can be with facial expressions and hand gestures!

After a bus ride from the train terminal, we finally arrived in Tvedestrand about 3:00 p.m., only to find that the Hotel Fram, the sole hotel in town, was closed for the New Year's holiday! We were rescued by a passer-by who spoke fluent English and who said that the hotel owner was a friend of his and that he would see if he could fix things up. It worked! Soon we found ourselves ushered into a comfortable, if somewhat frigid, bedroom room in the closed hotel.

Though it was already beginning to grow dark outside, we decided to begin our search for the Sorenson homestead immediately. Unfortunately, however, the only shred of evidence we had of its existence was the photograph Nancy had taken of the house that Grandpa Sorenson and his father had lived in until they emigrated to America in 1882 and that my great-grandfather, Mina Sorenson, had lived in until 1915. But luck was with us, and after a stroll of about 15 minutes we stumbled up on the little, white-frame house that matched the one in the photo.

After examining it from front and back, we rang the doorbell and were greeted by one of the three elderly Larsen sisters who presently live there. They invited us in with gestures and invited us to "sit down, say nothing" . . . which was the extent of their English. They quickly put their heads together and came to a solution for the language problem: they would call Captain Jorgen Jorgensen, Nancy's sea captain acquaintance, to come to the rescue! He was soon fetched and, voila!, we had an interpreter on the scene. For many years Jorgen had been a ship captain who had plied the seas between Europe and America. In the process he had learned to speak more than passable English.

For the next hour-and-a-half we talked about everything under the sun, drank strong black Norwegian coffee, and ate at least 10 different varieties of Norwegian cookies. But we learned little new about our family heritage beyond the fact that the three spinsters had lived in the house for 47 years since their family had purchased the house from Mina Sorenson in 1915. Nevertheless it was a delightful visit and in the end, Captain Jorgensen performed an invaluable service by telephoning our only known remaining Sorenson relative, Annette Andersen, who was living in an "Old People's Home" in the nearby village of Dypvaag, and arranging for us to meet her the next day.

The following morning we arose early, breakfasted, and took a taxi (the only one in town) to see Annette Andersen. As we walked up to the front door of the Old People's Home we passed several sprightly 80-year-olds shoveling snow from the driveway. Once inside, there was great excitement while everyone scurried off in all directions to find Annette. Finally, she came out to greet us. She was a sweet, elderly, white-haired lady who was slightly lame, but most gracious and obviously terribly excited. After much handshaking, we settled down in the living room close to the Christmas tree and began talking to each other through the medium of another old ship captain who spoke some English and vaguely remembered Mina Sorenson.

Yes, Annette Andersen knew all about us . . . she had loved receiving Dad's Christmas card and the photos of our family that had been enclosed. And, of course, she remembered her Aunt Mina Sorenson who had been very nice to her when she was very young. And so we had a wonderful conversation.

Some of her memories were a bit dim . . . and they weren't helped particularly by the old Cap'n whose English was a bit rusty. But she did remember a few additional facts that might be added to the patchwork quilt of family history. Mina Sorenson, my great grandmother, was born in 1832 and died in 1916. Annette, herself, was the daughter of Mina's sister Margarethe and she had two sisters, Grethe (who died in 1936) and Maria (who died in 1907), plus two brothers, Edward (who had two daughters still living in Oslo) and Bernard Morner (who had been a ship captain with 2 daughters and one son and who had just died in September 1961).

On great grandfather Lars Sorenson's side of the family, the only thing Annette could remember was that Lars had one sister, Karen, who married someone named Andreasen and had a son named Kristian who, in turn, had had two sons, Soren and Anthon, either or both of whom had had a tannery in Tvedestrand. So these are the only bits that we can add to the family history as a result of our conversation with Annette.

But the most important memory that we took away from our visit was that Annette was greatly pleased and happy that we had come to see her and I am sure that it added a bit of sparkle to her winter. Just as we were about to leave, she excused herself for a moment and then came back with a tiny wooden box with faded flowers burned into its sides and cover that latched cleverly at the top. She said that the little box was called a "tine" (pronounced tina) and that it had been given to her by Mina Sorenson when she was a little girl. She said that, as far as she knew, this was the only possession left that had been Mina's and she wanted us to have it. As you might imagine, we were quite touched. Shortly thereafter, we said our goodbyes and she hugged each of us and waved to us all the way out of the driveway.

After a short ride back to Tvedestrand, we arrived just in time to board the only bus to the station where we caught the train back to Oslo.

Thus, Dad, we had a beautiful 1962 New Year's adventure in your ancestral village of Tvedestrand.

All our love,

Bud and Char

. . . . .

Bud to the Sorensons

September 26, 1961

Dear Mom and Dad,

By this time you have heard about our BIG NEWS! As you can well imagine, we are terribly excited about the prospect of actually becoming PARENTS! Just think, that will make you GRANDPARENTS. Hard to believe, isn't it? So, filled with wonderment and armed with a trusty copy of Dr. Spock, we now look forward to the BIG DAY in April.

Actually, Char has made only one visit so far to the Doctor, who, after verifying her "delicate condition", told her not to try to climb the Matterhorn and to come back in one month. We will naturally keep you posted on this subject.

. . . . .

Char to the Sorensons (Same letter)

Speaking of babies, since everything is done naturally here, they have a strict program of taking care of the mother beforehand. One of my friends who is going to the same doctor has been forbidden to: wear heels, ride in her Volkswagen which bumps too much, eat cheese, and she must sleep until ten in the morning and take a two-hour nap in the afternoon! We are so excited about it that we are running in circles!! We are going shopping for clothes this afternoon.

. . . . .

Char to the Ripleys

October 18, 1961

Dear All,

Becoming a 'mere' really adds a deeper dimension to life and we love the whole idea! Don't know if it is of interest to you over there, but since *everyone here asks me, I feel fine! Especially in the morning. I haven't been to my new doctor yet, principally because after the initial visit, I found the doctor to whom I planned to go, is generally considered to be cold and impersonal. Through my friend, Betsy Wyman, I found another one who speaks only French, but who treats his patients gently and nicely and makes them feel as if having a baby is important. I shall visit him for the first time in two weeks, then from time to time after that, going regularly in the interims to a nurse for "treatments". It's all very exciting . . . Betsy has been wonderful in giving advice and in offering me cribs and things that her baby will have out-grown by April. Also we are very excited because one of our best friends has offered us an antique crib, a large one, for as long as we want to use it. We were hesitating at the thought of having to buy one.*

All our love,

Charlotte

. . . . .

Bud to the Sorensons

Pre-Christmas, 1961

Baby is doing just fine . . . lusty and lively. Has a pretty good kick, too!

Love,

Bud

. . . . .

Bud to the Sorensons

February 11, 1962

Dear Mom and Dad,

You will be pleased to know that everything seems to be progressing quite smoothly in the Sorenson baby department. We had our latest visit to the doctor on Wednesday of last week. He said that all was going very well . . . weight just as it should be, baby well-positioned, etc. Doctor Rossel is a wonderful person and an excellent obstetrician. We have complete confidence in him.

This coming week Char will begin a special course with Dr. Rossel in preparation for "l'accouchement san douleur" (birthing without pain) or natural child-birth. It involves breathing exercises and preparation in how to react to different types of contractions, etc. The course lasts for the final two months prior to the baby's birth. Char is also taking a short course in "puerioculture" or how to take care of the tiny tot after its arrival.

I must say that it is all very exciting. According to best estimates, the big day should be sometime between the 10th and 20th of April . . . though judging from the way the little thing kicks and moves about I shouldn't be surprised if there were an advance performance.

Much Love,

Bud

. . . . .

Bud to the Sorensons

March 1962

Dear Mom and Dad,

It's hard to believe that March is already here and that in just over a month our little visitor will arrive. Most exciting! Things continue to go along nicely. Char is right in the middle of her course with Dr. Rossel in which she learns special exercises. Every day she practices for about 45 minutes. I even get into the act in the evening by calling out the different breathing and relaxing exercises to her. We are both quite sold on the idea of natural childbirth and have full confidence in both the method and in Dr. Rossel.

We have been having fun lately thinking about possible names. Of course, we are still in the process of changing our minds every 2 or 3 days. We will no doubt will end up making our final decision on the way to the hospital.

It was thoughtful of you to send along the baby clothes. They haven't arrived yet but I'm sure they will be here before too much longer. We haven't bought very much yet ourselves . . . thinking we would wait until we found out whether it will be a boy or a girl.

Love, Bud and Charlotte

. . . . .

Charlotte to the Ripleys

March 11, 1962

Dear All,

M. et Mme. Moser brought the crib over yesterday. I wish you could see it. It is about 60 years old, dark wood with spiral "lattice" sides, and perfectly charming. They had it completely fixed and furnished with a brand-new mattress and quilt and pillow.

The "cours d'acccouchment" are going well and I practice faithfully (with Bud's help) every day. I just finished a book of testimonials of painless childbirth and I am convinced already that it is the only perfect method. Our doctor certainly doesn't have much faith in the zippy, druggy American methods, but from what I hear, little by little, American women want to do it in the more natural manner. It's interesting that the practice originated in Russia and only started to be used in France in 1951 by a Dr. Lamaze. So it is very recent even here and the doctors are taking great pains to educate their patients in the best possible way. Bud and I are so happy to be having the baby here. The whole process is so warm and friendly and normal.

Love, Charlotte

. . . . .

Bud to the Ripleys

Sunday, March 25

Dear George, Ruth, et al,

Just a few lines to let you know that Charlotte is a most radiant mother-to-be. We are both just as excited as we possibly could be at the thought that in two weeks (perhaps, if the little one arrives on April 5th, the "officially predicted day") we shall be PARENTS!! Oh my! It's hard to be patient and "just wait". But, I must say that Char has been wonderful and has done all of her exercises, taken "daily walks" and "daily naps", eaten all the "proper foods" . . . and only occasionally feels like shouting from inactivity or like going out and running a 100-yard dash.

In any case, it won't be long now—and, naturally, you will be the very first to know the moment anything happens. I have already arranged for IT&T to keep all trans-Atlantic cable lines cleared!

A bien tot,

Bud

. . . . .

CHAPTER FIFTEEN

IT'S A GIRL!!
(AND HER NAME IS KRISTIN!)

<u>Charlotte to the Ripleys</u>

April 15, 1962

Clinic de Charmettes

Chere Famille,

So . . . the most precious, tiny, black-haired, rosy-cheeked Kristin was born and is now sleeping sweetly in her basket of straw with the starched muslin curtains and a heart hanging above her head which says "ne me touchez pas" (do not touch me)! She is wrapped like a gift parcel in white with a little lace bib. The sun is streaming in the window, birds are singing, singing, and Bud is trying to keep himself from peeking under the curtain. It's all very wonderful!

When did it start? At about 2 a.m. on Saturday morning in the middle of a raging snowstorm. It felt like very persistent aching muscles and I'm afraid I wasn't a very "gentile femme" to Bud, making faces and such. We left for the clinic at 8:30 a.m., driving down the snowy route which we had memorized. The mid-wife or "<u>sage femme</u>", as they call them here, said that the opening was at "two francs". I think it is funny, the monetary values they give to the size opening . . . from 50 centimes to 5 francs.

From then until noon I don't remember too much except that from time to time the doctor said that things were progressing very rapidly and that sometimes when I opened my eyes, Bud was there, which was a great help. It was painful, but we were so prepared to do it that way that the idea of being drugged seemed impossible. Besides, it would have been embarrassing to admit to our kind doctor that I wasn't able to make it. We went into the delivery room at noon. Dr. Rossel instructed Bud to put on a white blouse and then told him that if he had need of it, there was a bottle of Cognac in the top drawer of the dresser against the wall. Next, to give Bud something to do, he showed Bud how to use the machine to administer oxygen to me.

Then began the "POUSSEZ, POUSSEZ, MADAME" that is such a famous part of the training over here. And, then, "VOILA"! les cheveux, les yeux, la bouche, l'epaule, etc. YES! Kristin Elizabeth Sorenson had arrived! It was terribly exciting. Kristin was so teensy, but very real. There was something funny about the placenta, so they put me to sleep for a few minutes afterwards while they went in to get it.

We were both so happy to have a little girl and we even expected to have one—a boy would have been a surprise. I spent yesterday afternoon watching the snow swirling down on the birds in the apple tree outside the window, smiling to myself and thinking of all the fun times we had when I was a little girl. Maybe, that is partly why I wanted a "petite fille". How I have changed from wanting five boys!

Bud was so sapped from the day's adventure that he went home early in the evening and fell into bed.

This morning, we received your wonderful telegram and were thrilled because: a) you liked the name, b) you sounded excited, and c) that you sent us word right away so that we all knew that everyone knew.

I am reading Benvenuto Cellini's autobiography and there is a fine radio in the room that fills Kristin's soul full of beautiful music.

So, we are happy, happy with our little girl and delighted that you are pleased, too. Many, many thanks and,

Much, much love,

Charlotte

p.s. Char gave me this letter to mail—but before putting it in the box, I just want to add that your daughter was absolutely wonderful while giving birth to our little Kristin. And now, with that part of it over, she is the loveliest mother imaginable. And you should see Kristin!! With all fatherly modesty I think she is absolutely adorable!

Love, Bud

. . . . .

<u>Bud to the Sorensons</u>

April 28, 1962

Dear Grandma and Grandpa,

Can you believe it? Yesterday we celebrated Kristin's birthday: two weeks old! She, of course, couldn't understand what all the fun was all about. She just yawned and blinked, ate mightily (as usual) and, from time to time, tried out her lusty little lungs to see if anyone would listen.

She's a lovely little Granddaughter. She is still no bigger than a minute (just under 7.5 pounds) but she's now beginning to gain quite regularly. We are not yet sure what color her eyes will be. Maybe blue . . . but then again, maybe brown. Another week or so and we should know.

Of course, everybody is trying to guess whether she will look like her mummy or her daddy. At the moment there seems to be a slight edge in favor of those who think she is the spitting image of her papa. But then, it is still a bit early to make definite predictions. In any case, we have already started to take a photo or two and as soon as we have finished the roll we will have them developed and send you copies.

In any case, so far everything is going beautifully. Mother and daughter both came home from the clinic last Monday. Kristin is really quite good as far as her meals are concerned. She thinks it is so nice that her mummy is feeding her and that she doesn't have to mess around with a bunch of bottles. Her mummy is one of those fortunate persons who, it seems, will be able to amply supply enough milk for even the hungriest little tike. Kristin started out eating 6 times a day, but now she is already down to 5 meals, starting about 5:30 a.m. and ending about 10 p.m.

All in all, Charlotte and I feel that having little Kristin is about the most wonderful experience we have ever had. I think Charlotte already mentioned that Daddy was right there during the "accouchement" or birth. What a moving moment when little Kristin actually appeared and suddenly there was a new and very special being in the world. Through it all, I felt very, very close to Charlotte and my respect for her grew tenfold. As Dr. Rossel afterwards said, seeing a pure and innocent new-born baby for the first time is most unforgettable, as if one has had a glimpse into the real meaning of life.

Very best love from all three of us,

Bud

. . . . .

Perhaps the best and most touching reflection on our whole experience of becoming parents for the first time is captured in the following letter that Charlotte wrote to her family two weeks after Kristin was born:

Monday, April 30, 1962

Dear, dear family,

Little Kristin is <u>un petit ange</u>, *fallen straight from heaven . . . there could be no other description. She was lovely from the moment she left her nine-month haven. Bud and the doctor confirmed that right in the delivery room. "Mais qu'elle est jolie!", ("But she is beautiful!") they both exclaimed on seeing her the first time. She has a pure, tiny heart-shaped face, large bright eyes, round, rosy cheeks and the most adorable . . . well, "kissing" mouth. She has lovely, rosy skin and well-shaped feet and hands. When she sleeps, her eyelashes make tiny stars on her cheeks. And when she smiles, her mother's heart trips with joy.*

She is gaining weight at a tremendous rate. Mme. Moser, our nurse friend, is astonished. In five days she gained more than normal babies gain in a week. Furthermore, says Mme. Moser, Kristin already shows tremendous character, vivacity, and precocity. (Mme. Moser having dealt with hundreds of enfants.) Kristin already knows more French than English, for, after all, in the clinic that is the only language that the nurses knew, and they gave her all sorts of funny names such as "le Poussin de Pacques" (Easter Chick), "le moinou" (monk), "le canari" (canary), and "le rossignol" (nightingale) for all the spring birds. Kristin is rolled up every morning into a fine little Swiss package—five layers with a little lace bib to top everything off. Granted, she can't kick too much, but then, do babies kick when they sleep all day?

The ten days in the Clinique were beautiful. It's a small place with room for only 25 babies, and the atmosphere is very cheerful and very personal. My room looked out in one direction over a garden that was bubbling with daffodils and tulips and in another over an apple tree toward Lac Leman.

Bud came every night for a delicious dinner complete with wine! Sometimes we even had guests, the food was so good and we felt so elegant. Kristin was always right beside me in her little straw and lace basket, and I couldn't resist 1000 or two peaks. I gained enormous respect for the nurses and the midwives there. There was something intensely real about them, intensely honest. My first thought when I was "thinking" again was that to be a nurse or maternity doctor would be the most beautiful thing in the world, for they are dealing with life in its purest form. The "sage-femmes" (midwives), in particular, have tremendously strong personalities; somehow their voices make you obey during the labor when they say "inspirez" (breath in), "expirez" (breath out), or "poussez" (push). I think I shall have to come back here for other babies, for I wouldn't know what to do in English!

Actually, my very first thought was a little prayer that Kristin would find just as wonderful a husband as Bud is, for I was full of love for him for having helped so greatly in putting such a sweet princess into the world.

Yet, another thought was that I loved being a woman and having seen my baby come into the world. It was most thrilling and indescribably fulfilling. The nurses here are amazed that in America one stays in the hospital only five days or so and, I must say, that I was so dizzy with beautiful and new thoughts that I needed all of the ten days to gain a bit of balance.

Easter morn was lovely. I woke at five (as I did every morning, so eager to see Kristin who was brought in at six) and thought I heard angels singing! It turned out to be the same choir that we heard last year at Christmas when we lived on Avenue Floreal . . . they are a church group who carol in that "quartier" (neighborhood) every Christmas and Easter. I got up and went out on the balcony. Down in the garden below (I'll never forget it), a bee and two tiny birds were all sitting in the same wide-open tulip. Then, when I looked up in the other direction, a little girl came out on the balcony of a building near-by. She had golden hair tied with a velvet ribbon, black shoes and the most delicious pink dress for Easter. She looked just like Spring and Happiness and Love!

We brought Kristin home last Monday . . . highly exciting. We dressed her in a green outfit, put a purple pansy in her bonnet, then drove down to Ouchy harbor and cruised, slowly, slowly along the quai. Everything was in blossom, even the sailboats, and the promenade was full of people and babies. We were highly self-conscious and certain that everyone <u>knew</u> that we had just had a baby girl named Kristin. But no-one looked. The excitement was intense as we carried the basket upstairs, put it on the bed, and then tiptoed around, wondering what in the world to do next.

The apartment looked beautiful. Bud had prepared everything, bought flowers, and made a delicious dinner. Mme. Moser came to see us in the evening. She lives 5 minutes away, and being a nurse and a good friend, she was very eager to make certain everything was in good order for the first night. She has since been invaluable . . . I really don't see how I could have got along without her in this past week.

I wish Kristin could stay as tiny as she is . . . she is such a darling. By the way, Kristin <u>is</u> a family name, something like a great-great-great grandmother on the Sorenson side. But we chose it because it sounded so musical and because it is a bit Norwegian. We were thinking about using Allyn as a middle name when we found somewhere that it meant "gift of the elves". But in the end, we decided upon Elizabeth. Don't we have an Elizabeth in the family tree somewhere?

P.S. From Bud

Well, Kristin Elizabeth's "fall from heaven" has been the most beautiful experience in the world. If each time is like it, why, one couldn't help but to become happier and happier as the years go on.

All our love,

Charlotte & Bud

. . . . .

And so we were launched as a couple into parenthood and, like millions of couples before us, found our lives were changed forever. Now we were a true family!

CHAPTER SIXTEEN

A TACK IN CAREER PLANS

Following the birth of Kristin, Charlotte and I began to think about where we wanted to raise a family. Did we want to stay in Europe or return to the United States? In a related vein, I revisited the subject of my long-term career plans.

While my work was going very well at Nestlé and I was learning new things every day, in the back of my mind I had begun toying with an idea that had originally taken root while I was still employed at IMEDE. One of my greatest joys as a research associate there had been the opportunity to actually teach some of the case studies I had researched and written on various management issues. Each of those teaching experiences had left me with a feeling of euphoria. On a couple of those occasions, the middle management participants in the IMEDE course had given me a rousing ovation at the end of the class. Could it be that I was destined to be a teacher? This was an idea that had never crossed my mind in any of my earlier career ruminations. And yet, while at Nestlé, I couldn't help remembering from time to time how satisfying those occasional teaching experiences had been.

Oddly enough, my thinking in this regard was actually spurred on by occasional conversations I had with Dr. Gloor, my boss at Nestlé. As a young man, he had earned a doctorate in law at the Ecole Polytechnique in Zurich with the thought of eventually becoming a university professor. While his career trajectory subsequently took off in a different direction, he confessed to me that he still harbored fantasies about being an academic. Hence, when I mentioned to him one day how much I had enjoyed my exposure to teaching at IMEDE, instead of trying to talk me out of any academic aspirations, he actually encouraged me to give serious thought to pursuing those dreams. I had the impression that he secretly regretted that he, himself, had not pursued an academic career and that he didn't want me to make the same mistake.

The result of my discussions with Charlotte, my conversations with Dr. Gloor, and my personal soul-searching was that I decided to tack in a different direction in terms of my career. I determined that I would become a professor!

Hence, in the winter of 1962-63 I applied for entrance into the doctoral program at Harvard Business School. With the help of recommendations from some of the Harvard professors with whom I had worked at IMEDE and as a result of having done well in my undergraduate studies at Amherst and my MBA studies at Harvard, I received an acceptance letter from Harvard saying my application had been approved and I had been accepted into the doctoral program beginning in September 1963.

Meanwhile, Charlotte had re-applied to Wellesley for permission to complete her final undergraduate year there by joining the senior class matriculating the coming September. She subsequently received a letter from the college saying her application had been approved. Curiously, however, the letter had a handwritten postscript from the dean of students asking her if, apart from attending classes, would she be kind enough to spend as little time as possible at the college. Implicit in her request was that she feared Charlotte, as a married woman with a newborn baby, would set a bad example for the single, unmarried female undergraduates on the campus! Clearly, in 1963, the spirit of women's liberation had not yet penetrated the culture at Wellesley and Victorian morals still reigned supreme!

The decision for both Charlotte and me to return to school in Boston involved some financial sacrifice on our part, particularly since Kristin was now also part of the family. We had managed to save up some money during our three years in Switzerland, but not enough to cover all of our projected educational and living expenses. Fortunately, however, the Ford Foundation came to our rescue. I applied for and was awarded a $5,000 per year grant from the foundation to cover living expenses while in the Harvard doctoral program. Meanwhile, Harvard itself granted me a full tuition doctoral fellowship. Hence, we calculated that, if we were willing to live frugally, we could just about scrape along financially for the time we estimated it would take for me to complete my doctorate and for Charlotte to finish up her bachelor's degree.

CHAPTER SEVENTEEN

BACK TO BOSTON

So it was that in August 1963 we said our goodbyes to all of the many friends we had made in Lausanne, settled up with our Swiss landlord, and packed up most of our belongings to be shipped by sea back to the U.S.

The settling up process that Charlotte had with our landlord proved to be devastating and ridiculous at the same time. Charlotte had spent days scrubbing and straightening up everything in the apartment so that it would be immaculate for the next tenants. When Mr. Jaccard, our landlord, came next door to inspect how we had left the premises, he proceeded to systematically examine every inch of every room. The first criminal act that he discovered was a tiny hole in the awning covering our balcony. He wanted us to pay him the cost of replacing the whole awning. After a series of other similar incriminating discoveries on his part, he finally fetched a small kitchen stepladder, climbed up and up on it and unscrewed the light bulbs in several ceiling sockets. He then informed Charlotte that he estimated that, on average, all of the light bulbs in the apartment had only about 30 percent remaining life left in them and that we, therefore, should reimburse him for an amount equivalent to 70 percent remaining of the original cost of all the bulbs! Upon hearing this, Charlotte burst into tears at what she considered the unfairness and absurdity of it all. I had previously rejected the stereotypical reputation some Swiss had of being obsessed with money and knowing the price of everything but the value of nothing. However, Mr. Jaccard's behavior reinforced that unfortunate perspective.

On the day of our departure, we bid a fond farewell to our next-door English neighbors and then were amused to observe all the rest of our Swiss neighbors in our building peeking out of their windows at us as we loaded up our little blue Volkswagen Bug and drove away. Not one of them came out of their apartment to say goodbye! It was not that they weren't friendly; it was just that they were demonstrating the Swiss trait of strictly respecting one's neighbors' privacy.

From Lausanne we drove to Paris where we stayed for a couple of days and then proceeded on to Le Havre where Charlotte, Kristin, and I boarded the *S.S. France* for an elegant voyage back to New York, courtesy of a generous going-away gesture on the part of Nestlé, which had paid for our fares.

Meanwhile, we left our car in Le Havre to be loaded aboard one of the freighters belonging to our ship-owning Norwegian friend, Yngvar Hvistendahl. Yngvar had thoughtfully volunteered to transport the Volkswagen free of charge back to a port in New Jersey.

On arriving back in Boston, we commenced a search for a place to live while Charlotte was finishing up at Wellesley and I was working on my doctorate at Harvard. We ended up renting the second floor of a house in Wellesley belonging to a widow of Irish extraction named Mrs. Barnacle. Its major advantage was its location in close proximity to the Wellesley College campus. Its major drawback was lack of privacy. There was no separation between us and Mrs. Barnacle. She simply lived on the first floor and we lived up the open staircase on the second floor with no doors or walls in between. This was a problem because Mrs. Barnacle turned out to be a lonely alcoholic (two or three bottles of gin per week) whose favorite pastime was eavesdropping on her upstairs tenants. Nor was she hesitant to poke her nose into our business and express her strong opinions on how we should raise Kristin and live our lives. It was a barely tolerable situation. Having signed a 10-month lease running from September 1963 to June 1964, there was little we could do about the situation but grin and bear it.

With the September opening of the academic year, Charlotte and I launched into our respective studies. Meanwhile, we enrolled Kristin, aged 18 months, in a pre-nursery school program run out of the house of an elderly one-legged lady named Mrs. Arsenault. Each day she had classes, Charlotte delivered Kristin to Mrs. Arsenault's house in a child's seat fastened to the back of her bicycle.

Mrs. Arsenault had some interesting ideas about the ideal way to raise small children. For example, to instill what she believed would be a lifelong love of classical music into the tiny tots under her care, she had Beethoven, Bach, and Mozart blaring out at them from loudspeakers all day every day. She had a kind heart and a love of children, however, and, as parents, we felt comfortable leaving Kristin in her care while Charlotte was attending classes at Wellesley and I was studying at Harvard.

The three years from mid-1963 to mid-1966 seemed to pass in a flash. Charlotte breezed through her final year of study at Wellesley without much difficulty. Having gained additional maturity and perspective from having lived in Switzerland, she was more than able to hold her own intellectually in her various courses.

One memorable classroom incident occurred in November 1963, during a political science class. Halfway through the professor's lecture that day, a Wellesley staff member slipped into the lecture hall and handed the professor a slip of paper. He looked at the message and then announced:

"I am sorry to report that it appears President Kennedy has been shot and killed in Dallas, Texas. It's a regrettable incident, but since he isn't the first president to be assassinated and since presidents come and go, I think it makes sense for me to continue today's lecture so we won't fall behind schedule in the course."

The other students who were present initially just sat stunned in their seats, waiting for the professor to pick up his train of thought from where he had left off. Charlotte, however, immediately stood up and admonished the professor saying, in effect:

"How can you possibly be so callous and insensitive? Do you honestly believe that continuing your lecture is more important at this moment than allowing all of us to begin processing the fact that our president has just been killed?"

She then picked up her books and walked out of the room. Soon, all the other students in the class followed her lead and left the professor looking stunned at the front of the lecture hall. Charlotte still wonders what possessed the professor that day. Was it academic arrogance, insensitiveness, or just plain cluelessness? Of course, it was an unprecedented situation and he may have been in shock, as all of us were at the time.

In spite of this great national trauma, life had to go on, and it did, but I am not sure we have, as a country, ever truly gotten over it.

Acquiescing to the somewhat bizarre postscript request appended to the acceptance letter Wellesley had sent her, Charlotte made it a point that academic year to spend as little time as possible on the campus, outside of attending classes. Some 40 years later, when we were living in Boulder, Colorado, she was reminded of this fact when she had a chance encounter with a woman who had been in the Wellesley class of 1964, the class that Charlotte ultimately graduated with following her return from Switzerland. On establishing the fact that Charlotte had come back to Wellesley to complete her bachelor's degree after an absence of three years in Switzerland, the woman suddenly exclaimed, "Oh, now I remember. You're the one we were warned about. The one who set a bad example for the rest of us by prematurely dropping out of Wellesley to get married and have a baby. They told us that if we weren't careful, that could happen to us and we could end up being dropouts who didn't have enough self-discipline to finish all four years of college."

Charlotte and her new Boulder acquaintance had a good laugh over the memory . . . but, nevertheless, the laughter had a touch of bittersweetness about it.

By the time Charlotte graduated from Wellesley in June of 1964, she was six months pregnant with our second daughter, Trina. As she walked across the stage to receive her diploma, the bulge under her graduation gown was clearly evident to all in attendance. Then, just as she was handed her diploma from Miss Clapp, Wellesley's president, a child's loud voice rang out from the audience, clearly saying:

"THAT'S MY MOMMY!"

It was, of course, Kristin, and she brought down the house. Charlotte, clearly, was the only Wellesley graduate that year who was already married and the mother of one child with a second on the way. Given how uptight eastern women's colleges still were in 1964, she might not have been considered a good role model for her fellow graduates, but to the Sorenson family she was a fantastic example of a true heroine who deserved greatly to be admired.

Following Charlotte's graduation in June 1964, we were relieved to move out of Mrs. Barnacle's house on the day our lease expired. By good luck, a Wellesley professor and his wife, who were friends of Charlotte and her sister Ginny, agreed to lend us their house for the summer. The house was located on the shore of Lake Waban in the middle of the Wellesley campus. It was heaven after living at Mrs. Barnacle's place.

(Ironically, it turned out that two days after we moved out, Mrs. Barnacle suddenly died of cirrhosis of the liver while at home alone. Since we were no longer living there, her body wasn't found until about a week later when her adult son, not having been able to reach her by telephone, stopped by to check up on her.)

Our summer interlude in the Gulicks' house on the shore of Lake Waban turned out to be a delight. We tended their organic garden, took occasional walks around the lake, and frequently went swimming or sailing as well. The only factor that prevented our stay at the Gulicks from being completely idyllic was that the summer turned out to be particularly hot and humid and there was no air conditioning in the house. Charlotte, in her third trimester of pregnancy, suffered greatly as a result.

At the end of the summer, we had the good fortune to move into a three-bedroom apartment in a brand new graduate student-housing complex in Cambridge called Peabody Terrace. Located on the bank of the Charles River, it was designed by José Luis Sert, a well-known architect who headed up the Harvard School of Design. Not everyone admired the modernist design of the complex. We, however, found it to be very comfortable and ideally located right next to the Weeks Walking Bridge, leading to Harvard Business School. Our apartment was located on the second floor with a balcony that looked out over a lawn and through some trees to the river.

Three weeks after we had moved in, on September 25th, Charlotte went into labor and we drove to the Boston Lying-In Hospital where Charlotte gave birth to lovely little Katrina Anne Sorenson, quickly nicknamed Trina. This second time around, the birthing experience wasn't nearly as pleasant as Kristin's birth had been in the Clinique des Charmettes in Lausanne.

To begin with, Charlotte's obstetrician, while competent, was not nearly as caring and friendly as her obstetrician had been in Switzerland. Second, the Lamaze method of natural childbirth had not yet been widely accepted in Boston and was not permitted at the Lying-In Hospital. Third, the hospital itself was cold and impersonal. In the recovery room after the birth, the nurses and other hospital personnel were insensitive and made crude jokes in front of the new mothers who were still feeling quite vulnerable. Finally, the moms with their newly born infants were shuttled out of the hospital after three days, quite a contrast to the 10-day delightful sojourn Charlotte had at the Clinique in Lausanne.

But no matter; we were totally thrilled to welcome tiny Trina into our family. Blonde, beautiful, and elfin in appearance, she had the bluest of blue eyes and, from the beginning, demonstrated a lively intelligence and strong sense of curiosity. She was adorable. When we brought Trina home, Kristin was fascinated to have a new little playmate. A second crib was moved into what had been Kristin's bedroom, the window of which looked out over a playground with swings and slides and teeter-totters, plus a large sandbox. Mid-mornings and mid-afternoons found the playground filled with married student mothers keeping track of their kinetic tots while trying to carry on friendly conversations with each other.

Just 13 months later, a third crib was added to the children's room. Its new occupant was Eric Ripley Sorenson, who was born on October 23rd, also at the Boston Lying-In Hospital. His birth mirrored that of Trina's: no natural childbirth permitted, no father allowed in the delivery room, only three days to recover in the hospital, and a hospital atmosphere that was still cold and impersonal.

Struck once again by the great contrast between giving birth in Boston and in Switzerland, Charlotte subsequently wrote a long letter to the administration of the Lying-In Hospital, describing in detail the contrast and making a number of thoughtful and constructive suggestions as to how the hospital's birthing process could be made to be much more mother-, father-, and baby-centric. She later learned that the administration had apparently taken her seriously and had subsequently implemented some of her suggestions.

The birthing process notwithstanding, Charlotte and I were ecstatic about the arrival of Eric. From the outset, he was a strong, handsome, intelligent, happy baby. He had a mind of his own and was all boy. Charlotte and I quickly concluded that we were totally blessed to have a boy and two girls in the family. We decided not to try to improve on perfection by seeking further expansion in the size of our household.

Peabody Terrace was an ideal setting to form friendships and bring up children. Since the complex was brand new and all of the married student residents were the first to occupy their apartments, there was a wonderful opportunity to create a new community and culture from scratch. Hence, the occupants banded together to form a community association that formulated an initial list of residential guidelines, launched a weekly community newsletter and established a nonprofit convenience store within the complex. Also established was an on-premise cooperative nursery and pre-school that proved to be a godsend for the many resident couples that had small children. Charlotte, in addition to being a great mom to three very young children, somehow found the time to teach a course in the fitness center that had also been created by the residents.

CHAPTER EIGHTEEN

DOCTORAL STUDIES AT HARVARD

Meanwhile, ever since returning to Boston, I had been diligently pursuing my doctoral studies at the Harvard Business School. The first year, I completed all of the doctoral courses required by the program. These turned out to be fewer than I had expected because I was granted a number of waivers as a result of several courses I had previously taken as a Harvard MBA student and also in recognition of some of the work I had as a research associate and case writer at IMEDE.

One of the doctoral courses that I remember well was a seminar in economic development taught by Professor John Kenneth Galbraith, who had recently returned from serving a stint as U.S. ambassador to India under President Kennedy. There were 14 of us in the seminar: two Americans and 12 foreign students, most of whom came from Southeast Asia, India, Egypt, and the Middle East. The other American was Sam Bowles, whose father, Chester Bowles, had recently taken Galbraith's place as ambassador to India. What sticks out in my mind was how Professor Galbraith seemed to derive almost sadistic pleasure from unmercifully browbeating the foreign students in the seminar, most of whom were completely cowed by Galbraith, to the point of almost total silence. To this day, I do not understand why such an accomplished and esteemed academic would behave in that way.

Meanwhile, neither Sam Bowles nor I was in the least cowed by Galbraith and we loved getting in heated debates with him. He seemed to respect us for being willing to challenge him. These debates often centered on the question of whether "top-down," centrally planned, foreign aid programs made the most sense or whether a "bottom-up" approach, involving greater involvement from the ultimate aid recipients themselves, was likely to be more successful in the long run. Professor Galbraith tended to argue the former point of view while Sam and

I argued the latter. I think that Sam and I gave as good as we got in these frequent exchanges. Ironically, more than 50 years later, this same question is still being hotly debated.

While completing my coursework in the spring of 1964, I began thinking about a topic for my doctoral dissertation. I had decided that, given the work I had done at IMEDE and Nestlé, my focus should be on international marketing. I wanted to choose a subject about which little was known, but one that would be of significant interest to international managers in their efforts to build multinational businesses and to local managers trying to compete successfully against multinational companies. If I could identify such a topic, the trick would then be to find a source of funding to underwrite the research project.

After toying with a number of possible subjects, I serendipitously stumbled onto the solution to my problem. One day, quite by chance, I engaged in a discussion with HBS Professor George Cabot Lodge. He mentioned that he was working on a project to help set up a new business school in Central America called INCAE (Instituto Centroamericano de Administracion de Empresas). Based on the request of President Kennedy before his death, the school was to be sponsored by Harvard Business School and underwritten by USAID. George mentioned that the school was interested in the development of indigenous teaching materials that would focus on some of the most important problems facing local Central American managers as well as managers of multinational companies operating in the region. He asked me whether I had any ideas and if I would be interested in the project. It didn't take long to see how this might be the solution to my dissertation dilemma.

I wrote a dissertation proposal suggesting that I would develop a series of case studies, together with an analysis focusing on the issue of marketing competition between purely local Central American companies and multinational companies operating in the region. Specifically, I would look at the question of whether there were certain industries where local companies could exploit their marketing advantages to compete successfully against the multinationals and if so, how. And at the same time, I would try to identify what, specifically, it was that gave multinationals their marketing strength and how they could leverage these factors in a region such as Central America.

Professor Lodge liked my proposal, as did Professor Hugo Uyterhoeven and marketing professor Ray Corey. All three agreed to serve on my dissertation committee and Lodge said he would authorize USAID to underwrite all expenses associated with the project. In one stroke, my dissertation problem had been solved. Now all I had to do was research the project, develop the case studies, analyze the data contained in them, develop some useful conclusions, and write the dissertation itself. Piece of cake? Hardly!

I spent much of the summer of 1964 taking a crash language course designed to help me learn enough Spanish to be able to read and converse in Spanish. Then, a week after Eric's birth on October 23rd, I left Charlotte to look after our three kids all by herself and flew to Central America to do my field research.

Central America was a whole new world for me. It was a place filled with bright primary colors, loud music, extremes of rich and poor, warm weather, and much sunshine. I was fascinated from the beginning. It was a particularly interesting time to be in the region. Five of the seven countries that comprised Central America (Costa Rica, Nicaragua, El Salvador, Honduras, and Guatemala) were in the process of trying to implement a newly formed Central American Common Market (CACM) that would permit internal free trade throughout the zone.

I began my research in San Jose, Costa Rica, where thanks to an introduction from Adolf Berle, a retired member of Franklin Roosevelt's brain trust and friend of Charlotte's family, I had an opportunity at the outset to meet with Pepe Figueres, the much-revered former president of the country. He was kind enough to give me an invaluable historical overview of Central America's political, economic, business, and cultural climate. Among other things, he pointed out that, while Costa Rica was democratic and stable, Nicaragua was run by the Somoza family dictatorship, and El Salvador, Honduras, and Guatemala had governments led by military leaders. He said that, although he believed the formation of CACM was a good idea, he had doubts that it would last very long, given the volatility of the region's political situation. It turned out that President Figueres was prescient. CACM subsequently became moribund in the mid-eighties, though at the time of my research, the alliance showed promise of succeeding.

Through the kindness of George Lodge, I had also been provided with an introduction to Walter Kissling, an entrepreneur who had started a local firm called Kativo, which had two main divisions: One produced and marketed detergents and soaps, while the second was a paint manufacturing and marketing company. Both of these organizations faced competition from several multinational corporations. In the case of the detergent company, the multinational competitors were Procter & Gamble, Unilever, and Colgate-Palmolive. In the case of paints, the main competitors were Sherwin-Williams and the Pittsburgh Paint Company, both from the U.S.

Kativo's paint company was thriving throughout all five CACM countries. Its detergent company, however, was facing an uphill battle against its multinational competitors. My quest was to understand why this was the case and to learn more about why it was possible for a local company to be so successful in one industry and why it was having so much difficulty in the second. I then hoped to be able to formulate some conclusions and generalizations that would be useful to managers both in other local companies and in the multinationals.

In the course of the two months I spent on-site in Central America, I gathered data and interviewed senior managers from all of the companies mentioned above plus several others based in the region. Most of the interviews were in English, since the majority of the executives in the various local companies were multilingual and the majority of executives in the multinationals spoke English as their native tongue. In some of the local companies, the interviews were in Spanish, with me limping along with my newly acquired rudimentary knowledge of the language. I was only able to understand every third or fourth word, so the research results of these interviews were hardly stellar. But it was good practice in my effort to learn a new language.

With my meetings every day and the necessity to transcribe my notes every evening, I had little time for sightseeing. The most memorable impression I carried away from my stay in San Jose, Costa Rica, was that the city was entirely covered by volcanic dust as result of the nearby Irazu Volcano having recently erupted. Apart from that impression, the only other time I can remember coming up for air was the weekend in Guatemala City that I spent with Joachim Lungarshausen, my old German friend from Lausanne.

Joachim was then working as a young executive for the German company, Bosch, overseeing its automotive parts operations in Guatemala. We had a rollicking good time together. Saturday morning, we set off to play golf on a nearby course. On my first drive off the tee of the second nine, I managed to hit my caddy, who failed to duck when I cried "fore" after my drive took a vicious slice into the rough to the right side of the fairway. The golf ball caught him squarely on the knee. After ascertaining that the caddy wasn't badly injured, Joachim and I concluded that perhaps it would be wise to call it a day before I, the gringo, was sued under Guatemalan law for attempting to murder my caddy. Instead, we decided to do a bit of sightseeing and drove to Antigua and Lake Atitlan. Both were lovely and provided me with a venue to purchase some handicrafts for Charlotte and the three little ones. We topped off the day back in Guatemala City with a delicious dinner, a copious amount of wine, and a lot of reminiscing about all that had happened to each of us since we last parted in Switzerland.

In early December 1964, I flew back to Boston for a most welcome reunion with my little family. I had missed them all terribly and they, me. Charlotte, barely 25, deserved a medal of honor for doing a brilliant, if lonely, job of single-handedly caring for three young children under the age of three, including one newly born, during the time I was away. It clearly was very hard on her and unfair of me to have left her totally on her own for so long, one week after the birth of Eric. But she was totally a good sport about the entire episode and I loved her all the more dearly for rising to the occasion.

The year 1965 was mostly devoted to working on my doctoral dissertation. The process was slow going, but I slogged through it day by day and ultimately completed it in the spring of 1966. I was happy to have the whole project behind me.

The finished document was entitled "An Analysis of Competition Among Local and Multinational Companies in Two Central American Industries." It included case studies and a considerable amount of original analysis. The conclusions I reached included a number of hypotheses concerning why local companies had a better chance of being successful in some types of industries than others. The thesis also identified how multinationals leveraged their size, marketing know-how, intellectual property, manufacturing scale, and strength of their brands across borders to gain competitive strength in international markets.

The end result was hardly a magnum opus or a brilliant, world-class piece of research. But it was a reasonably competent dissertation that my thesis advisors seemed to like and that, in the end, earned me a Harvard doctorate in business administration (DBA). The teaching cases that I developed and included in the thesis were used for many years in international marketing courses both at Harvard and a number of other business schools all around the world. Moreover, I think that some of the ideas developed in the thesis turned out to be of considerable practical use to many real-life executives in helping them to manage their international marketing efforts.

Apart from the tedium of writing the thesis, the other memory that stands out for me when thinking about my doctoral program experience at Harvard was being hired by the school as an instructor to help teach an MBA course entitled "Creative Marketing Strategy." The course had been developed by Ted Levitt, a world-renowned Harvard marketing professor and author of the best seller entitled *Marketing Myopia*. The course was an adventure in field-based experiential learning. Students worked in groups of four to seven as consultants to real companies confronting real problems. In advance of each semester, companies in the New York/New England area were invited to submit proposals describing an important marketing issue that they were facing. For example, the issue might involve designing a strategy for introducing a new product. Alternatively, it might require the design of an advertising campaign or how to respond to an emerging competitive threat.

Typically, Professor Levitt and I received about 20 such proposals that we then edited and presented to the 75 or so students enrolled in the course. The students, in turn, formed their own groups. Each group then listed its preferences with respect to the projects they would like to tackle. This resulted in 12 to 14 projects being distributed evenly among the groups. Professor Levitt and I then split up the projects; he served as a coach to half the teams and I took on the other half. Each of us met with our respective groups two or three times a week to give them guidance and serve as a sounding board for their ideas.

Part of the managerial learning experience for the group members was the process of deciding among themselves who would serve as overall team leader and what roles each of the other members would be assigned. At the end of the semester, each team was responsible for developing a written consulting report outlining their analysis of the problem they had been assigned, together with their specific recommendations to the client company. In addition, each team was expected to make an in-person presentation to the senior management of the company.

The course was a powerful learning experience for the students involved. Whereas the analysis and classroom discussion of case studies at Harvard constituted a good example of simulated reality, the Creative Marketing Strategy course offered an exercise in reality itself. I loved working with Ted Levitt and coaching the student groups during the two years I helped teach the course. To be honest, I think I learned as much, if not more, about management and marketing from the course as did my students.

For me, this was tangible proof of the old axiom that postulates the best way to learn about a subject is to be placed in a position of having to teach it. And, I might add, the best way for students to learn to be effective executives is through field-based experiences that give them an opportunity to work on real problems with real managers in real organizations.

Meanwhile, at home, Charlotte's life was consumed with the never-ending task of trying to keep up with the needs of three children in diapers while at the same time being a loving wife and striving to maintain her sense of humor and some semblance of sanity. The saving grace in the situation was that she was not alone in her situation. There were dozens of other student wives and mothers of young children living in the Peabody Terrace complex. Hence, we were able to make a number of good friends during this era of our lives. We formed a particularly close bond with one couple in particular, Peter and Peggy Gunness. They were the resident housemasters of the complex and Peter worked in the Harvard College admissions office while Peggy looked after their three small children, who were about the same ages as our three. Ours became a lifelong friendship. We named Peter to be one of our son Eric's godparents. Peter later went on to serve many years as headmaster of Buckingham, Brown and Nichols private school in Cambridge and Peggy became an ordained Episcopal rector.

Given our experience of living abroad, we were particularly drawn to other married student couples with international backgrounds. Donald and Margo Gibson from Australia and Leon and Ebbie Visser from South Africa stand out in this regard.

Having neither the money nor the time to engage in the various entertainments offered in the Boston area or to take family vacations, Charlotte and I tended to stay at home most of the time while I was working on my doctorate. We almost never ate out, went to parties, or saw a movie or play. Occasionally, we would drive out to Stockbridge for a weekend visit with Charlotte's family at Pilgrim's Inn. Other than that, we seldom came up for air. Our life was quite different from the one we had led in Switzerland.

In the winter of 1965-66, as I approached the end of my doctoral studies, I began to think of the next steps in my professional career. Having greatly enjoyed the teaching I had done so far, I decided I definitely wanted to stay in the academic field. I had received hints from Harvard that they might want me to stay on to teach at the business school. I had also received feelers from both the Tuck School at Dartmouth and the Darden School at the University of Virginia.

In the end, I received a very unorthodox offer from Harvard. It turned out that Harvard had recently received a major grant from the Ford Foundation to help three universities in the Philippines set up three separate graduate MBA programs in the Manila area. At the time, there were virtually no graduate business schools in Asia. However, during the late 1940s and the 1950s a number of Filipinos had earned their MBA degrees at the Harvard Business School. In the early sixties, at the request of these Harvard alumni and some other leaders in the Philippine business community, a number of Harvard professors had, for several years, conducted summer advanced management programs in the Philippines for senior executives. These programs had typically been oversubscribed and extremely popular.

Out of these summer executive programs grew the idea of establishing permanent MBA programs in the Philippines. At the time, the Philippine nation was considered to be one of Asia's up and coming "Asian Tiger" economies with a great future ahead of it. Business was booming there, and President Ferdinand Marcos had just been elected and was initially highly popular among Filipinos as a business-friendly "reformist" leader.

Hence, with the support of the Harvard professors who had taught in the Philippines and the backing of leaders in the Philippine business and academic communities, a proposal was made to the Ford Foundation to underwrite the efforts of the three leading Filipino universities to establish graduate MBA programs of their own. The Ford Foundation approved a multimillion dollar grant to be administered by Harvard Business School to implement the plan.

The plan called for sending a team of Harvard faculty members and research assistants to the Philippines to work with the universities in question and develop indigenous teaching materials. At the same time, the plan also called for granting a number of fellowships to Filipinos so that they could pursue doctoral degrees at Harvard and other business schools in the United States.

At Harvard, Professor Stephen Fuller, one of the professors who had taught in the summer executive programs in the Philippines and who was then serving as associate dean for external affairs at the school, was named by Dean George Baker to administer the Harvard side of the program. Thus, he was in charge of putting together the team of Harvard professors and research assistants who would go out to Manila as the Harvard Advisory Group in the Philippines.

It so happened that Steve Fuller had been one of the Harvard professors who had taught at IMEDE in Lausanne while I was a research associate there. Moreover, we had taken a liking to one another and he had served as an informal advisor and mentor to me while I was in Harvard's doctoral program. One day in March of 1966, he called me and invited me to meet with him in his office.

Imagine my surprise when Professor Fuller proposed that I join the Harvard faculty as an assistant professor and that I accept the position as head of the Harvard Advisory Group in the Philippines. He pointed out that I was one of the few people at the business school who had extensive experience in international business and that the two years I had spent at IMEDE in Lausanne made me an ideal candidate to head up the new Harvard project in the Philippines. Having spent time in the Philippines himself, he said he thought the new project had great promise and that heading it up would offer an exciting career opportunity for me. He finally pointed out that mine would be a regular tenure track appointment at Harvard and that on completing my assignment in the Philippines, there would be normal teaching assignments awaiting me back in Boston.

The offer was both unexpected and unorthodox. A week later, and after some soul-searching and a lot of discussion with Charlotte, I took a deep breath and, again, decided to take Robert Frost's "road less traveled." I said yes to the proposal. Miraculously, Charlotte, whatever qualms she might have had, took a deep breath as well and indicated that she also was willing to undertake the new adventure in a totally unknown part of the world.

During the rest of the spring of 1966, I tied up the loose ends of my work in the doctoral program and my teaching assignment in the Creative Marketing Strategy course and prepared for our new overseas assignment.

CHAPTER NINETEEN

ADVENTURES IN THE PHILIPPINES

In late June of 1966, Charlotte and I packed up our belongings and our three young tots (two of whom were still in diapers), said our goodbyes to our families and friends, and boarded a series of flights that ultimately landed us at the Manila airport in the Philippines. Overnight, our lives underwent a total change. From the moment we walked off the plane, we experienced culture shock to the nth degree.

First, there was the climate. On stepping onto the tarmac, we were hit by a blast of hot, humid, sultry, tropical air with temperatures near 100 degrees Fahrenheit. It was the beginning of the rainy season and for the first few months of our stay in the country it rained practically every day and flooded about once every two weeks.

Second, there were the throngs of humanity. Everywhere one looked, there were people, people, people. The population of the Philippines at that time was about 33 million, with 5 or 6 million living densely packed in metro Manila, the nation's capital on the island of Luzon. (Astoundingly, as I write these lines today, more than 50 years later, the population of the Philippines, a largely Catholic country, has more than *trebled* to about 100 million people! The country, which was already crowded in the 1960s, has had one of the highest rates of population growth in the world.)

Third, there were the sounds. Having been warmly greeted at the airport by local representatives of the Ford Foundation, we five Sorensons were bundled into a van for the 25-minute ride to San Lorenzo Village, the Manila suburb where the house we were to occupy was located. On the way, our ears were assaulted by a cacophony of blaring music and honking horns. Most of the music and honking came from the ubiquitous Jeepneys, the garishly painted and restored World War II jeeps that served as Manila's major form of public transportation and that monopolized the streets like swarms of angry hornets.

Fourth, there was the dirt. Looking out the windows of our van we saw an overcrowded metropolis whose streets were filled with trash, debris, and odiferous garbage.

By the time we arrived at what was to be our new home, we were in a condition of almost complete shock. I have a distinct memory of thinking, as we got out of the car, that perhaps we had made a terrible mistake and that we should climb back on the plane and return to the United States. What a difference Manila was from the familiar environs of Boston and the pristine, impeccable orderliness of Lausanne in Switzerland!

However, when we inspected the house the Ford Foundation had rented for us, our feelings began to mellow. While not elegant, it seemed like a palace compared with the married student apartment we had occupied for the previous two years in the Peabody Terrace graduate student housing complex. Light and airy, it had a large living room, three bedrooms, paneled study, kitchen, outdoor eating patio, and servants' quarters. Yes, you read right, servants' quarters! And not only that, the Ford Foundation supplied us with a full-time maid/laundress (Tina), cook (Freddie), and ya-ya (a nursemaid named Gloria) to go along with the servants' quarters. A car, full-time driver (Ruperto), and part-time gardener were thrown in for good measure.

Imagine our initial feelings. The week before we flew to Manila we were married graduate students with three tiny children, struggling to make ends meet on a very meager budget and doing absolutely everything for ourselves. Truth be told, Charlotte had often been at her wit's end trying to hold the household together. And now, suddenly, we were to have the luxury of a full-time staff that was ready to cater to our every need . . . including that of changing diapers. It felt like we had suddenly landed in heaven and were hugely relieved. Of course, given our respective New England and Midwestern egalitarian backgrounds and set of values, we felt an initial tinge of guilt. After what we had seen as we drove from the airport, it was difficult to accept the level of privilege we had been given.

Harry Case, the Ford Foundation's resident director, couldn't have been more gracious and hospitable in welcoming us to the Philippines. We were the first members of the Harvard Advisory Group team to arrive on the scene. The other members were three additional professors and a total of four research assistants/case writers. All of them arrived in Manila a few days after our arrival.

In short order, the Harvard Advisory Group, or HAG as we came to call ourselves, was set up in comfortable downtown Manila offices in a building on the waterfront boulevard that overlooked Manila Bay.

The Group's primary mandate was to help each of the three leading higher education institutions in the Philippines set up a graduate MBA program. The three were Ateneo de Manila University, De La Salle College, and the University of the Philippines. The first two were private Catholic institutions. The Jesuits founded Ateneo and the Christian Brothers founded De La Salle. The third, the University of the Philippines, was a public institution. All had previously established undergraduate business schools, but none had graduate programs.

HAG's secondary mission was to develop indigenous-based case studies and other teaching materials to be used in the new MBA programs and, further, to teach Filipino faculty members and case writers how to develop such case studies and use them on their own.

During the first weeks of our stay in the Philippines, we Harvard team members had a chance to meet with the presidents, deans, and faculty members of each of the grantee institutions. All were very excited about the project, greeted us cordially, and pledged to give us their full support. It quickly became clear to us that the name "Harvard Business School" was held in extremely high regard in the Philippines and served as an almost magical "open sesame" when it came to opening doors not only in academia but in business and government circles as well.

At the time, the president of the University of the Philippines was General Carlos Romulo, who came from a prominent Filipino family. He had gained some distinction in accompanying General Douglas MacArthur when the latter landed back in the Philippines in early 1945. MacArthur had proclaimed "I shall return" three years earlier on fleeing by submarine from the island of Corregidor in Manila Bay to Australia.

Father James Donelan was Ateneo University's president. He was a brilliant, wise, and personable Jesuit priest in his late forties who had been born in New York and who, after having studied at Fordham University and been ordained, had spent most of his adult life as a faculty member and administrator at Ateneo.

De La Salle was headed up by Brother Gabriel Connon, a jolly, rotund American who had also spent most of his working life in the Philippines and who, for several years, had guided De La Salle with a sure and steady hand on its tiller.

We spent the first several weeks getting acquainted with all three academic institutions, meeting with a number of leaders in the business community and the government and studying the Filipino economic and political scene. From these initial meetings and studies, it gradually became evident to me and to other members of our Harvard team that, given the limited faculty and financial resources available, it made little sense for each of the three grantee universities to establish its own separate graduate MBA program. Instead, we concluded that it would be far better for all three institutions to pool their resources and jointly establish one outstanding graduate business school.

The more we discussed this idea with the various parties involved, the more a consensus emerged within the academic and business communities in support of it. Harry Case from the Ford Foundation was also intrigued by the concept.

Hence, the Harvard Advisory Group was given the green light to draw up a Master Plan for creating a single free-standing graduate MBA business school that would have as its godparents all three of the original Ford Foundation grantee institutions.

We commenced the task by enlisting the pro bono assistance of Sycip, Gorres, and Velayo, the Philippines' largest and most successful public accounting and consulting firm. The principal founder of the firm was Washington Sycip, who was solidly behind the idea of creating a single high-quality graduate business school in the country and who volunteered to have SGV's consulting arm work on the project. At the time, the managing director of SGV's consulting practice was Roberto "Bobby" Ongpin, who had earned his MBA degree at Harvard. He and I immediately hit it off and became good friends. It was agreed that I, with input from my team and the three universities involved, would write the narrative part of the Master Plan for the new school and that he, with the help of his consulting colleagues, would develop all the pro forma financial and quantitative projections for the school. The subsequent financial modeling done by Bobby and his team turned out to be invaluable.

For me, the process of designing the Master Plan for the new school and then, working with others, helping to make the school a reality, was a fascinating and exhilarating experience. It was a great example of academic entrepreneurship. And as is the case with any entrepreneurial venture, we had to overcome a large number of challenges along the way.

The first and one of the most serious of these challenges involved the role of the University of the Philippines (U.P.). The original concept called for U.P., Ateneo, and De La Salle to be co-equal legal "godparents" of the new school. However, under Philippine law, U.P., a public university, was not permitted to participate in a public-private consortium with Ateneo and De La Salle, two private entities. This problem was solved when U.P. graciously agreed to withdraw from the partnership and renounce its share of the Ford Foundation grant funds. This outcome would not have been possible had it not been for the statesmanship of Carlos Romulo and Cesar Virata, respectively the president of the university and the dean of its business school. Parenthetically, Cesar had previously been a partner at SGV and many years later briefly became prime minister of the Philippines toward the end of the Marcos regime.

A second problem confronting the new school related to its basic mission. Should its mission be to prepare future business leaders solely for the Philippines or for Asia in general? Quite a lot of discussion took place around this question. The decision was to "aim high." The new school would be international in character and aspire from its beginning to be the most outstanding graduate business school in all of Asia. It should be called the Asian Institute of Management, not the Philippine Institute of Management. We thought it augured well that its acronym for the school would be AIM, which suggested high aspirations, rather than PIM, which somehow sounded less auspicious.

Formulating the overall plan for AIM involved considering countless details. How big a student body should the school attempt to accommodate and what should be its international composition? How many faculty members would it require? Where would they come from and what should be their backgrounds? What should be the design of the curriculum? What would the school's underlying teaching philosophy be? Like Harvard, should it be based mainly on the case study approach to learning? If so, what might be the balance of Harvard cases versus indigenously based cases? Who should develop the indigenous cases? Where should AIM be located and what should be the design of its physical facilities? What should the school's leadership structure be? What should its administrative and salary practices be? What, exactly, should the governance structure of the school be? These and myriad other questions had to be considered and resolved.

Finally, there was the really big question: How much was the entire project going to cost and where was the money going to come from? The Ford Foundation grant was merely meant to prime the pump. In the long run, the overall endeavor was going to require a very significant initial capital investment, together with a sizeable ongoing source of annual operating revenues.

By July of 1967, the Master Plan we had developed for AIM was complete. In the end, the plan addressed all of the foregoing issues. The process of putting it together was characterized by a remarkably high degree of good will and cooperation among all parties involved.

Now came the task of implementing the plan. The first step was to find the money required to make the dream of AIM a reality. It turned out that this needed to come almost entirely from the private sector. Thus, I was introduced to the world of big-time fundraising. In this, I had great partners from both the business community and the respective presidents of Ateneo and De La Salle.

Our first priority was to secure a physical location for the school and the capital to build a campus with classrooms, dormitories, dining facilities, a library, and administrative offices. In both regards, we ended up being extraordinarily lucky.

First, with respect to acquiring land on which to build AIM, we had the great good fortune to have had an excellent entrée into the Zobel de Ayala Group, the largest and most civic-minded real estate development group in the Philippines. At the time, they were in the early stages of developing the Manila suburb of Makati that subsequently was to become the heart of the Philippines' business and commercial community. Two cousins, Enrique and Jaime Zobel, headed up this family group. Father Donelan, Brother Gabriel, and I paid a visit to them and presented them with the audacious proposal that they donate a prime piece of land in Makati to house the new school.

To our total delight and amazement, they agreed. It helped that Jaime was a Harvard graduate and that both he and Enrique thought it was in their enlightened self-interest to donate the land. Not only were they convinced of the need for a business school like AIM to develop future leaders for the Philippines and Asia but they also had the vision to foresee that AIM could enhance the future prestige and commercial desirability of their Makati development. Hence, they donated a two-hectare parcel of land in an ideal location, right in the center of Makati.

Now all we had to do was to find a donor for the buildings to go on the "Promised Land." During my first year in the Philippines, I had met and become friends with Eugenio Lopez, Jr., who was a graduate of Harvard Business School and the oldest son of Eugenio Lopez, Sr., the patriarch of one of the two largest family-controlled industrial groups in the Philippines. Eugenio Jr., or "Geny" (pronounced "Henny") as he was more familiarly known, had become intrigued by, and enthusiastic about, the concept underlying AIM. It helped that he was also an alumnus of Ateneo's undergraduate program.

After some behind-the-scenes negotiations, Geny arranged a face-to-face meeting with his father for Ateneo's president, Father Donelan, and me. After discussing with Don Eugenio, Sr. the nature and importance of the project to the Philippines, Father Donelan and I screwed up our courage and asked if he would be willing to donate 5 million pesos to single-handedly underwrite the entire capital cost of constructing all the required buildings on the land that had just been committed to AIM by the Zobel de Ayala group. We pointed out to him that such a gift would represent an attractive naming opportunity for the family. We proposed that, if he were to make the donation, the new school would be permanently named the Asian Institute of Management, A Eugenio Lopez, Sr. Foundation. Geny had evidently prepared the way very well for our request to his father. Without a great deal of further discussion, Mr. Lopez agreed to make the gift.

The significance of this gift can hardly be overstated. It turned out to be the largest single charitable contribution ever made in the Philippines up to that time!

With the gift of the land and buildings in hand, the fundraising team was on a roll. We immediately set off to raise the remainder of the funds required to make AIM a reality.

When the Zobel de Ayala and Lopez gifts were publicly announced to the business community, it created leverage that led to a competition on the part of various companies and individuals to also make contributions to AIM. The result was that, among other gifts, different corporate and individual donors underwrote the creation of 18 endowed or semi-endowed faculty chairs, each of them named for its donor. This was quite remarkable given that, when AIM finally opened its doors in late 1968, it had only 12 faculty members!

Father Donelan, Wash Sycip, and I also paid a visit to President Ferdinand Marcos in the course of our fundraising adventures. At the time, President Marcos was still held in high regard in the Philippines. It was before he declared martial law and became corrupted by his wife, Imelda, and by his love of power and money. At the time, we saw no reason not to visit him and seek his support. We proposed to President Marcos that he approve the creation of an AIM student loan fund to be underwritten by the country's social security reserves. We explained that we wanted the school to be open to talented future leaders from all walks of life, regardless of income, and not just to students from wealthy families. He immediately saw the logic in our reasoning and agreed to establish the loan fund. In hindsight, it was very difficult for me to see the difficulties faced by the Lopez family as the Marcos regime grew increasingly authoritarian.

Entrepreneurial Insight #7: Overcoming Challenges and Starting AIM

The process leading to the conception and creation of AIM was truly extraordinary. Within the time span of two short years, the principal actors in the drama had dreamed a dream, translated the dream into a comprehensive Master Plan, and marshaled all the necessary resources—human, physical, and financial—to make the dream a reality.

There was no road map to follow, no precedent for such an effort. It was a hugely successful entrepreneurial venture and, for me personally, a wonderfully satisfying accomplishment. Among my professional experiences over the years, being a co-founder of AIM stands out as one of the most satisfying and one about which I am most proud. Today, 50 years later, I continue to be fond of the school and serve on its international board of governors.

Lesson Learned: Starting a new school is inherently an entrepreneurial venture.

AIM opened its doors in temporary quarters in 1969. Its first president was my old friend and mentor, Professor Steve Fuller from Harvard. Its initial faculty of 12 were mostly Filipinos who had done graduate work in the United States. AIM offered a two-year MBA program and its first class numbered about 75 students. Pedagogically, its teaching approach was based primarily on the inductive case study method pioneered by Harvard Business School. When the new AIM campus construction was complete at the end of 1969, the resulting facilities were the finest in all of Asia. Subsequently, AIM earned the distinction of being the first, and for a long time, the only graduate business school in Asia to be fully accredited by the American Association of Collegiate Schools of Business (AACSB).

With respect to the teaching materials used at AIM, it is noteworthy to mention that during our stay in the Philippines, the members of the Harvard Advisory Group researched, wrote, and published more than 150 indigenous case studies, complete with teaching notes for each case. These cases came to be heavily used not only at AIM but also at many other business schools around the world, including Harvard.

Two of the case studies that we developed in the marketing field, which was my area of responsibility, bear mentioning. When we first arrived in the Philippines, Ed Felton, my research assistant/case writer, and I determined that we should try to write marketing cases that focused on the most pressing economic and social challenges facing the country. We identified two such challenges in particular. They were as follows:

- How to develop self-sufficiency in the production of rice, which was the food staple on which the Filipino diet most depended. In the late 1960s, the country was a significant net importer of rice, a fact that, in turn, created significant food security and balance of trade problems.

- How to deal with the ever-increasing rate of population growth in a heavily Catholic country that was already over-crowded, but where the Church vigorously opposed any form of birth control.

My parents, Ralph and Verna Sorenson, after they were married in 1930 in Chicago, Illinois. My father was born on May 28, 1898, in Eau Claire, Wisconsin, and my mother on August 8, 1898, in Ada, Minnesota.

A photo of my sister, Nancy Sorenson Overman.

With my duck, Oscar, age one year and nine months.

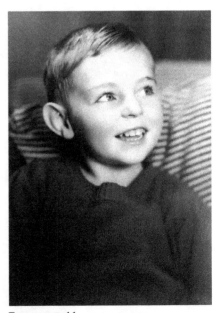

Four years old.

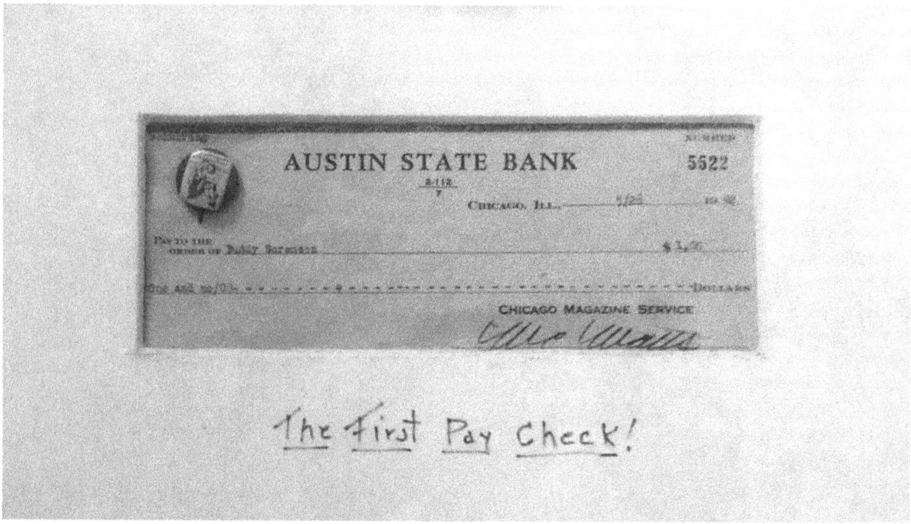
AUSTIN STATE BANK
5522
CHICAGO MAGAZINE SERVICE
The First Pay Check!

My first paycheck for one dollar earned when I was nine, by selling and delivering door-to-door the weekly magazines *The Saturday Evening Post* and *Ladies Home Journal.*

COOL DRINKS!
STRAWBERRY
RASBERRY
LEMON-AID

The next generation of young entrepreneurs in the Sorenson family. Our three children, Kristin, Katrina, and Eric, with their lemonade stand when we lived in Belmont, Massachusetts, from 1968 to 1974.

COOKIES
HOT COCOA
and
LEMONADE

The entrepreneurial gene apparently passed down to a third generation! Our grandchildren, Soren and Tessa Peterson, expanded their roadside product line to include hot cocoa and cookies.

Dancing the Charleston in the Varsity Varieties theater production. I graduated in 1951 from Mansfield Senior High School, Mansfield, Ohio.

My Amherst College yearbook photo. I graduated from Amherst in 1955 with an undergraduate degree in liberal arts and economics.

From 1959 to 1961 I worked as a research associate and case writer at the IMEDE International Management Development Institute in Lausanne, Switzerland.

Hooray! I married the extraordinary Charlotte Bacon Ripley in Stockbridge, Massachusetts, on June 25, 1960. Charlotte is 20 years old and I am 26.

Another red-letter occasion. Our first daughter, Kristin Elizabeth Sorenson, is born on April 14, 1962 in Lausanne, Switzerland. Here she is hitchhiking on her mother's back in the Swiss Alps.

Standing on the left with senior managers of Nestlé Alimentana. As executive assistant to Max Gloor, the worldwide head of marketing, I worked from 1961 to 1963 at Nestlé's headquarters in Vevey, Switzerland.

And then there were three! Katrina Anne Sorenson was born on September 25, 1964, and Eric Ripley Sorenson arrived on October 13, 1965. This photo was taken shortly before we, as a family, left Cambridge, Massachusetts, in August 1966 to live for over two years in the Philippines.

The Asian Institute of Management (AIM) in Manila, that I helped co-found as director of the Harvard Advisory Group in the Philippines. AIM celebrated its 50th anniversary in November 2018.

Don Eugenio Lopez, Sr. (fourth from right) has just announced a 1968 gift of 5 million pesos for the construction of buildings to house the new Asian Institute of Management. Left to right: Eugenio Lopez, Jr.; Aurelio Montinola, dean of Ateneo University Business School; Brother Paul, dean of De La Salle College Business School; Brother Gabriel, president of De La Salle College; Eugenio Lopez, Sr.; Father James Donelan, president of Ateneo de Manila University; Dr. Clark Bloom, director of the Ford Foundation; and me.

Delivering the inaugural address at Babson College in October 1974. Dr. Lawrence Fouraker, then the dean of Harvard Business School who sponsored me to be president of Babson, is sitting behind me to the left.

Larry Milas, Babson alumnus and trustee of the F.W. Olin Foundation; me; Charles Thompson, Babson VP of Development; and Jesse Putney, Babson VP of Finance, studying the architect's model of the Horn Library that was gifted to Babson by the Olin Foundation.

At the 1978 Babson College Founders Day, me, with Soichiro Honda (left), the founder of Honda Motor Company, and Royal Little, founder of Textron. They were among those in the first group to be inducted into the Academy of Distinguished Entrepreneurs.

With Edith Babson Mustard at the dedication of the Newton Room, Roger Babson Museum, and Babson Archives on October 17, 1980.

Charlotte and I at a Babson College reception. Charlotte took a special interest in helping to organize programs for Babson's international students.

Awarding diplomas at a Babson commencement.

Six former presidents of Babson College. Left to right: Brian Barefoot, Leo Higdon, William Dill, Leonard Schlesinger, and William Glavin. I am on the far right. Dr. Kerry Healey, not shown in the photo, is the current president of Babson.

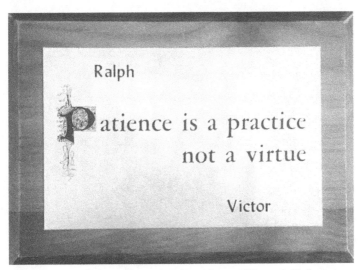

Victor Tomasso, Babson alumnus and benefactor of Tomasso Hall on the Babson campus, teaches me a lesson on being patient.

Chairman and CEO of the Barry Wright Corporation
from 1981 to 1989.

My 91-year-old father and I relaxing on the deck of a mail boat while cruising
with Charlotte in and out of fjords in Norway during the summer of 1989.
Later, we visited the islands in the Stavanger Fjord from which some of
Charlotte's Norwegian ancestors hailed, and the small seaside village
of Tvedestrand from which my father's father and my great-grandfather
emigrated to America in 1882.

Charlotte and I celebrate our 40th wedding anniversary in Boulder on June 25, 2000.

Ten years later, in July 2010, the whole Sorenson clan celebrated our 50th wedding anniversary sailing off the coast of Maine. For both of us, the occasion commemorated a remarkable half-century!

Charlotte and I enjoy a moment of repose in the lovely Lake Waban meditation retreat on the Wellesley College campus that Charlotte donated to the college.

Riding the annual University of Colorado Buffalo Bicycle Classic 100 Mile event at age 75. Of all the pleasures of longevity that I have enjoyed, none has been more satisfying than riding my bike.

Summiting Mount Ventoux in France to celebrate my 80th birthday in 2013. The family trip was a gift from Charlotte and my children.

QUATRE VINGT(OUX)! VIVE RAPHA! With Kristin, Charlotte, Trina, and Eric on my 80th birthday bicycle trip to France.

For many years, it has been the family custom to vacation together during the mid-winter holidays. Over the decades, these occasions have typically taken place in a sunny village near an ocean. This photo was taken on the beach in the little seaside town of Akumal, Mexico.

VICTORY! Trina, Eric, and I celebrate reaching Uhuru Point, the 19,340-foot summit of Mount Kilimanjaro in Tanzania. In Swahili, Uhuru means freedom and independence. We thought it symbolic that we summited at a moment that, given the time differential, was still July 4th, 1991, in the western time zone of the United States. We had reached Independence Point on Independence Day in the U.S., a universal symbol of freedom!

Together at the end of a rainbow near Victoria Falls in Zimbabwe. Charlotte and I feel we have been truly blessed to have lived the life we have had with each other and with our family.

With respect to the first of these issues, rice production self-sufficiency, we wrote a two-case series focusing on the work of the International Rice Research Institute (IRRI) that, at the time, had recently developed a new rice strain called IR-76. This strain was purported to achieve harvests that were twice as large as anything existing and to enable the planting of three rice crops a year rather than the traditional two crops. It was soon dubbed "Miracle Rice" by IRRI and by media throughout Asia.

Case A in the series focused on the question of how to commercialize and market this wondrous Miracle Rice. When the case was subsequently taught, students typically became quite excited about the marketing potential of Miracle Rice and its potential to help solve Asia's nutritional needs while at the same time enabling Filipino rice farmers to prosper. They typically came up with a wide variety of creative recommendations to address the commercialization and marketing challenge.

Then, in the next class session, along came Case B. In subsequent years, both at AIM and at other business schools around the world, this case became a classic example of the law of unintended consequences. It turned out there were a few problems with Miracle Rice. First, it required greater inputs of fertilizer, herbicides, and insecticides than the traditional rice grown in the Philippines. This required a greater up-front monetary investment than many subsistence-level farmers could afford. Second, when the more bountiful harvests came in, the farmers often had to hire additional outside workers to harvest the rice. Again, this imposed an additional financial burden on many family farmers. Third, it often was the case that there was inadequate appropriate land available for efficiently drying the harvested rice. As a result, much of the harvest ended up being improperly dried on dusty roadsides and was wasted in the process. Fourth, in many parts of the Philippines, there were inadequate milling facilities available to handle the more bountiful harvests. Fifth, for rice that farmers wanted to sell commercially, in some parts of the country the transportation infrastructure proved inadequate for efficiently delivering the bumper quantities of harvested rice to Divisoria, the central commodities market in Manila. Finally, and most important, if rice is the staple of one's diet—as was the case at the time in the Philippines—one cares deeply about its taste. It turned out that Miracle Rice never really passed the public's taste test in the Philippines. This ended up being the decisive factor in dooming the IR-76 strain of rice developed by IRRI. The miracle turned out to be an illusion. The moral of the story: It is vital always to think holistically about any new product or concept and to consider in advance *all* of the factors that are likely to influence the ultimate success or failure of the endeavor.

With respect to the second issue, that of the high birth rate in the Philippines in the mid-sixties, we wrote a case on the early marketing of birth-control pills that had come on the market internationally only a few years before. At the time, the Philippine population was about 33 million and the annual birth rate was about 3.4 percent, one of the highest in the world. The newly developed birth-control pills had the potential to slow down the exploding population of the country. However, the Philippine Catholic Church, then headed up by Cardinal Sin, adamantly opposed any form of artificial contraception. Nevertheless, five pharmaceutical companies were attempting to sell "the pill" there. One of these companies, Wyeth Suaco, agreed to permit us to develop a case study on its marketing strategy. The approach described in the case can be summarized as follows:

A woman with four or five children would go to her local parish priest, typically from the Dominican or Benedictine order, for advice, saying something along the lines of, "Father, I really don't know what to do. I already am having trouble feeding and caring for my children, but my husband doesn't seem to understand how hard it is for me. He would like to have more kids, particularly sons. I am just about at the end of my rope." The priest might then say, "My daughter, I really can't help you. But why don't you visit my Jesuit colleague who may have some suggestions for you." The woman would then go to see the Jesuit priest who was a bit more liberal in his thinking. After listening to the woman, he might suggest the name of a particular gynecologist for the woman to visit. At the doctor's appointment, the physician would typically listen to the woman describe her dilemma and then ask her how regular her monthly menstrual cycle was. She might then say it was usually fairly regular, but not always. Whereupon the doctor would say that he could prescribe a pill that she could take that would ensure that she would always be regular in her cycle. He then would explain that, as a side effect, it would also prevent her from conceiving additional children. In other words, the Wyeth Suaco marketing approach was based on the charade of emphasizing that "the pill" was mainly being prescribed medically to regularize the woman's menstrual cycle rather than as a method of birth control!

The approach failed to meet with widespread success. To this day, the Catholic Church continues to oppose artificial contraception and the use of "the pill." And to this day upwards of 90 percent of Filipinos and Filipinas are practicing Catholics. The result? From a population of 33 million in the mid-sixties, the Filipino population has more than tripled over the last 50 years to more than 103 million! And, while the annual birth rate has declined to about 1.6 percent, the country's population continues to grow and over half of pregnancies are still unintended.

Before leaving the subject of birth control in the Philippines, I might add an amusing aside. When we were writing the foregoing case study, it was ironic that the director of the Philippine Population Institute that set forth family planning and population policies in the country was a woman named Mercedes Concepcion. However, since she was heavily involved in the issue of birth control and was unmarried, she was fond of encouraging people to call her Miss Concepcion!

I should also mention that every professor in our group, including me, taught an evening graduate course in each of the four semesters we were in the country. I taught marketing courses and the other professors taught finance, organizational behavior, and operations courses respectively. Each of us also mentored one or more of the Filipino professors who ultimately made up AIM's initial faculty.

One of the lessons that I learned from my assignment in the Philippines is that if you truly believe in your mission, your work is not just a job but rather becomes a calling. This brings out the best of your talents. It makes you eager to get up each morning with a spring in your step and an eagerness to meet and resolve any challenges that the day might bring. The truly fortunate people are those who really believe in what they are doing and are in a position to make a positive difference in the world, however small it may be. In my view, belief is a much more powerful motivator than money.

The title of this chapter is "Adventures in the Philippines." Certainly, my work in helping to create the Asian Institute of Management was one such adventure. But the Sorenson family had many other adventures there as well. One of these related to Charlotte's role in the creation of another new school in the Philippines.

Entrepreneurial Insight #8: Creating the International Co-Operative Pre-School

When we arrived in the Philippines, Kristin had recently turned four years old and Trina was about to turn three. Had they been back in Boston, we would have enrolled them at a pre-school there. In Manila, however, there were, at the time, no pre-schools that were appropriate for the children of international families.

To meet this need, Charlotte, together with Joan Wilson, the wife of the U.S. ambassador to the Philippines, established what subsequently became known as the International Co-Operative Pre-School. In short order, they enlisted the support of other international families with small children. Within the space of a few months, they obtained the necessary permits, located an appropriate venue in the spacious, airy basement of a local Unitarian church, hired a head of school and a team of qualified pre-school teachers, developed a curriculum, and opened the school's doors to students.

From the beginning, the school was a success. Soon, 80 children from 25 countries were enrolled in the program. Kristin and Trina, of course, were among the first to be enrolled. Years later, when Charlotte and I were attending a 25th anniversary celebration at AIM, we had the pleasure of seeing that the International Co-Operative Pre-School was still very much in existence. In fact, it had been relocated to a new venue in a three-story building very close to AIM in Makati.

Lesson Learned: Entrepreneurship in thought and action has application at all levels of education.

Charlotte, freed by Gloria (our children's "ya-ya") and the rest of our household staff from her previous 24-hour-a-day job as mother, housekeeper, cook, and chauffeur, also found time to engage in two other educational endeavors.

In year two of our Philippine stay she taught part-time in the kindergarten of the American School in Makati. She also conducted a summer playschool program in our house for about 20 international and Filipino children who were brought daily by the chauffeurs of some of our family friends and were typically accompanied by their ya-yas.

From a family point of view, one of the most memorable occasions of our Philippine stay was the Christmas party we gave at our house for our kids and about 30 of their friends the second year we were there. Charlotte persuaded Brother Hyacinth Gabriel, president of De La Salle College, to stuff all of his 300 pounds of avoirdupois into a Santa Claus outfit that she had made for him. At the height of the party as the children were dancing around the heavily ornamented Christmas tree made of wicker, there suddenly was a commotion on the street outside. All the children exited the house to see what it was all about. And what to their wondering eyes did they see, but a tiny brown pony pulling a two-wheeled open calesa (cart) down the street, with an enormous white-bearded Santa Claus in the back.

Brother Gabriel was so heavy that when he had climbed into the cart, he had shifted the balance so much that the little pony pulling the cart literally levitated slightly off his feet! As the cart approached the house, Santa cried: "HO, HO, HO! MERRY CHRISTMAS! MERRY CHRISTMAS!" He then lumbered down out of the cart (much to the relief of the poor little pony) and came into the house with his huge bag of presents. The children were wildly excited. After ascertaining that all of the children had been extremely good during the past year, he passed out Christmas treasures to each of them. The party was a smashing success!

Adventures in the Philippines

Charlotte and I had a far livelier social life in the Philippines than at any time before or since. The Filipinos knew how to work hard, but also how to have fun and enjoy themselves. They looked for any excuse to entertain. They were constantly giving going-away parties (despididas), welcome home parties (bienvenidas), birthday parties, anniversary parties, and any number of holiday celebratory parties. Given the omnipresence of household help among well-to-do and upper-middle-class families, entertaining in the Philippines was clearly much easier than in the United States.

As a consequence of these local customs, two or three times a week, we went to cocktail parties, dinners, dances, or other forms of entertainment. Most of the events were very elegant affairs, many of them involving black-tie outfits for the men and formal dresses with elaborate hairdos and lots of jewelry for the ladies. Charlotte, with her reserved New England background, was not a particular fan of these extravagantly lavish events. Nevertheless, she was a good sport about attending them and found that they provided a fascinating insight into the Filipino culture. When she did attend them, she typically charmed everyone with her warm smile, gracious manner, and intelligent conversation. It helped that, in her party finery, she always looked absolutely beautiful and glamorous.

Not all of our time in the Philippines was spent in the rarified atmosphere of the upper-class stratum of society. While we had many friends in the international, academic, and high-level business communities, we also made it a point to learn something about the rest of Philippine society, culture, and economy. One memorable adventure in this regard involved our visit to the aboriginal Mangyan tribe on the island of Mindoro in the Philippine archipelago.

Several months into our stay in the country, Charlotte and I met a Filipino lawyer who, as a hobby, pursued a secondary career as a passionate anthropologist. When we met him, he was very excited about the fact that in his explorations around the Philippines he had recently stumbled upon a hitherto unknown aboriginal tribe of people living deep in the heart of the jungle on Mindoro Island. They called themselves "Mangyans."

Our friend stated that he and a few of his anthropologist colleagues had been the first, and to date, the only people from the "civilized world" to interact with this tribe. We expressed great interest and asked him to describe the tribe's culture. He replied that reality was worth a thousand words and that if we were really serious about wanting to learn about these aboriginal people, he would be willing to have us accompany him on his next visit to them. We were thrilled by the idea and immediately accepted his invitation. He said the only condition of our going with him was that we had to promise not to later publicize our visit or spread the word about the tribe's existence. The Mangyans had made clear to him by signs that they wanted to keep their existence a secret from the outside world. We duly made the promise.

So it was that, several weeks later, we set off on an expedition with him. Our journey involved an eight-hour trip by bus to the southern coast of Luzon island, followed by a three-hour ferry boat ride to the island of Mindoro, and then a two-hour trek by pony and on foot to the jungle venue of the Mangyans.

Our first glimpse of them made an indelible impression. All of them were quite small. The tallest of them were perhaps 5'1" or 5'2" in height. The men were clothed only in loincloths. The women wore wrap-around woven skirts, and either were bare-breasted or had "bras" consisting of a simple band made of woven plant fibers. The insides of their mouths were all beet red from chewing the betel nut that they used as a mild stimulant. They kept their betel nut supplies inside corked bamboo containers about six inches long. The outsides of the containers were carved with stick-like hieroglyphics that our anthropologist friend thought was an ancient language yet to be deciphered. Several of the men we met carried pet monkeys on their shoulders. Most also carried wooden bows with bowstrings made of twisted plant fibers and had arrows with tips made of sharpened flint stone or quartz.

There was no "village" or community center. Rather, the huts they lived in were widely scattered two or three hundred yards apart in the tropical rain forest. Most were within a short walking distance of a broad river that was their source of water for drinking, cooking, and washing. The huts were extremely simple structures made of clay or bamboo with "palapa" type thatched roofs. Some of the huts were perched in trees.

During our three-day stay, we met about 30 or 40 Mangyans. About half were adults and half were children, from babes in arms to teenagers. All were very friendly to us . . . mainly because our anthropologist friend, whom they had come to trust over a period of many of his visits, had vouched for us and indicated that we were his friends. Both the men and women seemed to be relaxed and enjoying life and one another's company. There was lots of smiling and frequent bursts of laughter.

During our visit, we could discern little community structure or governance. To the extent that there was a headman, he appeared to be a respected village elder named Agau.

His hut was the one most visited, and whenever there was an audience, Agau seemed to love telling stories in the Mangyan language that none of us visitors from the outside could understand. Many of Agau's stories evidently had a funny punch line that brought out uproarious laughter on his part and many red-toothed smiles from those gathered around. It appeared to us that most of the Mangyans took great joy in life. Of course, much of this is surmise, since our communications with them consisted mainly of sign language and a few words of their language that our anthropologist friend had picked up.

The Mangyans led a subsistence-level life and survived mainly on a few edible crops that they planted around their huts and the bananas, papaya, mangoes, and other tropical fruits that grew in their rainforest. Some of them also had a few chickens, goats, or domesticated boars.

At the suggestion of our anthropologist friend, we had brought along, as gifts, little packets of laundry detergent and a number of small packages of unstrung multicolored beads. The first had a practical value, since the Mangyans commonly suffered from lice and ringworms. On receiving the detergent packets, many immediately went to wash themselves under a waterfall in the river to rid themselves of their lice and to cleanse their ringworm adhesions. They seemed to greatly enjoy this cleansing ritual, since they thought it was great fun to play in the bubbles created by the interaction of the water with the strange and wonderful new powder called "detergent." The colored beads were also a great hit, since the women, in particular, loved to wear colorful baubles.

The visit to the Mangyans was an extraordinary experience for us. It created a fascinating memory that is still with us. Today, though the Mangyans are no longer unknown to the outside world, they are still trying to preserve their largely isolated culture and way of life in the jungle.

Apart from visiting Indigenous people, we also traveled extensively in various parts of the Philippines. A favorite destination was the mountain village of Baguio in the north of the island of Luzon. Because of its altitude and geographic location, Baguio was always cooler and less humid than sea-level Manila. Hence, it was a resort-like refuge for those seeking an occasional escape from the heat, humidity, and clamor of the capital city. For a number of years after World War II, it was the site of Fort John Hay, which served as an "R&R" resort for American military personnel stationed at other U.S. military bases scattered around the country. The town was also home to the Baguio Country Club, which had an excellent golf course, a number of clay tennis courts, and a well-equipped playground for small children.

Everyone in the Sorenson family enjoyed the occasional long weekends that we spent in Baguio. Kristin, Trina, and Eric loved going for pony rides and playing in the playground. Charlotte and I made good use of the golf course and tennis courts. And we all loved wandering around the colorful market area of the town, where local craftsmen, artisans, and artists displayed their handicrafts and works of art.

During one of our family stays in Baguio we experienced a sample of Mother Nature's power and fury. While asleep one night in a small wooden bungalow, we suddenly awakened to find the entire structure shaking and rocking violently. The bedroom dresser and a standing lamp were knocked over and the mattresses on our beds were heaving up and down. After what seemed like minutes, but actually was probably only about 30 seconds, the shaking stopped and was replaced by an eerie stillness. We had been in the midst of a full-scale earthquake! Fortunately, none of us was hurt. But the earthquake had wrought extensive damage on the town and its surrounding area. We were happy to have escaped relatively unscathed.

On another occasion, Charlotte and I spent a hilarious weekend camping out overnight with our friends, Bobby and Monica Ongpin, on a disappearing beach on a tiny island in the Hundred Islands area off the coast of Luzon. Bobby had been my partner in formulating the Master Plan for AIM. His wife, Monica, was Chilean by birth and had met Bobby while she was studying at Mount Holyoke College in the U.S. and Bobby was earning his MBA degree at Harvard. They had become good friends of ours and we occasionally got together socially.

On the weekend in question, we drove to the Hundred Islands and hailed some local fishermen who agreed to paddle us in their wooden outrigger boat to one of the islands in the bay. There they dropped us off, promising to pick us up for the return trip to shore the following afternoon. The island was tiny, but it had a small sandy beach at the base of a vertical stone cliff on one of its sides. Provisioned with a bit of food and sleeping bags, we pretended we were shipwrecked and determined to play Robinson Crusoe for 24 hours.

After taking a swim and watching a beautiful sunset in the early evening, we dined on a cold roasted chicken we had brought with us. Afterward, having brought along an astronomy book of stars, we floated on our backs in the water and, looking up at a sparkling canopy of stars, tried to identify as many constellations as possible. Later, we climbed into our sleeping bags and went to sleep to the sound of lapping waves in the open air under the crystal-clear skies.

The only problem was that we had failed to take the tide into account in our planning. As the tide rose toward two in the morning, what had been a 25-foot beach from the water's edge to the base of the vertical cliff in the afternoon, was now only a 10-foot beach! And still the tide continued to rise. Awakened by the water lapping at our feet, we kept moving our sleeping bags closer and closer to the base of the cliff. Soon we had only nine feet. Then eight. Then seven. The situation was becoming dire. Finally, with only about four feet between the cliff and the water, the tide peaked and slowly, slowly began to subside. The beach had all but disappeared! We managed to get some sleep the rest of the night while huddled under our sleeping bags in a sitting position, with our backs pressed against the wall of the cliff.

The following morning, after a largely inedible breakfast of "salt-water soup" prepared by simmering the chicken bones from the previous night's dinner in seawater, we spent a lazy morning reading, talking, and swimming. In mid-morning, I put on my snorkeling gear and flippers and swam away from the island to explore the underwater marine life around some neighboring islands in the bay. The area was teeming with a great variety of tropical fish and beautiful coral reefs. After about 30 minutes, I looked down and about 12 feet down on the ocean floor, spotted what initially looked to me like a submerged ceramic Etruscan vase encrusted by barnacles. "Wow," I thought, "I've found a sunken treasure in the form of an ancient artifact!" I dove down to give it closer scrutiny. Imagine my puzzlement when I discovered that the vase had what appeared to be some tentacles sticking out from it. Then, I suddenly realized what I was seeing. It was a metal explosive underwater sea mine that was no doubt left over from World War II! Scared witless and having no idea whether it might still be active, I gingerly avoided touching the wires protruding from the mine and swam away from it as quickly as possible. So much for discovering sunken treasure!

Other travels in the Philippines spanned the country from the northern tip of Luzon to the city of Davao on the southern island of Mindanao. We explored the famous rice terraces near Baguio, the Ifugao headhunting territory, large sugar, coconut, and pineapple plantations, small rice farms, and many rural villages scattered around the country.

We also shot the river rapids in a dugout canoe for a visit to the locally famous Pagsanjan Falls. The falls were indeed impressive. At their base was a freshwater pool that beckoned all visitors for a swim in its cool, clear water. It was even possible to swim in the turbulent water under the falls and between it and the rock face behind it. This I did. Imagine my dismay when, climbing out of the pool, I discovered that the turbulence had loosened the wedding band on my ring finger to the extent that it had evidently dropped off and sunk to the very bottom of the pool some 20 feet below the surface. Always thinking on the positive side, Charlotte and I convinced ourselves that the pool was like a wishing well and that leaving the ring on its bottom as an offering was a good omen that foretold a long and happy marriage for us. More than a half-century later we have concluded that the omen must have, indeed, been a very powerful one!

CHAPTER TWENTY

TRAVELS IN ASIA

Our travels from 1966 to the end of 1968 were not confined to the Philippines. On one occasion in early 1967, Charlotte and I left Kristin, Trina, and Eric in the capable hands of Gloria and the rest of our household staff and traveled to Cambodia, Burma, India, and Nepal.

Our flight from Manila to Cambodia included a brief refueling stop in Saigon, Vietnam, where the Vietnam War was still in full swing. As passengers on a commercial flight, however, we neither saw nor heard any signs of military activity while we were on the ground.

In Cambodia, we had the privilege of visiting the famous site of Angkor Wat shortly before it was closed to the public for more than 20 years. Angkor Wat is an extraordinary temple complex that was serially constructed from the 9th to the 15th centuries by both Hindus and Buddhists. The largest and best-preserved temple was built by the Hindus in the early 12th century and is called Angkor Wat, after which the whole complex is named. By the end of the 15th century, the entire complex had been re-enveloped by the jungle and literally disappeared. It was not rediscovered until 1860.

When we visited Angkor Wat, it had not yet been developed for tourist purposes. There was only one tiny guesthouse outside the walls of the complex where a team of French archaeologists was staying. The operators of the guesthouse were kind enough to rent us a room there for our overnight stay. We were practically the only tourists on the site.

The sight of the temple complex filled us with awe. Upwards of a hundred Buddhist monks, all clad in colorful saffron robes, inhabited the site and spent their days and much of their nights praying, meditating, and chanting. The temples and other structures had originally been constructed of stone with wooden lintels above their doors. Termites, causing many of the structures partially to collapse, had long since devoured the wooden lintels. Thousands of bats darted in and out of all the structures. There was an overpowering stink of bat droppings. The entire scene was a massive mish-mash of Hindu and Buddhist architecture with many of the temples and other structures still being totally imprisoned in the root structures of gigantic jungle trees. It was all quite eerie. We have never seen anything like it either before or since. We felt it a privilege to be witness to the interplay between the indomitable force of nature and the ambitious, but impermanent, works of humanity.

Following our visit to Cambodia, we made a one-day stop in Burma (now called Myanmar) where we were deeply impressed by the grandeur of its many Buddhist temples and pagodas and with the golden glitter of their pointed roof spires. Then it was on to India.

On landing in New Delhi we were met by a representative of the Ford Foundation, who settled us into the colonial splendor of the famous Imperial Hotel. Built in the mid-1930s, the hotel personified all the pomp and elegance of the British Raj. We felt we were in a different world. Inside its walled-in grounds, with its expansive lawns and gardens, impressive colonial architecture, gracious lobbies and restaurants, tradition of high tea, and army of impeccably mannered staff members, guests were made to feel totally pampered. Outside its walls, one immediately encountered the sights, sounds, and smells of deep poverty. The contrast was stark and difficult to absorb.

Nevertheless, we were intoxicated by all that New Delhi had to offer. Its horse- and human-drawn conveyances, bazaars, ubiquitous beggars, curry-laden foods, and the general clatter of densely packed humanity were all new and fascinating to us. What I remember best about that first trip to India was its many different smells, its hot and humid climate, and its overall feeling of poverty punctuated by occasional displays of opulence and great wealth.

After spending a few days in New Delhi, we headed out of the city to explore a bit more of India. The Ford Foundation delighted us with the loan of a car and driver to facilitate our travels. We followed the well-worn Indian tourist route by visiting Jaipur, Jodhpur, and Agra. In Jaipur, Rajasthan's largest city, we stayed in what formerly was a maharaja's palace that was complete with an ancient indoor swimming pool that had a large knotted rope strung from its ceiling on which one could swing out over the middle of the pool and drop with a splash into the water. Naturally, both Charlotte and I tried it! The standout of our stay in Jaipur was our visit to the remarkable Jantar Mantar outdoor observatory. Built in the mid-1730s, it houses the world's largest sundial, as well as a number of geometric devices for measuring time, predicting eclipses, and tracking stars' location.

In Jodhpur, we were duly dazzled by visits to the massive and well preserved Mehrangarh Fort and views of the Blue City of Brahmpur, where almost all houses are painted the same shade of light blue.

Then there was Agra, where the beauty of the Taj Mahal stunned us. It is perhaps the single most beautiful edifice I have ever seen. Viewing it almost literally took our breath away. Completed in 1653 after 22 years of construction by 20,000 workers, it was conceived and built by Shah Jahan, Emperor of the Mughal Empire, as a tribute to his beloved wife, Mumtaz Jahan. It remains one of the "Seven Wonders of the World." Almost equally memorable for us was a visit to the palace where Shah Jahan was held under house arrest by his sons for eight years until his death in 1666. From the balcony of the suite of rooms in which he was imprisoned, he had a daily view of the magnificent monument that he had built for his wife. It must have aroused poignant memories for him. After his death, he was quietly buried next to Mumtaz in the Taj Mahal.

The final stops on our Indian tour were visits to Calcutta (now called Kolkata) and Benares (now called Varanasi). On the first morning of our stay in Calcutta, we were totally shocked and dismayed when, following breakfast, we exited our hotel and observed men with carts picking up bodies of street dwellers who had died—mostly of starvation—in the course of the night. Rats also infested the streets. It was a sobering sight. Later that day, in our wanderings around the city, everywhere we looked we saw devastating poverty and hungry people. The memory is still indelibly etched in my mind. After just a day in Calcutta, we couldn't wait to leave the misery behind.

Far and away the most striking experience in Varanasi was the visit we made to the sacred Ganges River. As we drifted downriver in a small boat, we witnessed sacred Hindu cremation ceremonies taking place all along the shores. Smoke wafted up from the funeral pyres where dead bodies were being burned into ashes in front of mourning family members and friends. When the cremation process was complete and the soul of the deceased had been released from its body, the ashes that remained were scattered over the waters of the Ganges. It was said that, in Varanasi, there is a riverside cremation every minute of every day of the year. Our Varanasi experiences brought home to us how varied the customs and belief systems of different cultures around the world are.

The last country we visited on our visit to the Asian subcontinent was Nepal. We stayed at the Palace Hotel, a cold, drafty, and somewhat run-down former maharaja's palace. It was in the process of being renovated by Boris, an eccentric expatriate Russian. We slept on a creaky bed with a lumpy mattress in a cavernous room overlooking a courtyard. Our bathroom was vast in size but, unfortunately, had no hot water and a toilet that didn't work.

The hotel and Boris were well known to the Himalayan mountaineering community. Most of the climbers attempting to scale the peaks of Mount Everest or K-2 in the late 1960s stayed at the Palace Hotel when in Kathmandu. While we were there, we met Barry Bishop, his wife, Lila, and their two small children. Barry had been a member of the first American team to scale Everest in 1963. He had lost all of his toes and the tip of a little finger on the expedition because of frostbite and, as a result, he had given up technical climbing. When we met him, he had returned to Nepal to do cultural/ecological research on an area in western Nepal for his University of Chicago PhD dissertation. He was also a gifted professional photographer who was employed by the National Geographic Society for much of his life.

Kathmandu itself was wonderfully colorful. In our wanderings around the town we encountered very few tourists, but quite a few monkeys, colorfully dressed women and children, turbaned men, and lively bazaars. The streets were made of dirt, and in many places, they were muddy and awash with sewage or littered with trash. There were almost no cars or trucks.

We were struck by the number of ornate Hindu temples, austere Buddhist stupas, and other religious pagodas and shrines scattered throughout the city. The elaborate erotic stone fertility carvings on some of the Hindu temples were particularly intriguing. We learned that the majority of Nepalese practiced both Hinduism and Buddhism, but that many other religions also were tolerated and actively practiced in the Kathmandu Valley. These included Jainism, Sikhism, Islam, Bahai, and Christianity. We felt lucky to be able to visit Nepal when it was still largely undeveloped and free of the commercialization and rampant tourism that have characterized the country in recent years.

Midway through our two-year stay in the Philippines, the whole family made an around-the-world trip back to the United States, with intermediate stops along the way.

The first such stop was in Kashmir. We ended up loving Kashmir, but flying both to and from there turned into harrowing experiences. Having flown from Manila, we arrived at the New Delhi airport close to midnight the same day. Having a connecting flight to Srinagar at 7:00 a.m. the following day, we first stopped at the Indian Airlines desk in the airport to reconfirm our reservations and to be told that we had to check back at the same counter five and a half hours later at 6:00 a.m. Then all five of us took a taxi to a nearby hotel where we napped for a few hours. Bright and early, we were back at the Indian Airlines airport counter as we had been instructed at 6:00 a.m. to check in for the flight to Kashmir. Imagine our dismay when the agent behind the counter said:

"Oh, I am so sorry, Mr. Sorenson, but that flight already took off about 15 minutes ago."

With incredulity in my voice, I replied:

"What do you mean 'the flight just took off'? I was here at this counter just six hours ago to reconfirm that the flight would depart at 7:00 a.m. and that we should be back here to check in at 6:00 a.m., which we are! How could the flight have already departed?"

Agent: "Well, I don't know what you were told. All I know is that the plane has already left."

I then spotted behind the counter the very man who had been there the night before, had reconfirmed our flight, and told us to be back at 6:00 a.m. to check in. So I then pointed to that man and expostulated:

"Look, there is the agent with whom I spoke last night. Ask him if what I am telling you is correct."

The agent before me turned his head to look and then returned his gaze to me and said to me in a voice he might have used to explain something to a child: "Oh, that's Mr. Singh. That explains everything. Mr. Singh did not know that the departure time for the flight had been changed, so naturally he could not have told you the correct time to arrive back here to check in. The five of you will just have to wait and take the next flight that has space on it."

Me (by this time getting hot under the collar):

"Well, that's an absurd explanation. In any case, what time does the next flight to Srinagar leave?"

Agent: "At 2:30 p.m. this afternoon, but one never knows for sure. And then, we have to make sure we have space for you."

Me (almost ready to explode):

"Look, I'm traveling with my wife and three very small children, all under the age of five. All of us are totally exhausted, having flown from Manila and slept only about three hours last night. And now you tell us that the next flight for Kashmir doesn't leave for more than eight hours and that you are not even sure there will be room for us on that flight! Surely, you can do better than that!"

Agent: "Now calm yourself, Mr. Sorenson. We will do the best we can. Meanwhile, you are welcome to try to find some seats until this afternoon in the cafeteria or in the airport waiting areas. And do try to learn how to calm yourself. Getting upset is not good for your well-being."

Clearly this conversation was going nowhere. So, with Charlotte also trying to convince me that "getting upset was not good for my well-being," I dutifully followed her, Kristin, Trina, and Eric up some stairs to a mezzanine where we found seats in the dingy cafeteria and sat down to wait. And wait. And wait!

At this point, I should add that even though it was still only a little past seven in the morning, the temperature was already above 95 degrees Fahrenheit and the air in the non-air-conditioned airport was both extremely hot and fetid.

Moreover, even though we were sitting in a cafeteria, we were almost paranoid about the children eating Indian food or drinking Indian water. We were sure that doing so would lead to food poisoning and possibly even to instant death. Soon, however, our exhausted kids were howling that they were tired and hungry and that they desperately wanted something to eat and drink. So we ordered some hardboiled eggs, toast with jam, and what ended up being countless bottles of Coca-Cola that we knew wasn't good for the teeth but at least, we rationalized, wouldn't lead to dysentery.

On one occasion during our ensuing wait, Trina wandered off and attached herself to an Indian family with young children and we spotted her from a distance as she was leaving the terminal with them. I dashed after her, grabbing her just before she disappeared with them in the milling crowds outside the exit. On another occasion, we had to spring to the rescue of Eric who almost fell over the edge of the mezzanine, which had no railing, onto the floor below. The terminal was still under construction!

Shortly before 1:00 p.m., after we had been waiting in the sweltering heat for about six hours, a representative of Indian Airlines found us still in the cafeteria and said:

"Ah, Mr. Sorenson, there you are with your fine little family. I have very good news for you. We have found a place for all of you on our 2:30 p.m. flight to Srinagar and, not only that, I am to take you out to board the flight immediately, ahead of all of the other passengers."

"Great!" we thought. "That's very nice of them to arrange a special boarding for us."

Our guide proceeded to lead us out on the tarmac and up the stairs and into the airplane. The only thing he hadn't told us was that the airplane had been parked all day in the sun. Since the outside temperature was by now 105 degrees, it was like entering an oven! Our escort led us to the very first row of seats right behind the cockpit and told us the entire row of seats was ours and to make ourselves comfortable. This meant that four of us could have seats of our own and we could hold two-year-old Eric on our laps. Then our escort left. Thereupon, we sat down in our seats, one of which promptly fell out of its moorings and onto the floor. Although a mechanic came aboard and re-attached the seat, we nevertheless ended up sitting in the sweltering heat (by this time at least 115 degrees inside the plane) for almost an hour and a half! By the time the other passengers boarded the plane, we all felt totally dehydrated and miserable.

Then came the straw that almost broke the camel's back. At 2:25 p.m., five minutes before the plane's scheduled departure and after we thought all the other passengers had boarded, there was a stir at the back of the plane. Whereupon the flight attendant came up to our row and said that she was sure we would understand, but at the last minute, the wife of the co-pilot was coming on board because she had had an emergency in the family back in Kashmir and, consequently, we would have to share our seats with her and her three children! We were incredulous. It ended up that she and one of her children occupied two seats on one side of the aisle and held her other two children on their laps. Charlotte and I, in turn, occupied the other two seats in the row with Kristin and Trina on our laps and we farmed out Eric to another accommodating woman passenger in the row behind us. It was like the famous television commercial showing nine people stuffed into a Volkswagen Bug. The situation was so outrageous it was funny. We ended up accepting it all in good humor and were thankful for the Good Samaritan Indian woman who held Eric on her lap for the entire flight.

When we finally landed in Srinagar, the door of the plane opened and sweetly perfumed breezes from scented flowers growing in the Vale of Kashmir greeted us. Outside, green fields and fruit orchards in full bloom covered the entire valley. The temperature was perfect, 30 degrees cooler than what we had experienced in New Delhi. Our first impression was that we had landed in paradise.

We were met at the airport by Gulfar, a Muslim-born Kashmiri, who drove us to the beautiful wooden flat-bottomed houseboat where we were to stay during our week-long sojourn in Kashmir. Named the *Merry Dawn*, it was exquisitely furnished inside by intricately woven oriental rugs on which colorful pillows were strewn in great profusion. Low tables adorned with flowers and candles dotted the main salon. A faint and delicate scent of incense wafted through the air. Large windows that overlooked the Jhelum River, on whose banks the *Merry Dawn* was moored, rounded out the ambiance. The whole ensemble was like a scene straight out of the *Arabian Nights*. We suddenly felt like Oriental potentates or maharajas.

Each morning, shortly after sunrise, long, slim boats (called shikaras) would sidle up to the *Merry Dawn* with smiling Kashmiris offering fresh fruits and vegetables, bouquets of flowers, exquisite handmade jewelry, semi-precious stones, handwoven shawls, vividly painted lacquered boxes, and a variety of other local artisan handicrafts. Moored behind the *Merry Dawn* was its small "kitchen boat" in which our cook was able to whip up the most delicious meals imaginable, prepared over an open wood fire. Our favorite specialty was his light and airy walnut soufflés that were worthy of any five-star restaurant. Their delicate flavor literally melted in one's mouth.

Gulfar, the owner of the *Merry Dawn*, was a great storyteller. The most memorable tale he told us was autobiographical. It seems that when he was a young man in his twenties, his Muslim parents had arranged a marriage for him with the young daughter of another family who was willing to commit to paying a substantial dowry to the groom. Gulfar's family evidently thought it would be a good match, even though neither they nor Gulfar had met the young bride-to-be in person until the day of the wedding, when she arrived for the occasion completely dressed in a black burka with only her eyes showing. The bride and groom duly went through the marriage ceremony and were pronounced man and wife.

A celebratory dinner followed with many guests in attendance. Toward the end of the evening, with the festivities still going on, the bride and groom ceremoniously retired to the nuptial chamber. There, Gulfar finally had the opportunity to unveil his new bride. Which he did. And when he did, he evidently took one look and said to himself, "Oh, no! This isn't going to work."—or words to that effect. Whereupon, he gathered up his clothes and wallet and climbed out the back window of the nuptial chamber. Dropping to the ground, he surreptitiously sneaked off under cover of night and ultimately made his way undiscovered out of Kashmir. He then embarked on a series of travels that ended up in Australia, where he subsequently served as the "batman," or servant, to a colonel in the British Army.

About a dozen years after his flight from Kashmir, Gulfar evidently decided that the coast was sufficiently clear for him to return home. This he did, having saved enough money in the interim to buy the *Merry Dawn* and establish himself as a local entrepreneur. He also married again, only this time it was to a bride of his own choosing. According to his account, he had subsequently been living happily ever after.

At the time, Charlotte and I were amused by his tale and laughed heartily along with him after he told us the story. In retrospect, however, the episode now seems more tragic than funny. First, there is the custom of arranged marriages that are still prevalent in many parts of the world and in which families offer large dowries to the families of prospective grooms to take their daughters off their hands. Second is the fact that the brides and grooms themselves often have little or no say in the matter and, as in the case of Gulfar, sometimes haven't even had a chance to meet and become acquainted with one another prior to the wedding.

Finally, in the particular case of Gulfar, one can only imagine the devastation, embarrassment, and humiliation that the bride herself, along with both families involved, must have felt for years following the wedding incident.

I realize that my views are colored by the fact that I come from a Western culture and should tread lightly when judging the cultural and religious practices in other parts of the world. On a very human level, however, no matter what one's belief system, the custom of arranged marriage without the full support of both bride and groom seems wrong to me.

During our stay in Kashmir, one other notable cultural incident involving Gulfar occurred. One day we decided we would like to go with our kids to visit the tiny mountain village of Gulmarg, located about 50 kilometers outside of Srinagar near the still-disputed border between India and Pakistan. This involved a bus ride each way of about one and a half hours. Gulfar kindly agreed to drive us to the bus station in his rickety car. He proceeded to help us buy tickets and to accompany us onto the bus to make sure we were comfortably seated. Much to his chagrin, when he boarded the bus he found that there were only three open seats left on the bus for the five of us. Thereupon, in a voice loud enough to be heard throughout the bus, he called out for two volunteers to give up their seats so that all of the foreign visitors could be seated. No one moved. Becoming visibly upset, he confronted a turbaned Indian Sikh and held up his hand with fingers spread out in front of the man's face. The following verbal exchange ensued.

> Gulfar: "My friend. Please to notice the five fingers of my hand. You see that they are not all of the same length. And so it is with humans. Some should be treated with greater deference than others. In the case of foreign visitors that is the case and they should be given preference when traveling on the bus. So please to give up your seat to them."

> Sikh: "Ah! It is true that not all of the fingers are of the same length. But what is more important is that it is the same blood that runs through all of the fingers. And so it is with humans. Under the skin we are all equal and since I got here at the head of the queue I am staying in my seat."

Gulfar was clearly ready to rise to the bait and carry on the disputation, but Charlotte and I, both embarrassed and wanting to avoid an international incident, insisted that we didn't mind standing and implored him to not worry about us. Though he clearly would have preferred to carry on the philosophical debate, he finally stepped off the bus and waved us goodbye.

The exchange was less about the differences between Muslims and Sikhs and more about differences in caste and social position.

In Gulmarg, Kristin, Trina, and Eric all delighted in riding horses with the spectacular Himalayan mountain range as a dramatic backdrop. Meanwhile, Charlotte and I were fascinated by the vignette of an Indian woman in a beautiful silk sari falling off her horse as a result of the inattention of a young Kashmiri boy who was holding the horse's reins and allowed it to buck its rider off. The unfortunate lady's sari flew up over her head as she hit the ground, allowing all the onlookers to learn that some Indian damsels wear nothing under their saris. Meanwhile, the tall, stern Kashmiri man who was in overall charge of the horses paid no attention to the lady in distress, but rather attacked the young inattentive groom and beat him ferociously across the face with his fur cap. The real casualty of the incident was the mortified woman's sense of dignity.

Back in Srinagar, we enjoyed exploring the city. We had a magical visit to the fabled Gardens of Shalimar, where many Kashmiris were spending a lazy afternoon strolling about or sitting on oriental rugs spread on the grass chatting and smoking their hookahs. While there, three-year-old Trina managed to fall into a pool with a fountain in its center. Since her clothes got soaked, I took off my T-shirt and gave it to her to wear while they were drying. It hung down to her ankles and made her look like a little tow-haired ghost dressed all in white. She immediately became the center of attention for many of the visitors to the park, who surrounded her and gaped at the little foreign apparition. The mishap had a happy outcome in that a friendly Kashmiri family invited all five of us to have afternoon tea and shortbread with them in the gardens.

Other explorations took us to a workshop where three generations of a single family were busy weaving intricately patterned rugs. The process fascinated us and led to our purchasing our first-ever genuine oriental rug. We still have it to this day. Knowing the family that had woven it has lent special appeal to it. Of course, it didn't cross our minds at the time that some of the nimble fingers that helped create the rug belonged to 10 or 11-year-old children who might have been better served spending their time going to school. If Kashmir had child labor laws in those days, they certainly weren't being enforced.

We also spent time just walking through the town, visiting bazaars, sampling restaurants, haggling with street merchants, and generally enjoying the universal sport of people-watching.

Our visit to Kashmir had an unexpected ending. On the day we were scheduled to fly back to New Delhi, a cold front settled in that brought rain and a heavy cloud cover. When Gulfar drove us to the airport, we learned that all flights out of Srinagar had been cancelled since, given the lack of visibility, there was a risk that the planes couldn't gain altitude fast enough to fly above the 20,000-foot mountain passes that surrounded the Kashmir Valley. We were secretly happy at the delay since we were enjoying our stay so much.

We were less pleased when the same thing happened the following day, given that we had to make connections in New Delhi for the next leg of our journey that was to take us to Europe. Finally, on the third day of the delay, Gulfar drove us once again to the airport where we learned that the airport was still closed but that there was a slight chance that the weather might clear toward the end of the afternoon when there was still enough daylight to make a visual takeoff (nighttime takeoffs and landings were not permitted). After we waited at the airport for much of the afternoon, there finally was an announcement that a 30-minute window of visibility prior to sunset was anticipated, during which they were going to permit all of the 11 aircraft that had been stranded at the airport to attempt takeoffs.

On hearing the announcement, I rushed up to the Indian Airlines counter to make sure we knew which airplane to board. On my way back to where Charlotte and the children were waiting, I passed a counter where you could buy flight insurance. Imagine my dismay when I heard a rather large Englishman shouting at the insurance agent saying: "WHAT DO YOU MEAN, YOU WON'T SELL ME ANY FLIGHT INSURANCE?" In a calm voice, the agent said, "I am very sorry, sir, we have been notified by our Delhi headquarters that all of these upcoming departures have been determined to be much too dangerous for us to be willing to sell insurance on them. I'd advise you not to fly on any of them."

What a dilemma! What should I do? There I was with my entire family, more precious to me than anything else in the world. Should we take a chance and fly? Or should we cancel and wait until the next day when it still wasn't certain that planes would be flying? In the end, without saying anything to Charlotte about my qualms, I decided to "breathe deeply in faith" and have all of us board the plane. It turned out I made the right choice. Despite my white knuckles during takeoff, the plane rose successfully through the clouds into the clear sky where we were suddenly treated to one of the most spectacular sunsets we had ever seen. It cast a rosy light on the entire Himalayan mountain range, including Mount Everest and K-2, in all its majestic glory.

With a huge sense of relief, we landed in New Delhi and transferred within the hour to a British Airways-operated airliner bound for Vienna, Austria, via Beirut, Lebanon. We were greeted on board with hot face towels, refreshing drinks, comfortable seats, and extremely gracious flight attendants. Whew! What a relief!

Despite our hazardous adventures flying on Indian Airlines, I would be remiss in closing the chapter on our Kashmiri visit without mentioning that of all the more than 60 countries I have visited so far, Kashmir is the one area I most crave to visit again. That's how much of a hold it continues to have on me. Unfortunately, as I write these lines, the Muslim/Hindu political conflict is still sufficiently tense that a second visit isn't, for the moment, prudent.

The rest of our around-the-world, home-leave trip went smoothly. After touching down briefly to refuel in Beirut, our flight took us on to Vienna where we had a several-hours wait between flights. During the layover, our Viennese friends, Herr and Frau Guschlbauer, met us at the airport and took the five of us for lunch in an outdoor restaurant on the shores of the nearby Danube River. Dining on fresh fish from the river and sipping wine, we spent a restful interlude exchanging news about our respective families and various current events of the day.

Then it was on to Lausanne, where we spent a few days renewing acquaintances with our friends from our time living there during the first years of our marriage. Little had changed. Switzerland was as beautiful as ever. The Swiss, with the exception of our friends, were as reserved as ever. And the country was as prosperous as ever . . . quite a contrast from the poverty we had witnessed throughout Southeast Asia.

From Switzerland, we flew back to the U.S., where we had welcoming visits with Charlotte's family in Stockbridge and my family in Mansfield. The two sets of grandparents were thrilled to see Charlotte and me and even more thrilled to see Kristin, Trina, and Eric.

After returning to the Philippines for the second year of my assignment there, we had one more family trip that took us to Japan and Hong Kong. The Japanese portion of the trip led to a lifelong love affair with traditional Japan. We were less charmed by modern Japan, with its overuse of concrete and the din and clatter of its large cities like Tokyo and Osaka.

We were especially captivated by Kyoto, with its exquisite gardens, its well-preserved classical architecture, and its overall sense of quiet beauty. We also became enamored of the aesthetic simplicity embodied in its delicately crafted works of art and ceramics. That trip resulted in the first of many subsequent purchases of antique "tansu," or Japanese chests and handcrafted ceramic bowls and vases.

One night while in Kyoto, Charlotte and I left Kristin, Trina, and Eric in the care of the daughter of the proprietor of the "ryokan," or traditional Japanese inn where we were staying, while we went out to have dinner with some friends. As was typical in Japanese inns, our adjoining bedrooms had tatami mat floors, futons for beds, shoji screen sliding doors, and little else. They were models of simplicity.

While we were gone, the children decided they would entertain each other and the babysitter by putting on a stage show using some hand puppets they had collected during the trip. Kristin went first and instructed her sister, brother, and the babysitter to sit in one room facing the shoji screen sliding doors that separated it from the other room. She then went into the other room and punched holes right through several of the paper panels so that she could entertain her audience with her hand puppet play. Of course, Trina and Eric then wanted to get into the action and thrust their hand puppets through a number of other shoji screen panels. The innkeeper's daughter, perhaps intimidated by her high-spirited foreign charges, did nothing to stop the carnage.

Suitably appalled when we returned to the inn that evening, Charlotte and I immediately apologized for our unruly children and offered to pay the innkeeper for all damages. He just laughed and said not to worry about it, the shoji screens could be easily repaired.

On the way back to Manila, we had a brief stopover in Hong Kong, where we stayed at the Kowloon YMCA in rooms overlooking the water. We were impressed by the many colorful Chinese junks sailing about in the harbor and by the overall hustle and bustle of the city. Hong Kong, at the time still a British dominion, was clearly on an economic roll. I came away from the visit with the impression that Hong Kong was to China and Asia what Switzerland was to Europe.

As we headed for home, I reflected on how extraordinary it had been to observe so many critical events taking place in our home country from afar, and on two different occasions and from two different continents. While we were abroad, the Cuban Missile Crisis took the world to the brink of war, the assassinations of Robert Kennedy and Martin Luther King shook the country, and social unrest reached an unprecedented level. The Apollo moon missions tended to restore our sense of hope and possibility, while the ongoing war in Vietnam was a source of constant tension.

It was difficult to be away from home during difficult times, but it gave us a unique and broadened perspective on the U.S. that we would never have obtained if we had never left the country.

We found that, in general, the people we met abroad might not like American policies, but they did not blame individual Americans, including us, for the mistakes of our government. That is a distinction we brought home with us and it was one of the most valuable lessons from our travels.

CHAPTER TWENTY-ONE

TEACHING AT HARVARD

Year two of our stay in the Philippines passed quickly and soon it was time to return to Boston and my teaching assignment at Harvard. Thanks to the sleuthing of our friends Peter and Peggy Gunness, whom we had met when we lived in Peabody Terrace, we found a rambling Victorian house to rent that was conveniently located right next to Cambridge in Belmont, Massachusetts. Though we were hoping to eventually purchase a home, we thought that it would make sense to rent for a year or so until we could find just the right house for us. In the meantime, our Belmont house on Hillside Terrace suited us just fine. Large and comfortable, there was plenty of space for Kristin, Trina, and Eric each to have a bedroom of their own. The neighborhood school was only a block away and had a good reputation. And the commute for me to the business school took less than 15 minutes by car.

We arrived back in Boston at the end of October 1968. I returned with the satisfaction of having fulfilled and surpassed the expectations established by Harvard and the Ford Foundation at the outset of my assignment to the Philippines. Now my focus was to be on building a more traditional academic career through teaching, research, and consulting at HBS itself.

My agreement with Harvard Dean George Baker, Associate Dean Steve Fuller, and Chairman of the Marketing Department Walter Salmon was that on my return to the school, I would have a tenure track position as an assistant professor and initially teach the required first-year MBA marketing course, along with a team of five other instructors. Collectively, we would teach eight sections of the course, each with 90 students. Ultimately, the idea was that I would develop an International Marketing course. Harvard had never had such a course, but it was timely that one be developed, given the increasing internationalization of business in the world. My background seemed ideal for taking on such an assignment.

I took on the first-year marketing course assignment with a great sense of anticipation and enthusiasm. I especially loved the teaching part of my academic career. At Harvard Business School, the role of a teacher using the case method was more one of being a skillful orchestra conductor than that of a professor giving lectures to a classroom full of students. Case method teaching requires that instructors do their best to help students develop the ability to think independently for themselves and then learn to articulate their thoughts and reasoning in a clear, persuasive fashion to their fellow learners. Given that classes consist more of discussions and debates than of listening to lectures, one never knows what is going to happen. That makes it a lot more interesting and fun for both the teacher and the students. It also leads to better learning.

I took naturally to teaching using the case approach. Judging from the feedback I got from student evaluations at the end of each semester, I was pretty good at it, too.

In the second year of my teaching the required MBA first-year marketing course, I was asked to become chairman of the course. This involved coordinating the schedules of the five other professors teaching the course and chairing our twice-weekly meetings, in which we discussed the pedagogical approach that each of us planned to use in teaching various cases comprising the course. It also involved leading course design efforts and case development activities related to the course.

Simultaneously during this period, I began working on designing and writing case teaching materials for the international marketing course I launched in my fourth year back at Harvard. In the meantime, I was promoted to the rank of associate professor.

The International Marketing course was a success from the beginning. Each semester that I taught the course, it was fully subscribed with the maximum allowed number of 90 students signing up. In addition to the new cases that I developed after I returned to America, I also used the international marketing cases I had written in Central America as part of my doctoral dissertation as well as many of the cases I wrote or supervised during my stay in the Philippines. The object of the course was to help students understand how social, cultural, and economic differences from country to country can profoundly affect how one should go about marketing their goods or services in an international context.

In addition to developing my international marketing course, I was given the assignment of chairing a faculty committee set up to look at how the teaching skills of HBS faculty members could be further enhanced.

Then and now, doctoral programs in the U.S., and indeed throughout the world, have been notorious for how little attention they have paid to helping future instructors develop their teaching skills. Rather, they focus almost exclusively on teaching doctoral students how to perfect their research skills. What these candidates pick up about effective teaching they learn mainly by their experience as unsupervised teaching assistants, a hit-or-miss affair at best. Moreover, at most institutions of higher learning, whether or not one is an effective teacher is not given much weight when it comes to making tenure decisions. These decisions are made mainly on the basis of one's research skills as measured by the number of books written or articles published in refereed academic journals. This is true not only in the arts and sciences, but in the field of management as well.

In the early 1970s, Harvard was one of the few business schools where good teaching, while not as important as research, was nevertheless considered important and taken into consideration when it came to making tenure decisions. Thus, the mandate of the committee I chaired was to explore whether there were ways to improve the classroom skills of its faculty members and, particularly, of young faculty members.

At the culmination of its deliberations, the Committee on Methods of Instruction, as it was called, published a report containing several common sense recommendations.

During this period of my career, I also did some marketing consulting for a number of well-known companies and joined some boards of directors. The latter included General Housewares Corporation (a diversified manufacturer of housewares and outdoor furniture), Star Markets, Inc. (a New England regional supermarket chain), and Knapp King-Size Corporation (a retailer of clothing for big and tall men). Faculty members were granted one day a week to engage in such outside activities. Taking on these activities enhanced both my business acumen and my effectiveness as a teacher. They also enhanced our family bank account.

The third and weakest leg of my career activities during this period was research. Here, partly because of inclination and partly because of the effort I was putting into teaching and my other endeavors, both professional and personal, I was not spending a lot of time on scholarly research. Yes, I was a prolific writer of cases and teaching notes. And I researched and wrote a couple of articles that appeared in the *Harvard Business Review* and one or two other publications. But, I wrote no books and accumulated only a skimpy record of scholarly articles in refereed academic journals.

Which brings me to my first and greatest career disappointment.

At the time, faculty members at Harvard Business School were typically considered for the granting of tenure and full professorship in the ninth year of their academic appointment. I had been promoted to associate professor after my fourth year on the faculty. This had been a good sign because most of the weeding out of young faculty members had typically occurred between the assistant and associate professor appointment levels.

My case was a bit unusual, however, because my first two years as an assistant professor had been in the Philippines and did not involve the expectation of any academic research. Thus, by the ninth year of my appointment I had had less time than normal to compile a research record. Nevertheless, the faculty appointments committee decided to follow normal procedure and put me up for a tenure vote in the ninth year of my appointment. The final decision was to be made by a vote of all of the full professors on the faculty.

When the decision occurred in the spring of 1973, I was devastated to learn that there had been a split vote by the full professors and that since there had not been a substantial enough majority of ayes, I was not to be granted tenure at that time. Instead, Larry Fouraker, then dean of the school, informed me that I was to be granted a two-year extension as an associate professor to give me an additional period to strengthen my research record. At the end of the two years, my tenure decision was to be reconsidered. He added that my teaching record and my other service to the school had been considered outstanding, but that my research output had been inadequate.

I was enormously hurt and disheartened when I heard the news. I had thought that the tenure decision would be positive and would sail through without a problem. Thus, I was crushed to learn that this was not to be the case. Up until then, everything I had accomplished in my career had been done with flying colors. Now, suddenly, I had failed, and it rattled me to my core.

However, the decision turned out to be a blessing. To begin with, it made me see how fortunate I was to have Charlotte as my wife. From the moment we heard the negative news, she was totally loving and supportive every step of the way during the succeeding months when my self-confidence was badly in need of support. So, too, were the kids, although they were still too young to understand fully what the fuss was all about.

Second, it was a great lesson for me to learn that when one door closes in life, a second one almost always opens. So it was in this instance. And the new door that opened turned out to be one of the best things that happened to me. In short, it taught me that there is truth in the adage that crises often represent opportunities. In this case, my tenure crisis totally changed the future trajectory of my professional life and, in every way, for the better.

It also taught me that change, more often than not, leads to renewal. Like potted plants, we humans run the risk of becoming root-bound if we don't "repot" ourselves from time to time into more fertile soil. Renewal often has the ability to re-awaken one's curiosity and zest for life. It also can lead to new learning and the development of new skills.

CHAPTER TWENTY-TWO

A NEW PROFESSIONAL CHAPTER

What was this new door that opened for me?

One day in the late fall of 1973, I received a call from Mr. Jarvis Farley, chairman and CEO of the Massachusetts Indemnity and Life Insurance Company, a person whom I did not know. He asked me if I would join him for lunch at the Harvard Club as he had a matter he would like to discuss with me. We set a date and time for the lunch and I duly arrived at the Harvard Club on Commonwealth Avenue in Boston at the appointed hour. However, Mr. Farley wasn't there. After waiting about 15 minutes for him to show up, I made a series of telephone calls and finally discovered from his secretary that while I was waiting for him, *he* was waiting for *me* at the Downtown Harvard Club located in Boston's financial district. We had both forgotten to specify which of Boston's two Harvard Clubs would be the venue for the lunch. Having told his secretary that I would come to him, I took a taxi to the downtown club where we finally met up in person. I recount this mix-up because, had it not been resolved, the course of my life might have taken a different turn.

I liked Jarvis Farley from the outset. In his mid-sixties, he had a patrician look and cordial manner. We both laughed about the mix-up in lunch venues. After introductions, he stated that he was not there in his professional capacity, but rather in his role as trustee and chairman of the Presidential Search Committee of Babson College, located in Wellesley, a town with which Charlotte and I already had considerable history. He said that Babson was engaged in a search for a new president, and that Harvard's dean, Larry Fouraker, had put forth my name as someone who might be an attractive candidate for the position. Hence, he had invited me to lunch to get acquainted.

My reaction was one of total surprise. I knew little about Babson and had no idea that it was searching for a new president. Nor had the idea of becoming a college president crossed my mind. I was only 40 at a time when most college and university presidents were in their fifties or sixties. Moreover, I still had my nose to the grindstone at Harvard trying to create some publishable research that would qualify me for tenure upon reconsideration a year later.

I expressed my surprise to Mr. Farley and asked him why Dean Fouraker had suggested to him that I might be a good candidate. He replied that the dean had cited my experience in leading the effort to design, fund, and implement the establishment of the Asian Institute of Management, my knowledge of management education, my success as a teacher, my chairing of the faculty committee on improving the quality of teaching at HBS, my ability to get along well with people, and my overall leadership qualities as the reasons underlying his recommendation.

I told Mr. Farley I was flattered that he had reached out to me, but that the idea of a college presidency had not been on my radarscope and was totally new to me. As a consequence, I would need time to give it serious thought and talk the idea over with Charlotte. I indicated that, once I had done this, I would get back to him to let him know whether I was willing to have my name thrown in the hat as a potential candidate for the position.

There followed several days during which I researched Babson, spoke with several of my Harvard colleagues, and discussed with Charlotte the pros and cons of becoming a candidate for the Babson presidency. In the end I agreed to be considered.

In my research into Babson and its background, I learned that it had been in existence since 1919, that it was coed, that it offered both an undergraduate BS degree and a graduate MBA degree, and that it was focused primarily on management education, though at the undergraduate level it also required students to take courses in science and the liberal arts. Small in size, it had about 1,200 undergraduate students, 250 full-time graduate MBA students, and 1,300 part-time evening MBA graduate students. It had an attractive campus on a gorgeous 550-acre tract of land, half in Wellesley, half in Needham. I also learned that it was not very well known and had a mediocre academic reputation. Further, Babson had a tiny endowment and was almost totally dependent on tuition revenues to support its operations.

I concluded that the new president would face a daunting leadership challenge if he or she were to succeed in helping the college to significantly improve its overall quality and reputation in the future. On the other hand, I also became convinced that, despite its problems, the college might actually be a diamond in the rough that, with some skillful polishing and reshaping, had the potential to emerge as a shining academic gem.

The more I thought about it, the more Babson began to appeal to me. This would be an opportunity to help build an institution that had not yet arrived, but had considerable upside potential, as opposed to being an institution that had already arrived, where the president's job would be more one of maintaining than one of building.

Thus, with some trepidation, and with Charlotte's support, I took a deep breath and decided to become a candidate for the president's position.

There followed an intense round of interviews and discussions with Babson's presidential search committee and its faculty, students, senior administrators, and alumni. The process culminated in my being offered the job and my accepting the offer. Appendix A contains newspaper articles announcing my acceptance of the position as president of Babson College. With the decision made to go to Babson, I opened the door on the next chapter of my professional life.

CHAPTER TWENTY-THREE

FAMILY LIFE IN BELMONT

Six years had passed since we had moved back to the United States. From a family point of view, those years had made a tremendous impact.

After returning from the Philippines in 1968 and living for a year in our large, comfortable rental house on Hillside Terrace in Belmont, our lease was about to run out. We had been keeping our eyes open for a home we could buy. In the fall of 1969, we fell in love with what we concluded was an ideal house to purchase in another part of town called Belmont Hill.

The house was on Pinehurst Road, a quiet street shaped like a tennis racket. One entered from Concord Avenue at the handle end of the street and then the road circled around on itself and doubled back onto Concord Avenue. Our new house, number 16 Pinehurst Road, was halfway up the handle. The house cost $145,000. With the help of a hefty 11 percent interest mortgage from the Harvard Trust Bank in Cambridge, we were able to make the purchase.

The new house and neighborhood proved to be a perfect place to make friends and raise a family. A large number of couples with young children lived there. We and our children formed lifelong friendships with many of them. We still keep in touch with the Webb, Barss, Brosio, Harris, Hastings, Perkins, and Laskaris families, as do our children with many of their children.

The house had a large yard that backed up against historic Old Concord Road that was once the only road that connected Boston with Concord. Still unpaved, it was the road that Paul Revere reportedly took during his historic ride to Concord at the outset of the Revolutionary War to alert the citizens along the way that "the British were coming."

We loved our life in Belmont. The town's inhabitants comprised an interesting mix of academics, doctors, lawyers, other professionals, business executives, blue-collar workers, and service workers. It was also diverse from an ethnic, religious, racial, and socioeconomic point of view. Belmont had an excellent school system and other public amenities, including parks, athletic fields, and a conveniently located public library.

Kristin, Trina, and Eric attended the Winn Brook School, where many of their classmates were the children of professors or other professionals. Its academic standards were high, and it provided our children with a good start to their educations. Charlotte and I did a stint there as co-presidents of the Parent Teacher Association. Charlotte was also a frequent parent classroom volunteer there.

From the beginning of our stay in Belmont, Charlotte threw herself into the profession of being a great mother to our children. She organized myriad activities designed to help them increase their interests and their knowledge. She was always challenging them to learn and try new things. She encouraged them to set their sights high, both figuratively and literally. For example, she encouraged each of them in turn to climb to the very highest limbs of the huge hemlock tree that stood on our front yard, while she stood at the bottom egging them on and hoping they would succeed, but not fall and break a bone.

Wanting to expose our children to a variety of ways of thinking, Charlotte took them on visits to various places of worship in Belmont, Cambridge, and Boston, including Protestant, Catholic, Jewish, Greek Orthodox, and Quaker places of worship. As a family, we ultimately became attendees for a time at the Unitarian church. Though we never became "true believers" or regular in our attendance, we were attracted by its ecumenical approach to religion as well as the simplicity of its services. It also had the advantage of being conveniently located a short walk down Old Concord Road.

Charlotte became the ringleader of the mothers in the neighborhood. She was the one who was always organizing community events: plays starring the children, skating parties, soccer games, Easter egg hunts, May Basket celebrations, excursions to museums, and other diversions for children and adults alike. Everyone in the neighborhood loved her.

We encouraged all three children to become active in a variety of sporting activities. While in Belmont they learned to swim at the nearby Belmont Hill Club, which had an excellent swimming pool and both indoor and outdoor tennis courts. By the ages of seven, eight, and ten, all of them were competing in youth swimming meets. They also became proficient soccer players, bike riders, ice skaters, and skiers. The last of these sports they learned by first skiing down the snow-covered gentle slope in our back yard and then graduating to honing their skills on some of New England's many ski resorts.

Naturally, the children also had a pet dog during the Belmont years. Tasha, a mixed-breed canine fugitive from the local dog pound, became a much loved and appropriately spoiled sixth member of our family. A series of cats, gerbils, hamsters, and other household pets joined her from time to time.

Apart from being a great mother, Charlotte expanded her professional horizons while we lived in Belmont. She was hired by Earthwatch Institute to be the part-time head of its museum services department. Earthwatch was a nonprofit organization that recruited citizen volunteers to assist scientists, archaeologists, and naturalists in a wide variety of Earth-related projects that it sponsored in countries all around the world. Charlotte's job was to foster cooperative relationships for Earthwatch with science and natural history museums throughout America.

Toward the end of our sojourn in Belmont, Charlotte also enrolled in a master's degree program in education jointly offered by Lesley College and the Shady Hill School in Cambridge. The program involved graduate-level classes at Lesley coupled with extensive apprentice teaching as an intern at the Shady Hill School, a venerable local private day school. She completed the degree in 1973 and was invited by Shady Hill to stay on and teach in its reading program for children with learning disabilities. She continued to teach there for a period of time after I became president of Babson and we moved to Wellesley.

During the years we lived in Belmont, we tended to spend part of each summer traveling. On successive summers, I taught in executive programs back in the Philippines, at IMEDE in Switzerland, at Cambridge University in England, and at Keio University in Japan. Typically, Charlotte accompanied me and we took one or all of the children with us. Later in our lives, Charlotte and I were fond of saying that, for the first 20 years we were married, we never spent the summer on the same continent where we lived in the winter. Apart from our foreign travels, we also typically spent part of each summer visiting our families in Stockbridge or Mansfield, as well as making trips to various vacation spots on the New England coast.

Our years living in Belmont were happy ones for each member of our family. Kristin, Trina, and Eric all gained a solid foundation on which to base their future educations. At the same time, they made many lifelong friends and had their horizons stretched in myriad other ways. Charlotte and I also formed a number of enduring friendships and appreciated being part of an interesting and vibrant community.

It continued to be a time of great change for America. While the sixties had been a time of tragedy, with the assassinations of three national leaders, the seventies ushered in a different kind of transition, with the Watergate scandals and a continuing disillusionment with all forms of government and authority. It was also a time when various movements for social change gathered momentum, including environmentalism, women's rights, and civil rights. It was against this unique societal setting that I set off to lead a small educational institution.

CHAPTER TWENTY-FOUR

BABSON COLLEGE

The move to Wellesley toward the end of the summer of 1974 brought about traumatic changes in all of our lives. At the time, Kristin, Trina, and Eric were 12, 10, and 9, respectively. From their point of view, they felt totally uprooted from their best friends, their familiar schools, and their beloved neighborhood. Charlotte and I, too, shared some of their pangs. Wellesley was a less diverse and decidedly more economically upscale community than Belmont. It was populated by a large number of high-net-worth executives, entrepreneurs, doctors, lawyers, and other successful professionals, plus a smattering of academics from Babson and Wellesley Colleges. Despite having spent a year as students in Wellesley earlier in our marriage, we knew very few of its residents when we arrived.

The president's residence that we were to occupy was a comfortable, large, but not pretentious, brick house with a big fenced-in back yard on the corner of Wellesley Avenue and Whiting Road. We were fortunate in that, unlike many academic presidential residences, it was not located in the middle of the college campus. Rather, it was in a nice neighborhood adjacent to the campus and only a seven-minute walk from what was to be my office. This meant that we did not have to live the fishbowl existence that many presidential families have had to endure. For this we were most grateful, particularly for the sake of our children, who were able to lead normal lives similar to other kids in the community.

Though the transition to new friends, new schools, and a new community presented a challenge to Kristin, Trina, and Eric, each in his or her own way handled it well and over time they all came to thrive in their new surroundings.

The day of our move to Wellesley was marred by only one negative incident. Charlotte's treasured diamond engagement ring somehow disappeared in the moving process. She had taken it off and put it on the windowsill above the kitchen sink while she was washing dishes and it was presumably stolen when she stepped out of the room, perhaps by one of the movers, though we never found out for certain. It had great sentimental value for both of us, given the story of its original purchase in Brussels 15 years earlier. Hence, we both felt its loss. The ring was never recovered. However, apart from that incident, the rest of the move went smoothly and we quickly settled into our comfortable new home.

We both rapidly became immersed in our respective new lives, I as Babson's new president and Charlotte wearing multiple hats as mother, part-time teacher and, now, as presidential spouse.

An incident had occurred in the spring of 1974 that helped set the stage for my presidency, before I officially assumed my job. One day, I received a call from Dick Nichols, immediate past chairman of Babson's board of trustees, suggesting that the two of us meet with Henry Kriebel, my about-to-be predecessor as president. Dick was a crusty but wise and well-respected senior partner at the venerable Boston law firm of Goodwin, Procter and Hoar. I accepted his invitation. Shortly after, we paid Henry a visit in his office. After greeting us, Henry invited us to sit down for a chat. The following is the gist of the conversation that ensued:

> Dick: "Henry, what do you intend to do after Ralph, here, comes in as president and you step down?"

> Henry: "Well, I think I'd like to stay at the college and go back to teaching and being chairman of the accounting department, which is what I did before becoming president. And then, of course, I'd like to stay on the board of trustees. Finally, I thought I would help show Ralph the ropes and get him started off on the right foot."

> Dick: "That's interesting. By the way, Henry, how long have you been at the college?"

> Henry: "This is my 26th year."

> Dick: "Wow! That's a long time. And you love this place, don't you?"

> Henry: "I sure do. It's been the heart and soul of my professional life."

> Dick: "Well, Henry, I'll tell you what. If you truly love Babson, you will not stay on the faculty. You will not chair the accounting department. You will not continue as a member of the board of trustees. You will not hang around to show Ralph the ropes. Instead, what would be best for the college would be for you to leave Ralph a clean slate so that he can put his own distinctive leadership stamp on the college without having to live in your shadow."

Henry suddenly looked stricken. He sat silent for perhaps half a minute. Then, to his great credit, he replied more or less as follows:

"In my head, I know that you are right. It's my heart that I'm having difficulty with. But, in the end, I'll do as you suggest, because deep down I believe it is the right thing to do, both for the college and for Ralph."

Henry was as good as his word and totally retired from Babson when he left the presidency. He was 65 at the time. He subsequently accepted an appointment from then Governor Michael Dukakis to participate in a commission studying higher education in Massachusetts and moved off the Babson campus to new offices at Northeastern University in Boston.

I am sure that, on my own, I would not have had the chutzpah to initiate such a candid discussion with Henry. However, in retrospect, I was enormously grateful and indebted to Dick Nichols for his forthrightness in tackling the delicate issue of what the outgoing leader should do when his successor assumes his position.

The moral of the story is that, no matter what type of organization is involved, a lot of heartache would be avoided if every major changing-of-the-guard included such a conversation. In my particular situation, the exchange between Dick and Henry cleared the deck for me to have an open field of action from the first day I began my term as president of Babson. Two years later, when I was fully established in my position, I had the great pleasure of inviting Henry to once again become a trustee of the college. He was delighted and touched by the invitation and agreed to come back on the board. I think that the gesture meant a lot to him.

From the beginning, what was accomplished during my tenure as president resulted from a team effort. I saw my role as that of helping to create a culture and vision for Babson that would bring out the best in everyone associated with the college and that would allow it to make significant strides forward in achieving excellence in all that it did.

I embarked on a crash course to learn everything I could about the college and to become personally acquainted with members of all its stakeholder groups. The first thing I did on assuming my responsibilities was to schedule one-on-one meetings with every faculty member, administrator, and supervisor at the college. I also tried to personally meet as many students as possible. I initiated efforts to reach out to alumni of the school so as to understand their dreams and aspirations for Babson's future. Finally, I had conversations with members of the Boston business community and with various community leaders in Wellesley.

Since the students were Babson's raison d'être and, thus, its primary stakeholder group, I felt they deserved special attention. Unfortunately, on most college and university campuses, there is a huge divide between students and senior administrative officers. At Babson, however, I found a great way to bridge that gap. Almost all of the students ate lunch in Trim Dining hall. At least twice a week, I made it a practice to have lunch with them there. I would first initiate conversations while waiting with them in the cafeteria line. Then, having made my lunch selections, I would carry my tray into the big dining room and randomly pick a table of students to join for an exchange of ideas.

When I first began the practice of these weekly lunches, some of the students were surprised to be joined at their table by the president and were intimidated into silence. But, before long, they grew accustomed to my weekly presence and most came to appreciate the opportunity to share their observations, suggestions, and gripes about me. As for me, I gained interesting insights from the students that I otherwise wouldn't have been able to obtain.

Several weeks after my arrival on campus, a formal presidential inauguration event took place. In addition to a full complement of invitees from all of Babson's various constituencies, the auditorium was packed with representatives from a number of other colleges and universities, together with many of Charlotte's and my family and friends. It was an opportunity for me to articulate my overall views with respect to the college as a whole: its strengths, its challenges, its future opportunities, and my philosophy of leadership. The text of my address is contained in <u>Appendix B</u>. The talk speaks for itself and provides the most accurate insight into my hopes and dreams for the future of Babson at the time that I assumed its presidency.

As was suggested in my talk, my highest immediate priority was to put in place a mechanism for the college to look ahead, define its future direction, and develop an "evergreen" Master Plan for achieving its goals. By "evergreen," I meant a plan with a five-year future horizon, but one where, at the end of each year, we would evaluate our progress to date and then, based on what we had learned, roll out the plan for an additional year into the future.

From the beginning, this process of formulating and then implementing a long-range plan involved input from every stakeholder group at the college. In September 1974, we established a Master Planning Steering Committee made up of faculty members, administrators, trustees, students, and alumni. To facilitate the process, we hired a gifted independent educational consultant named Matt Cullen. He was an invaluable resource for us.

By making sure that all of the stakeholder groups were involved in the planning process, we increased the odds that there would be buy-in from those who subsequently would be responsible for implementing the plan.

By the end of the 1974-75 academic year, we had a final draft of the new Master Plan ready to be presented to the trustees for approval. The approval, when it came in the fall, was unanimous. The highlights of the plan are summarized in Appendix C.

The plan summary, of course, is but a broad overview of the Master Plan we put together in my initial year at Babson. Each of the sections of the plan was backed up by considerable detail and contained specific, measurable one-year and five-year goals. The plan also contained a complete set of financial goals and projections, as well as projections of student enrollments for each program, tuition rates, size of faculty and staff, salary increases, annual giving goals, and capital fundraising goals.

Subsequently, working together as a team, we accomplished the near impossible in the world of higher education. As a result of our master planning process, we formulated an ambitious long-range strategy and plan that turned out to be an excellent road map for our future actions. We identified several educational niches to occupy that ended up giving us significant competitive advantages in the decades to come. We achieved enthusiastic buy-in from nearly all members of the Babson community. And we avoided much of the vicious squabbling and internal politicking that all too often characterizes most college and university decision-making. Finally, and most important, we accomplished almost everything in the Master Plan we set out to achieve.

Of all the decisions embodied in the Master Plan, the one that had the greatest positive long-term impact on Babson, was that of identifying *entrepreneurship* as an underserved area of management education.

At the time, very few business schools had courses aimed at helping to educate future entrepreneurs. Harvard Business School, for example, had only a single elective course called "Management of New Enterprises." It was not very popular with students. Instead, Harvard saw its greatest strengths in what it called the "general management" area. The faculty there was concentrating on preparing future captains of industry for what I was fond of calling the "giant generals": General Motors, General Electric, General Foods, General Dynamics, General Tire and Rubber, etc. At the same time, they were also focusing on educating students to go to work for major consulting companies such as McKinsey or Booz Allen Hamilton, or to head to Wall Street to become "Masters of the Universe" at investment firms such as Goldman Sachs, Morgan Stanley, and J.P. Morgan.

When I first arrived at Babson, some were afraid that I might try to imitate HBS and "Harvardize" the place. This never entered my mind, since to try to compete directly with Harvard or some of the other top business schools would have been folly. Instead, my thought was to identify an underserved niche that had potential and that would give Babson a distinctive competitive advantage.

During my early weeks as president, when I immersed myself into trying to learn everything possible about Babson, I made it a point to study what past graduates of the school had done with their careers. When looking through the alumni catalogue, I began to notice that a large number of graduates had the title of "president" or "founder" or "CEO" after their names. Typically, however, they were not large companies or organizations that they were leading. Instead, they tended to be the self-employed heads of small enterprises such as car dealerships, retail establishments, accounting firms, construction companies, and small manufacturing firms. In many cases, these were companies they had started themselves or that had been started by their families. That was when the light bulb went on in my head. Why shouldn't Babson pick as its niche an explicit focus on entrepreneurship education?

Several faculty members reinforced this idea in the planning process, and in particular, Professor Jack Hornaday, who was already teaching a course in entrepreneurship and who thought that such a focus made sense for a variety of reasons. First, it built on a historical tradition already in place at Babson. Second, there were no other business schools with such a specialty. Third, such a focus had a good chance of winning the support of most of the management faculty, regardless of their functional area. Entrepreneurship education would require good marketing professors, finance professors, operations professors, organizational behavior professors, and policy professors. Thus, it wouldn't lead to a situation such as existed at other business schools where one functional area often tended to overshadow the others; for example, finance at Wharton, marketing at Northwestern, and general management at Harvard. This functional focus, in turn, sometimes resulted in internal rivalries and unhealthy faculty pecking orders at these institutions. To the greatest extent possible, we hoped to avoid such rivalries at Babson.

Entrepreneurial Insight #9: Babson Finds Its Niche

The final reason for focusing on entrepreneurship was perhaps the most important one. Namely, as the Master Planning Task Force thought about the future and the needs of the coming decade, we concluded that there would be an expanding need for growing numbers of entrepreneurs capable of creating new enterprises that, in turn, would be the source of jobs, new inventions and innovations, and additional wealth. We also were convinced that, while many believe that entrepreneurs are born and not made, there was much that we could teach those with the entrepreneurial gene that would significantly increase the odds that they would be successful when the time came for them to actually start a new enterprise.

Hence, we determined to develop entrepreneurship education as a major focus of the school. Toward that end, we created the first Center for Entrepreneurship Education in the world.

Lesson Learned: Entrepreneurship can be taught and it can be learned.

The Center, as it developed, encompassed a whole suite of activities.

First, it involved the development of more courses in entrepreneurship at both the undergraduate and graduate MBA levels, together with offering entrepreneurship as a major in both programs.

Second, thanks to the generosity of the Babson family, it fostered the creation of the Roger Babson Professor of Entrepreneurship, the college's first fully endowed faculty chair in the entrepreneurial area.

Third, it led to the eventual creation of the Symposium for Entrepreneurship Educators at Babson. This was a short, non-degree outreach program designed to enhance Babson's impact on entrepreneurship education by helping professors at other business schools to better teach entrepreneurship. This program was very practical in nature and had as its mission to teach its participants very specific classroom skills. Its design was unique. One week in length, its applicants applied to the program in pairs, with one participant being a faculty member experienced in teaching and the other an experienced entrepreneur who was interested in sharing his or her "real world" experiences with others by becoming a practitioner/teacher. The symposium has proven to be immensely successful and is still in existence decades later. Its alumni roster now includes thousands of entrepreneurship teachers, many of whom are continuing to teach at business schools all around the world.

A fourth activity of the Center for Entrepreneurship was its creation and sponsorship of an annual research conference at which scholars and researchers doing work in the field were invited to present the results of their work to their academic peers. This conference also still exists and has become the premier conference of its type in the academic world.

Finally, we created the "Academy of Distinguished Entrepreneurs." This represented an effort to give long-overdue public recognition to successful and innovative entrepreneurs from around the world. It was also intended to draw attention to the fact that Babson was staking out a claim as a leader in the field of educating future entrepreneurs. At the time, a number of business schools and business publications had various "Hall of Fame" programs to honor outstanding CEOs of large companies and to give recognition to various successful Fortune 500 companies. But there were no programs to pay homage to outstanding entrepreneurs who had been successful at creating jobs, innovative new businesses, and wealth.

The Academy worked like this: Once a year, Babson students were invited to submit a list of names of individuals whom they felt had excelled as entrepreneurs. This list was then submitted to a panel of credible judges who were asked to make the final selection of up to five outstanding entrepreneurs on a worldwide basis to be honored.

This second step in the process initially posed a challenge. Who should the "credible judges" be? At the time, Babson was not very well known and there would have been little incentive for the selected entrepreneurs to accept induction into an unknown academy sponsored by an obscure college. We solved this problem by resorting to "borrowed credibility." Namely, we asked the editors and/or publishers of five leading business publications to be the judges and to lend their names to the invitations that would be sent to the winning honorees.

Hence, I contacted Malcolm Forbes, founder and publisher of *Forbes* magazine, Bob Bartley, editor of the *Wall Street Journal*, Bernie Alexander, publisher of *Business Week*, Ralph Lewis, editor of the *Harvard Business Review*, and Anthony Lewis, the American editor of *The Economist* magazine, to serve on the judges' committee. All accepted the invitation and Malcolm Forbes volunteered to host a lunch where he and his fellow judges would discuss the nominees and select the top five. Professor Hornaday, who had been named the initial director of the Babson Center for Entrepreneurship, and I were also to attend the judging sessions.

Malcolm Forbes' first judging lunch was quite something. It was held at the elegant brownstone building in New York City that was headquarters to *Forbes*. On our arrival, we were first treated to a showing of Malcolm's famous Russian Fabergé egg collection. We were then ushered into an elegant private dining room and seated around an exquisitely arranged round table complete with solid 24-carat gold table settings. Thereupon, the five publishing moguls, some of whom had not met each other before, hit it off with one another immediately and soon were engaged in animated discussion. All were fascinated by the idea of the newly established Academy. To a person, they felt that it was high time that more recognition be given to successful, innovative entrepreneurs. They all also applauded Babson's decision to give greater attention to the field of entrepreneurship education.

After a cordon bleu lunch and over coffee, the judges got down to business, and for the next couple of hours discussed the pros and cons of various nominees to the Academy. They finally settled on five individuals to be honored. They were Ray Kroc, founder of McDonalds; Soichiro Honda, founder of Honda Motor Company in Japan; Berry Gordy, Jr., founder of Motown; Ken Olsen, founder of Digital Equipment Corporation (DEC); and Royal Little, founder of Textron, Indian Head Mills, and Amtel, Inc. Together with me, the judges subsequently were all signatories to the letters announcing the awards to the recipients. Much to our collective delight, the five recipients all accepted the honor and agreed to come to Babson to be inducted into the Academy in person.

When the date of the recognition ceremonies came, all five honorees and all five judges showed up. The daytime events included a public convocation for the students and faculty members in which a different student host introduced each honoree. In turn, each honoree told his own story and shared his observations on entrepreneurship with the audience. Afterward, there were smaller simultaneous sessions at which each distinguished entrepreneur met more intimately with different groups of students. The day was a smashing success, matched only by what happened in the evening.

We had sent out invitations for a formal, black-tie dinner celebration to all leaders of the business and academic community in the Greater Boston area. The opportunity to be exposed to the five well-known inductees into the newly formed Academy of Distinguished Entrepreneurs proved to be irresistible. Almost everyone we invited came to the standing-room-only dinner at one of Boston's leading hotels.

It was a sparkling evening, one that few in the audience were likely to ever forget. Again, student hosts introduced the honorees, each of whom gave a short and entertaining talk to the assembled diners. It was clear that all of the honorees were pleased by the whole affair. Much of their enjoyment was the opportunity they had to meet, get acquainted with, and share stories with one another as well as with the students, the judges, and leaders of the Boston business community. The event was a win-win-win for all involved, not the least of which was Babson itself, whose public reputation was greatly expanded and enhanced in the process. It didn't hurt that all of the judges' publications gave great coverage to the formation of the Academy and to the events of the day!

The Academy helped put Babson on the map and symbolically announced to the world that Babson was on the move and carving out a niche in entrepreneurship education. During my tenure as president at Babson, the annual Academy ceremonies were a highlight of each year for students, faculty members, judges, and leaders of the Boston business community alike. And no one enjoyed both the annual judging lunches and yearly induction ceremonies more than me.

My tenure as Babson's president was the single most fulfilling period of my professional career. I loved my job, believed in the mission of the college, and felt that what I was doing was making a positive difference. It was not totally a seven-year honeymoon, but it came very close. It had its serious moments, its humorous moments, its frustrating moments, and its truly satisfying moments.

With respect to serious moments, let me speak for a moment about relationships with the faculty. In my experience, more college and university presidencies founder on the shoals of the faculty than for any other reason. At Harvard, when then President Derek Bok once began to explain his view of the role of the university at one of his first faculty meetings, the voice of a faculty member in the audience was famously heard to say, "We are the university." President Bok later went on to opine that: "Nothing works around here without the cooperation of the faculty," and "The faculty is the building block on which everything else rests." I believe this is true at all colleges and universities.

The problem is that faculty members typically are a feisty lot. All too often, university faculties are characterized by petty squabbles, professional jealousies, large egos, and overbearing intellects. Fortunately, to a large extent, this was not the case at Babson. Nevertheless, from the beginning I took great care to develop a positive relationship with every member of the faculty. This meant frequently meeting with them both one on one and in small groups to listen to their concerns and to try to get buy-in from them for their part in helping to achieve the college's goals. It also meant that, each year, Charlotte and I hosted a series of small dinners at our house and made sure that all faculty members and their spouses were included at one or another of them on an annual basis.

At Babson, I was greatly helped in the effort to ensure the support of the faculty by Professor Walter Carpenter, who was vice president for academic affairs at the college. Walter had been appointed to his position prior to my arrival at Babson. He and I hit it off from the beginning and I decided to keep him in his job as chief academic officer. He was an astute and seasoned academic leader who was wise to the ways of the faculty and had a wonderfully witty sense of humor. He was responsible for the overall care and feeding of the faculty and he handled his responsibilities with great skill. He was universally well regarded and possessed the ability to handle the most sensitive faculty issues in an insightful and thoughtful manner. However, he could also be tough-minded when the situation called for it. He was a perfect fit for his job.

I learned a lot from Walter. The most important lesson was that for college presidents to succeed in their jobs, it is essential to have a Walter Carpenter-like person overseeing the faculty. Walter did the majority of heavy lifting when it came to faculty issues, which enabled me, as president, to be the "good guy" . . . at least most of the time.

CHAPTER TWENTY-FIVE

BABSON VIGNETTES

The good times, the bad times, and the funny times during my seven years as Babson's president were too numerous to recount in this memoir. But perhaps a few vignettes will suffice to give a feel for what the job entailed.

The Great Ice Cream Protest

Being president at Babson had its lighter moments. For example, there was the episode of the "Great Ice Cream Protest." In the seventies (and indeed to this day), it was typical every spring for students on campuses across the country to find some issue or grievance about which to go on strike, or at least to organize a public demonstration. Sometimes these strikes or demonstrations were about quite serious matters: the war in Vietnam, women's rights, racial discrimination, lousy housing conditions, etc. In 1980, however, Babson students found a different kind of issue about which to protest: ice cream!

It began with Jesse Putney, Babson's very conservative and very effective vice president of finance. Jesse was always looking for ways for the college to operate more efficiently and save money. As students were fond of saying, "Jesus saves, but Jesse saves more!" In the spring of 1980, Jesse concluded that students were abusing the campus dining hall's "unlimited ice cream" policy. They were bringing empty quart containers of ice cream to the dining hall, filling them with ice cream, and taking the food back to the refrigerators in their rooms. As a result, the college's ice cream costs were skyrocketing. Jesse decided something needed to be done. He issued an order summarily terminating the "unlimited ice cream policy." Henceforth, the order stated, all ice cream had to be consumed within the dining hall.

The collective student reaction was one of shock, disbelief, dismay, and anger. Immediately, a widespread protest movement began. The leaders of the movement circulated a petition stating that unlimited ice cream was a basic student right and demanding that the college immediately reinstate its "unlimited ice cream policy." After about a week of agitation on the campus, a large student delegation arrived in my outer office and insisted that my wonderful longtime assistant, Dottie Caddick, admit them immediately to see me. She did so and in came about a dozen or so leaders of the rebellion. After vociferously voicing their collective outrage, they presented me with a petition signed by over a thousand students demanding that Jesse Putney's new policy be rescinded.

I took the document from them and studied it page by page for a minute or two. When I reached the final page, I took out my pen and signed my name in the blank space below the last student's signature. Not having spoken a single word until then, I handed the petition back to the students and suggested that they take the petition to Jesse Putney and present it to him for his decision.

The next day, the college's "unlimited ice cream" policy was formally reinstated. Would that all of the campus-wide issues I confronted in my seven years as Babson's president were as easy to resolve!

The Heist of "Big Bird"

On another occasion, the head of the campus police informed me that a car with three students in it had flashed by the attendant at the campus exit gate with a huge metal bird's head hanging out of the back window. The attendant called the local police, who immediately sent a squad car that intercepted the fleeing vehicle and arrested its occupants. It turned out that the students had pushed over and decapitated "Big Bird," a 12-foot-tall metal sculpture of a bird that was on loan from a local Boston sculptor and that had been on display on the lawn next to the library.

One of the student perpetrators of the heist was the son of a Babson alumnus who ranked high among the college's largest financial benefactors. It also turned out that the statue was quite valuable and worth many thousands of dollars. Finally, it became known that the sculptor (understandably) was not happy that his statue had been decapitated and its head had been stolen. He was seeking a substantial amount of cash as remuneration.

The police brought criminal charges against the three student perpetrators. The prominent alumnus hired a defense lawyer to defend his son and the two other students. The lawyer argued in municipal court that the caper was nothing more than a college prank. The judge was having none of that argument and found the three guilty of theft and desecration of a valuable piece of art. However, he said that if the students made full restitution to the artist for the loss, he would sentence them to probation for two years, at the end of which time their criminal records would be expunged, provided they fully abided by the probationary terms. The wealthy father reimbursed the artist for the destroyed statue and paid the court costs and legal fees of all three students.

Meanwhile, back at the college, the student judicial court also brought charges against the three students, found them guilty, and banned them from living on campus for the remaining one and a half years until their graduation. The wealthy father was furious about this action and personally importuned me, as president, to overturn the student court verdict. He said that if I didn't, he would never donate another cent to the college. I told him I was sorry he felt that way, but that I would let the student verdict stand because, after reviewing the case, I felt the verdict was just. I also suggested to the father that, in the long run, he would be doing no favor to the character development of his son if he continued to try to protect him from the personal consequences of his own actions. This line of reasoning clearly didn't persuade the father. True to his threat, he cancelled his substantial gift pledge to Babson. To the best of my knowledge, he never gave another penny to the college.

In retrospect, the "Big Bird" caper had its humorous side. But it also had its serious side and is illustrative of the kind of situations frequently faced by college and university administrators as they are called upon to make a choice between doing what is right, on the one hand, and the financial well-being of their institution on the other. Of course, these kinds of dilemmas between doing what is right and doing what is expedient constantly confront individuals in leadership positions in every other type of private and public sector institution as well.

A Sad Telephone Call

College presidents are called upon to deal with many other difficult situations, as well. One evening, when Charlotte and I were hosting an alumni reception in our house, I received another call from the head of the campus police. He said he had sad news. One of our students had just been killed in a one-car accident less than a quarter-mile from our house. With another student as his passenger, he had been driving his sports car at a relatively high speed when, coming over a ridge on the road running past the Wellesley Country Club, he had evidently lost control of the car and crashed head-on into a tree. He was killed instantly, while his passenger had been injured, but would survive.

It fell to me to make the call to notify the deceased driver's parents of the tragedy. That was very difficult for me. He had been a fine young man and a good student. What made the call particularly hard was the fact that I had met his parents when they had visited the campus and had begun to develop a friendship with them. How does one compassionately inform parents that their son's life has suddenly been snuffed out? One does the best one can, but for me this instance was a truly heartrending experience.

Babson's Niche Strategy as Applied to Athletics

As I write these lines, a number of other memory snippets come back to me relating to our family's seven years at Babson.

One relates to the role of athletics at Babson. Most colleges have football teams on whom they rely to generate funding for other team sports. Babson, ever the iconoclast, had no football team. Instead, it had a "futbol" team, also known as a soccer team. And what a soccer team it was! Thanks to the efforts of Coach Bob Hartwell and a talented combination of American and international student players, Babson reached the NCAA Division 3 national championship finals five times during our Babson years. And it won the national championship three of those five years. It was an example of Babson's niche strategy of focusing on a lead sport where it could truly excel and which was relatively cheap (cleats, shorts, ball, and a soccer field) rather than committing resources to a sport like football, which is expensive and where Babson College would no doubt have been little more than mediocre.

Wearing a Fundraiser's Hat

Part of the job description of all college presidents is raising money—or "development," as it is euphemistically known. Babson was no exception. During my tenure as its president, perhaps 20 to 30 percent of my time was devoted to fundraising.

Babson faced a somewhat unique challenge in this regard. From the time that Roger Babson founded the college in 1919, he pledged that the college would never ask any alumnus for a charitable contribution. He also pledged that the college would never accept any government funding. His rationale was that any business school that couldn't balance its budget and operate without creating a deficit was not worthy of the name. As long as he lived, these pledges were honored.

He, himself, however, generously reached into his own pocket to help fund the college at the outset by donating the 550 acres of valuable land on which to build its campus and by funding the construction of a number of buildings over a long period of years. Moreover, throughout his life, he fostered the unspoken understanding that on his death, he would, in his will, leave the lion's share of his considerable wealth to create an endowment sufficient in size to permanently ensure that the college could function in a healthy financial condition. Unfortunately, upon his death in 1967 at age 91, the expected gift to the college never materialized.

This created a dilemma for the college. Tuitions alone were beginning to prove insufficient to permit Babson to operate with a balanced budget. This prompted the decision on the part of the trustees at the end of the sixties to abandon Mr. Babson's lifelong pledge and to initiate annual alumni fundraising drives. This proved to be a challenge, since for almost 50 years, Babson's alumni had never been asked to direct charitable contributions to the college. Indeed, the college didn't even have a complete directory of the current addresses of its graduates.

When I arrived at the college in 1974, the results of the newly instituted annual giving efforts had been less than stellar. Consequently, part of the Master Plan that we established shortly after my arrival called for a greatly stepped up effort to bolster annual alumni giving and at the same time to launch an ambitious capital campaign.

We brought in a new vice president for development, Charles Thompson, who previously had been a development officer at Harvard. He subsequently led a successful effort to professionalize our annual giving record, beginning with an effort to compile an up-to-date directory of the names, addresses, and phone numbers of all of Babson's alumni. We then appointed annual fundraising chairs from each class and attempted to give them the tools they needed to step up annual giving from their classmates. This effort met with considerable success. Alumni began to become accustomed to including their alma mater in their annual gift giving. This resulted in a significant increase in the number and size of the annual gifts received by the college.

In addition to bolstering our annual fundraising efforts, in 1977 we launched what was, for then, an ambitious capital campaign to underwrite the cost of constructing and/or renovating buildings on the campus, create endowed faculty professorships, and underwrite the cost of launching new academic programs, including the creation of the new Center for Entrepreneurship Education. This campaign turned out to be a great success. By the time I stepped down from the Babson presidency, it had surpassed its targeted goals by 50 percent!

The largest single gift generated in the capital campaign came from the F.W. Olin Foundation. It was a $4.8 million grant to build a new library on the campus. It came about as the result of a fortuitous coincidence. The Olin Foundation, headquartered in Minneapolis, had for many years been one of the few foundations that made capital grants for buildings on private college campuses. When the foundation's name came up on our radar screen at Babson, I discovered, quite by chance, that Nancy Horn, the wife of one of the foundation's three directors, William Horn, had been my sister Nancy's roommate at Northwestern University. Following a phone conversation between the two Nancys, Nancy Horn kindly opened the door for me to meet with the three directors of the foundation in Minneapolis and made sure I had a favorable reception.

When I arrived at the meeting, I discovered, much to my delight, that another of the three directors of the foundation, Larry Milas, was a Babson alumnus. I made a presentation to the board members asking them to approve a capital gift to Babson for the construction of a much-needed new library and presented a comprehensive written proposal to them in support of the request. The directors apparently liked the idea and subsequently agreed to make the gift. At $4.8 million, it turned out to be the largest capital construction grant made to any college in America by a private foundation that year. In 1978, $4.8 million was still considered to be a lot of money!

I later learned that, apart from the proposal itself, the decision was influenced by three additional factors. First, the personal relationship between Nancy Horn and my sister, Nancy. Second, the fact that Larry Milas was an alumnus of Babson. And third, the fact that Babson had never sought nor received any government funding. This final factor resonated with one of the Olin Foundation's fundamental conservative principles that the foundation should not make grants to institutions that were receiving financial support from the government. This experience opened my eyes to the realization that fundraising is as much an art as it is a science and that luck, coincidence, and serendipity typically play a major role in any successful capital campaign.

Thus it was that, at Babson's outdoor commencement ceremony in the spring of 1978, we held what was intended to be a dramatic groundbreaking ceremony for what was eventually named the Horn Library. The plan was to detonate a dynamite charge in front of the entire commencement audience on the hillside site of the new library. When the big moment came, I as president of the college, together with the chairman of both the Babson board and the Olin board, simultaneously pushed down on the detonator plunger and . . . nothing happened! But then big Eddie Sullivan, head of the buildings and grounds department, came to the rescue. After fiddling with some wires, he shouted to us, "Shove it down again. This time harder"! We did, and . . . KABOOM! The audience and we were rewarded by the noise of a most satisfyingly loud explosion that left a surprisingly big hole in the ground. A great cheer went up and the new construction project was duly launched.

The Practice of Patience

Perhaps my favorite fundraising story has to do with Victor Tomasso, an alumnus from the Babson Class of 1949. I met Victor during my first year at Babson and we hit it off from the beginning. After graduating from Babson, he and his brother, Angelo, had started a large and successful construction company based in the metro New York City area, plus a sand and gravel company as well as a barge and tugboat business that operated on the Hudson river. All of these ventures had thrived. As a result, the brothers had become quite wealthy and Victor had retired to Florida.

In our initial visit together, Victor told me how much he had enjoyed his years at Babson and how valuable the education he received there had been to him in his subsequent entrepreneurial ventures. Seeing how enthusiastic he seemed to be about the college, I planted the idea with him that he might want to consider making a capital gift to the college in recognition of the role that Babson had played in his life. He said he would give the matter some thought, but it might take some time and I would have to be patient.

A year went by and I heard nothing from Victor. So I visited him again and we had a delightful lunch together in Florida. But when I broached the question as to whether he had come to a conclusion with respect to making a capital gift to the college, he said that he and his brother had given it some thought but were not yet ready to decide. However, he did indicate that, given their background in the construction industry, if they were to make a gift it would probably be to fund a building construction project on the campus. "As a matter of fact," he said, "I understand that your Master Plan calls for building a new library, which means that, eventually, you no doubt will have to renovate the current Sir Isaac Newton Library building and repurpose it for another use. That's a project that might interest us in view of the fact that Angelo and I have always liked that building and it would be nice if, once renovated, it could be renamed Tomasso Hall."

I responded that I thought his idea was an interesting one and well worth pursuing. Victor, who had a sly sense of humor, then proceeded to wonder aloud whether all the New England "Wasps" associated with the college would react positively to replacing Sir Isaac Newton, a famous English name, with an Italian name like Tomasso. I laughed and told him not to spend too much time worrying about that issue and that I thought Tomasso was a perfectly good name. In fact, I pointed out that America was a melting pot and had been built by people of all different nationalities. Victor then closed out the conversation by saying that, in any case, he and his brother still had to give the matter more thought and that I shouldn't be impatient.

A third year went by and I still didn't hear back from Victor. Whereupon, I visited Victor once again, and once again he said that he and Angelo still weren't ready to decide and that I should be patient. The only problem was that I was growing increasingly impatient. To add to my frustration, two *more* years went by with a repeat of the same annual charade. At that point, I concluded Victor was just leading me on and all but gave up hope that he and his brother would ever make a capital gift to the college.

Then, in the spring of 1981, my final year as president of Babson, I was sitting in my office one morning when I heard a huge noise outside my window. When I looked out I saw a low-flying helicopter circling the campus. I didn't think much more about the matter until about 15 minutes later, when my assistant, Dottie, knocked on my door. She said that the helicopter I had heard had landed on Babson's soccer field and there was a delegation from it in my outer office waiting to see me. Whereupon, in walked Victor Tomasso, his nephew Michael Tomasso, an MBA student at Babson, Paulo Fantacci, a Babson undergraduate, and Rocco Russo, also an MBA student.

With little or no preamble, Victor said, "Hi Ralph. We have some things for you." Whereupon, he snapped his fingers and said, "Rocco!" Rocco Russo then came over and gave me a jacket that had TOMASSO CONSTRUCTION embossed on its back. Before I could try it on and thank him, Victor snapped his fingers a second time and barked, "Paulo!" Paulo Fantacci dutifully stepped forward and handed me a 6" by 8" brass plaque on which the following was neatly engraved:

RALPH

PATIENCE IS A PRACTICE, NOT A VIRTUE!

VICTOR

As I was trying to take this all in, Victor snapped his fingers a third and final time and said: "Michael!" Michael Tomasso then came up and presented me with a certified check made out to Babson College for $1,250,000! Thus it was that I learned the additional lesson that the practice of patience also has a role to play in any successful fundraising endeavor. And so it was that Babson was able to renovate its old and outdated Sir Isaac Newton Library into an elegant new classroom and faculty office building suitably renamed Tomasso Hall.

I might add one significant after-note to this vignette. When the Tomasso family made their capital gift to the college, they specified that $1 million should be for renovation of the building and that the additional $250,000 should be used to create an endowment fund to underwrite the permanent maintenance of the building. Prior to the Tomasso gift, maintenance endowments of this type were very rare in the realm of capital gifts for construction purposes. Today, such maintenance endowments are more common, but at the time, the Tomassos, with their backgrounds in the construction business, showed considerable foresight in creating an endowment ensuring that Tomasso Hall would be properly maintained in the decades to come.

A Behind the Scenes Look at Entertaining

While at Babson, we did a considerable amount of entertaining in our home. Over the seven years we were there, we hosted more than 14,000 guests at college-related dinners, lunches, receptions, and garden parties. We made a major effort to extend hospitality to students, faculty and staff members, alumni and alumnae, trustees, Babson Corporation members, local officials, and members of the business community. Charlotte typically bore the brunt of all this entertaining. As an "unpaid volunteer," she did the planning, and worked closely with the college's catering staff and the campus building and grounds crew to ensure that the functions at the house went smoothly. Though it wasn't always easy, given all the other demands on her time, she was invariably a gracious hostess at these events. She had a wonderful knack for making every guest feel welcome and wanted.

I personally learned an important lesson by observing Charlotte in her role as presidential spouse. Namely, I learned how important it was to pay attention to and be thoughtful in one's dealings with the myriad people who operated behind the scenes at the college. These included all the members of the buildings and grounds department, everyone on the food service and catering staff, the college medical staff, and members of the security force. On most campuses, these are the "invisible people" who are absolutely essential to the smooth functioning of the institution. Yet, all too often, they are underappreciated, underpaid, and underrecognized. These were the people that Charlotte paid the *most* attention to. She went out of her way to get to know them personally, to listen to them thoughtfully, and to treat them with respect and in a kind and friendly manner. Moreover, she was always considerate in the requests she made of them. As a result, Charlotte became much appreciated by them and they would often bend over backward to be helpful to her. Although I tried my best to emulate Charlotte's approach with these "behind the scenes" people, I was never nearly as successful as she was in this regard. While most of these workers came to like and respect me, almost all of them loved her and would willingly go the "extra mile" for her.

The Babson International Student Olympics and a Related Ethical Learning Moment

Charlotte developed a particularly soft spot in her heart for the international students at Babson. I think this came from having lived for five years as a foreigner in Switzerland and the Philippines. As a result, she became co-founder, along with a number of foreign students, of the Babson International Student Organization. Initially, this was an organization designed to help international students feel more comfortable and at home at Babson. It organized a variety of extracurricular and social events and supported students for whom English was a second language and to whom the American college culture initially seemed strange and daunting.

Shortly after its founding, the Babson International Student Organization decided to create the Babson International Student Olympics, or BISO. This was a two-day charitable event that brought together international students from 18 Boston-area colleges and universities at Babson for friendly competitions in a variety of sports and games ranging from soccer to track and field events to chess and other board games. Evening social activities followed the competitions. From the beginning, the Student Olympics were a success and fostered a spirit of fun and friendship among Boston's international student community.

To help benefit UNESCO, students sold lottery tickets at all the participating academic institutions. One year, the grand prize was a Toyota Celica sports car donated to the Student Olympics by the Toyota Company. The gift was arranged by Akio Toyoda, then an MBA student at Babson who was living in our home at the time. Wanting to support the Olympics, Charlotte and I bought a bunch of lottery tickets in the names of our kids.

When the time for the lottery drawing came, Charlotte was asked up onto the outdoor stage to hold the large fishbowl into which the purchased lottery tickets had been placed. Then Akio Toyoda, representing Toyota, was asked to draw the winning grand prize ticket. He reached in and picked the ticket out of the bowl. As he was handing it across to the master of ceremonies, Charlotte suddenly shot her hand out, grabbed the ticket, and tore it in half. Startled, the master of ceremonies, who was the student chairman of the Olympics, asked Charlotte to give him the ticket that she had torn in half. When he put the two halves together, he saw that the name on the ticket was Katrina Sorenson, our daughter, and announced her as the winner.

At the time, I was standing with Trina on the lawn in front of the stage. When she heard her name, she was ecstatic. She was 16 and had just the previous week received her first driver's license. Meanwhile, the master of ceremonies was totally nonplussed, not knowing whether he had done the right thing by announcing Trina's name. Finally, he looked to me for guidance. I signaled for him to ask Akio to draw again. It just didn't feel right that the daughter of the college's president should be the winner, when his wife was holding the bowl out of which the ticket had been drawn, and the person drawing the ticket was living in his home.

So Akio drew another ticket, and the new winner was declared to be a Venezuelan student from a wealthy family who already had a sports car. That fellow was quite happy to have won, but later when it came to claiming his prize, he said he didn't like the Celica model and asked the local Toyota dealer if he could get another model in exchange! No such luck! He had to settle for the model on display on the stage.

Trina, of course, was totally dismayed. She turned to me in disbelief. She said, "What happened? I won, didn't I? Akio pulled my name out of the bowl. Why did they draw a second name out of the bowl?"

I explained to her that it wouldn't have been right for the president's daughter to have won, given that Akio, our houseguest, had pulled her name out of a bowl held by her mother. She replied, "But Dad! You bought and paid for the lottery ticket just like everyone else. And it was a totally random process when Akio reached in and pulled out the ticket with my name on it. Isn't that how you taught us the free enterprise system works? You pay your money, you take a risk, and if you win, you win."

Of course, she had a point. I told her I totally understood her feelings and empathized with her disappointment. But I also tried to explain to her that in some cases it is better to err on the side of discretion and that this was one of those cases. That one's reputation is one's most valuable possession and that it would not have been worth it to have the rumor going around that the lottery was rigged so that the president's family would win. I told her that her mother had a very strong moral compass and that was why, as soon as she had seen Trina's name, without hesitation she had instinctively reached out and torn the lottery ticket in half. I also told her that was why I had indicated to the master of ceremonies that he should draw the second ticket. This didn't console her. Nor do I think it convinced her. But, being Trina, she accepted the decision, and over time she came to understand why her mother and I had acted as we had. In any case, it was an ethical learning moment that I still remember more than three decades later.

As a postscript to this incidence, I might add that Akio Toyoda subsequently became a close friend of our family and ultimately went on to become president and CEO of the Toyota Motor Company that had been founded by his great-grandfather. As I write these lines, Akio's son is an MBA student at Babson.

What It Means To Be a "Presidential Spouse"
In the 1970s, at the time the Sorenson family went to Babson, it was typical that when a college or university appointed a new president, the position would be a "two-fer," as in two for the price of one. That is, there was the expectation that the president's spouse, although unpaid, would take on and perform a wide range of official duties and responsibilities.

In the vast majority of cases, "presidential spouse" meant president's wife, since there were few women presidents at that time. Moreover, unlike today, few presidential wives had active professional careers of their own. So it was just naturally assumed that they would willingly team up with their husbands and devote much of their life to furthering the interests of the college or university where their husband was president. Unfortunately, there was rarely a written job description that described what the job entailed. It was a "learn as you go" situation.

Toward the end of our stay at Babson, Charlotte decided to do something about this situation. When the college eventually formed a search committee to find my successor as president, she decided to write a "white paper" describing her experiences at the college and making suggestions that might be helpful to future presidential spouses. Not only did this white paper prove helpful in the Babson search but it also became a widely circulated document that was read by other presidential spouses and that was used by presidential search committees at other educational institutions.

The document is reproduced in Appendix D.

CHAPTER TWENTY-SIX

CORPORATE AND CHARITABLE DIRECTORSHIPS

Starting in 1969, when I was teaching at Harvard, I began serving on corporate boards of directors. The first company that asked me to become a director was Star Markets, a New England-based regional chain of grocery stores. In the ensuing years, I have also served on the boards of more than a dozen public companies and about an equal number of private companies.

The public companies have included the following: Whole Foods Market, Inc.; EMC Corp.; Houghton-Mifflin Company; Eaton Vance Corp.; Affiliated Publications, Inc. (parent of the *Boston Globe*); Polaroid Corp.; Exabyte, Inc.; Springs Industries, Inc.; Foxboro Company; Amtel, Inc.; Barry Wright, Inc.; General Housewares Company; Mammoth Mart, Inc.; Sweetwater, Inc.; and Xenometrics, Inc.

What does serving on a corporate board of directors entail? It is my observation that most people have little idea of what boards of directors do. Indeed, my own ideas about what boards can and should do have evolved significantly. Today, when asked about the role of boards, I reply that public company boards, acting on behalf of the shareholders of the company, have responsibilities in four main areas. These responsibilities are as follows:

- **Leadership:** Make sure an effective leader is in place as CEO who is mission-driven, sets a positive "tone at the top," and fosters a culture designed to bring the best out of everyone associated with the enterprise. Set appropriate compensation for that CEO and the company's senior leadership team. Ensure that proactive management succession programs are in place to produce excellent internal candidates to fill future senior management positions.

- **Control Systems:** Provide oversight of the company's financial, accounting, and control systems to ensure the company's books are kept with accuracy, honesty, and integrity. Further, ensure that risk is being managed properly.

- **Strategy and Planning:** Participate in formulating and approving the long-term strategy of the company and in reviewing and approving annual company plans and budgets, major capital expenditures, and M&A (Merger and Acquisition) activities.

- **Crisis Management:** "Be there" when crises occur to make sure any actions taken are wise, timely, effective, and constitute "the right thing to do."

Of these four areas of responsibility, I have concluded over the years that the most important is number four. Notice that I use the phrase, "To be there *when* crises occur," not "*if* a crisis occurs." That is because in my experience it is almost inevitable that, sooner or later, every company goes through crises. In fact, I would say that it is axiomatic that just as all of us, as individuals, periodically face crises in our lives, so too do organizations of every type. It is in these moments of crisis that directors who serve on company boards really earn their salt. Or, as the case may be, *fail* to earn their salt.

I have been fortunate in that most of the boards on which I have served have functioned effectively and acted with foresight and integrity. There have, however, been exceptions. In several of these situations, the board's shortcoming was in failing to ensure that management acted quickly and decisively enough when confronted with the threat of a disruptive technology, a new form of competition, or an incident that could seriously damage the company's reputation.

Polaroid is a good example of this type of failure. For many years, Polaroid was an extraordinarily successful company. Edwin Land, its founder, led a team of chemists and marketers that invented and then brilliantly exploited the technology of instant photography. For several decades, its strong patent protection gave it a virtual monopoly in its field. The Polaroid brand became one of the top 10 most recognizable brands in the world. Sales skyrocketed and shareholders thrived. Then, in the late 1980s and early 1990s, along came what proved to be a disruptive technology: digital imaging. Polaroid was slow to recognize and react to the new threat. Management thought that consumers would always place a high value on being able to create a tangible instant image on photographic paper and that digital imaging did not present a serious threat. As it turned out, they were wrong.

The situation was exacerbated by the fact that the core of Polaroid's R&D's staff was made up of talented scientists and technicians who, with their predominantly chemical backgrounds, knew a lot about photographic imaging based on chemistry, but very little about developing products based on digital imaging technology. The latter would have required computer scientists and electrical engineers, which Polaroid was slow to hire. As a result, Polaroid missed out on the digital revolution and its sales increasingly suffered as a result.

Meanwhile, Polaroid was facing growing competition from another quarter. Some of Polaroid's patents on its instant film had begun to expire, and the Japanese company Fuji had introduced a competitive instant film that had begun to put additional downward pressure on sales.

In the face of all this increased competition, the Polaroid board was as slow as management to recognize the overall gravity of the situation. By the time management and the board fully woke up to the true significance of the digital revolution, it was too late. The company was headed toward financial failure. Efforts to sell the company to Eastman Kodak or the Fujifilm Company failed. As a result, at 9:00 a.m. on the morning of September 11, 2001, a meeting of the board was called to declare Chapter 11 bankruptcy. Just as the meeting was called to order, the CEO's secretary slipped into the room and handed him a note. He read the note, turned pale, and announced that one of the World Trade Center towers in New York had just been hit by an airplane.

The Polaroid board meeting was immediately cancelled, and the attendees reassembled in an adjoining room with a television set. The group then watched, in real time, the second World Trade tower being hit by another plane. What was to have been a sad and disastrous day for Polaroid turned out to have been an even sadder and more disastrous day for the world. A few days later, the Polaroid board met again and formally voted to put the company into Chapter 11 bankruptcy. The once-proud organization was subsequently sold at a fraction of its peak value and was never again able to rise from the ashes of its failure.

I cite this episode at some length, because since the turn of the century, a growing number of once-powerful companies in industry after industry are facing competition from innovative "disruptive technologies" that are threatening their very existence. Indeed, Eastman Kodak, which for most of the 20th century dominated the photography industry, declared Chapter 11 bankruptcy in January 2012. Like Polaroid, it had failed in its efforts to successfully make the transition to digital imaging. Other examples of companies that have struggled to cope with disruptive technologies are Hewlett-Packard (office equipment), Nokia and Research In Motion (cell phones), Best Buy and Circuit City (electronics retailing),

Borders and Barnes & Noble (book stores), General Motors, Digital Equipment Corporation and Wang Labs (computers), Storage Technology (data storage), Blockbuster (movie rentals), and many print newspapers and magazines.

In the following chapter I shall discuss why I believe higher education will be the next major industry to be impacted by the "disruptive technology" phenomenon. Stay tuned.

During the many years that I have served as a board director, I have been involved in a number of other "crisis management" situations. Two of these involved the behavior of board chairmen. The first was a company named Amtel, the third public company founded by Royal Little. The first two companies that he founded were Indian Head Mills and Textron. Amtel was a conglomerate that produced and marketed everything from auto parts, steel products, and nuts and bolts, to jewelry and book stores (at the time, Amtel owned Barnes & Noble). After retiring from Textron, Roy Little had created a venture investment firm called Narragansett that had, in turn, put up the seed money to form Amtel.

By the time I went on the board in the mid-seventies, Amtel had grown in sales to about $250 million, was publicly traded, and Roy Little was its chairman. Roy at the time was in his mid-eighties and still vigorous. He was also still ambitious. Having started Indian Head Mills and Textron, both of which had reached $1 billion in annual sales, he was determined to start a third venture that would also hit $1 billion in sales before he died. His chosen vehicle for reaching this goal was Amtel. The problem was that Amtel's annual sales were at the time only in the $250 million range and it might have taken years to reach his goal. What to do? He concluded that the quickest way to realize his ambition would be to merge Amtel with a larger company. However, all the other members of the board, together with the current CEO of Amtel, felt that Amtel was making good progress on its own and had no interest in such a merger. As a consequence, it had unanimously voted against such a merger.

Not to be deterred and despite being its sitting chairman, Roy decided to defy the board and launch a hostile takeover of Amtel, his own company. He had teamed up with a Canadian-based firm called Dominion Bridge for this purpose. Together, they made an unsolicited public all-cash offer of $15 per share. This created a dilemma for the board. After voting initially to make a pro-forma rejection of the offer, the board hired Goldman Sachs to do a more thorough evaluation of the offer and to explore a possible sale of the company to another buyer. There ensued a royal brouhaha involving lawyers and investment bankers and a fair amount of posturing and acrimony on both sides. I remember one meeting when, looking out the 20th floor windows of Amtel's corporate headquarters, we watched two helicopters land side-by-side in a nearby field, one bearing the Amtel legal and banking team, and the other, the opposing team.

In the ensuing battle, tempers flared, shareholder lawsuits were initiated, and millions of dollars were paid in legal and banking fees. In the end, Amtel was sold to Dominion Bridge through its American subsidiary for $16.50 per share. The Directors and Officers Insurance policies carried by both companies covered the huge legal and banking fees associated with the litigation and the takeover. However, because the Amtel board had terminated Roy Little as chairman and director when he launched his hostile bid for the company, his legal fees were not covered by the company's D&O insurance. Hence, he ended up personally paying some $300,000 in legal fees and suffered considerable reputational damage. For him, the whole episode was a pyrrhic victory. The following year, in 1979, he published a book entitled *How to Lose $100,000,000 and Other Valuable Advice*. It contained the following quote: "If you're on an acquisition binge—slow down! Be more careful than I was . . . !"

Oddly, some 20 years later, I experienced an eerily similar situation while serving on the board of another large publicly owned company. In this case, the chairman of the company was its largest shareholder and had been a driving force behind the firm's early growth. Now in his early seventies, he had already stepped down from active management of the company but continued to serve on its board. His partner and longtime CEO of the firm had also recently retired from active management and had left the board. To prepare for the future, the two of them had personally groomed a very promising internal candidate to become the firm's new CEO. The board and its voting shareholders had approved this new CEO's appointment and he was now serving in his first year in that position and appeared to be off to a good start.

Evidently, however, the chairman began to have doubts about the new leadership. He somehow concluded that the best way to maximize his personal return on investment in the company while he was still alive would be to arrange a near-term sale of the firm at a large cash premium to a bigger company in the industry. When he broached this idea to his fellow directors, they were unanimous in their opposition to the concept. They explicitly enjoined the chairman from seeking a buyer and thereby "putting the company into play."

However, the chairman didn't know how to take no for an answer. He walked into the next board meeting with his personal lawyer and with a team of investment bankers from a prominent Wall Street firm. He called the meeting to order and stated that while the matter wasn't on the agenda, he continued to think that the sale of the company made sense and had engaged the investment banking firm to make a thorough study of the concept. They were at the meeting to present their findings.

On this announcement, a palpable tension arose in the room. The new CEO immediately requested that the board go into executive session and that the team of investment bankers and the chairman's personal lawyer be asked to leave the room. Whereupon, the bankers stepped out but the lawyer did not. It was a tense moment and silence initially ensued. Then, the CEO spoke up and reminded the chairman that the board had explicitly enjoined him from exploring a sale of the company. The chairman aggressively rejoined that he had not agreed with that decision and insisted vehemently that the board had an obligation to hear the presentation of the investment bankers. Whereupon, one of the board members made a motion that the chairman be stripped of his title and dismissed from the board. The motion was seconded and, with the exception of the chairman's vote, passed unanimously.

Stunned, the chairman continued to sit at the head of the table and refused to leave. Finally, the CEO picked up the phone, dialed building security, and asked that a security officer be dispatched to the boardroom to escort the chairman, his lawyer, and the team of investment bankers out of the building. That amazing eviction then occurred!

The crisis had passed. But it had been one of the most dramatic moments in all my years of serving as a public company board member. The episode had been most regrettable and extremely painful for all concerned. In the end, however, it turned out that the board had made the right decision in this crisis situation. In subsequent years, the company remained independent and the new CEO did a stellar job of growing it rapidly, serving its customers well, continuing to keep it as a great place to work, and returning an outstanding profit to its investors. Ironically, in the long run, the former chairman prospered far more handsomely from a financial point of view than he would have if his previous hostile attempt to sell the company for cash had been successful.

I could recount many other stories of my adventures as a public company board member over the years. But the foregoing should give a flavor for what company boards do and what being a director entails. Suffice to say, I have greatly enjoyed my service as a director and learned a lot about both business and human nature from the experience.

Before leaving the subject of board service, I should also point out that, by and large, I have also enjoyed my experiences as a director and/or advisory board member of a number of private startup firms. Here, much of the satisfaction comes from having the opportunity to both mentor and learn from the entrepreneur/founders of these early-stage ventures. The responsibilities of early-stage private company boards tend to be broader than those of public companies. Earlier, I described the public company board responsibilities as falling into four categories: picking the right leadership, overseeing the integrity of financial reporting and control systems, being involved in formulating long-term strategy, and taking appropriate actions when crises occur. In startup companies, board members have all of those responsibilities, but they also tend to get much more involved in raising capital, providing business contacts, and giving personal help and advice to the founding entrepreneur and his or her team.

In my case, I have tended to play a special additional role as a company director or advisor. Namely, I have often served as a buffer between the founder/entrepreneur and the venture capital firms that become investors once it is clear that the startup company has proved it has the potential to prosper. In my experience, it often occurs that the venture capitalists, having made their investment and with their superior financial leverage, begin to apply pressure on the founder in terms of telling him or her how to better run the firm or when to push for the sale of the company. This can lead to tension, particularly if the venture firm's objectives and timetables differ from those of the founders and the other earlier stage "angel" investors. In these instances, I have often acted as the entrepreneur's "representative" in making sure that the entrepreneur and the earlier stage investors are being treated fairly by the VCs. I enjoy this role and I think it can be valuable to all parties.

Under the heading of "directorships," I should also say a word about my service over the years on the boards of a number of not-for-profit organizations. Dating back to the early 1970s, when our family lived in Boston, I began to be asked from time to time to play a governance role in a variety of not-for-profit educational, civic, and cultural entities.

The earliest of these was the invitation that Charlotte and I received to serve as PTA co-presidents of Winn Brook Elementary School in Belmont, which our kids attended. This we did, and, during our tenure, we pushed, with limited success, for Winn Brook and other Belmont schools to adopt more of the "open classroom" approach to teaching that was becoming popular at the time. The idea of the open classroom was that a large group of students of varying skill levels would be in a single, large, open classroom with several teachers overseeing them. Rather than having one teacher lecture to the entire class at once, students were typically divided into different groups for each subject according to their skill level for that subject. The students then worked in these small groups to achieve their assigned goal, often in a cooperative system. Teachers served as both facilitators and instructors.

Both Charlotte and I were convinced that this approach to learning was preferable to the highly structured and regimented classroom approach that both of us had experienced when we were growing up. Later, based on the educational experiences of our own children, our thinking evolved to the conclusion that while the open classroom approach worked well in helping students develop their creative and artistic skills, it was not as effective at teaching the traditional "hard" skills of reading, writing, arithmetic, and basic science.

Later in the seventies, there followed invitations to serve on the boards of trustees or overseers at the Boston Museum of Science, Massachusetts General Hospital, the Boston Symphony, the Boston Museum of Fine Arts, the Massachusetts Trustees of Reservations, and Earthwatch. In the early nineties, I served a term as chairman of the board of trustees at the Museum of Science and am still a life trustee of that institution. To this day, I feel a strong commitment to the museum and believe strongly in the work it is doing to instill a love of science, nature, and technology in the next generation of Americans.

In the 1980s, I also served on the Visiting Committees of both Harvard's Graduate School of Education and its School of Continuing Education. I came away from these assignments with a greater respect for both of these schools within Harvard. The School of Continuing Education particularly intrigued me. Most of its faculty were retired Harvard professors, some of them outstanding teachers and scholars in their fields. One of Harvard's best-kept secrets is that the HSCE can be a wonderful back-door way to get a great education and earn a bona fide Harvard degree in the process.

More recently, I served a number of years as a trustee of The Nature Conservancy in Colorado (TNC) and as Colorado's representative on the Conservancy's National Trustee Council. TNC is the largest not-for-profit environmental conservation organization in the world. In this era of environmental degradation and global climate change, its work is vital to the preservation of what TNC terms "the world's last great places." These include our oceans, freshwater rivers and lakes, grasslands, forests, mountains, and the atmosphere. In my view, it is a race against time to see whether we humans are intelligent enough, committed enough, and capable enough to avoid long-run global environmental Armageddon. I enjoyed my work as a trustee of TNC and, to this day, the entire Sorenson family is very much committed to the work it is doing.

One interesting institution on whose board of directors I served in the late eighties was that of the Federal Reserve Bank of Boston. This turned out to be a fascinating assignment and I'm afraid I learned more than I contributed to the workings of this board. I learned, for example, that the boards of the 12 individual regional Federal Reserve Banks in the system have little impact on interest rates or on federal monetary policy. Rather it is the Federal Open Market Committee (FOMC), composed of the seven members of the Fed's board of governors in Washington plus five rotating presidents from the regional banks, who are empowered to vote on those issues and are the real decision-makers. The regional banks can make recommendations, but have no power to act. However, the 12 regional bank presidents and boards do provide supervisory oversight of all the state-chartered banks and bank holding companies in their respective regions.

During the time I was a Fed bank director, almost all of the New England banks were thriving and had few problems. Hence, we were seldom presented with real issues to resolve. The only votes we were called on to cast at each meeting were perfunctory ones to rubber-stamp the bank's discount rate recommendation to the FOMC in Washington. Our board meetings consisted mainly of presentations and tutorials on how the banking system worked and what the current and future economic outlook was for New England and the U.S. as a whole. I found these sessions interesting and educational.

Before leaving the topic of not-for-profit boards, I should also mention that in addition to serving as a trustee of Babson College, I have also served on the board of governors of the Asian Institute of Management (AIM), the school that I helped found in the 1960s. Finally, I have served on the President's Council of the Olin College of Engineering and as a trustee of the Deming Center for Entrepreneurship at the University of Colorado, a center that I helped to create when, in later years, I was dean of the University of Colorado's business school.

CHAPTER TWENTY-SEVEN

THE FUTURE OF HIGHER EDUCATION

In the previous chapter, I stated my conviction that one of the next industries to feel the impact of the "disruptive technology and innovation" phenomenon in a major way is that of higher education. I am not alone in this belief. Indeed, Professor Clayton Christensen, the well-known Harvard Business School professor who is the father of the theory of "disruptive innovation," has opined that as many as half of American universities and/or colleges could face closure in the 2020s.

Christensen bases his prediction mainly on his belief that the advent of evolving technologies such as Internet-enabled online learning and artificial intelligence (AI) will undermine traditional colleges and universities to the point that many won't survive.

I concur that MOOCs (Massive Open Online Courses) are destined to have a profound impact on education at all levels. Colleges and universities, in particular, will be increasingly impacted by the proliferation of online courses. These courses are becoming more widely used in the U.S. and worldwide. They can be interactive, they are convenient, they are increasingly effective, and they are considerably less expensive than on-campus courses. They clearly represent a disruptive technology destined to change the whole landscape of higher education in America, particularly in the STEAM (Science, Technology, Engineering, Arts, and Math) disciplines.

The other fast-evolving technology that deserves a special call-out in terms of its potential future impact on higher education is that of artificial intelligence, or AI, as it is more commonly called. I will discuss this phenomenon in greater detail at the end of this chapter.

But, in my view, there are other reasons, beyond technology, why traditional colleges and universities are endangered.

First, the cost of a college or university education continues to rise at a dramatically higher rate than the average rate of inflation in the U.S. Many studies have documented this fact. For example, according to a 2012 *Forbes* report: "College costs have been rising roughly at a rate of 7% per year for decades. Since 1985, the overall consumer price index has risen 115% while the college education inflation rate has risen nearly 500%." In general, this trend has continued in the years since then.

Despite the existence of scholarships, financial aid packages, and 529 Plans, these rising costs have impacted students in several negative ways. Many are graduating with a serious level of debt resulting from having borrowed significant amounts of money via student loan programs. Others have decided not to go to college or to drop out before completing their degree because they simply can't afford it. And still others end up graduating in six or seven years, instead of four, because they need to take time off to earn enough money to pay for their tuition, room, and board.

In short, the rising costs of attending college and/or graduate degree programs are causing many would-be students to seriously question whether it makes sense to enroll in these programs. This is beginning to impact enrollments in both public and private institutions. For example, according to the website statista.com, total university and college enrollments in the U.S. peaked in 2012 at 21.64 million. By 2017, total enrollments were 19.74 million, a decline of 8.8 percent.

Second, most colleges and universities, be they private or public, are extremely inefficient institutions. Classrooms tend to be used only five or six hours a day for only eight or so months a year due to summer, winter, spring, and other holiday breaks. Dormitories and campus cafeterias are underused during summer months and other break periods. The same is true for other campus facilities such as libraries, faculty offices, and athletic facilities.

These inefficiencies, coupled with rising administrative and faculty costs, are placing many private colleges, community colleges, and public universities in a serious financial bind. Administrative overheads, in particular, have been a culprit in driving up spending. According to the Department of Education, administrative positions at colleges and universities grew by 60 percent between 1993 and 2009, which was 10 times the rate of growth of tenured faculty positions. And this trend has continued. There are now two non-academic employees at public universities and two and a half at private universities for every full-time tenure track member of the faculty.

Third, the almost universally used system of "faculty tenure" has led to unintended negative consequences on many campuses. University tenure in the U.S. dates back to the early 1900s, when three universities—Harvard, Columbia, and the University of Chicago—first adopted the concept. By mid-century, almost all American colleges and universities had formally adopted the tenure system. The concept underlying tenure is two-fold. First, it is intended to ensure that faculty members who have been granted tenure have the academic freedom to express and teach their ideas, no matter how controversial, without the fear of being fired. Second, it is intended to ensure that, once having been granted tenure, professors have a guaranteed academic position for life at the granting institution.

In my view, the unintended negative consequences of the tenure system stem from the way the system works in actual practice. Typically, the system begins with an academic candidate enrolling in a PhD program designed primarily to teach him or her how to do original academic research. In most programs, much less attention is devoted to helping the candidate learn how to become a skilled and effective teacher.

Once having earned a PhD degree, the candidate typically lands a tenure track position as an assistant professor at a college or university. He or she then spends the first seven to ten years of his or her academic appointment focused primarily on producing research articles for publication in "refereed" academic journals. This is because the ultimate tenure decision tends to be based primarily on the quality of the professor's academic research output. The individual's teaching prowess is typically assigned a lower priority by the senior professors who make up the tenure committee. Hence, tenure track professors throughout their career often end up treating teaching as a "burden," compared with their research "opportunities."

The result is that in most colleges and universities, low-paid non-tenure track instructors, teaching assistants, and/or adjunct non-academic professors do much of the teaching. While these individuals can often be gifted teachers, in many cases they are not. Students often become the losers in this situation and feel they are short-changed in the process, given what they are paying to attend college.

Fourth, in America, much of the teaching in universities and colleges continues to be based on the traditional "lecture method." This involves "God, the professor" or the "sage on the stage" standing in front of a room full of note-taking students and imparting information, often based on outdated lecture notes. Even in online courses, this format is often followed.

The problem with this method is that in today's world, the information being imparted is not necessarily "knowledge" and, in this digital age, often has a short half-life. Moreover, it is frequently information that is readily available online. Finally, it is a passive approach to learning that is increasingly ineffective.

In my inauguration talk upon becoming president of Babson College (see Appendix B), I elaborated on why I believe that true learning must be an active process, not a passive one. The following is an excerpt from my talk.

> The fundamental truth, of course, is that in the last analysis, the initiative for learning must rest with the learner and not the teacher.
>
> The second premise, corollary to the first, is that effective learning tends to be both active and interactive and is seldom, if ever, passive.
>
> The Greek philosopher Aristotle recognized the active nature of learning 2,400 years ago when he observed that: "What we have to learn, we learn by doing." And Alfred North Whitehead picked up on this theme in 1929 when he suggested in his book, The Aims of Education, that: "Celibacy does not suit a university. It must mate itself with action."
>
> As for the interactive quality of learning, it was Ralph Waldo Emerson who, in the mid-1800's, aptly observed: "You send your child to the schoolmaster, but 'tis the schoolboys who educate him." He also observed that "Conversation is the laboratory and workshop of the student."

Roger Babson, founder of Babson College, also subscribed to the active and interactive nature of learning when in the late 1930s he wrote his book *Looking Ahead Fifty Years*. In an especially perceptive passage he stated:

> Facts alone are not readily retained in memory. It is easier to remember facts when they are accompanied by acts—particularly if the acts are our own. Therefore, lectures have been supplemented by laboratories. Students visit industries, sometimes to work there part-time. Industries visit the school. The conference system and the case system have come into vogue. It is all typical of the swing toward dynamic training instead of the older method of teaching by rote. The new education will firmly follow this modern trend. The teacher's main function will be not to impart information but to implant wisdom.

Mr. Babson was certainly prescient in his thinking.

For all of the foregoing reasons, the American higher education system is at risk. In my view, small private colleges are particularly vulnerable—especially those that don't have a large endowment and/or those without a distinctive niche strategy like that of Babson College, which, of course, has focused on entrepreneurship and management education.

Lest I be guilty of painting too grim a picture of the future of American colleges and universities, let me hasten to add that most public institutions and upper-tier private institutions, such as the Ivy League colleges and universities and those with strong brands and well-padded endowments, will no doubt continue to survive and perhaps even thrive. But even they must be prepared to address and resolve the serious challenges that I have outlined above.

This brings me to some additional thoughts on the future of education in America and the rest of the world. In 2017, the journalist and author Thomas Friedman published his book titled *Thank You For Being Late*. In the first third of the book, he describes the many ways in which the whole STEAM (Science, Technology, Engineering, Art, and Math) world is exploding exponentially and, in the process, profoundly influencing the way we live and learn.

These developments are calling into question our whole traditional approach to education. This traditional approach—which has existed for centuries—has been based on the premise that "formal" education begins in pre-school, followed by elementary school, middle school, high school, then perhaps undergraduate college and, in some cases, graduate school. Once we have a certificate stating that we have earned a high school, college, or graduate degree, our "formal" education is at an end. These are typically called "terminal degrees," suggesting that henceforth we are on our own in terms of learning in later life.

In my view, this traditional approach to education has to change. We humans will increasingly have to become *lifelong* learners to keep up with the exponential explosion of information, ideas, concepts, and knowledge being generated in the world each day. Fact: As of 2018, more data has been created in the last two years than in the entire previous history of the human species! And in this Internet era of AI (artificial intelligence), computer science, medical research, space exploration, and global interconnectedness, our traditional "formal education" system will become increasingly obsolete.

There is, however, a potential silver lining for existing colleges and universities in the face of the disruptive forces I have just described.

First, and most obvious, they have the opportunity to find creative ways to increasingly weave MOOCs, AI, and other forms of online learning and technology into their curricula.

They can explore opportunities to identify and then focus on unique educational "niches" where they can strive to become the educational leader in that field. This is what Babson did in identifying entrepreneurship education as its area of particular educational expertise, what Olin College of Engineering has done in the field of engineering, and what Berklee College of Music has done in the field of music.

They can step up efforts to control the growth of institutional costs in general and administrative costs in particular.

They can find ways to make more efficient use of their physical facilities. For example, they can offer three-year undergraduate degrees that operate on a year-round basis, including during summer. They can place more emphasis on one-year master's degree programs that have summer sessions.

They can strive to place more emphasis on interactive "learning-by-doing" courses and less emphasis on lecture-oriented courses.

They can take steps to phase out the tenure system and instead adopt the approach of periodic performance reviews used by almost every other industry in the country.

They can place more emphasis in their PhD programs on helping candidates learn how to develop into gifted teachers.

They can further step up their development efforts with the goal of increasing alumni giving and increasing their endowments.

They can redouble their efforts to recruit talented foreign students who are able to pay the full tuition.

They can seek to form partnerships with other educational institutions, or in some cases, with corporations that desire to provide continuing education opportunities for their employees.

Finally, and in my opinion the most important and promising market opportunity of all, they can initiate a full-court press on developing non-degree, lifelong learning programs for citizens aged 25 to 95, enabling them to understand and keep up with the exponential explosion of information, ideas, concepts, and knowledge being generated in today's world. These programs can take place on campuses or they can take place online.

Business schools, in particular, have an attractive opportunity to address this growing market. This is because many, if not most, senior and midlevel managers are woefully behind their younger colleagues in their understanding of how "big data," AI, and the many other developments in the rapidly changing STEAM world are impacting their enterprises. Business schools that have not already done so can form partnerships with these enterprises to provide lifelong learning programs for executives at all levels within their organizations.

It is interesting to note that at Harvard Business School, revenues from its non-degree executive education programs for senior and midlevel managers are already larger than the tuition revenues generated by its MBA degree program. And at Babson College, revenues generated by non-degree executive education programs held at its Executive Conference Center continue to represent a significant percentage of its overall institutional revenues.

Similar opportunities exist in almost all other academic disciplines: engineering, science, liberal arts, law, medicine, nursing, and so forth. Picture a world in which all adults spend the equivalent of at least a month each year enrolled in online, campus-based, or field-based learning programs. Some of these might be related to one's profession and some just related to one's need and desire to keep up with developments in the ever more rapidly changing world in which we live.

I realize that not everyone will be excited by this concept. But I know that I, in my mid-eighties, have to keep learning every day just to remain current in the use of my laptop computer, my iPad, and my iPhone. The same is true in terms of my trying to keep up with the ever-evolving geopolitical scene and with developments in the socioeconomic, environmental, cultural, literary, and artistic spheres. And, of course, new concepts are constantly evolving with respect to the health-related fields of medicine, nutrition, exercise, and nutrition.

In short, the need to continue to learn in no way stops on our graduation from high school or college. In fact, this need continues to grow throughout our lives. Given this fact, there is no reason why our existing educational institutions cannot, through innovative thinking, expand their non-degree curricular offerings so as to take advantage of this huge market opportunity. If these nonprofit institutions don't rise to this challenge, it is likely that for-profit enterprises will. In this case, it is possible that Clayton Christensen's prediction that as many as half of American universities and/or colleges could face closure in the 2020s may come true.

By the way, my primary computer and iPhone consultants are my grandchildren . . . aged 13 to 22. I suspect this is true for many other seniors as well. Imagine that! It is probably the first time in human history that children have become mentors to their parents and grandparents!

Before I close this chapter, I would like to elaborate on one of the most disruptive forces looming on the horizon of education: artificial intelligence (AI). Most of the technologies discussed so far focus primarily on how content is delivered. For example, the Internet makes it possible for students from all over the world to congregate with a teacher. This is new and innovative, but once the class has come together, the educational material is delivered quite often in the old-fashioned way: from teacher to student in a lecture or seminar type of format.

The difference with artificial intelligence is that it can transform the teaching function itself. In fact, it raises the question, "What is the role of a teacher today?"

For example, one of the most important tasks of any teacher or teaching assistant (TA) is *grading*. The instructor is not only responsible for delivering information to students but also assessing the extent to which they have integrated this new knowledge and actually *learned* something of value.

We might think that only a knowledgeable professor or TA could perform this assessment function. However, AI programs have been "trained" to do human tasks by "watching" a person do it. After many hours of such training, AI has the potential to translate languages, diagnose diseases, analyze business problems, check the logic of a legal argument . . . and do much more. AIs are already adept at grading multiple-choice tests and/or subjects with a clear answer, like physics. The next step is to teach them how to evaluate student essays or case study analyses. This will be more difficult, but I have no doubt that it will be done, because the payoff will be huge. Teachers around the world will have thousands of hours liberated to improve their courses, meet with students, and keep up with their own fields of knowledge. Students will benefit as well. Because the software can work 24/7, they will receive their grades and feedback more quickly. Also, since the AI will never get tired or hungry, there will be a consistency in the grading patterns that humans could not easily achieve.

Please note, too, that an AI grading system does not imply that the teacher is eliminated from the process. The teacher or TA can "stay in the loop," checking the validity of the AI system's grading. Because the AI will learn from corrections made in its procedures, its fidelity to the human instructor's grading rubric will improve daily.

A second example of how AIs could improve education is one-on-one tutoring, or customized learning. Every teacher knows that, in a class of 20 students, five or so will be far ahead of the others, five will be behind, and 10 will fall somewhere in the middle. The differences might be connected with prior experiences, cognitive abilities, home life, or many other factors. Whatever the cause, the teacher must modulate his or her instruction to take into account the range of knowledge and capabilities the students bring to the class.

Ultimately, no one gets quite what they need, which is why professors have office hours and TAs have sections. It is also why parents often hire private tutors to help their children keep up in subjects that are difficult for them.

This problem can be solved with the same AI system that does the grading. When the course starts, each participant could interact with the AI software, providing information about themselves and how much they know about the subject. The AI would then be available around the clock to answer questions from the individual students and provide advanced topics for those who are dashing ahead.

Once again, the teacher can stay in the learning loop, checking periodically to see how the AI is interacting with each student and following up if the system is missing important points.

To be honest, though, such a system could eliminate not only the teacher but the course structure itself. Let's say I want to take a course in fundraising for nonprofit organizations. In our imaginary future, I could find such a course online, pay the fee, and enroll. The AI teacher could then take me through the process of learning about fundraising at my own pace, connecting me with other students and with experts in the field as I moved along. I could have as much or as little human interaction as I wanted throughout.

Finally, an AI system could provide a form of *immersive learning* that is powerfully experiential in nature. Fans of the *Star Trek* television series often cite the "Holodeck" as the type of learning they would like to have in real life. Crew members of the *Starship Enterprise* would go to the Holodeck when they wanted to learn anything at all, from the plays of Shakespeare to the mechanics of a warp drive. To learn about Shakespeare, for example, they might find themselves transported back to 16th century England, spending time with the Bard himself. They could ask "him" (an AI-powered avatar, of course) questions directly, rather than read someone's analysis of his works.

We would probably need to combine virtual reality with artificial intelligence to get the full "Holodeck" experience. However, a great deal of it could be simulated in two-dimensional virtual environments similar to today's video games. Plenty of research shows that direct experience is the best way to learn anything, so education that feels immersive and experiential would be optimal. As with the other examples, the professor or instructor need not be eliminated. He or she could go along on the meeting with Will Shakespeare or other historical figures, for example.

I don't think anything like this exists today, but I do know that there are so-called "bots" present in virtual-reality settings to help people use VR.

These are just a few ideas of how artificial intelligence could disrupt education. The grading algorithm would certainly be a positive disruption for most teachers, at any level of education.

The more I learn about AI, the more I see potential applications and then find that many are already being developed. As a lifelong educator, I am both awed and a bit intimidated as I consider this highly disruptive technology! In particular, I believe that AI is destined to have a huge impact on the colleges and universities of the future. As in other industries that have been affected by radical technological innovations, there are bound to be winners and losers in the world of higher education. The winners will be those institutions that find effective ways to incorporate AI into their teaching programs. The losers will be those that do not.

CHAPTER TWENTY-EIGHT

A CAREER FORK IN THE ROAD

One of the public companies on whose boards I have served was the Barry Wright Corporation. I became a director of this company in 1976, having been recommended by my friend, Dick Nichols, former board chairman of Babson College, who had been a longtime director of Barry Wright.

Barry Wright, based in Watertown, Massachusetts, a Boston suburb, was a public firm traded on the NASDAQ exchange. Founded as Barry Controls during World War II, its initial focus was on the manufacturing of products designed to minimize the harmful effects of shock, noise, and vibration caused by the recoil of anti-aircraft guns on naval ships. Later, the product line was expanded to include shock, vibration, and noise control devices for commercial and military airplanes, helicopters, ships, submarines, tanks, trucks, computers, and various other applications.

By the late seventies, when I joined the board, the company had merged with Wright Line, Inc. Wright Line products were used to organize, file, access, and protect all types of computer-generated data and other information.

In 1979, the founder and CEO of the company, Erwin "Pete" Pietz, had reached the age of 65, the mandatory retirement age that he had established earlier in the life of the company. In anticipation of his retirement, Pete had groomed a successor to take his place. Unfortunately, and unexpectedly, the potential successor had died of a brain tumor earlier that year.

The company formed a search committee made up of several members of the board to seek a new CEO. After hiring an executive search firm and screening both internal and external candidates for several months, the committee approached me in the summer of 1979 to ask whether I would consider taking the job. My initial reaction was one of incredulity. To begin with, Barry Wright was primarily a technology company. For the most part, its products were technical in nature and required considerable engineering and manufacturing knowledge and experience. Not being an engineer by training, I had little or none of this knowledge. Second, most of my background was in the world of management education and academic administration. While I had earlier worked with Nestlé in the private sector and had done a fair amount of marketing consulting, I had no actual executive management experience in the private sector.

Most important, however, was the fact that I was immensely enjoying my work as president of Babson and had much unfinished business to do there before we could declare victory in terms of accomplishing all of our major Master Plan objectives. Thus, I told my fellow directors that I was flattered that they should think of me, but my answer was no.

Thereupon, the board and the executive search firm renewed their search. Pete Pietz said that he would be willing to postpone his retirement date until a satisfactory replacement could be found. If truth be told, I learned that he was secretly pleased to remain as CEO for a bit longer. Although it was he who had established the mandatory "retirement at age 65" policy, he had done so in his early fifties when he felt that having a mandatory retirement age would constitute good management practice. As often happens, however, the closer he, himself, got to 65, the less the policy seemed to be a good idea.

For months, the search continued until, almost a year later, in mid-summer 1980, the search committee came back to me and said they would really like me to reconsider and take the job. They pointed out that I was well known and liked by all of the executives in the company, that they felt I had gained outstanding executive experience as president of Babson, that the company already had plenty of technical and engineering talent, and that I would bring to the job the kind of visionary leadership that the company needed for the next phase of its development. Finally, they pointed out that a very attractive compensation package went along with the job . . . particularly when compared with the academic salaries that were being paid in the 1970s.

This time Charlotte and I gave their proposal serious thought, based on several factors:

I had been at Babson for six years, which was already longer than the average five-year tenure typical of college presidents at the time.

As a family with three children approaching college age, we could use the additional financial resources for future tuition payments.

Barry Wright was headquartered only a short distance away from our home, and would not require a move away from the Boston area that we so loved.

Most of all was the fact that the position offered a tempting new personal career challenge. I had taught business administration and managerial leadership for many years. I had served as president and CEO of an academic institution. But could I handle the job of being CEO of a midsized publicly traded company in the "real world" of business?

It was this last factor that finally convinced me to respond positively to the Barry Wright offer. But I did so with one big string attached. Namely, I indicated that I would accept the job, but only on the condition that I could delay taking on my new responsibilities until the end of the 1980-81 academic year.

I pointed out that I couldn't just leave Babson in August with a new academic year starting in September. In the academic world, boards of trustees typically required at least a nine-month academic year lead time to conduct a search for a new president.

I also pointed out that we required a final year to accomplish the remaining major goals that had been laid out in Babson's Master Plan, which I had initiated when I had first arrived at the college. These included successfully concluding the college's capital campaign, completing a number of major building projects that were underway, winding up the academic accreditation process that was scheduled for the upcoming academic year, and completing a number of curriculum and faculty initiatives that were in process.

To my considerable surprise, the Barry Wright board agreed to this nine-month delay. Again, the fact that Pete Pietz was willing to postpone his retirement for a second year was a factor in their decision.

The delay permitted me to have a "shadow year" as Barry Wright's CEO, during which I attended all of the company's annual and long-term budgeting and planning sessions. Since the company's headquarters were only a 15-minute drive from Babson, it was easy to fit these sessions into my schedule. As a result, when the time actually came for me to take on my new responsibilities on a full-time basis, I was able to hit the ground running.

So it was that, in June of 1981, I vacated my office at Babson and moved my base of operations to the Barry Wright headquarters. Fortunately, my very capable secretary/assistant, Dottie, was willing to make the move with me. She had been a godsend to me at Babson and continued to play the same role at Barry Wright.

I left Babson with a very good feeling about what we had collectively accomplished during my tenure as its president. Virtually all of the major Master Plan goals that we had laid out following my arrival at the college had been achieved. Moreover, they had been accomplished as the result of a cooperative effort on the part of all the college's stakeholders: faculty, students, staff, trustees, overseers, alumni, town officials, and supporting foundations and corporations. Finally, we had created and carved out a distinctive academic niche for ourselves in the area of entrepreneurship education. To this day, thanks to the creativity and hard work of successor presidents and successive generations of the aforementioned stakeholders, Babson has maintained its "first mover" advantage and continues to be ranked the number one global educational institution in this increasingly important area. Appendix E contains an overall review of my Babson presidency as reported in the Fall 1980 issue of the *Babson Quarterly Bulletin*.

As we prepared to leave the college, the whole Sorenson family received a heartwarming sendoff from the faculty, staff, students, trustees, and alumni of Babson. Among other events, there was a wonderful farewell dinner that featured a video slideshow depicting the highlights of our stay at the college. Of course, there were also the usual speeches. But the highlight of the evening was being presented with two leather-bound volumes containing some 200 personal letters from the many friends we had made during our seven years at Babson.

From a family point of view, my transition from Babson to Barry Wright brought about a number of significant changes. Perhaps the most significant of these was our physical move from the college president's residence in Wellesley to a house located at 117 Brattle Street in Cambridge, Massachusetts.

The family had debated whether to move back into the house that we still owned on Pinehurst Road in Belmont or whether we should move closer to Boston. Serendipity played a role in our final decision to opt for the latter.

It happened this way:

One day in the early spring of 1981, I had taken the airline shuttle to New York to attend a board meeting. That evening, on the return flight, I encountered a friend of mine, Richard McAdoo, who was a senior executive at Houghton-Mifflin, the publishing company on whose board I also served. I had left my car parked at Logan Airport and, since Dick had not, on our arrival in Boston I offered to give him a ride to his home in Cambridge. On the way, I mentioned that Charlotte and I were exploring the possibility of moving back to Cambridge, which was Charlotte's hometown and where we had happily lived as married graduate students.

"That's funny," he said, "my wife and I have some friends, Arthur and Jean Brooks, who own a carriage house located behind their big home on Brattle Street. The other day, they mentioned that they were in the process of renovating the carriage house so that they can rent it out. Before dropping me off at my home, why don't you drive west from Harvard Square on Brattle and I'll show you where it is."

This we did, and when I saw the location of the house, I was immediately interested. Situated on Brattle Street, the most historic street in Cambridge, it was just four blocks from Harvard Square and one block from the Charles River.

A Career Fork in the Road

Brattle Street, sometimes known as Tory Row, was where a number of the leading English families lived in beautiful 18th century Georgian homes during pre-revolutionary colonial days. When the revolution began in 1775, many of these families, being loyal to the British Crown, fled. Their homes were then occupied by elements of the Continental Army. The largest and most beautiful of these homes served as General George Washington's headquarters during the first year of the war. Other houses were turned into army hospitals or administrative offices.

Years later, in the early 19th century, the poet Henry Wadsworth Longfellow and his family resided in the house that General Washington had occupied during 1775-76. While living there, he built two very large houses next door for his two daughters. Then, in 1886, the family built a carriage house/barn behind these two houses to serve the whole estate. It was this carriage house that Dick McAdoo mentioned to me on our drive to his home that night in the spring of 1981.

The next day Dick called Arthur Brooks, the current owner of the carriage house, and provided an introduction to him for Charlotte and me. When we contacted Arthur, he said that yes, indeed, he was renovating the carriage house and he would be happy to show it to us as prospective renters. Arthur was an architect and he had done the design for the renovation himself and was personally overseeing the required construction work.

When Charlotte and I came to look at the carriage house, we immediately fell in love with it and said that we would be happy to rent it beginning July 1, 1981. The deal was struck. The nice thing about it was that, since there was still nearly three months of construction work to be done on the renovation, Charlotte and I had the opportunity to suggest some design changes to better suit our family's needs. Specifically, we requested that the living area be divided into two sections. The larger section would be where Charlotte and I would live. The second section would be a smaller apartment over a four-car garage where our three teenage kids would hang out and have some privacy. Arthur readily agreed to the changes. The resulting setup turned out to work well for us.

Later, in 1986, the Brookses agreed to sell us the carriage house and it is a residence that our family still owns today.

When we first moved into 117 Brattle Street in 1981, Kristin had just completed her freshman year at Kenyon College in Ohio, Trina had finished her junior year at Wellesley High School, and Eric had completed his sophomore year at Saint Paul's boarding school in New Hampshire. In the fall, following our move to Cambridge, the plan was for Trina to complete her senior year of high school as a boarding student at Phillips Academy in Andover, Massachusetts, and the other two kids would continue their educations as boarders at their respective schools. This meant that Charlotte and I would be "empty nesters" almost immediately following our move into Cambridge. This is why the concept of a separate apartment for Kristin, Trina, and Eric when they were home from school turned out to be a great idea. They enjoyed their relative privacy and we enjoyed the comfort and convenience of knowing that they were still under the same roof with us.

Thus began yet another chapter in our lives.

I subsequently spent eight years heading up Barry Wright, the first four as president and CEO and the last four as chairman, president, and CEO. These were the Reagan years. They started with an economic downturn in 1981, followed by a period of relative prosperity until another downturn that reached its nadir in 1987 when the Dow Jones Industrial Average experienced its largest single day crash in history. This, in turn, was followed by another period of relative growth in the late 1980s. Barry Wright's fortunes during this decade, being tied to the underlying economic cycle in the U.S., followed a similar pattern.

As I look back over that period of my life, the professional aspect of it seems to have passed in a blur.

On my arrival at Barry Wright, I initially focused on getting better acquainted with all aspects of the company's operations and with all of its key managers. From the beginning, I was particularly interested in further fostering a culture that would bring out the best in everyone associated with the firm. Toward this end, and working together with our entire management team, we formulated and articulated the following set of what we subsequently called our "Corporate Values and Management Commitments":

1. We are committed to excellence and a high degree of professionalism in all phases of our operations.

2. We believe the fundamental strength of our company is based on the quality of our people. Consequently, we are committed to providing all our employees with satisfying, challenging and rewarding career opportunities. We are also committed to engendering a sense of pride, excitement, and loyalty on the part of all who are associated with the company.

3. We have a strong customer orientation and are committed to dependably meeting our customers' needs in an effective, timely, supportive fashion. We believe we shall benefit in the long run if we are willing to "go the extra mile" to help customers solve their problems.

4. Hiring and advancement within the company will be based primarily on merit and will reflect our commitment to pursue an active program of affirmative action.

5. We are committed to high standards of business ethics in our dealings with employees, suppliers, customers, competitors, shareholders and the public at large.

6. We are committed to being responsible and respected corporate citizens both nationally and abroad.

7. We are committed to work continuously toward improving productivity in all phases of our operations. This is an effort that should involve every employee. Our objective is to find the simplest, most cost-effective approach in every phase of our operations. This objective will receive particularly high priority during the 1980's.

8. We believe in using common sense in dealing with management problems. Consequently, we prefer simple, straightforward solutions to problems, and we seek to avoid an excess of bureaucracy, red tape and over-complexity in our operations.

9. Within the framework of our annual and long-term plans and budgets, we believe in granting a high degree of autonomy to the managers of our operating units. Centralized management will be confined to those areas where company-wide coordination and control is vital. These areas include planning, accounting, finance, legal, risk management, compensation and employee benefits.

Our internal "champions" are those who excel in carrying out their responsibilities and who consistently make positive things happen in a creative, constructive, dependable manner. During the 1980's, we shall look with special favor on individuals who excel in any of the following ways:

- Generating creative ideas that result in successful new products, marketing programs or manufacturing systems.
- Reducing costs and improving productivity.
- Surpassing sales targets through using particularly effective selling techniques.
- Inspiring others by deed and example to strive toward excellence and true professionalism in the accomplishment of company objectives.

It was partly with these values and commitments in mind that in 1983 I wrote an op-ed article in the *Wall Street Journal*. Entitled "A Lifetime of Learning to Manage Effectively," it describes how my thinking about management and leadership had evolved over the years. The contents of the article are reproduced in Appendix F.

The management team I inherited at Barry Wright was strong and experienced. Consequently, as was the case at Babson, I was fortunate not to have to make any significant personnel changes during my first few years at the company. Of course, over the period of my tenure as CEO, there was some turnover as a result of retirements or resignations, but with only a few exceptions, none of the senior management changes in the company was performance-related.

In many ways, Barry Wright could be considered a mini-conglomerate. It comprised two main operating groups (the Industrial and Aero Products group and Wright Line, Inc.) and seven diverse manufacturing divisions, each operating as a separate business entity. Each entity served a different and distinctive industrial market. The only thread that ran through all of these entities was that each had a number one or two competitive share of the particular market sector it served. In the 1980s, there were many such manufacturing conglomerates in the United States, with General Electric being a prime example. Today, although GE still exists, many of the other U.S.-based entities of this kind have been broken up or dismantled as more and more manufacturing activities have been shifted abroad.

During the years I spent at Barry Wright, I was often asked how being a company CEO compared with being a college president. Appendix G contains a talk that I gave during that era that, with a certain amount of "tongue in cheek," addresses that question.

In keeping with what I said in that talk, my job as CEO of Barry Wright was to ensure that the company had a strong and viable long-term strategy, that it had the right people in place doing the right things, that it met the targets of its annual operating plans and budgets, and that it "walked the talk" when it came to living by its "Corporate Values and Management Commitments." Put another way, my job was to lead the company and create a culture designed to make everyone associated with the company a winner.

The goal was to make customers winners by serving them well and meeting their needs at a fair price. Employees would be winners by having jobs they felt were fulfilling and by being paid compensation that was fair. Partners in the supply chain would win by being treated well by the company and being paid fairly for the goods or services they provided to the company. Investors would be winners by realizing an attractive long-term return on their investment in the company. And the communities where we operated would be winners by our having provided attractive jobs for their residents and by their receiving significant tax revenues from the company and its employees that could be used to provide needed municipal services.

Accomplishing all these goals was easier said than done. In retrospect, I give myself mixed marks as a private sector corporate leader. During my tenure as CEO of Barry Wright, I think I did well in leading the effort to put into actual practice a culture that adhered to the basic tenets outlined in the company's statement of "Corporate Values and Management Commitments." Customers, employees, supply chain partners, and the communities were all "winners" during those years. While I led the company, we also continued to successfully defend our record of being either number one or number two in market share in each of the major markets in which we competed. In addition, we also made a successful transition from having our common stock shares traded on the NASDAQ Exchange to having them traded on the New York Stock Exchange.

I was less successful in two areas. The first was failing to avoid the negative impact on the company of the two major economic and industrial downturns in the 1980s. Our sales and profits tended to seesaw up and down with the ups and downs of the U.S. economy as a whole.

The second was in not recognizing and reacting early enough to a major disruptive technology that subsequently affected the business of our Wright Line computer products operating group. During most of the 1980s, computer data was stored either on reels of computer tape or on perforated computer printout paper. Wright Line's major family of products in the 1980s was related to these modes of data storage. It manufactured and marketed a patented product called TapeSeal, comprising a plastic belt that wrapped around the computer reel and snapped shut to protect the tape on the reel. The snap had a hook attached that could be used to hang the reel on a "universal hanger bar" in specially designed metal OptiMedia cabinets that Wright Line manufactured in its plant in Worcester, Massachusetts. In the decade of the eighties, more than 95 percent of all computer tapes around the world employed TapeSeal belts for protection and storage purposes. As a result, data centers worldwide were filled with OptiMedia data storage cabinets containing computer tapes sealed with the company's TapeSeal belts.

The company also made patented plastic three-ring binders to store computer printout paper. The covers of these binders had hooks molded into them that enabled the binders to be hung on the "universal hanger bars" in the same OptiMedia cabinets used to store the computer tapes.

Finally, Wright Line made and marketed a patented DataFile information filing system that comprised specially designed color-coded manila file folders that could be stored in compatible DataFile filing cabinets.

The problem was that the world of computer data storage began to change rapidly during the 1980s. Computer tapes and paper printout documents began to be replaced first by smaller cartridges, then by hard discs and floppy discs, then by flash drives, and more recently by cloud storage. The result was that computer tapes and printout paper became increasing obsolete, together with the custom cabinets used to protect and store them.

At Barry Wright, we were slow to react to this disruptive technology threat. When we did begin to react, we were not innovative enough to develop cutting-edge new products that responded effectively to the fast-developing technology trends in the data storage field. In part, this was because most of Wright Line's product development staff were mechanical engineers and traditional design technologists. None of them had backgrounds in electrical engineering or computer science. Consequently, they were unable to fully understand the significance of the profound changes taking place in the world of computer science and data storage. Metaphorically, they were designing buggy whips at the dawn of the automobile age.

So, like Polaroid, Blockbuster, Digital Equipment Corporation, Hewlett-Packard, Nokia, and similar companies I noted earlier in this memoir, my own company, Barry Wright, was guilty of failing to keep up with the rapidly developing technological changes in its industry. In the end, the ultimate responsibility for this failure was mine, as CEO.

The result was that, in the latter half of the 1980s, the Wright Line half of Barry Wright began to experience downward pressure on its sales revenues, margins, and profits. While this pressure was gradual and the Industrial and Aero Products half of the company continued to grow and thrive, the overall company's stock price was clearly affected.

To cope with this situation, in the fall of 1988, we hired a consulting team from the Boston Consulting Group to do an in-depth study of our Wright Line group in light of projected future developments in the computer data storage field. Their conclusion and recommendation was that we spin off and sell Wright Line and focus our future efforts on continuing to develop and grow our divisions in the Industrial and Aero Products group, where we were on the cutting edge of the technological developments occurring in the various industries we served.

We were in the middle of this process, when late one Wednesday afternoon in the early spring of 1989, I received a telephone call from the CEO of a

Milwaukee-based company called Applied Power, Inc. After a bit of introductory chitchat, he suggested that I might want to read the next morning's *Wall Street Journal*, since it would contain a half-page ad making an unsolicited all-cash offer from his company to buy *all* of Barry Wright's stock. This was familiarly known as a "hostile takeover bid" in an era that was the heyday of such bids. The phone call was a short one.

Sure enough, the ad appeared in the *Journal* the next morning. And so, the fat was in the fire. In financial parlance, Barry Wright was "in play."

The irony of the situation was that I was personally familiar with Applied Power. It was a publicly traded firm that made and marketed industrial products somewhat similar to those of our Industrial and Aero Products group. It was approximately the same size as Barry Wright. In fact, it was a company that I had considered acquiring for Barry Wright a couple of years earlier when it had a different CEO. However, some preliminary, cordial conversations with the family that owned the largest interest in Applied Power revealed that they were not interested in selling at that point. I, in turn, responded to them that I appreciated their candor and accepted their position. I further told them that they need not fear that I would pursue the matter, since I did not approve of hostile takeovers and would never consider initiating one.

Now the shoe was on the other foot and the relatively new GE-trained CEO of Applied Power had no compunction about initiating a hostile bid in the other direction. However, under the Barry Wright company charter and bylaws, for the bid to be successful, it had to be approved by at least two-thirds of the outstanding common shares in the company.

In response to the ad in the *Wall Street Journal*, our Barry Wright management team and board of directors sprang into action. Fortunately, the company had in place a variety of legal defenses that provided us with time to consider what line of action to pursue. Among other things, these defenses included having a "staggered board of directors," a "poison pill" provision in our company charter, and an Employee Stock Option Plan ("ESOP") in place.

The staggered board meant directors were elected to serve three-year terms and, therefore, that only one-third of the board seats were up for election in any given year. The poison pill provision meant that once a hostile party had acquired 20 percent of the outstanding shares through public market transactions, the company's board could trigger the "pill," which meant that each of the remaining outstanding shares was deemed to have super-voting rights equal to two votes per share rather than one vote per share. Finally, the ESOP meant that a significant percentage of the company's shares was held by employees of the company and that block of shares would be voted in such a way that was presumably friendly to the interests of the current management team and board of directors.

In the end, the experience of other public companies with such protections against hostile takeovers in place had shown that they were mainly helpful in buying time for the target to explore other alternatives to the hostile bid that had been made. Seldom, however, were they successful in preventing the sale of the company if shareholders considered the offering price to be high enough. This proved to be the case with Barry Wright.

The same day the announcement of the hostile bid appeared in the *Wall Street Journal*, we received delivery of the documents confirming the offer. I immediately assembled our management team and called a special meeting of the board of directors. At the time the bid was made, our stock was selling at $4.50 per share. The Applied Power offer was at $8.00 per share. Despite the considerable control premium represented by the bid, the board and management concluded, after considerable discussion, that the bid was inadequate in light of the long-term prospects of the company. We therefore decided we should seek bids from other potential buyers who might be willing to pay more for Barry Wright. Toward that end, we ran an ad in the *Journal* recommending that shareholders reject the Applied Power bid.

Thereupon, there ensued a tense game of cat and mouse. Having bought time as a result of the legal protections we had previously established, we put out feelers to other potential "white knight" corporate buyers to see if they would be interested in making counter offers. Two or three expressed possible interest and began discussions with us. This evidently made Applied Power management nervous and they increased their offer to $10 per share.

Meanwhile, the *Boston Globe* and the *Wall Street Journal* began to cover the drama. Despite the fact that we, at Barry Wright, were bound by SEC rules from revealing non-public details and information to the media, a number of speculative articles appeared in the press, some of them based on information leaked to them by Applied Power executives who were not legally enjoined from speaking openly to reporters. In one such case of leaked information, a *Globe* journalist wrote a highly critical and uncomplimentary article about me, personally, criticizing my management style and saying that I should accept the Applied Power bid. The independent Barry Wright directors promptly wrote and signed a public letter to the editor of the *Boston Globe* strongly rebutting each of the points made in the article.

Some of the articles that appeared contained speculation about who the potential "white knight" corporate rescuers might be that would make higher bids for the company.

Other articles pointed out that Barry Wright was an important Massachusetts employer and that it would be regrettable if control of the company passed out of the state (at the time we employed approximately 3,000 people, of whom approximately 2,000 worked in the state). Then, Massachusetts Governor Michael Dukakis got into the act. He, too, was concerned about the possibility that the headquarters of Barry Wright might pass out of the state and that Massachusetts would lose jobs as a result. He suggested that the Massachusetts legislature pass legislation that would make it more difficult for that to happen.

The climax of the drama occurred in early June 1989 when, with the unanimous backing of our board, I agreed to have a face-to-face negotiating session with my counterpart at Applied Power. The session started at 7:00 p.m. at the Boston offices of Goodwin, Procter and Hoar, our lawyers. It ended with a handshake at 2:00 a.m. The result, after hours of heavy-duty discussion and, at times, intense bargaining, I agreed to encourage our board to accept an offer from Applied Power to pay $12.40 per share to buy all of the stock of Barry Wright. Given the huge price premium over the $4.40 share price on the day we first learned of the Applied Power hostile bid, our board and most of our shareholders considered this to be a significant victory from an investor point of view.

Ultimately, the sale was consummated with the unanimous support of the Barry Wright board.

From my personal point of view, it was a bittersweet victory. While the deal was excellent from a shareholder's point of view, in retrospect it did not turn out to be beneficial for some of the various businesses we operated or from the perspective of many of our employees. The problem was that the eyes of the Applied Power's CEO appeared to have been bigger than his stomach. As a result, he had ended up paying more than he should have for Barry Wright. It had been a case of his making up his mind that he had to have Barry Wright at almost any price and feeling that his reputation would have been at stake if he had not been able to consummate the deal. It is a syndrome I have seen again and again in the world of business. CEOs often become obsessed with completing a particular deal or acquiring a particular company. This, in turn, clouds their judgment and they end up paying too much when the wiser course of action would have been to walk away from the deal.

In order to finance the acquisition, Applied Power had to sell off several of the smaller divisions in the Industrial and Aero Products group and to downsize some of the other operations in the remaining divisions. Several years later, they also sold the profitable Barry Controls division that had been the cornerstone of Barry Wright from the beginning.

What also saddened me was that the Applied Power culture turned out to be significantly different from the culture we had worked so hard to establish over the years at Barry Wright. Without going into detail, the feedback I subsequently received from former employees who stayed on after the sale of the company was that many of the practices at Applied Power were not as enlightened as those outlined in Barry Wright's statement of "Corporate Values and Management Commitments."

Again, it is my observation that the reason so few corporate mergers and acquisitions are truly successful is because of the clash of cultures that subsequently occurs. In biological terms, it is analogous to the human body as a whole rejecting an organ transplant because of incompatible DNA. In like terms, if the cultural DNA of two organizations is significantly different, it is highly unlikely that a corporate transplant of one into the other will work in the long run. As Peter Drucker, the management guru, purportedly said: "Culture eats strategy for breakfast."

The lesson to be learned by CEOs and corporate leaders is "buyer beware." Before saying marriage vows, make sure to do extensive due diligence to ensure that the culture of the organization or company that you are considering merging with or acquiring is reasonably compatible with the cultural DNA of your own organization.

As for me, the sale of Barry Wright brought about a number of changes in my life. The most immediate was that, upon the closing of the deal, I resigned from the chairman and CEO positions at the company. The year was 1989 and I was 56 years old. Even before the sale of the company, I had concluded that after eight years as its CEO, the time was approaching when I should step down from my position. Toward this end, I had already begun making preparations. In terms of management succession planning, I had concluded that John F. Quinn, the longtime head of the Industrial and Aero Products group, would be an excellent person to succeed me. With this in mind and with the enthusiastic support of the board, I had promoted him to the position of president of Barry Wright in 1988 with the thought that he would become CEO in 1990.

Also, I had already had discussions with my friend, John McArthur, then dean of the Harvard Business School, about the possibility of my returning to HBS to teach. He was enthusiastic about the idea and had offered to hold a position open for me on the faculty beginning in the fall of 1990. With the sale of Barry Wright consummated in June of 1989, we merely moved the date of my rejoining HBS up by one year to the fall of 1989.

Thus in September of that year, I went back to doing what I had always loved doing: teaching.

CHAPTER TWENTY-NINE

NORWAY

The timing of the Barry Wright sale had a serendipitous side to it. Charlotte and I had made previous plans to take my 91-year-old father on his first trip to Norway to get in touch with his Norwegian heritage. With the Barry Wright chapter in my life now completed, I could make the trip with a completely carefree mind.

My mother, Verna Sorenson, had died the year before at age 90. Her last few years had been difficult. She had suffered from a severe case of shingles that had covered a broad swath of skin from her back around to her chest. Shingles are excruciatingly painful. To deal with the pain, her doctors had overmedicated her. This, in turn, affected her mentally and she lived in a constant state of disorientation. When my father, sister Nancy, and I all insisted that the doctors cut back on her medication, they finally complied, and she became considerably more alert. But the pain never totally left her.

Because of the care required for my mom, she and Dad had moved into the Woodland Nursing Home in Mansfield, Ohio, where they shared a room together. However, they continued to own their home at 390 West Third Street in Mansfield, and my father, who was in good health and could still drive his car, periodically stopped by the house to ensure that everything was in good order.

In the early fall of 1988, my mother experienced fatal heart failure and succumbed peacefully in the local Mansfield hospital. Following her death, my dad decided to stay on in the nursing home. While he didn't require nursing care, he felt at home there and had made a number of friends among its other residents. "Besides," he told us, "some of the other folks there need me for companionship and I think I can be helpful to them." That was typical of my dad.

In any case, early in 1989, Charlotte and I had invited him to go on a trip with us to Norway, where his ancestors had lived. He was immediately enthusiastic about the idea. Thus, in mid-June, he flew to Boston, where he joined us for a connecting overnight flight to Oslo. During our half-day Oslo layover, the three of us visited our Norwegian friend, Ric Larsen, who took us to rest up at his family's beautifully preserved folk-style home. My father, who had dreamed of Norway all his life, was thrilled and deeply touched to see this picture-perfect traditional house.

Then we took another plane for a flight to the town of Kirkenes in northern Norway near the Russian border. There we spent the night and then boarded a mail boat for a voyage around the North Cape and down the western coast of Norway.

The first night on board was the occasion of some excitement. My father and I were sharing a tiny interior "stateroom" on the boat. Dad, who in the past 24 hours had traveled through eight different time zones and found himself in one of the northernmost towns in the world in mid-June when the sun shone at midnight, was totally disoriented and had no idea what time it was. Nevertheless, both of us were tired and decided to try to get some sleep.

At about 4:00 a.m. I was awakened from my slumber by persistent knocking on the stateroom door. When I opened the door, I saw a stewardess standing alongside my father who was impeccably dressed in sport jacket and necktie and looking a bit confused. As it happened, he had risen at 3:00 a.m. thinking it was morning, so he got dressed and went out on the deck for a stroll. Even though it was totally light outside, he evidently thought it odd that he was the only one on the deck. So he decided to return to our room. The only problem was he couldn't remember the room number, so he tried a number of stateroom doors to see if he could get the right one. It was in the corridor that the stewardess found him, asked his name, looked on the roster to see what the proper room number was, and guided him to the appropriate door. Relieved to have found me, he reentered the room, undressed, and returned to his bed, where he finally got a bit of sleep.

In the morning, we arose at about eight, and joined Charlotte, who had been sleeping in the stateroom next door, for breakfast in the dining room. Most of the tables were full, but we found space at one where a woman in her seventies invited us to join her. By way of making conversation, midway through breakfast she confided to us that during the night she had had a scary experience. She said that about 3:30 a.m. someone had rattled her door and vigorously tried to get into her room. At that point my father began to blush and sheepishly related that he was likely the guilty would-be intruder. Whereupon, the stylish lady turned to him and in a coquettish voice said: "Oh, if I had only known it was you. You would have been most welcome!" It was a lovely way to start the new day on shipboard!

Our mail boat cruise took us above the Arctic Circle and then south all along the west coast of Norway, exploring a number of fjords along the way and also visiting several towns, including Hammerfest, Tromso, Trondheim, Stavanger, and Bergen. In the Stavanger Fjord, we stopped on the island of Fogn to meet some of Charlotte's distant relatives, who operated Norway's largest tomato farm out of greenhouses scattered across the island.

The serenity and incredible scenery that we experienced while cruising up various fjords were accompanied by the majestic music of Edvard Grieg's *Peer Gynt* musical suite, issuing forth from the ship's loudspeakers.

The high point of our trip was our visit to my father's ancestral village of Tvedestrand on the southwest side of the Oslo fjord. As described earlier in the book, the last time Charlotte and I had visited Tvedestrand was over the Christmas holidays in 1961, 28 years earlier. We found the village much unchanged, apart from seeming even more picturesque in its overall charm and coastal setting. This time, what made our visit thrilling was to see how charmed and excited my dad was to experience, for the first time, the village where his father and grandfather had lived before emigrating to America.

We easily located the small white house with its red door where the Sorenson family had lived for many years. Its elderly occupant was the only remaining daughter of the family that had bought the house from my great-grandmother, Mina Sorenson, in 1915. Therein lies a tale.

When my grandfather, Anton, and great-grandfather, Lars, emigrated to the U.S. in 1882, they temporarily left my great-grandmother and grand-aunt behind with the thought that they, too, would emigrate to the U.S. once the men of the family were established there. For various reasons, that never happened. As a result, Mina lived out the rest of her life in the little white house with the red door. It delighted my dad to be visiting the family homestead for the first time and to be talking with its current occupant, who had distant memories of meeting his grandmother in person.

Though the Sorenson men left the women of the family behind when they left Norway, a 20-year exchange of letters ensued between the women in Norway and the men in America. The letters written by the men were subsequently lost to posterity, but the 100 or so letters written by the women to the men were all carefully preserved through the years by my grandfather and great-grandfather. These had been passed down to my father and his brothers, who subsequently had them translated from Norwegian into English. On this trip to Norway, my father had brought along both the original letters and their translations with the thought that someone in the village might be interested in them.

That someone turned out to be the local town historian, with whom we arranged a meeting. When the historian began reading through the letters he reacted with growing excitement. One would have thought he had discovered buried treasure. The letters written by the women were tantamount to a monthly chronicle of all the significant happenings in Tvedestrand in the 20 years between 1882 and 1902. They contained town news on such subjects as how good the yearly crop harvests had been, what fishing vessels had been lost at sea, what building activity had occurred, what issues the town fathers were confronting, and so forth. They also contained town gossip: which couples had been married, who was having an affair with whom, what babies had been born, who had died, as well as who had left town and for what reasons.

The town historian couldn't have been more enthusiastic. This, in turn, pleased my father immensely, and he then had the pleasure of presenting the originals and the translations of the letters to the historian as a permanent gift to the town. The historian gratefully accepted them and said they would become a treasured part of Tvedestrand's archives, shedding needed light on an important era in the town's history.

We spent a couple of more enjoyable days in Tvedestrand. Over the years, the seaside town had been transformed from a sleepy little fishing and farming community to a chic site of gentrified summer homes and harbor-front retreats for families and boat-owning individuals from Oslo and other parts of Scandinavia. One of the nights we spent there was the summer solstice, when the sun almost never went down. There was raucous celebrating all night long, complete with bonfires, fireworks, lots of singing, laughing, drinking . . . and even more drinking!

Then it was on to Oslo for a weekend of sightseeing, followed by a plane ride back to America.

On our return home, Charlotte and I reflected on how fortunate we were to have been able to travel so extensively throughout our married life and to have seen so much of the world. On the subsequent occasion of our 50th anniversary, a number of years later, we created a digital presentation entitled "Around the World in Fifty Years" that was set to music and comprised a compilation of images depicting highlights of the adventures we had experienced in 35 of the 60-some countries that we had visited as a couple over the course of a half-century. Our Norwegian trip is appropriately chronicled in the video.

Following our Scandinavian odyssey, my dear father stayed with us in New England for the rest of the summer of 1989. We had a lovely time with him. In September, he returned to Ohio, promising to come back later in the fall to spend Thanksgiving with us. Hence, on the Monday of Thanksgiving week, "Grandpa," as we called him, flew to Boston, where Charlotte met him at Logan Airport. When he climbed into the car, Charlotte asked whether he had everything he had brought with him. He replied, "Well, let's see. I've got my hat, my coat, and my suitcase . . . and I've got my excitement! So, let's go."

That evening, Kristin joined us at our house for a candle-lit supper. We reminisced about our trip to Norway and Grandpa entertained us with some of his favorite family stories from his childhood. We then tucked him in bed for the night. The following morning, he never woke up. He had peacefully died in his sleep at age 91. It was a beautiful ending for a man who had been a beautiful human being. To this day, I miss him dearly.

I tried to capture my feelings about him in a eulogy I delivered at his memorial service. The following is an excerpt of what I said.

> Grandpa was the foundation of our family. We loved him dearly and we knew that he loved us dearly . . . with no strings, no conditions, and no wavering. It was just plain and simple love.
>
> In our eyes . . . and perhaps in some of your eyes as well . . . Grandpa defined and personified what it meant to be a good man. He was kind, he was caring, he was gentle, he was generous in his thoughts, he was unselfish, he was unfailingly thoughtful of others. He never made a big deal out of it. He was just naturally, instinctively all of these things. In short, he was a true "gentle man" in the most genuine way imaginable.
>
> For us in the family, he was our ultimate role model. Much of what we have learned about living, we learned from him . . . partly from what he said . . . but even more so from just observing the way he acted and how he treated others. Just being with him made us all feel good. We loved his gentle and whimsical sense of humor. And we loved his unfailing optimism. Even during the darkest of times Grandpa used to invariably say: "You know I think things are going to get better." Whenever we called him on the phone and would say: "How are you, Grandpa?" he would cheerily reply: "Able to be here!" All through his life, he was just thankful for each day.

CHAPTER THIRTY

BACK IN THE CLASSROOM

My return to the Harvard Business School as an adjunct professor in the fall of 1989 had very much the feel of a homecoming for me. Despite the 17 years I had spent away from the school, I had remained in contact with it during my absence. In 1984, for example, I had attended the 25th reunion of my MBA class and had written a piece for the *HBS Alumni Bulletin* in which I responded to several questions I was asked regarding my life since graduating from the school in 1959. This article is reproduced in Appendix H.

The physical setting and many of the faces on the faculty were still very familiar to me upon my return. Moreover, Dottie, my wonderful long-term colleague at Babson and Barry Wright, agreed to come with me to HBS to serve as my assistant and secretary. This, too, helped smooth my reentry to the school.

My faculty assignment was to teach an MBA course called *Management Policy and Practice* or "MPP" as it was more familiarly known. It was the only required course in the second year of the MBA program. Since there were approximately 900 second-year students, this meant there were 10 sections of the course, each comprising about 90 students. There were seven of us in the group that taught the course. Three were tenured HBS professors, while four of us were adjunct professors who had served as CEOs or senior executives of actual companies.

The course focused on the job of a CEO or that of other leaders or general managers who had overall responsibility for any type of organization. Its emphasis was on implementation and execution rather than on strategy formulation. The primary questions posed in the course were: What do CEOs actually do and how do they do it? What leadership styles do they bring to their jobs and which of these styles works best in various industries, various situations, and various organizational cultures?

It was great to be back in the classroom. This time around, I found the Harvard students to be more sophisticated, cockier, worldlier, and more diverse than those I had in the 1960s and 1970s. There were more women, minorities, and international students. But the fundamental dynamics of what went on in the classroom were basically unchanged from the last time I had taught at HBS.

As before, the objective was to teach students to reason independently and think for themselves. The second goal was to help them develop the ability to discuss their reasoning and ideas verbally in a clear and persuasive fashion in front of their peers in a public setting. Third, the course was designed to expose students to a variety of leadership styles and help them decide which particular style best fit their own talents and personalities. Finally, we wanted to familiarize students with a wide variety of companies and organizations, both large and small, in many different industrial, not-for-profit, and public sector settings.

What I had conveniently forgotten since my last period at Harvard was just how hard it was and how much work was involved in teaching. For every hour in the classroom, I ended up spending six or seven hours in preparation. But I loved every minute I spent on my métier.

Being back in the classroom reminded me just how important the role of education is in our society. Earlier, during my presidency at Barry Wright, I had written the following op-ed page article for the *Boston Globe* on this subject. It poses a number of unanswered questions concerning education and was based on a talk I had given on the occasion of being granted the "Citizen of the Year" award by the Boston area council of the Boy Scouts of America in 1986.

THE BOSTON GLOBE
AUGUST 9, 1986
<u>Misplaced Priorities in Education, in Life</u>
<u>Ralph Z. Sorenson</u>

When I was growing up I was a Boy Scout. I learned many things about the out-of-doors and getting along with other kids. But most of all, I learned about fundamental values and a personal code of conduct. The tenets of that code are embodied in the Boy Scout Law.

It says a scout is "trustworthy, loyal, helpful, friendly, courteous, kind, cheerful, obedient, thrifty, brave, clean and reverent".

In this age of cynicism, words and traits such as these tend to be viewed as "goody-goody". But the future of our civilization may depend on how well we human beings can continue to transmit from one generation to the next the traits and values of the type embodied in the Boy Scout Law.

Let us pursue a simple chain of logic:

Postulate No. 1: The world in general, and the United States in particular, is beset by complex and vexing problems on all sides: breakdown of law and order, decay of cities, racial and religious tensions, economic pressures, threat of nuclear holocaust, international conflict, corrosion of the family, drug abuse and many other problems.

Postulate No. 2: There are many possible individual approaches and solutions to each of these problems and we are deploying vast resources, both financial and human, to find these solutions. But despite these efforts, we often joust ineffectively with symptoms rather than with causes. And what are these causes?

This leads to Postulate No. 3: In most instances, the causes can be traced back to the existence of a large and perhaps growing segment of the citizenry who, when they were young, never learned good values, never got an adequate education, and never received effective training for responsible citizenship.

And, finally, Postulate No. 4: If the foregoing is true, then it is evident that the best long-term way to solve, or at least alleviate the most vexing of our social problems, is to ensure that the next generation of young people receives adequate preparation and education for responsible citizenship.

If children can learn a simple code of ethics and set of values in their earliest years and can combine them with a first-class primary school education, beginning with the three R's, they will have a good foundation upon which their education in high school, college and beyond can build. The result will be a responsible adult citizenry made up of people better equipped to deal with society's fundamental problems.

All this sounds self-evident. But now comes the interesting part. If it is so self-evident, why is there such a mammoth inconsistency in the way we appear to be ordering our social priorities?

Why are we placing the primary school teachers, to whom we entrust our children's early education, at the low end of our educational and social totem pole. Why do we pay college graduates who begin teaching in public elementary schools significantly less than we pay the starting accountant or engineer? Why do we not pay first-grade teachers more than we pay college professors? The overall impact of the first-grade teacher on a student is probably more important than that of the college professor. Why is not as much prestige attached to being a grade-school teacher as to being a college professor?

And why is the quality of many of our teacher-training colleges so low and the SAT scores of the diminishing numbers of students attending those well below the national average?

Why have we relegated to television, with its questionable programming, so much of the task of raising our children and imparting values to them.

And why are we going more and more in the direction of single-parent families with that parent typically having to work full-time? Or, in the case of two-parent homes, why do both parents so often work full-time with their primary commitments to their careers rather than to their children. Why is it that men and women alike increasingly appear to be putting self-fulfillment and the quest for material gain ahead of family fundamentals? Why are so many women, when asked the inevitable question, "What do you do?"—embarrassed to say, "I'm a mother and a housewife". Or why are so few men willing to say, "My wife is the primary bread-winner, and I'm devoting most of my time to raising our children." Indeed, why do so many men abdicate responsibility for spending quality time with their sons and daughters and imparting values to them?

And, finally, as we worship at the altar of careerism, is there a risk that we shall no longer enjoy the benefits of volunteerism? Volunteerism—the willingness to give generously of one's money and, more important, one's time for the good of others—has been one of the characteristics that have set the United States apart from the rest of the world. It has been an extraordinary phenomenon.

This force has benefitted the Boy Scouts and Girl Scouts, community youth groups, the YMCA and YWCA, Little League, youth church groups and other organizations that help to impart a healthy set of values and skills to the next generation. We should not risk losing it.

Back in the Classroom

Re-reading this article recently made me realize that, while the teaching I was once again doing at Harvard was worthwhile, it probably was not as important or essential as the teaching being done in American primary and secondary schools. In turn, as the article suggests, the prestige and compensation associated with being a university professor was greater than it should have been, as compared with that enjoyed by our elementary and high school teachers. For me, a university professor, this was a somewhat disturbing and humbling thought, but it didn't detract from my enjoyment at being back in the classroom. Today, more than two decades later, I believe the imbalance in the way society values university teachers compared with elementary and high school teachers still exists and perhaps always will.

In addition to my teaching, I also embarked on an ambitious program of case writing. I had observed that almost all the case studies that had been used in the MPP course the previous year involved the CEOs or senior executives of large, well-established, publicly traded corporations.

Case studies involving entrepreneurs and CEOs of small emerging companies were clearly lacking. I set out to do something about this situation.

Based on my experience at Babson and in the private sector, it was my conviction that the future health and growth of our economy would depend in large measure on the innovations, jobs, and wealth created by entrepreneurs. Hence, I wrote or supervised the writing of a number of case studies that focused on the leadership role of the entrepreneurial CEOs in startup or early-stage companies. These cases were subsequently woven into the syllabus of the MPP course and proved to be popular with students.

One of the case studies I wrote involved a company called Overseas Adventure Travel. Based in Cambridge, it was operated by its CEO, Judi Wineland, and her husband Rick Thompson, the entrepreneurial couple who had founded the company. OAT offered adventure travel excursions to destinations all over the world and, most particularly, to Africa. The case focused on Judi's leadership style and values as she dealt with a variety of strategic and tactical issues facing the company.

I was so intrigued by the company that I decided to do some field work on my own to experience what it would be like to go on one of their travel adventures as a client. The trip I chose was a safari to Tanzania and Kenya in Africa in the summer of 1991. It featured a climb up Mount Kilimanjaro and visits to a number of game parks. When I floated the idea to the rest of the family, Trina and Eric jumped at the chance to accompany me. Charlotte took a pass because she was involved that summer in a course in Cambridge on conflict resolution. Kristin was also unable to join us because she had just started a new job.

So in late June of 1991, Trina, Eric, and I set off for Africa. In Arusha, Tanzania, Susan and Nate, two of Trina's classmates from Dartmouth's Tuck School, from which all three had just graduated, joined us. The next morning, following a thorough briefing, we were driven to a small hostel at the base of Mount Kilimanjaro, where we were introduced to OAT's head guide and two local bearers who were to accompany us on our attempt to climb the mountain.

The next six days of climbing were exhilarating. The highlight was our ultimate summiting of "Mount Kili." Appendix I contains excerpts from my contemporaneous journal description of our final climb to the 19,340-foot top of the mountain. In addition to the thrill of summiting the mountain, our subsequent safari adventure in Tanzania included unforgettable visits to the Serengeti Plain and Olduvai Gorge where, in the 1950s, Louis and Mary Leakey, after 28 years of searching, discovered the skull of "Zinjanthropus Man" and also that of "Homo habilis," both estimated to be between 1.6 million and 1.8 million years old. We also saw an extraordinary variety of birdlife at Lake Manyara and camped on the floor of Ngorongoro Crater, where the wildlife was spectacular. We saw cheetahs, leopards, rhinoceros, lions, hyenas, zebras, antelopes, Thompson gazelles, ostriches, warthogs, jackals, cobras, and hippopotamus.

By the time Trina, Eric, and I arrived back in Cambridge, we had become fans and admirers of OAT. In the fall of that year, when I taught the OAT case in my course at Harvard, both Judi Wineland and Rick Thompson came to my class, and I had the pleasure of showing the class the video we had taken of us reaching the summit of Kilimanjaro and planting OAT and Harvard flags on the summit. The class loved it!

In addition to my work at Harvard Business School, I continued to be active as a board director of half a dozen companies as well as a trustee, overseer, or member of the corporation of a number of not-for-profit organizations in the Boston area. However, I began increasingly to feel as though I was being stretched too thin. It was a case of being a mile wide and an inch deep. I needed to learn to say no to new invitations.

In terms of my personal and family life, the eighties and early nineties had brought about a number of changes.

By 1991, Kristin, Trina, and Eric had all graduated from college. Kristin was an alumna of Kenyon College, where she had majored in comparative religion and languages. She initially found work as an assistant in the Impressionist Department at Christie's art auction house in New York. Subsequently, she became executive director of the Fundacion Simon Bolivar, a not-for-profit foundation that supported adult literacy and community development projects in various Latin and Central America countries. As its executive director, she resided in New York City.

Trina had graduated with a political science degree from Princeton and, after brief stints working at the Conservation Law Foundation in Boston and teaching outdoor education at Albuquerque Academy in New Mexico, completed an MBA degree at Dartmouth College's Tuck School of Management. She had just accepted a job as executive vice president at Evergreen Management, a small venture investment firm based in Boulder, Colorado, that focused on investments in startup firms in the environmental, outdoor, and recreational fields.

Finally, Eric had graduated from Yale with a history degree. After several years of teaching at the Berkshire Country Day School in Lenox, Massachusetts, and Sidwell Friends School in Washington, D.C., and after a stint as a ski instructor at a mountain ski resort in Santa Fe, New Mexico, he was in the process of relocating to Boulder to pursue opportunities in residential construction and real estate development.

Meanwhile, Charlotte had become interested in the field of alternative dispute resolution (ADR), a concept that had been developed by Harvard professor Roger Fisher, author of the book *Getting To Yes*. She had attended a seminar course taught by Professor Fisher and was spending the summer of 1991 putting some of the concepts she had learned in the course to work as a volunteer in a Cambridge-based program called The Multi-Door Courthouse. This program was aimed at encouraging parties involved in various lawsuits to reach resolution of their differences through mediation or arbitration and thus to avoid the trauma and expense of litigating their dispute in a courtroom trial.

Part of this interest stemmed from an unfortunate event that had greatly affected our family and caused both Charlotte and me considerable heartache. The incident had its origins in 1988 and involved the property next to ours on Brattle Street in Cambridge. For many years, the large home on the property housed New Prep School, a small one-year post-high school program for boys designed to better prepare them to attend college. A wing had been added to the house to accommodate the program. In the spring of 1988 there were about 25 day students enrolled in the program. Most of the students either took public transportation or rode their bikes to the school each day. The property was zoned for one-family residential use in the Historic Brattle Street Neighborhood district, but because the house had been used for educational purposes since before the current residential zoning regulations had been adopted, it was "grandfathered" in for this purpose for as long as it was being operated as the New Prep School.

In 1988, the owner/headmaster of the school was approaching retirement age and had decided to close the school and sell the property. In advance of the sale, he informed us and other neighbors that he had received an offer from an architect who wanted to convert the property back to a residence and use it both to live in and for his home-based one-man professional architectural practice, a use that was permitted under the Cambridge residential zoning regulations. He said he felt the offer was fair and that the neighbors would be pleased that the property was being returned to residential use. Therefore, he informed us that he had accepted the offer.

What he did not tell us—or perhaps what he did not know—was that the architect was merely a "straw" purchaser for another party. Hence, on the same day the papers were signed consummating the sale of the house, the property was immediately resold to an entity called the "Commonwealth Day School."

The Commonwealth Day School was a private kindergarten located at the time in the Back Bay neighborhood in Boston. The owner of the school, Janice Cuddy, both oversaw the operation of the school and simultaneously was active in buying and selling commercial real estate. Evidently, she had received an attractive offer to sell the commercial building in which the Commonwealth Day School was at the time located, but to realize the gain on that property, she had to find another location for the school.

The location she chose was the house next to ours in Cambridge. Knowing that the idea of locating another school on the property rather than having it revert back to single-family residential use would probably be controversial in the eyes of neighborhood residents, she used the ploy of purchasing the property through a "straw" intermediary. It was several months before we and other neighbors became aware of the true identity and intent of the real purchaser of the property. This we learned when the new owner opened up a new school on the property in the fall of 1988 under the Commonwealth Day School name with students transferred from the school's old location in Boston. At the time, the new owner claimed that, despite the fact that the location was within Cambridge's single-family residence zoning overlay district, she was within her rights to open the new school there because the property had previously been "grandfathered in" for educational use.

On hearing the news, the reaction of the Brattle Street neighborhood was almost universally negative. The primary issues were those of size, safety, traffic, and appropriateness. In terms of size, the school planned to expand into the elementary grades and ultimately to have 150 students, almost six times as many as its New Prep predecessor. In terms of safety, the school had but one means of entrance and egress onto busy Brattle Street. There was only a single, one-way driveway in and out of the property and no place on the street for cars to stop and drop off students. Further, the property was in the middle of a block with no crosswalk to the other side of the street. As a result, since children would be delivered to and from school by both cars and buses, it was likely that there would be troubling traffic jams in the morning and afternoon of each school day as the vehicles waited in line to maneuver in and out of the single lane driveway. In addition, there was no room for an outdoor playground on the property. Thus, at recess time, the children would have to walk the equivalent of four city blocks to the Cambridge Common for their outdoor play, crossing at least one busy street on the way. Finally, the neighbors felt that the residentially zoned location was intrinsically ill-suited to accommodate a large kindergarten and elementary school for small children.

As a result of these concerns, neighbors met to discuss the situation. The consensus was that, unlike its small and low-key predecessor, the proposed school would represent an inappropriate use of the property in question. Neighbors were also upset that they had been duped by the previous owner's assurances that the buyer of the property intended to convert the house back into a single-family residence and thus bring it back into conformance with the residential overlay zone district within which it was located.

Based on these concerns, a petition stating the neighborhood's objections and opposition to the new school was drawn up and circulated for signatures. Over 200 Brattle Street neighbors and other Cambridge residents signed the petition. Many of the signatories were prominent members of the Cambridge community, including such local luminaries as Harvard constitutional law professor Larry Tribe, TV chef Julia Child, and David Ives, president of the public television station WGBH. The signed petition was turned in to the Cambridge City Council that, in turn, directed the city's zoning board to hold a series of hearings on the matter. Based on these hearings, the city said the school could operate but imposed a number of restrictions on it in terms of its size and its mode of operation. These restrictions were objectionable to the owner of the school.

In response, she hired a well-known Cambridge politician/lawyer to argue for allowing the school to operate without the restrictions. He, together with the owner and a number of parents of the children attending the school, decided the best tactic they could use to defend the school's existence was to claim that the real reason the neighbors opposed the school was because a number of its students were black or members of other racial minorities. In other words, they claimed that the city and the Brattle Street neighbors were racists who were guilty of public discrimination motivated by the NIMBY or "not-in-my-back-yard" syndrome. They not only argued this point of view in the zoning board hearings but they, with the support of the Massachusetts attorney general, also filed a civil lawsuit in the Boston federal district court against the city of Cambridge. In addition to the city, the owners of the two closest neighboring houses to the school were personally named in the suit. Charlotte and I were owners of one of these houses and Arthur and Jean Brooks were the owners of the other.

It should be remembered that this episode took place at the height of public debate about school busing and racism in all its forms. As a result, the Boston news media were quick to pounce on the story. Articles appeared in local newspapers and on Boston radio and TV stations. They drew attention to the lawsuit that had been filed and identified Charlotte and me, together with the Brookses, as individuals who had been cited as racists in the suit. This was hurtful to both of us, but particularly to Charlotte, who was devastated that a zoning issue was being so wrongly depicted. Discrimination had nothing to do with either Charlotte's or my opposition to the school and to have our names publicly associated with racism in the media seemed inconceivable. We learned the hard way that once such a charge gets out in the public, many people accept it as true, regardless of the actual facts.

To defend ourselves against the lawsuit, we, together with the city of Cambridge and the next-door neighbors named in the suit, hired attorneys to represent us. Three years of excruciating legal wrangling ensued. The end result was that in 1994, Judge Douglas Woodlock, a federal district court judge in Boston, issued a rare summary judgment in the case dismissing all of the allegations in the lawsuit without ever going to court. This meant that we, our neighbors, and the city of Cambridge were exonerated of all charges. This was more or less equivalent to opining that the allegations were frivolous, without merit, and had no basis in fact.

Although we were greatly relieved to have the case behind us and although our liability insurance policy had covered most of our legal costs, Charlotte and I considered the outcome to be a pyrrhic victory. The whole episode had been a painful experience from beginning to end. Despite the fact that virtually all of our friends had stood by us during the entire ordeal, we felt the case had tarnished our reputation. It had also been mentally exhausting, particularly for Charlotte, who had worked hand-in-glove with our lawyers throughout the entire process. The one silver lining to the case was that Charlotte had grown to have a fascination with the law, enough so that she gave serious consideration to attending law school. Although, in the end, this didn't happen, the episode did lead to her taking Roger Fisher's course on alternative dispute resolution and, subsequently, to enjoying her work as a volunteer in Cambridge's Multi-Door Courthouse program.

CHAPTER THIRTY-ONE

WESTWARD-HO!

The winter of 1991-92 brought another dramatic change in our lives.

Through the years, it had been the tradition in the immediate Sorenson family to spend the Christmas season together. In 1991, we opted for a ski holiday in Vail, Colorado. By that time, Trina and Eric were both living in Boulder, Colorado, where Trina was continuing work with her venture capital firm and Eric was partnering with a friend to learn the residential construction and real estate trade. The two of them suggested that Vail would be the perfect venue for our family get-together. Charlotte, Kristin, and I, the eastern contingent of the family, enthusiastically agreed.

The day before Charlotte and I boarded our flight to Denver, I received a letter at my Harvard office asking if I would consider becoming dean of the business school at the University of Colorado. During the previous several years, I had received several such inquiries from various institutions, including the Tuck School at Dartmouth, the Haas School at Berkeley, and my alma mater, Amherst College, which was looking for a new president. Being happy in my teaching position at Harvard and in our life in Boston, I had ultimately decided not to pursue any of these opportunities.

Normally, the letter of inquiry from the University of Colorado would have also gone into the round file. However, since we were flying to Colorado the next day, I thought I might show the letter to Trina and Eric. So I folded it and stuck it into the inside breast pocket of the sports coat I planned to wear on the plane. I then promptly forgot all about it.

We had a glorious time skiing at Vail during Christmas week. We had rented a small log chalet, complete with deer, elk, moose, and bear heads mounted on the wall, where we enjoyed lots of après-ski eating, drinking, and laughter in front of a blazing fireplace.

On the morning of New Year's Eve, we drove to Boulder, where, thanks to Trina and Eric, the entire Sorenson family had been invited to welcome in the new year at a New Year's party hosted at the home of one of their friends. When donning my sports coat to go to the party, I suddenly remembered the letter in its inner pocket. I took it out and showed it to our kids, saying to Trina and Eric something akin to the following;

"I thought you might get a kick out of the fact that the University of Colorado wants to know if I would be interested in coming out here to become dean of their business school. What do you think? I'm not sure about exploring the idea, but if I did, I'd need your blessings. This is your home territory, and we wouldn't want to barge into your lives out here."

They responded to the following effect:

"Come on, Pop, you guys aren't so bad. We'd be delighted to have you move out here! It would be great to be closer to you. Besides, Boulder is a fantastic place to live. You'd love it. So we think you should definitely pursue CU's offer to explore the deanship here."

As a follow-up to this conversation, on New Year's Day, we asked the kids to give us a guided tour of both the CU campus and what they considered to be the nicest residential areas in town. As we drove around, we spotted a couple of homes in the Mapleton Hill neighborhood that had particular appeal. Neither was on the market at the moment. But that didn't matter, because we were still a long way from being convinced that it would make sense to seriously consider the CU offer.

As we drove around, Trina and Eric shared what they liked about Boulder. They began by pointing out that Boulder had a wonderful high, dry climate where the sun shone 300 days a year. It was an incredibly healthy community that had attracted world-class runners, bikers, triathletes, rock climbers, skiers, and other athletes to train there because of its mile-high altitude and excellent air quality. It was a university community with more people with advanced academic degrees per capita than in any other comparable-sized city in the U.S. It was a hotbed of entrepreneurial activity, particularly in the high-tech, biotech, and organic foods sectors. It was a friendly town inhabited by a lot of interesting people. And so on.

By the end of our visit to Boulder, Charlotte and I decided that perhaps we should give serious consideration to exploring the CU offer and moving to Boulder. Hence, after returning to Cambridge, I responded to the head of the dean's search committee at CU and told him I would be willing to enter into discussions with respect to the job.

Over the following weeks, I made two or three in-person visits to the university, during which I met with faculty, students, administrators, and various members of the dean's search committee. I liked some of what I saw and heard, but had serious reservations about other aspects of what I learned during these visits.

What I liked were most of the people I met, the fact that the business school was located right next to the engineering school, its physical facilities, and the beautiful overall setting and architecture of the university. I concluded that the business school was a work-in-process with considerable potential for future development. I also was intrigued by the fact that the Front Range of Colorado was the site of considerable tech-based entrepreneurial activity and that, given the physical proximity of the business and engineering schools, there could be potential synergy between the two institutions that could help accelerate this movement.

I had qualms about the fact that the school had a mediocre reputation and had recently had a troubled past marked by considerable internal faculty dissension and friction. A symptom of this discord was that the school had run through four deans in the previous six years. The fundamental issue seemed to be whether the school should focus primarily on academic research or on excellent teaching aimed at preparing students to become effective managers and leaders in the real world of business, government, and not-for-profit organizations. The faculty reportedly was split into two factions concerning this issue. The old guard favored focusing on their teaching mission. The Young Turks were almost single-mindedly focused on their research mission.

I was also concerned about the fact that not only was the University of Colorado a state institution but it was also a politicized one in which members of its board of regents ran for public election as either Democrats or Republicans. Moreover, the state of Colorado ranked 49th nationwide in financial support of its higher education institutions and, in the case of the University of Colorado, contributed less than 10 percent to its annual budget. Coming, as I did, from Amherst, Harvard, and Babson, all private and relatively non-politicized institutions, the CU culture was unfamiliar territory to me.

In thinking about whether to accept the CU deanship, were it to be offered to me, the philosophy of "repotting" figured heavily into my thinking. I had long held the opinion that we humans are like plants. If we stay stuck in one place, one profession, or one mindset for too long, we, like plants, tend to become root-bound. The best way to cure this problem, both for plants and humans, is to repot them. As Charlotte and I deliberated about the decision, it became more and more evident that it might be healthy for us to repot ourselves before it would be too late in our lives to do so.

Hence, spurred on by the urgings of Trina and Eric, and despite any misgivings we might have had, we took a deep breath and decided to take the plunge and accept the job if offered it and if the terms of employment were acceptable.

In March of 1992, Charlotte and I flew to Colorado for a final interview with the dean's search committee. During that trip, we met with committee members, the provost, and the chancellor of CU Boulder. Following the meetings, the chairman of the committee and the provost told me they would let me know in a few days the outcome of their deliberations and whether I would be their first choice for the deanship. I told them in response that they should only offer me the job if they were sure there was universal support for my candidacy from the faculty. This was because I had long ago concluded that more university presidencies and deanships had foundered on the shoals of the faculty than for any other reason.

Meanwhile on that trip, Charlotte and I also explored various housing options, were we to move to Boulder. To our immense delight, it turned out that the owners of one of the two houses we fell in love with during our New Year's visit to Boulder, when informally approached by our broker, said that even though their home was currently not on the market, they were contemplating a move to Denver and would, thus, be willing to discuss selling their house to us. When we met the owners, an architect and his wife, our discussions went well. The owners said they would seriously consider a sale to us, if it turned out that I was finally offered the dean's job and decided to accept it.

And so it came to pass that, a few days after returning to Cambridge, I received two phone calls within 30 minutes of one another. The first was from the CU provost saying that, with the unanimous support of both the search committee and the faculty, he was calling to offer me the dean's position on terms that were acceptable to me. The second was from Alan and Laura Ziegel, the owners of our dream house, offering to sell to us at a price that was also acceptable to us. In the space of half an hour we said yes to both offers and launched ourselves into a whole new adventure in life.

We moved to Boulder in June of 1992. Our new house was at 603 Spruce Street in the beautiful and historic Mapleton Hill neighborhood. Constructed of brick and built in 1891, it was situated on a half-acre corner lot. In the previous 100 years, the house had only had four owners. Ideally located, it was only a 10-minute walk east to the tree-lined walking mall in the center of town and a 10-minute walk west to the isolated Mount Sanitas hiking trail in the Rocky Mountains foothills.

Much of the charm of the house derived from the fact that a delightful stream ran along one side of it. "Irrigation ditch rights" came along with the purchase of the house, which allowed us to draw water from the stream to irrigate the lawn and gardens during the months that there was running water in the stream. At first, this meant little to us. As time went on, however, we learned that these rights were enormously valuable, given how scarce water is in the West.

During our first year in Boulder, we built a studio guest apartment above the existing detached garage on the property. Once this was completed, we moved into it while we renovated the 100-year-old main house by adding a new wing that housed a master bedroom suite and an up-to-date kitchen/family room. We also gave the original part of the house a facelift, all the while preserving the historical exterior charm of the residence. Since the house was situated within the Mapleton Hill historic district, we were required to obtain permission from the Boulder Landmarks Commission for the renovations that we accomplished. This presented no problems. In fact, when the project was completed, we were pleased to hear that the members of the commission were very happy with the end result.

Today, more than 25 years later, Charlotte and I are still living at 603 Spruce Street, the longest we have lived in any one house during the 55-plus years we have been married. It has been a wonderful home to us and we still love it.

CHAPTER THIRTY-TWO

ACADEMIC FIREWORKS

July 1, 1992 was my first day on the job as dean of the University of Colorado School of Business. I was initially greeted by a warm welcome from the 15 or so members of my administrative staff. On my arrival that morning, they all showed up wearing T-shirts with my photo embossed on the front over a caption saying, "THIS BUD'S FOR US." I was touched by their gesture.

That day, however, a second event occurred that turned out, in retrospect, to be a portent of things to come. On that same morning, someone had stuck an anonymous note in the mailbox of every faculty member. The not-too-subtle message in the note was a quote from Machiavelli's book *The Prince*. It read as follows:

> "When an innovator arrives on the scene, he makes enemies of all those who prospered under the old order, and only lukewarm support is coming from those who would prosper under the new. Whenever those who oppose the changes can do so, they attack vigorously, and the defense made by the others is only lukewarm. So both the innovator and his friends come to grief."

Welcome to the University of Colorado! It was clear that there might be some at the business school who were not pleased about my arrival on the scene. At the time, however, I didn't think too much about the incident. Instead, I embarked on my new position with both vigor and enthusiasm. My approach was similar to the one that had worked so well when I was president of Babson. Put most simply, it involved listening, learning, engaging the ideas of others, planning, ensuring buy-in from those who ultimately would be responsible for implementing the strategy, executing, learning from mistakes, continuously improving, and trying to lead by example.

An Entrepreneurial Journey Through Life

The following excerpt from an article from the University of Colorado alumni magazine in the fall of 1992 captures a sense of the mindset I brought to the job:

> Sorenson is emphatic, though, that no matter what the business college does to improve, it cannot, by itself, create tomorrow's business leaders.
>
> "It's terribly important that our graduates be full, rich human beings." Sorenson says, "that they have some exposure to the humanities and to the arts and to the sciences, that they learn other languages. It's important that they understand the cultural context in which they're going to be working and the historical context of this society. It's important that they be equipped to be citizens of the world."

As was mentioned in this article, shortly after my arrival at CU we put in place a process to develop a Master Plan that could serve as a blueprint for determining the future of the business school. This was meant to be a group effort that involved input from all of the school's stakeholders: faculty, students, administrators, alumni, and members of the business community.

From the beginning, it became evident that this effort was not going to be as smooth and harmonious as it had been during my earlier experience at Babson. Almost immediately, it became clear that there was a deep philosophical schism within the faculty participants engaged in the process. As mentioned earlier, one faction, comprising a majority of the faculty, had a vision for the school that corresponded, to a large degree, with my own. This vision postulated that the primary mission of the school should be to do a superb job of preparing students to be successful leaders and managers in the private, public, and not-for-profit sectors of the economy. This involved placing a strong emphasis on teaching excellence. The second faction, comprising a small, but vocal, faction, believed that, in selecting and promoting faculty, teaching should take a back seat to research. After all, they argued, CU was primarily meant to be a research university. They were clearly in the "publish or perish" camp of academics.

My own view was that both good teaching and good research were important: good teaching because it was essential to accomplish the primary mission of the school, good research because it had the potential to change the way management was practiced for the better. However, I had a caveat when it came to research. I believed that much of the research currently being conducted by faculty members in business schools was overly academic in nature and was primarily aimed at publishing articles in refereed academic journals so as to be able to build a record that would justify promotion and the awarding of tenure.

Too often this research was focused on esoteric subjects that had little practical application. So, my caveat to the faculty was: "By all means, do research, but be sure that it is research that has the short- or long-term potential to be useful to practicing managers and professionals in the real world of business."

In the fall of 1992, after the academic year began, it soon became evident that the schism within the faculty over this "teaching versus research" issue was very real and went very deep. What is more, the discussions concerning the issues were far from civil. Rather than engaging in collegial dialogue, some of the faculty members resorted to the practice of making open ad hominem attacks on other faculty members and leaving nasty anonymous notes in the mailboxes of those who disagreed with them. A number of the attacks were personal rather than professional in nature. Many faculty members just plain didn't like or trust one another. The overall atmosphere became increasingly tense and unpleasant.

After about four months on the job, I realized that the current faculty culture at the school was fundamentally dysfunctional. I began to understand more fully why the school had gone through five deans in nine years. What is more, I also began to conclude that under CU's existing faculty charter, the situation probably wasn't fixable. More than two-thirds of the faculty members were tenured and could not be disciplined or dismissed for poor performance or for non-collegial behavior. Moreover, the university as a whole treated the business school as a cash cow. It was expected to generate twice as much revenue from student tuitions and research grants as it was given in its operating budget to run the school. Thus, as dean, I had neither carrots to provide financial incentives to faculty members for good performance, nor sticks to discipline them for poor performance or for not behaving in a collegial manner. Moreover, as members of the AAUP (the American Association of University Professors), most of the faculty were unionized—a fact that also limited the discretionary powers of the dean. It appeared to me to be a no-win situation.

As the fall wore on into winter, the members of the research-oriented clique increasingly began to direct their attacks toward me personally, believing that, in my leadership of the master planning process at the school, I was placing too much emphasis on its teaching mission and not enough on its research function. They were also nervous about the fact that I was spending a fair amount of time trying to build stronger direct relationships between the school and Colorado's business community. They were afraid that, in the process, I was turning the School of Business into a trade school.

Despite these intensifying attacks, I was determined to make the best of the situation and press on with the master planning process in the hopes that the faculty would ultimately coalesce around a mutually acceptable set of goals and a well-conceived plan to achieve them. Along the way, some small victories were achieved. For me, the most significant was the creation of what subsequently became the Deming Center for Entrepreneurship. This center in many ways mirrored the center that we had earlier established at Babson. However, in the case of CU, the center was created with the enthusiastic support of Professor Richard Seebass, dean of the CU engineering school located right next to the business school. Given the strength of the high-tech and biotech entrepreneurial activity in Colorado, this engineering school partnership represented a significant plus for the new center. In my view and that of many others, the Deming Center has, thanks to my successors, evolved over subsequent years into the crown jewel of the CU business school.

Despite these and other small victories, by the spring of 1993, it became clear to me that under my leadership there was little or no chance the faculty, as a whole, would harmoniously coalesce around a mutually acceptable set of strategic goals. The internal factions and frictions were just too strong. The atmosphere within the school had become toxic and I was no longer enjoying my job.

I discussed the situation with Charlotte, who said she had never seen me so frustrated and unhappy. She suggested that, given the intransigent obstacles I was facing at the school, I should stop metaphorically beating my head against the wall and resign. I also conferred with the university's president, chancellor, and provost, as well as the chairman of the business school's Dean's Advisory Council (DAC). All were understanding of my situation and not surprised to see me. They pointed out that the seeds of internal faculty discord at the business school had been planted long before my arrival and that it was likely the discord would continue long after my departure unless drastic action was taken by the administration. All of them tried to persuade me to continue as dean, but I told them that the position had become intolerable for me and that I had made up my mind to resign.

Following these discussions, at the beginning of May, I called a college-wide meeting of all faculty members and senior administrators. In it, I initiated the session by reminding the attendees that, prior to accepting the deanship, I had personally indicated to all of them and to the dean's search committee that I would accept the dean's job only if I could be assured that my nomination had the unanimous support and backing of the faculty and administration. At the time I was given this assurance. Now, however, it had become clear to me that I no longer had that level of support within the faculty. I told them that since a healthy atmosphere of collegiality was very important to my style of leadership, the current toxic atmosphere at the school was making it increasingly difficult for me to function effectively. As a result, I informed them that, for the good of both the school and me personally, I was tendering my resignation as dean, effective as of the end of the academic year on June 30th.

My announcement reverberated through the business school, the university, and the business community like a bombshell. It generated a flurry of press attention, some of it hostile, but most of it supportive and sympathetic toward me. A number of prominent business leaders, in particular, wrote letters and op-ed pieces thanking me for my efforts to improve the CU business school and to build stronger links between the school and the business community . . . efforts that they pointed out had been missing in the past.

Following my resignation, the board of regents and university administration took the unprecedented step of declaring the temporary equivalent of martial law at the CU School of Business. They appointed a special committee of seven professors to hold the fort until a new dean could be named and to make recommendations for change to the college's governance structure. The most important recommendation that was made and approved was that the powers of the deanship be strengthened so as to permit future deans to take appropriate disciplinary action against faculty members for egregious "non-collegial" behavior. Heretofore, such behavior was protected under the "academic freedom" statute of the university. Had such powers been in place during my deanship, it is possible that my tenure in the position might have been longer.

CHAPTER THIRTY-THREE

THE MAGICAL KINGDOM OF BOULDER

Despite my serving as dean of CU's business school for only one academic year, my experience there turned out to have a huge silver lining. Namely it had provided Charlotte and me a great excuse to move from Cambridge, where we had begun to become root-bound, to Boulder, where a whole new world of wonderful experiences opened up for us.

There is a legend in Boulder known as "Niwot's Curse." According to the legend, there once was a Native American chief named Niwot. He presided over a tribe that lived in the shadow of the aptly named Haystack Mountain, located in Boulder County just north of town. Chief Niwot is reported to have cast a spell decreeing that he or she who once lays eyes on Haystack Mountain is destined never to leave and to spend the rest of their life living within sight of the mountain. In our case, the spell seems to be working. Charlotte and I are still living in Boulder, 25-plus years after we first laid eyes on Haystack Mountain in the summer of 1992. Clearly, Niwot's Curse is working its magic on us. We came, we saw, and we decided to stay.

What keeps us in Boulder? To begin, we have loved living closer to Trina and Eric and their families. While we respect their separate lives and their privacy and they respect ours, there nevertheless are many opportunities for us to get together informally for family fun and laughter.

Since we moved here, both Trina and Eric have married and had children. In 1994, Trina married Jess Peterson, a native of Santa Fe, New Mexico, who majored in mathematics at Saint John's College and Colorado College and who earned graduate degrees in geophysics and computer science at the University of Colorado and the University of San Diego. Today, Trina and Jess have two children, Soren and Tessa, and live at 9,000 feet on Glacier Lake in the mountains, about a 35-minute drive west of Boulder. Jess has held various positions in fields related to computer science and investing. Trina currently serves as policy director for the Colorado Forum, a 40-year-old nonprofit organization comprising civic and business leaders committed to finding solutions for major challenges facing Colorado.

In 1996, Eric married Jeannine Fox, who grew up in California and was educated at Sarah Lawrence College. Eric and Jeannine, recently divorced, have two children, Emily and Felix. Professionally, Eric is focused on real estate development and residential home construction.

Meanwhile, Kristin remains in the east and resides in Garrison, New York, where she serves as the vice president of development for West Point. She is married to Eric Stark, a retired art dealer. They have two children, William and Sophie, and two stepchildren, Evan and Alexa.

Apart from family, Boulder has many other delights. One is its climate. High, dry, and sunny, with clean air and clear water, it is a quintessentially healthy place to live. The residents of Boulder are, on average, purportedly the thinnest and most fit people in America. It's hard to live in Boulder without being physically active.

Shortly after we arrived there, I discovered the joys of cycling. While in the Boston area, I had tried to stay fit by running and playing tennis. However, by the time we moved to Boulder, I was beginning to experience a considerable amount of pain in my right hip. The impact of running had clearly begun to take its toll on the cartilage there. So I decided to cut back on running, bought a good road bike, and began biking instead. Making this decision ended up postponing my need to have hip replacement surgery for a number of years.

Boulder is a biker's paradise. In Boulder County, there are 300 miles of bike paths, trails, and lanes. To the west, there are five canyons that present challenging climbs. To the east there are scenic, little-trafficked country roads that offer opportunities for high-speed biking on flat, paved surfaces. I not only found that the smooth motion of cycling was much kinder on my hip, I also found that being on a bike brought considerable joy to my life. In addition to being good exercise, it provided me with an opportunity for meditation, exploration, and inspiration.

I joined a bike club called the Gutgrinders, made up of a bunch of guys who had been biking together for years. In addition to biking on weekends, they sponsor a weeklong tour each year to different venues in the Rocky Mountain region. I have participated in trips that included routes in Colorado, New Mexico, Utah, Wyoming, South Dakota, and Nebraska. Every two years or so, the Gutgrinders also organize biking trips to Europe. I have gone on two of these trips. On the first, we biked all the significant mountain passes in the French Alps that are on the route of the Tour de France annual cycling competition. On the second, we climbed all the Pyrenees Mountain stages of the Tour. Both trips were exhilarating experiences for me.

To this day, weather and schedule permitting, I cycle early every morning when I am in Boulder. Typically, I cover 75 to 125 miles per week. It's a great way to start the day and stay in good physical condition. Once a year, I bike in the annual one-day Buffalo Classic cycling event sponsored by the University of Colorado to raise scholarship funds for CU students. In 2013, the event was held during the week of my 80th birthday in September. To celebrate the occasion, Trina and I completed the event's 110-mile mountainous "century route" that included about 7,500 feet of elevation climbs. It was an exhausting, but exhilarating experience! I ended the day with a satisfying sense of accomplishment.

Earlier that summer, Kristin, Trina, and Eric, as a surprise advance birthday gift, organized a weeklong biking odyssey in the Vaucluse region of France with a company called CycleVentoux. The highlight of the trip was the day the three kids and I, with Charlotte in support, cycled up Mount Ventoux, one of the most, if not *the* most, demanding mountain stages on the itinerary of the Tour de France. From bottom to top it was an unrelenting 22-kilometer climb with an average uphill grade of 8½ degrees. Eric was the rabbit who made it to the top in one hour and forty-eight minutes. I was the tortoise who huffed and puffed all the way up, but who finally had the satisfaction of reaching the summit. The last five-kilometer stretch presented the toughest challenge. All above tree level on the barren, wind-blown top of the mountain, it comprised a twisting series of uphill hairpin curves. Every time I tacked around a corner to the right, I encountered a 35 mph headwind. It was exhausting going. So, for me, summiting was a triumph. While reviving over cups of hot chocolate on the mountaintop, we learned that the strongest wind velocities ever officially recorded, 270 mph, were measured at the weather station on the summit of Mount Ventoux.

Entrepreneurial Insight #10: Entrepreneurial Regions

We have found many reasons to validate our decision to stay in Boulder and not move back to Cambridge, where we still have our house at 117 Brattle Street. One reason relates to what might be called the "Boulder way of thinking." Unlike Boston, a city steeped in tradition, formalism, and what might be called a certain sense of stuffiness and intellectual superiority, Boulder is less formal, stuffy, tradition-bound, and intellectually pompous. However, like Boston, Boulder tends to be quite liberal in its political leanings. Just as

Cambridge has been known as "the People's Republic of Cambridge," Boulder has been known as "the People's Republic of Boulder." As for my personal political leanings, I have always tried to avoid party labels. I would describe myself as an economic conservative and a social liberal. I guess that makes me a "libcon" or a "conlib." But I am perfectly happy to be known as a moderate in the middle.

Driving around Boulder, one sometimes sees bumper stickers proclaiming: "Keep Boulder Weird." This harkens back to the notion that Boulder has always tried to march to the beat of its own drummer and to be on the forefront of change—sometimes for the good and sometimes for the not-so-good.

For example, Boulder has been on the forefront of the whole sustainability movement. It was a pioneer in the field of open space preservation, with 200,000-plus acres of land in Boulder County set aside for this purpose. It is the epicenter of the organic and natural food renaissance, with myriad organic farms and food processing firms springing up in the area over the past several decades. It is in the process of attempting to condemn the city's current investor-owned electric utility and replace it with a municipal system that would hasten the use of renewable sources of energy. It voted overwhelmingly to legally permit the open sale and use of recreational marijuana. It has been a magnet for homeless indigents who know they will be reasonably well treated in the city. It long ago embraced the concept of same-sex marriages.

At the same time, Boulder has been a hotbed of entrepreneurial ferment for private sector startup companies, particularly in the high-tech, biotech, and organic food industries. It is the home of a number of important government-supported scientific laboratories and agencies such as NCAR (the National Center for Atmospheric Research), NIST (the National Institute of Standards and Technology), and NOAA (the National Oceanographic and Atmospheric Administration). And, of course, it has the University of Colorado, an institution strong in science, physics, chemistry, geology, technology, and engineering.

Lesson Learned: Certain places foster entrepreneurial thinking "across the board."

While Boulder's cultural, musical, and artistic scenes are not as extensive or vibrant as those in Boston, they nevertheless are quite active. Moreover, one's interests in these areas can always be supplemented by visits to nearby Denver, which has rich offerings in all of these sectors.

Finally, we have found that Boulder is home to many interesting and friendly people. These range from well-educated "millennials" and midlife professionals to a variety of vintage individuals who have been attracted to the city by its overall quality of life.

In short, Charlotte and I have found Boulder to be a wonderful place to live. Having great kids and grandkids around and loving our very special house are the frosting on the cake!

CHAPTER THIRTY-FOUR

PROFESSIONAL LIFE ON MY TERMS

Having stepped down from the deanship at the University of Colorado in 1993 at the age of nearly 60, I had no intention of abandoning my professional life to twiddle my thumbs in retirement. In fact, provided one continues to be healthy in mind and body and to enjoy the professional side of one's life, I don't believe in the concept of retirement. Of course, if you hate whatever work you are doing or if your body or mind is slipping, that's a different story. Also, if you are passionate about some new activity or adventure that you want to undertake, by all means, shed your former professional skin and redirect your energies and talents toward achieving your goals in that new field of endeavor. But that is more akin to re-*treading* than re-*tiring!*

I was also committed to continuing my service on a number of corporate boards of directors and my involvement in several not-for-profit institutions, including The Nature Conservancy, the Boston Museum of Science, Babson College, and the Asian Institute of Management. In the case of corporate board work, I remained a director of Eaton Vance Corporation, Houghton-Mifflin, Affiliated Publications, the *Boston Globe*, Polaroid, and Exabyte. In addition, in 1994, I was invited to serve on the board of Whole Foods Market, Inc., a company that, at the time, was emerging as a leader in the organic and natural food retailing industry. I accepted this invitation, little knowing what a profound impact my involvement on the Whole Foods board would have on my whole philosophy of management and my fundamental understanding of the capitalist system.

Entrepreneurial Insight #11: Becoming an Angel Investor

In terms of my professional life, I decided to nourish my longstanding interest in the world of entrepreneurship by establishing a small family limited partnership to do "angel" investing in early-stage startup venture companies. The new entity is called the Sorenson Family Limited Partnership.

As managing general partner, I have made most of the investment decisions. I have also had the fun of working with the entrepreneurs/ founders of companies in which the partnership has invested. This typically involves serving on their boards of directors or on their advisory boards and/or acting as an informal coach or mentor to members of their management team. The part I have enjoyed most is the opportunity to learn from these entrepreneurs and their colleagues and to share my ideas and experience with them concerning the best way to manage, finance, and grow their enterprises.

Apart from any financial returns it has produced, the Sorenson Limited Partnership has also generated handsome psychic returns for me, personally. I have thoroughly enjoyed both the intellectual stimulation and the friendships within the entrepreneurial community that have resulted from my involvement as its managing general partner.

Lesson Learned: You can be an entrepreneur at any age.

Over the years since its founding, the Sorenson Family Limited Partnership has made modest minority investments in approximately 15 startup businesses. With me serving as managing general partner, Charlotte is also a general partner. Kristin, Trina, and Eric are the limited partners.

The investment record of the Sorenson Limited Partnership has been typical of other similar venture partnerships. We have had some winners. We have had some losers. And the jury is still out in the case of several of the investments we have made but that have not experienced a so-called "liquidity event"—that is, they haven't yet been sold or launched an IPO (Initial Public Offering) so as to become publicly traded companies.

Earlier, I mentioned that my service on the board of Whole Foods Market, Inc. has had a profound impact on my thinking about business and the concept of capitalism. That is because Whole Foods has developed and evolved an approach toward business that it terms "Conscious Capitalism." I believe that if this approach is more widely adopted by other companies, it has the potential over time to fundamentally transform the way capitalism works, and for the better.

What is Conscious Capitalism? John P. Mackey, the visionary founder and co-CEO of Whole Foods, originated the term and the concept. Along with his fellow team members and colleagues at the company, he has put the concept into practice. In the process, Whole Foods has demonstrated that this approach to management can be enormously successful. In 2013, John and a co-author, Dr. Raj Sisodia, currently a chaired professor at Babson, authored a book entitled *Conscious Capitalism* that describes the concept in considerable detail. What follows is my personal attempt to describe what the concept means, in its essence, to me.

Put most simply, the concept of Conscious Capitalism rests on three basic pillars.

Pillar number one postulates that companies should be driven, first and foremost, by their fundamental purpose and their mission, rather than by the single-minded goal of maximizing shareholder profits. This might sound self-evident. But in a country with laissez-faire laws that ordain that the only legal responsibility of management and boards of directors is to maximize returns to investors, it is by no means an obvious principle.

Pillar number two postulates that the most successful companies are those that are led by "servant leaders"—as opposed to "command and control" leaders—whose primary responsibility is to help create and foster a culture and atmosphere that will release the creative energies and bring out the best in everyone associated with the enterprise.

Pillar number three postulates that companies should be stakeholder-focused rather than stockholder-focused. More specifically, this means working hard to *optimize* the returns to *all* stakeholders and not just to *maximize* the return to stockholders. And who are these stakeholders? In the case of Whole Foods, they are, first and foremost, their customers and their team members or employees. They also include partners in the supply chain (at Whole Foods, this includes farmers, food venders, distributors, and other service providers), investors, the communities in which stores are located, and the environment. The whole idea is to create a win-win situation for all these stakeholder groups, rather than a situation where stockholders win, but do so at the expense of the other stakeholders.

By continuing to practice and evolve the concept of Conscious Capitalism over the years, the company has emerged as the clear leader in the field of natural and organic food retailing. Ironically, over the long term, Whole Foods has also generated attractive returns for their stockholders . . . but they have done so as the *end result* of creating a win-win for all other stakeholders. In short, the company, while not perfect, has amply demonstrated that, by practicing Conscious Capitalism, it is possible for a private sector corporation to do well, *and*, simultaneously, to do good things for all of their other stakeholders.

In recent years, the common sense lesson that "win-win" works much better than "win-lose" has resonated strongly with me and has increasingly informed my thoughts and actions not only vis-à-vis my dealings with the business world, but in my personal life as well. Treat others as you would like to be treated yourself. It's as simple as the Golden Rule. Easy to understand, but oh so hard to always follow! However, with more and more companies beginning to join Whole Foods in practicing Conscious Capitalism, I am optimistic that capitalism, in an evolved form, can become a kinder, gentler, positive force in helping to make the world a better place for all.

As has been widely publicized, in the fall of 2017 Whole Foods was sold to Amazon, Inc. As a result, the Whole Foods board of directors was disbanded, thus ending my 23 years of service on its board. Our entire board, however, had supported the sale.

We believed that significant potential two-way synergies could be realized by the merging of the two companies. We also thought that the merger had the potential to revolutionize the entire grocery retailing industry. Finally, we believed that Amazon would respect and preserve Whole Foods' very special culture of Conscious Capitalism. So far, all of these predictions are proving to be true. Truth be told, it is my secret hope that, over time, Whole Foods can accomplish a reverse cultural takeover of Amazon. Only time will tell!

CHAPTER THIRTY-FIVE

THE PLEASURES OF LONGEVITY

It hardly seems possible that I have already lived more than four-score years. In my mind, it feels more like I am still in middle age. What is surprising to me is how much I have enjoyed the most recent 20-plus years of my life. It is as though a great weight was lifted off me at age 60.

About that time, I think I began subconsciously to say to myself, "I've actually 'been there and done that.' " I've nothing to prove to the world or myself anymore. So now I can turn my curiosity and zest for life in new directions. While continuing to pursue various professional activities of my own choosing, I can also begin to explore some of the more existential issues that confront all of us in life. I can read more. I can spend more time with Charlotte and my kids and grandkids. We can travel freely. I can develop a deeper appreciation for nature and the out-of-doors. I can put more miles on my bike. I can try to distill wisdom from what I have learned and experienced. I can become better acquainted with myself. I can begin to concentrate on living each moment of each day more fully.

Finally, I can pursue my ongoing personal spiritual journey. In this regard, I continue to be filled with awe at the beauty and wonder of our world. I choose to believe that a positive force was behind the "Big Bang" that fashioned our Earth and the cosmos. I see the influence of this life force everywhere I look. However, though I subscribe to the tenets of the Golden Rule and humanism, I am disillusioned with most human-invented organized religions. It is my belief that, since the advent of humankind, there has been more bloodshed in the name of "my religion is better than your religion" than for any other reason. If I had to attach a label to myself, it would probably be "agnostic pantheist." I am still like the four-year-old boy I once was when, told by my dear father that God created the heavens and earth, I inquired: "Who gave him the idea?" I am continuing to search for the answer to that question, even though I can never know what it is.

In the meantime, I have found that it is much more satisfying and enjoyable to live life as an optimist than as a pessimist.

And so, I have passed the last 20-plus years with all of the foregoing as my focus. In the process, I have continued to learn from many others and to develop new insights of my own. The following list is a distillation of some of those thoughts and concepts that have guided me in my daily life. Even though I don't come close to living up to these guidelines, I have found the list to be helpful to me as a personal set of aspirations.

This I Am Learning

1. We are all spiritual beings having a human experience, rather than human beings having a spiritual experience.

2. When you are kind and loving to others, you are being kind and loving to yourself.

3. We are all part of each other and of all other living things.

4. Develop generosity toward others and be mindful of their needs.

5. Avoid being judgmental.

6. Be accepting; what happens is what is meant to happen.

7. Nourish your sense of humor; laughter *is* the best medicine.

8. Live in this very moment, not in the past or for the future.

9. There are no ordinary moments; just extraordinary moments.

10. All the answers you need to know are within yourself.

11. Enjoy the journey; it's at least as important as the destination.

12. Use your creativity and talents to make a difference.

13. Work to live; don't live to work.

14. If you don't enjoy your work, find work that you do enjoy.

15. The mind, like steel, is kept bright through use.

16. Simple solutions are usually the best solutions.

17. Whatever you choose to do, do it to the best of your ability and make something beautiful of it.

18. The collective creative power of the team is far greater than that of any one team member.

19. Keep your body as healthy as possible.

20. Do an hour of vigorous exercise and stretching each day and eat a nutritious diet.

21. Meditate and breathe deeply every day.

22. Be awestruck by the extraordinary beauty and diversity of nature and do your bit to preserve the planet.

23. When listening, looking, or touching, do so with intention.

24. Seek an inner stillness and listen for the song.

25. Never lose your curiosity or your passion for living and learning.

26. Have many friends and especially many young friends.

27. Forgiving others is the key to healing oneself.

28. Try to live your life with a happy heart.

29. Love is the very essence of life.

30. Dying is no big deal if you have lived your human life fully.

Entrepreneurial Insight #12: "Being Entrepreneurial"

Years of living, raising a family, and, of course, working with entrepreneurs and their ventures has led me to a simple insight: Being entrepreneurial includes, but is not limited to, starting a business. Being entrepreneurial is a mindset, a worldview, a way of approaching life itself.

"Being entrepreneurial" means being:

- **A self-starter:** You can't wait for others to make things happen.
- **Flexible:** If unexpected events derail your initial plans, try something different.
- **Resilient:** The question is not whether you will have setbacks, but how you will respond to them.

- **Open to suggestions:** Other people may have good ideas you can use.

- **Willing to learn:** Accept the fact that you don't know everything.

- **Optimistic:** Opportunities are everywhere for those with the right attitude.

- **Persistent:** The only sure way to fail is to give up.

- **Curious:** It's amazing what you can learn if the world is interesting to you.

There are more qualities you can discover for yourself, of course. However, this is the kind of mindset we tried to teach at Babson and it is the kind of worldview that makes for a happy and interesting life, no matter what your profession or your family situation.

Lesson Learned: You don't have to be an entrepreneur to be entrepreneurial.

APPENDIX A

ANNOUNCEMENT OF PRESIDENCY

Ralph Z. Sorenson Named New President of Babson College
Babson Free Press

Ralph Z. Sorenson, associate professor at the Harvard Graduate School of Business Administration has been elected seventh president of Babson College by a vote of the college's Board of Trustees. Sorenson's appointment will become effective September 1, 1974.

The election of Sorenson was made on the recommendation of the Presidential Search Committee chaired by Jarvis Farley, Chairman of the Babson College Corporation. This committee made its final report after a year of investigation and the screening of over 200 candidates.

Sorenson is a magna cum laude and Phi Beta Kappa graduate of Amherst College and received his M.B.A. and D.B.A. degrees from Harvard University Graduate School of Business Administration.

He has been a faculty member at Harvard since 1964, when he came to the university to complete his doctoral work as a Ford Foundation Fellow. From 1966 to 1968, Sorenson was Director of the Harvard University Advisory Group in Manila, Philippines.

As director of this operation Sorenson worked with three Philippine universities under a Ford Foundation grant to strengthen graduate level management education in that country. His efforts culminated in the creation of the Asian Institute of Management.

An expert in international marketing, Sorenson has been in charge of that course of study at Harvard since 1971. His background in international business includes having worked as an executive for Nestlé Alimentana S.A. in Vevey,

Switzerland, and as a research associate at IMEDE Management Development Institute, Lausanne, Switzerland.

Sorenson is currently director and consultant to General Housewares Corporation, Knapp King-Size Corporation, Star Markets, Inc. and Mammoth Mart, Inc., and he is a trustee of the Habitat Environmental School. He has also done consulting and management development work for General Electric Corporation, Polaroid Corporation, SOHIO, ITEK, and several firms in Europe, South America and the Far East.

Sorenson is married to the former Charlotte B. Ripley, has three children (Kristin 11, Katrina 9, and Eric 8), and resides in Belmont, Mass.

. . . . .

The special edition of the *Babson Free Press* carried a number of related articles as well, including the following:

New President Brings Unique Administrative Skills To Babson
By Harvey Firemen
Babson Free Press

"He's a distinguished colleague, with a particular strength in administration. He's impressed almost all of us with his remarkable combination of human skills and the ability to get the job done. He has a good sense of what is educationally important, and he can make things happen under very unlikely and unfavorable conditions. I have great admiration for him as an administrator, faculty member, and as a human being."

This is the respect accorded to Ralph Sorenson, next president of Babson College by the man who recommended him to the Presidential Search Committee, Lawrence Fouraker, Dean of the Harvard Business School.

The respect is well accorded.

At age 40, Dr. Sorenson is an associate professor at the Harvard Business School, with many outstanding qualities and qualifications.

For two years beginning in 1966 Sorenson was director of a Harvard Advisory Group in the Philippines which helped to establish the Asian Institute of Management. As the director of the group, Sorenson "had responsibility for providing overall project leadership and for maintaining close contact with the Philippine academic and business communities," according to Sorenson's biography. He also helped to raise $6 million to finance the Institute.

"The unanimous view of the people who worked with Sorenson was that he was more instrumental in bringing about the school than any other person. It was a remarkable educational achievement", said Fouraker. "He worked in a setting where that degree of cooperation had not been the standard; where the level of philanthropy from private sources had never been recognized in the past. He had to bring church, state and private groups together to reach agreement on common purposes and interests. There was an almost endless number of tasks, often in areas where there were wide differences of opinion, and substantially conflicting interests. And Sorenson, working through all that maze of complexity in a culture not his own, helped to bring about a very superb educational institution.

"He has had an interest in international marketing since his days in graduate school. As I remember, his doctoral thesis is on multinational corporations in Central America. In addition to the thesis, he wrote a series of cases on multinational companies. He also spent time at IMEDE, Switzerland, where he did research and developed teaching material in the international field. So Dr. Sorenson has always had a very warm interest in other people of different countries—what their problems are, and how he could help them", explained Fouraker.

Sorenson's international background doesn't end with his thesis, cases, and work at IMEDE. He is a consultant to many foreign companies, and Fouraker thinks this is a reflection of his classroom ability.

"I think his overseas consulting is an indication of breadth of mind and interest, and his capacity to reach those who have a slightly different view of the world than his own. It takes an outgoing intellect to do that well. I think that's one of the reasons that Dr. Sorenson is a great teacher. He can identify with the student—with the student's perspective."

Whatever the reason for Sorenson's classroom abilities, it is clear that he has them, for he was asked to chair a committee on methods of instruction for new professors at Harvard.

"Harvard places more emphasis on teaching effectiveness than perhaps do other graduate business schools. We're conscious about transmitting that excellence to our new faculty. One of the problems of teaching is how do you teach new faculty from other educational institutions what is considered to be an effective and successful teacher. Dr. Sorenson was recognized as a superb teacher, and he chaired that committee, working with new faculty, to capture experienced professors' insights to help solve the problems of those just beginning their careers here," said Fouraker.

In Dean Fouraker's eyes, Sorenson is a great professor of marketing. But he also feels that Sorenson's contributions as a teacher aren't restricted to the classroom.

"I think that the best single summary of Ralph and Charlotte Sorenson is that they are superb human beings. And that's perhaps the best qualification a man should have to be president of Babson College. Their values, approach to life, the way they resolve issues, both in the family and on the job, and their relation to people provide a standard that's worth emulating. And perhaps that is ultimately the most effective teaching method of all".

. . . . .

To this day, I remain indebted to Larry Fouraker for recommending my name to the Babson presidential search committee in the first place and for the extraordinarily generous appraisal that he subsequently gave to the committee.

Finally, among other articles that appeared at the time concerning my appointment, there was this one in the February 23, 1974 issue of the *Boston Globe:*

Sorenson Eager to Tackle Babson Job
By Angus Twombly
Boston Globe

Sometime this summer when Ralph Sorenson moves his family from Belmont to the big brick house in Wellesley that is home to the president of Babson College, he'll be making good on a thought that he had had years back that he'd "like a chance to help administer and shape the future of a school".

It was quite by chance that the school turned out to be Babson, training ground for graduate and undergraduate students in business management.

"The contact with Babson came totally out of the blue," said the 40-year-old Harvard Business School marketing professor last week. "I'd really had very little contact with Babson and had a very limited knowledge of what the school was and what it did.

"My initial contact," he continued, "came by a phone call from the chairman of the presidential search committee and chairman of the Babson College Corporation, Jarvis Farley, asking if I would be interested in exploring the presidency there. It was at that point that I began to try to educate myself about the school. The more I saw, the more I liked it."

His efforts culminated with the February 8th announcement that he would succeed Henry A. Kriebel as Babson's seventh president.

Sorenson admits that he still has a "tremendous amount of learning to do about the school," but his detailed outline, his easy conversation and his copy of the Babson catalogue in which the names of many trustees are meticulously checked off all indicate he has made careful preparations to move into the top administrative spot.

A concern for precision and detail probably will characterize much of what Sorenson does as he prepares for the Babson presidency. He dresses in a neat conservative style, chooses his words carefully as he describes his preliminary plans.

"I think that in the mid- and late 1970s," he says, "it is going to be absolutely critical for every educational institution to have a clearly thought out strategy for where it is going. It should have a long-term plan, a strategic set of objectives and then some annual expression of the actions required to achieve those objectives."

"I think that my first tasks as president of Babson are going to be to establish the mechanism to do this long-term planning, to pose the critical kinds of issues that this planning must address, and to find the right people to do this planning."

Formal planning will not be new to Babson. Among the accomplishments of Dr. Kriebel in his 13 years in office was the "Babson Master Plan", a guideline for the five-year period just ending. It provided a framework within which Babson became coeducational, expanded its management and liberal arts curriculum and built six new buildings.

"It just makes good common sense and we're going to do it again," said Sorenson of the planning process. "I think one change, though, is that I see the planning process as being a much more continuous process."

To Sorenson's marketing students at Harvard and to Babson students, that latter point is the classic marketing concept of "finding a niche"—doing something that differentiates you and your market from the competition.

The competition in this case will, of course, include Harvard.

"I'd like to see it much more in complementary rather than competitive terms, although inevitably there is some overlap in the mission of the two institutions," Sorenson said.

Apart from his marketing concepts, however, Sorenson will bring a rich background of teaching and administrative experience to Babson. He spent nearly two and a half years in the late 1960s as director of the Harvard Advisory Group in the Philippines to create the Asian Institute of Management, a graduate management school that has the backing of three Philippine universities.

Working on that program involved about $6 million to endow teaching chairs, obtain land, and construct the buildings.

Sorenson's career in management and management education was partly influenced, he says, by his father, a marketer for Westinghouse. When he was growing up in Evanston, Ill. and later in Mansfield, Ohio, Sorenson said he came to realize the power vested in the business community to allow anyone who had an interest in having an impact on one's environment a lot of opportunity.

Sorenson, a Phi Bata Kappa graduate of Amherst College, earned an MBA and DBA from Harvard and put in four years in private industry and research before coming back to the business school in 1963. He has specialized in international marketing and had done consulting work for General Electric, Polaroid, and ITEK. He is a director of General Housewares Corporation, Knapp King-Size Corporation, Star Market, and Mammoth Mart, Inc.

Sorenson says that much of his life outside school is spent in "sharing the growing up period with my kids (Eric 7, Katrina 9, and Kristin 11)—that's pretty important to me."

Education is an interest he does take home and shares with his wife, the former Charlotte Ripley, a Wellesley College graduate. She is finishing a full-time apprentice teaching program with Lesley College and the Shady Hill School in Cambridge. Together they serve as co-presidents of the Winn Brook School PTA in Belmont.

"One of the priorities we have set for ourselves is an understanding of what the public education system in Belmont is all about," he said. "It's fair to say that, as a family, we really care about the education process both professionally and as it affects our family personally."

Mrs. Sorenson may do some part-time teaching while she doubles as a college president's wife. "We're really going to have to stretch the hours in a day," Sorenson said with a smile.

Perhaps in keeping with his emphasis on planning, Sorenson has done some thinking about just how long he might be at Babson. "For a president to have an impact on an institution requires a minimum of four or five years," he said.

"I'd like not to have an abiding set of rules governing the time an individual has in a chief executive's job. One can observe, though, that it's often the case that chief executives after eight or ten years need a new challenge and the institutions reach the stage when it would be healthy to have new leadership."

APPENDIX B

BABSON COLLEGE INAUGURATION SPEECH

President Ralph Sorenson

There is on this campus an enormous globe. It stands three stories high, and I am told it is the largest ever constructed by man. Ever since arriving at Babson, I have been intrigued by that globe. The other day when I went to look at it, I was struck by two powerful feelings. The first was one of wonder, for the world when seen and contemplated in its entirety is truly extraordinary. The second was more sobering. For looking at the globe, one realizes that the world is finite, and one begins to comprehend at last that it can indeed be true that the world's seed capital, in the form of land and water and natural resources and raw materials, is being consumed faster than it is being replaced.

Therein lies one of the many monumental challenges for both the now and future manager. For managerial skills and analytical thinking, as practiced individually and collectively by all those, whatever their title, who direct business, scientific, agricultural, social and governmental activities, must lie at the heart of our ability to use wisely the world's remaining seed capital.

There are other major challenges. One has only to think of the recent economic summit meetings in Washington to realize that, after all this time, we still do not know how to deal effectively with recessions, depressions, or inflation. We still do not know all we need to know about how to make work meaningful or how to create organizational environments in which individuals can truly thrive and develop their maximum potential. We have much to learn about combining beauty and function, cultural pursuits and industrial necessities. And we have much to learn about ourselves as human beings; how best we learn; how to match talent and desire with career; and how to make effective personal decisions in a world of great choice.

Each of us, of course, could easily expand this list of challenges. But the point I want to make is that managers and the management profession can, and must, play a central role if challenges such as these are to be met effectively.

Thus, the thoughts that ran through my mind the other day as I looked at that globe served to reconfirm my conviction that, despite the current clouds on the economic horizon, there will continue to be an increasing need for effective, well educated, tough-minded, but humane and moral managers who will be willing to tackle with zest the exquisitely baffling major challenges that confront our world.

To add a more earthy dimension to these worldly challenges, there will also be an increasing need for competent managers who are proud of their profession and who will be able to mind the store on a day-to-day basis. By this I mean properly educated managers at all levels of responsibility in all kinds of organizations who will be able to handle their individual jobs with skill, humor, sound judgment and common sense.

All of which brings me to Babson. I want each of you to know that I am very excited about coming to Babson College. For I believe that this institution is poised to play an increasingly important role in the education and development of the managers I have just described. Why do I believe this?

Let me begin with the factor of momentum. There is no such thing as a steady-state institution. All institutions are either alive and vibrant and gaining momentum or they are stagnating and—little by little—dying. I believe that the facts indicate that Babson College is today alive and vibrant. And here, at the outset, I would like to pause to pay special tribute to my predecessor, Dr. Henry Kriebel, who since 1961 has been president of Babson and under whose sound and thoughtful guidance the school has, in recent years, made steady progress.

Back in 1967 and 1968, faculty, administrators, students, alumni, incorporators, and trustees of Babson joined hands to formulate a master plan that was subsequently implemented with what, in my judgment, was remarkable success.

Since others were totally responsible for the results, I think I can report to you, without risk of being thought immodest, that since 1968 the college has:

1. Significantly improved its cornerstone undergraduate program by curriculum revisions that strengthen offerings in management areas and broaden course work in the liberal arts.

2. Doubled the size of the faculty and, in the process, strengthened it significantly so that today we have an excellent nucleus of extremely capable teachers.

3. Dramatically increased applications and enrollments in each of its major programs.

4. Improved the quality and mix of its student body and in the process became co-educational.

5. Developed the graduate MBA program so that, with 275 full-time students and 1080 part-time students it now stands as one of the largest in the New England area.

6. Created an active School of Continuing Education for practicing managers.

7. Built several new educational buildings and dormitories, as well as making extensive additional improvements on the campus.

8. Finally, I am pleased to be able to say in this age of educational red ink that the foregoing accomplishments have been achieved while pursuing sound and sensible financial policies.

All of this suggests that Babson, as an educational institution, does indeed have momentum. And this is a momentum that I firmly believe can be accelerated in the future.

To make this happen, the time has now come for the Babson community to join hands once again in an effort to plan systematically for the years ahead. I bring with me to this new office a deep conviction that it is imperative for all educational institutions, regardless of their present state of health, to establish explicit strategic long-term objectives and then to formulate specific plans to achieve these objectives.

In the next decade, the need for such systematic planning by private, Massachusetts-based colleges and universities in particular, will become even more acute in the face of inflation, a declining birth rate, an uncertain economic outlook, increasing educational competition, and a current tendency on the part of government to pump funds into state schools at the expense of private institutions.

To thrive in such an environment—and thrive we shall—Babson College must have a sensible set of long-term objectives, a clear sense of direction, and detailed annual plans of action. In assuming the presidency of Babson, I intend to assign the highest order of priority to the establishment of such objectives and plans, as well as to the creation of a mechanism for systematically reviewing and revising these objectives and plans on a periodic basis. In so doing, I shall be seeking an approach to planning that will, on the one hand, encourage active and thoughtful involvement by interested, respected and capable individuals from all of Babson's internal and external constituencies, but which will, on the other hand, still be sufficiently streamlined and well-organized to get the job done in a sprightly and expeditious way.

What, then, are some of the starting assumptions that might be made as we jointly begin to look toward our future? I would like to share with you some simple propositions that, without in any way prejudging the end results of the planning process, might perhaps serve as a starting point for our future planning dialogues.

The first of these simple propositions is that it is better for Babson to do a few things superbly than many things poorly. Too many educational institutions have, in my view, courted disaster by attempting to be all things to all learners and to all researchers. The curse of over-diversification that has come back to haunt many industrial corporations in recent years has also invaded academia. Colleges that have attempted to become miniversities and universities that have sought to transform themselves into multiversities now are beginning to pay the price in terms of both deflated quality and inflated overheads.

Appendix B

So, I would side with Alfred North Whitehead who, in his landmark treatise on the AIMS OF EDUCATION, commented on what he called the "mental dry rot" which characterized many educational institutions. "How are we to guard against this mental dry rot?" he inquired. "We enunciate two educational commandments: do not teach too many subjects. What you teach, teach thoroughly."

I believe that Babson has an advantage in this regard, in that it is already specialized with a clear unified thrust to its activities. Its central mission is first and foremost to be a school of <u>management</u> education. The management program is not and, in my view, should not be buried among other programs.

Thus, as a starting point for our future planning I urge that we consciously place quality before quantity and reaffirm our commitment to specialize and seek excellence in a few areas rather than adequacy in many.

Let me now turn to the role of teaching and learning at Babson. To our own students who are here today and to all of you who are teachers—both at Babson and at sister institutions—I would like you to know that I share with you a deep love and a reverence for good teaching that leads to effective learning. This love, coupled with what I believe to be a hard-headed assumption that students—whether they be undergraduates, graduates or adult practicing managers—will in the future be increasingly attracted to those education institutions that openly and demonstrably are characterized by outstanding teaching and a vibrant learning climate, leads me to my second proposition. Namely, I suggest that Babson would be well served if it officially and in practice were to continue to assign top priority to excellence in teaching and in learning. This means putting the needs of students clearly in the center of our institutional orbit. I hasten to add that provided this priority is recognized, strong encouragement can and should also be given to those types of research, consulting, campus and community activities that will resonate in the classroom and that are so necessary for a faculty member's professional and intellectual growth.

In referring to excellence in teaching and learning, I fully realize that I am speaking of a wonderfully mysterious process that defies categorical definition. I suspect, however, that as we join together to plan Babson's future, we might all agree at the outset on certain premises concerning the elements that must be present for effective learning to occur. We can then attempt to insure that these elements will be built into any educational programs offered by the school.

The first and most basic of these elements is deceptively simple: in order to learn, one must first want to learn. As far back as the first century the Greek philosopher Epictetus observed that: "It is impossible for a man to learn what he thinks he already knows" or, we might add, what he has no desire to know. Wags of a later era changed the phrase but not the thought when they said: "You can lead a man to college, but you cannot make him think."

The fundamental thought truth here, of course, is that in the last analysis, the initiative for learning must rest with the learner and not the teacher. Babson's educational approach must continue to reflect this fact.

The second premise, corollary to the first, is that effective learning tends to be both active and interactive and is seldom, if ever, passive.

Another Greek philosopher, this time Aristotle, recognized the active nature of learning 2,400 years ago when he observed that: "What we have to learn to do, we learn by doing." And Alfred North Whitehead picked up on this theme when he suggested that: "Celibacy does not suit a university. It must mate itself with action."

As for the interactive quality of learning, it was Emerson who aptly observed: "You send your child to the schoolmaster, but 'tis the schoolboys who educate him." He also observed that: "Conversation is the laboratory and workshop of the student."

Certainly Roger Babson was aware of the active and interactive nature of learning when in the late 1930's he wrote his book LOOKING AHEAD FIFTY YEARS. In an especially perceptive passage he stated: "Facts alone are not readily retained in memory. It is easier to remember facts when they are accompanied by acts—particularly if the acts are our own. Therefore, lectures have been supplemented by laboratories. Students visit industries, sometimes to work there part time. Industries visit the school. The conference system and the case system have come into vogue. It is all typical of the swing toward dynamic _training_ instead of the older method of _teaching_ by rote. The new education will firmly *follow this modern trend. The teacher's main function will be not to impart information but to implant wisdom."*

Mr. Babson's comments, I suggest, are equally valid today and offer a good model for us to emulate as we seek in the future to enhance further the quality of our teaching and the rigor of the learning experience at this college.

Before I depart from the subject of teaching and learning, let me touch briefly on the role of liberal arts in the undergraduate program. Upon occasion, questions have arisen, particularly on the part of freshmen, as to why a college of management requires liberal arts as an essential part of its undergraduate program. There are many ways to respond to that question, but I think that the answer I like best is the one given by the French author, Antoine de St. Exupery, when he spoke through the lips of the title character in his delightful book, THE LITTLE PRINCE: "I know a planet," said the Little Prince, "where there is a certain red-face gentleman. He has never smelled a flower. He has never looked at a star. He has never loved anyone. He has never done anything in his life but add up figures. And all day he says over and over: 'I am busy with matters of consequence.' And that makes him swell with pride. But he is not a man—he is a mushroom!"

Thus, the liberal arts courses are included as a vital part of the undergraduate management program out of a conviction I firmly endorse, that Babson should not grow mushrooms. Instead, it is important for us to try to help educate perceptive managers who will be fully sensitive to the social, cultural, ethical, and historical implications of their future decisions.

The third proposition that I would like to put forth is that we should begin almost immediately an effort aimed at developing ways to strengthen dramatically Babson's direct ties with the business community, as well as with the growing number of nonbusiness organizations in this area. Here I would like to address specifically those of you in the audience who represent these kinds of businesses and organizations. Six weeks ago, President Ford, speaking at Ohio State University, called on higher education and industry to form a more active alliance. I would like those of you today who are business executives and practicing managers to know that Babson is interested in just such an alliance.

I believe that such an alliance can be a two-way street and will result in significant value to both parties. For example, Babson, on its side, might benefit by:

1. Having access to your ideas and opinions as we approach the task of master planning, curriculum development, and course design.

2. Having an opportunity to develop realistic case and teaching materials based on the experience of your firms.

3. Having a real-life, decision-making laboratory for students who might work with you in project work or in some form of rigorous work-study program or internship.

4. The intellectual stimulation afforded to faculty members who work with you as consultants or as instructors in continuing education programs.

5. Having executives come to the campus on a frequent basis as speakers and seminar participants or to work with us in our career development efforts.

6. Enjoying your support and confidence as we go about the continuous task of developing our resources and our reputation.

All these things and more are needed in order for Babson to be certain there will be a sense of sound realism and excellence in its curriculum.

Meanwhile, the quid-pro-quo for industry can take several forms:

1. Industry can have access to a valuable pool of better-educated graduates who will have a sounder grasp of the way business actually works in the real world.

2. Both profit and non-profit corporations can help solve their internal management problems by availing themselves of Babson's part-time MBA program and its various continuing education programs, as well as by utilizing the services of Babson faculty members as consultants or for certain types of in-company training programs. It might interest you to know, by the way, that there are already more than 30 firms in this area that currently have at least five employees enrolled in our part-time evening MBA program. In fact, several of these firms such

as Raytheon, Honeywell, and Polaroid each have more than 25 employees enrolled in that same program.

3. As time goes on, firms might increasingly use small groups of students on an ad hoc basis who, as a learning experience, would analyze various management problems under the supervision of a faculty member and make recommendations to management.

4. Teaching materials developed at Babson might be used for in-company training programs.

And the list might be expanded. It should be clear from these examples, however, that closer ties between Babson and both business and non-business organizations can have significant tangible benefits for all concerned.

My fourth proposition is that Babson, in its coming planning deliberations, should carefully examine the potential opportunities that are arising as a result of certain basic trends occurring in the fields of education and management. Let me mention three such needs.

First, I believe that one of the single most powerful education developments in the last part of this century will be the increasing recognition that education is not something to be relegated to one's youth, but rather can and should be a continuous process throughout one's life. Roger Babson was ahead of his time in perceiving this development many years ago when he wrote: "The need of the hour is that students shall sooner become men and that men shall longer remain students."

As we look ahead to the late 1970's and 1980's, nowhere will that need be greater than in the field of management education. Thus, I suspect that Babson, with its already active start in continuing education programs, would do well to explore actively further opportunities in this area.

A second major development is the progress being made by women in the management profession. While women have clearly not gained overnight acceptance in the ranks of management, they nevertheless are beginning to make slow but steady progress which I predict will accelerate in the future. Babson has already begun to be responsive to this trend. For example, almost 20 percent of all new students in the undergraduate program were women this year. And the School of continuing education is already offering its highly promising Managerial Skills (MS) program that is aimed specifically at women who are already employed and who are considered by their employers to have strong management potential. In light of this encouraging start, I would hope that we could, in a very natural way, continue to be responsive to the growing demand for management education on the part of women.

A third growth opportunity that I believe should be explored is the international area. A substantial number of students in each of our programs already come from outside the United States. An even greater number of our students will, at some time in their careers, be called upon to deal with international management problems as business becomes increasingly multinational. With my own international background, I would be less than honest if I didn't confess that I have a certain natural interest in things international. Indeed, I was not terribly unhappy to hear that Babson faculty voted last spring to develop international business as a partial field of concentration for certain of our MBA students.

This list of possible opportunities is by no means meant to be exhaustive. There are obviously other areas that we can and perhaps should study in the course of our strategic planning. It bears reemphasizing, however, that as we examine these opportunity areas we must be sure that we build toward the future on the solid foundation of our existing undergraduate and graduate strengths. This means, as I suggested earlier, not trying to do too many things, but instead, being highly selective and concentrating on a few "critical mass" programs in which we are sure that we have, or can develop, the necessary resources to do an outstanding job.

Finally, let me turn from planning and strategy and opportunities to what I consider the most important subject of all. Ever since coming to this campus, I have sensed a very special quality about the Babson community. The people who make up this community—and most of you are here today—really seem to share a great love for and loyalty toward Babson. There is an esprit and an air of friendliness and a ring of laughter about the campus that I find totally refreshing. It is this shared sense of esprit and love and loyalty that will be the single most important ingredient in the future progress and development of this school. All great institutions, whether they be colleges or corporations, churches or communities, have at their core an intangible spirit that is absolutely essential if they are to thrive and grow and endure.

The Little Prince of St. Exupery, to whom I referred earlier, had a nice way of putting it: "And now here is my secret" he said, "a very simple secret. It is only with the heart that one can see rightly; what is essential is invisible to the eye".

And so it is with Babson College. What is really essential is invisible to the eye. But I believe that invisible esprit is here in great abundance and can translate itself into the shared sense of excitement and commitment that comes from being part of an educational institution that has tremendous potential and that is only now beginning to mature and blossom.

Let me at this point inject a personal note. When I was growing up, my father and my mother, who are with us today, communicated to me, in gentle ways and by example, a very simple message. The message was that whatever work one undertakes in life—be it as manager or worker, teacher or learner—one can make something beautiful out of it. I believe that this is true for each of us here today.

And so I close by inviting all who care about this college—teachers and students, staff members and incorporators, alumni and parents, business executives and public officials, friends and family—to become informal trustees of this school and to join with me in the challenging and exciting adventure of building something beautiful at Babson College.

APPENDIX C

HIGHLIGHTS OF THE BABSON COLLEGE MASTER PLAN
1975 – 1980

OVERALL

- Seek Excellence in a Few Fields . . . Rather Than Adequacy in Many
- Remain Specialized in Management Education
- Primarily Business-Oriented, But Long-Term: Attention to Public & Nonprofit Sectors
- Strong Emphasis on Practical . . . But Also Underlying Concepts
- Focus on Entrepreneurship as an Underserved Area of Management Education
- Strong Emphasis on Effective Learning and Excellence in Teaching
- Help Students Develop a Strong Sense of Responsibility Toward Themselves, other Individuals, and Society
- Build Direct Ties with Management Community
- Build National and International Reputation
- Stay in Four Current Educational Programs

UNDERGRADUATE PROGRAM
Overall:
Grow in Quality, Not Size
Emphasize Good Teaching
Strive To Be the Finest Undergraduate Management College in Country

Students:
Stabilize at about 1200
More Selective
More National and International, Fewer Regional
More Women
More Minority Students

Curriculum:
Better Integration of Management and Liberal Arts
More Emphasis:
- Independent Analysis and Decision-Making
- Real-Life Learning Experience
- Communication Skills
- Bridge Gaps Among Major Curricular Areas

Faculty:
Assure That Faculty's Expectations of Students Remain High and That Rigor and Demands of Program are Met

Accreditation:
Seek AACSB (American Association of Collegiate Schools of Business) Accreditation

FULL-TIME GRADUATE PROGRAM
Overall:
High Quality All-Around MBA Program
But With Special Emphasis on Entrepreneurship Education
Differentiate Through Field Experience
Create "Living MBA" Based on Concept of Learning by Doing

Students:
Stabilize at about 300
More Students with Work Experience
More National and International Students

Curriculum:
Complete Review of Core Curriculum
Design More Field Project Work
Improve Overall Quality
Engage in More Concentrated Planning Effort

Facilities:
Better On-Campus Study Facilities

Environment:
Provide Greater Contact with Leading Professionals

PART-TIME GRADUATE PROGRAM
Overall:
Strong Continued Emphasis on Part-Time MBA Program
Strengthen Ties with Sponsoring Employers

Students:
Stabilize at about 1100 for Next 3 Years
Focus on Special Interest Areas (e.g. Entrepreneurship)
Step-up College to Company Recruiting

Faculty:
Gradually, More Full-Time Faculty to Teach in Part-Time Program
Better Course Planning – Especially by Part-Time Faculty

Facilities:
Improve and Provide Better Study and Lounge Facilities

CONTINUING MANAGEMENT EDUCATION PROGRAM
Overall:
Lay Groundwork for Strong Future Growth
Become Education Arm for a Few Organizations
Provide Alumni with Engagement-Career Development Programs
Long Term: Build On-Campus Executive Education Center

Potential Market Niche:
Differentiated Middle Management Programs for Small to Medium-Large
  Companies and Organizations
Entrepreneurship Programs
High Repeat Business
High Spillover Benefits to Faculty and Other Programs

Faculty: Make Executive Education Programs a Mainstream Faculty Activity

SPECIAL CONSIDERATIONS
<u>Faculty:</u>
Single Faculty to Serve All Programs, But Concentrated Planning
Emphasize Good Teaching and Activities That Lead to It
Reflect Emphasis in Recruiting, Promotion, Compensation, and Recognition
Salaries: Midpoint Among 7 New England Business Schools
Better Logistics Support
More Resources to Research & Faculty Development

<u>Staff:</u>
Complete Review of Personnel Policies:
(Hiring, Compensation, Benefits, Evaluation, Career Development)

<u>Students:</u>
Better Career Planning and Guidance
Better Program of Meaningful Cocurricular Activities:
(Social, Athletic, Professional)

<u>Employers & Business Community:</u>
Much Greater Two-Way Involvement
Positive Sense of Community
Open Communications
Subscribe to Spirit of Equal Opportunity and Affirmative Action

PHYSICAL FACILITIES
<u>Renovations:</u>
Quiet Study Places
New Terminals and Other Computer Resources
Better Lounge Facilities
Interactive Classrooms

<u>New Construction – College Resources:</u>
Learning Resources Center – <u>Top Priority</u>
Athletic and Recreational Facilities
Interactive Classrooms
Student Union and/or Other Community Facilities
Facility for Service Vehicles and Storage

New Construction – With Rental Income:
Additional Housing
Executive Education Center

DEVELOPMENT
Very Critical:
Stepped-Up Annual Giving
New Corporate Fellows Program
Major Capital Program

PLANNING
Institutionalize the Long-Range Planning Process to Provide Continuous
Review And Updating of Master Plan

Establish Planning Review Committee of Board of Trustees

Create Planning Office

Prepare Annual Review to Measure & Assess Progress Toward
Accomplishment of Specific Program & Financial Goals

Annual Roll-Out of Five-Year Strategic & Financial Goals Based on Progress
Made in the Previous Year & on New Consideration

APPENDIX D

THE ROLE AND THE JOB OF A COLLEGE PRESIDENT'S SPOUSE

(Remarks prepared for the Babson College Presidential Search Committee)

Charlotte Ripley Sorenson
Wife of President Ralph Z. Sorenson
(1974-1981)
Babson College
Wellesley, Massachusetts

To the members of the Babson College Presidential Search Committee:

Thank you for inviting me to your meeting. I am grateful for the opportunity to share with you my views on what is involved in being the wife of a college president.

I would like to begin by saying that the last seven years have been for me marvelous and happy ones.

We became involved with Babson College at a time when my first priority was our family of three children whose ages when we arrived at Babson were 11, 9, and 8. I considered our Babson activities to be a natural extension of our family activities, an enhancement, in fact, of our family activities. Fortunately, everyone entered into this spirit, and Babson College and the family seemed to mesh nicely.

My intention this morning is to describe to you both the ROLE that I have played and the JOB that I have done for Babson College.

I will also describe for you how other spouses are handling their positions at other academic institutions. (In these remarks, "spouse" means "wife," as college presidents have traditionally been men.)

And I will offer some suggestions to you as members of the search committee so that the spouse of the president whom you select will be aware of what is involved in this new position and will look upon it as an opportunity.

THE ROLE

The traditional college president's spouse has tended to adopt an attitude, assume a posture. You will recognize her.

- She is gracious, hospitable, tactful, discrete, and pleasant;
- She is quietly but totally supportive of her husband and of the institution that he has chosen to represent;
- She takes pains to learn about the college, keeps up on the day-to-day events, and tries to learn everyone's name and position. Somehow, however, she remains detached. She is well-informed, but diplomatically does not get involved in college matters. She does not embarrass the president.
- She accepts the responsibility of being a public person. She works hard at protecting her privacy and that of her family, if there are children involved.
- She makes herself available for college functions. She doesn't seem to mind that she does not have extended periods of time that she can call her own.
- She listens well, especially as her husband's confidant;
- She keeps her sense of humor and her perspective;
- She is aware.

These qualities comprise what I call the ROLE. This is the image that comes to the minds of most people when they think of a college president's wife. The ROLE is an attitude that the wife assumes. But it does not answer the question: "But what does she *do*?"

THE JOB

I would like to suggest today that, in addition to playing what sounds like a rather passive ROLE, the college president's wife is often expected to take on a substantial JOB.

It is job that requires physical energy and quantities of time. It requires organizational, administrative, and public relations skills—in abundance. It requires commitment.

As it is not understood, this JOB is seldom outlined by search committees or college trustees. It is probably seldom understood or discussed in advance by the presidential candidates and their wives.

Appendix D

The JOB that I am about to describe is unavoidable. Especially, if the president and his wife are encouraged to live on campus in a college-owned house, the expectations are there.

This JOB has to be done, whether by a bewildered wife who is overwhelmed, by an informed spouse who finds that this is just her thing, or by a professional housekeeper *cum* executive secretary *cum* hostess (to be supervised, of course, by the spouse,) if, of course, she is lucky enough to find such a package.

For me, for the past 7 years, this JOB has meant:

- Being willing to take on the responsibility of being the caretaker of college property, the president's house and grounds. This has meant dealing almost daily with the college's buildings and grounds staff and knowing what is necessary and how things should be done;
- Being willing to take on the responsibility of being the chief caterer. Not much cooking is involved, but there is much planning, preparation, and working with and supervising the kitchen staff sent from the college as well as the occasional outside caterer;
- Being willing to take on the responsibility of being chief housekeeper, supervising the help that comes to clean, making sure that house is always ready for guests, expected and unexpected;
- Planning, preparing for, and supervising over 20 scheduled events in the president's house during the school year;
- Preparing for quickly and supervising about 15 college-related but unscheduled events in the president's house during the school year.

During the past seven years, we have entertained over 14,000 guests in the president's house, the house that is also our home and the home of our three young children who, of course, have their own very definite demands and needs.

Students, parents of students, faculty members, members of the staff and the administration, trustees, alumni, members of the community and other neighboring academic institutions, and sometimes the spouses and families of these groups . . . all have been made welcome.

This JOB has also meant:

- Attending, as a representative of the college, about 25 scheduled events a year on the campus, including appearances at trustee meetings, dedications and such:
- Attending, as a representative of the college, about 30 unscheduled but college-related functions a year both on and off the campus, including

athletic events, dinners with students' parents, dinners with VIPs, visiting firemen, administrators from neighboring colleges, etc. (I have purposely separated the scheduled and unscheduled events to imply the state of readiness that has to exist.)

- Being available and active on behalf of the college almost every weekend from the beginning of September to mid-October, for several weekends during the holiday season and during the weekends in late April and May.

- Being on-call and active for entire weekends: Parents' Weekend, Winter Weekend, Homecoming Weekend and Commencement;

- Traveling to meet alumni. I haven't done as much of this as there was to be done, but it could have been a substantial part of the JOB;

- Attending seminars in which my husband was often a participant, partly out of interest, but often because I needed a chance to be with him, away from the college;

- Keeping careful records of the way that I spent college money;

- Making the extra phone call, writing thank-you notes, sending or arranging flowers, etc.

- Keeping not only the college house and grounds, but also myself and the children ready at all times, so that we would all reflect positively on the college.

This is the JOB that is there. This is the JOB that is unavoidable. Each individual who takes on this JOB may emphasize a different area, but each aspect of the JOB must get some attention.

This is the JOB for which I could not be hired, from which I could not be fired, but which I could not quit.

In addition, not because it was part of the JOB but because I got into the swing of things and because I enjoyed it:

- I spent nearly a thousand hours of my own time enhancing the gardens and the grounds of the president's house. I laid out the design for the property, so that it would accommodate both the formal and the informal entertaining that had to be done. I worked in the gardens myself, selected all of the plants and supervised the planting and maintenance of the grounds;

- I worked with the landscape architects hired by the College and was responsible for some improvements in the landscaping around the College, in particular around the new library;

- I developed and ran the Host Family Program for international students, a program that has involved 30 neighborhood families with Babson international students;

- I helped to organize and run (as chair of the advisory committee) the International Student Olympics that for two years brought 400 students from 13 Boston-area colleges and universities to the Babson College campus for one day of athletic and social events;

- I helped to design and run the orientation program for the wives of Babson international students;

- I helped to select works of art for the new library as a member of the Art Committee;

- I believe I made some contribution to developing a relationship between Babson College and Wellesley College, my alma mater, Class of '61.

Each college has its own setting. Each is in a different stage of growth. For each institution and for each time, the needs are different.

The needs of a small, suburban or rural, undergraduate college are different from those of a large, urban, established institution. Amherst, Swarthmore, and Babson Colleges have needs that are different from those of Harvard, Boston University or Northeastern.

I believe that the smaller, the more isolated a college is, the younger it is, or the harder that it is trying to grow, the more personal attention it needs. The more it needs people at the top who care about providing informal settings where faculty and students, alumni and trustees and community members can be brought together to get to know one another and to build friendships and trust . . . to build college spirit, loyalty and pride.

It doesn't matter, perhaps, that at Harvard the wife of the president is not deeply involved in the life of the College in the ways that I have outlined above or that, at the graduate level, at the Harvard Business School, the Dean's wife decided to have little involvement with the school, in fact declined to live in the house on the campus provided by the School.

These institutions are established. There are many built-in ways for their constituencies to communicate. The sense of pride is there and loyalty. The money is flowing in.

In your search for the new president of Babson College, you, as members of the search committee, will be assuming, whether you are aware of this or not, that the spouse will play a ROLE in representing the college.

You may not be aware, however, of the nature of the JOB that you unconsciously may be assuming that the president's spouse will undertake. The expectation is there, I can testify, even though it is not specifically outlined.

THREE RECOMMENDATIONS

My *first* recommendation to you as members of the search committee is to decide before you narrow your choice of candidates whether you think that the kinds of service to the college that I have outlined above will continue to be valuable to the college at this stage in its development.

My *second* recommendation is to be honest not only with your candidates but also with their spouses. Lay your cards on the table early in your discussions.

If you decide that the services outlined above are *not* essential to the College at this stage in its development, then don't have any expectations. Don't be disappointed if the spouse has a job of her own that demands her full attention. Above all, don't encourage the presidential couple to live in the president's house. The beautiful walls exude tradition—and expectations!

If you decide, on the other hand, that you would like to have a continuation of the kinds of services outlined above, then level with your candidates and their spouses. Respect their need to know and their right to know what you will expect of them—at least your minimum expectations. It will help your candidate and his spouse make an informed decision. It will allow them to consider options:

- If, for example, the spouse has a full-time profession and has no time for the kind of college-related job that she is being asked to do, offer a full staff (which, of course, you would do anyway if there was no spouse.)

  - The president of Wellesley College (a woman) has a permanent housekeeping staff of three.

  - The president of Bryn Mawr hired an executive assistant to supervise and manage her household staff.

- If the spouse is willing but lacks either the physical energy or the necessary administrative and organizational skills for the job that she is being asked to do, be prepared to back up her efforts with a supportive staff.

- If the spouse wants to become involved in some aspects of the job, but not in others, try to accommodate these preferences.

Once you have selected a president, my *third* recommendation to you as members of the search committee is to suggest that the trustees provide an advocate for the spouse. There should be someone on the board of trustees who is responsible for meeting with the spouse for an hour or so before each meeting of the board to answer questions and to offer support. This person would also be available between meetings and would be able to take information and recommendations from the spouse to the board. The president is not in a position to do this.

During these past seven years, I have been fortunate. I have been happy. I have loved the house, the grounds, all of the wonderful people at the College. I have learned a great deal. I have grown. Playing the ROLE and doing the JOB has been an opportunity, full of high points and rewards. It has been fun!

Tell that to your candidate and his spouse. But tell them, too, that for the spouse, there will be more than a ROLE to play. There will be JOB to do.

Acknowledge it. Give it dignity.

Chances are that the College will be rewarded by an appreciative presidential couple that will join Babson College with pride in the jobs that they both have been given to do.

Thank you.

APPENDIX E

REVIEW OF RALPH SORENSON'S PRESIDENCY OF BABSON COLLEGE

Babson Quarterly Bulletin
Fall 1980

"Barry Wright Picks Sorenson" declared the headline in the *Boston Globe* on the morning of August 26th.

Four days earlier, members of the Babson community had learned the news in a letter from Jarvis Farley, chairman of the Board of Trustees. Ralph Sorenson, Farley wrote, would resign as president at the end of the 1980-81 academic year to accept an appointment as president and chief executive officer of Barry Wright Corporation. The firm, with headquarters in Watertown, manufactures computer accessory equipment and other industrial equipment.

Babson has been strengthened both academically and financially since Ralph Sorenson came to the college in the fall of 1974. Outstanding teachers have joined the faculty, curricular innovations have been introduced, and the Center for Entrepreneurial Studies has been established. The college has received wide publicity for its annual Founder's Day programs at which internationally known entrepreneurs have been inducted into the newly formed Academy of Distinguished Entrepreneurs. In the graduate program, several internships have been introduced. And new programs are being offered by the School of Continuing Education.

This year the undergraduate program received additional professional accreditation by the American Assembly of Collegiate Schools of Business (AACSB). The graduate program is scheduled to receive similar accreditation at the end of the 1980-81 academic year.

Since 1974, ten major building or renovation projects have been completed. Last spring the new three-story Horn Library opened, replacing the Sir Isaac Newton Library built more than forty years ago. The Newton Library, after renovation, will become the Tomasso Hall teaching center.

At the end of next month, the college will conclude its $12 million capital campaign, the largest fund-raising campaign ever undertaken by the college. President Sorenson has assumed a leading role in this campaign, and it appears that the original goal will be surpassed.

During Sorenson's tenure as president, leading members of both the business and academic communities have joined Babson's governing board. Alumni, too, have become more influential in the governing of the college, and alumni committees now maintain closer communication with the college community.

Jarvis Farley described Sorenson as "the right person in the right place at the right time . . . Ralph's years of leadership have carried Babson College a long way on its road to preeminence in management education."

In his letter of resignation addressed to Farley, the president said in part, "When I first came to Babson in 1974, I indicated that I thought five to ten years was the ideal tenure for a college president at an institution such as Babson . . . I have now come to the conclusion that with the completion of the coming academic year, my seventh year as Babson's president, it would be a good time for me to relinquish my duties at Babson . . . "

The president said he believed the college was "in healthy condition and is well positioned to meet the challenges of the 1980's. Given this fact, I believe that next year would be an excellent time for me to step aside to make room for new leadership."

His years at Babson, Sorenson said, have been "the most satisfying of my professional career. Charlotte, the children, and I have all come to love the college and the people who make up the Babson community. We shall always think of our years here with special affection."

A LIFETIME OF LEARNING HOW TO MANAGE EFFECTIVELY

Ralph Z. Sorenson
The Wall Street Journal
February 28, 1983

Years ago, when I was a young assistant professor at the Harvard Business School, I thought that the key to developing managerial leadership lay in raw brain power. I thought the role of business schools was to develop future managers who knew all about the various functions of business—to teach them how to define problems succinctly, analyze these problems and identify alternatives in a clear, logical fashion, and, finally, to teach them to make an intelligent decision.

My thinking gradually became tempered by living and working outside the United States and by serving seven years as a college president. During my presidency of Babson College, I added several additional traits or skills that I felt a good manager must possess. The first is the ability to express oneself in a clear, articulate fashion. Good oral and written communication skills are absolutely essential if one is to be an effective manager.

Second, one must possess that intangible set of qualities called leadership skills. To be a good leader one must understand and be sensitive to people and be able to inspire them toward the achievement of common goals.

Next, I concluded that effective managers must be broad human beings who not only understand the world of business but also have a sense of the cultural, social, political, historical, and particularly today the international aspects of life and society. This suggests that exposure to the liberal arts and humanities should be part of every manager's education.

Finally, as I pondered the business and government-related scandals that have occupied the front pages of newspapers throughout the seventies and early eighties, it became clear that a good manager in today's world must have courage and a strong sense of integrity. He or she must know where to draw the line between right and wrong. That can be agonizingly difficult. Drawing a line in a corporate setting sometimes involves having to make a choice between what appears to be conflicting "rights." For example, if one is faced with a decision whether or not to close an ailing factory, whose interests should prevail? Those of stockholders? Of employees? Of customers? Or those of the community in which the factory is located? It's a tough choice. And the typical manager faces many others. Sometimes these choices involve simple questions of honesty or truthfulness. More often, they are more subtle and involve such issues as having to decide whether to "cut corners" and economize to meet profit objectives that may be beneficial in the short run but that are not in the best long-term interests of the various groups being served by one's company. Making the right choice in situations such as these clearly demands integrity and the courage to follow where one's integrity leads.

But now I have left behind the cap and gown of a college president and put on the hat of chief executive officer. As a result, my list has become still longer. It now seems to me that what matters most in the majority of organizations is to have reasonably intelligent, hard-working managers who have a sense of pride and loyalty toward their organization; who can get to the root of a problem and are inclined toward action; who are decent human beings with a natural empathy and concern for people; who possess humor, humility, and common sense; and who are able to couple drive with "stick-to-it-iveness" and patience in the accomplishment of a goal.

It is the ability to make positive things happen that most distinguishes the successful manager from the mediocre or unsuccessful one. It is far better to have dependable managers who can make the right things happen in a timely fashion than to have brilliant, sophisticated, highly educated executives who are excellent at planning and analyzing, but who are not so good at implementing. The most cherished manager is the one who says "I can do it," and then does.

Many business schools continue to focus almost exclusively on the development of analytical skills. As a result, these schools are continuing to graduate large numbers of MBAs and business majors who know a great deal about analyzing strategies, dissecting balance sheets, and using computers—but who still don't know how to manage!

As a practical matter, of course, schools can go only so far in teaching their students to manage. Only hard knocks and actual work experience will fully develop the kinds of managerial traits, skills, and virtues that I have discussed here. Put another way: The best way to learn to manage is to manage. Companies such as mine that hire aspiring young managers can help the process along by:

- providing good role models and mentors
- setting clear standards and high expectations that emphasize the kind of broad leadership traits that are important to the organization, and then rewarding young managers accordingly
- letting young managers actually manage

Having thereby encouraged those who are not only "the best and the brightest" but also broad, sensitive human beings possessing all of the other traits and virtues essential for their managerial leadership to rise to the top, we just might be able to breathe a bit more easily about the future health of industry and society.

APPENDIX G

COMPARING THE ROLES OF COLLEGE PRESIDENTS AND COMPANY CEOs

Tonight, I thought I might share some thoughts with you about what it's like to be a company CEO compared to being a college president. It is the question that I'm most frequently asked when I meet people, even though it has been almost five years since I left the academic world. They always ask: "What's it like out there in the real world?" So tonight, I thought I might try to answer the question.

Now, lest I incriminate myself in the process, let me begin with an important disclaimer. Namely, I want to make it clear from the outset, if it is not already obvious, that I loved being president of Babson—most of the time—and I love being CEO of Barry Wright—most of the time. Both are highly acceptable activities. Having made that clear, let me proceed.

My short answer to the comparison question is that the jobs of a company president and a college president are 90 percent different... but the same in all <u>essential</u> elements. Now that answer typically provokes some rather puzzled expressions on the faces of the questioners, just as I see some quizzical expressions out there right now. Let me in the next few minutes try to elaborate a bit on the 90 percent differences and wind up by telling you why, despite these differences, I have concluded that the two jobs are essentially the same in all important elements.

Let me begin where most good organizations begin: with the customers. One difference is that at Barry Wright we don't make our customers apply for admission. We may check their credit, but if that's good, we sure don't send them letters of rejection! Instead, we ship them the product. Of course, it could just be possible that from a marketing point of view, perhaps some colleges are way ahead of their corporate brethren. Having learned one of the oldest marketing lessons of all, namely if you make something scarce enough, everyone will want it.

Sticking for the moment with customers, let me point out that there is one big similarity between our Barry Wright customers and the students who are Babson's customers. Both demand excellence and good value for their money and are vociferous when they don't get it. But the big difference is that Barry Wright's customers are not all located on a campus and don't publish a student newspaper to air their complaints with free-swinging public opinions and feisty editorial comments about almost anything and everything connected with the running of the organization and their degree of satisfaction as customers. To student editors, nothing is sacred! And nothing is too trivial to be commented on. So in that respect, the company CEO's life is somewhat less onerous and less delicate than that of his college counterpart.

Score one for the company president in terms of relative ease of management.

But there is a flipside to that coin. For in terms of intrinsic satisfaction, from the president's point of view, having students as customers all located on one campus where one can have virtually daily contact, wins hands down over having one's customers scattered all over the world. For all their foibles and hijinks, students are great! And in my personal opinion, there is nothing more important or worthwhile than working with young people in their quest for a good education. Being around students keeps one young and flexible in both mind and spirit.

So chalk one up for the college president in terms of the fun and intrinsic satisfaction of working with one's customers and in terms of feeling good about one's basic mission. Although there are a number of things I miss about being a college president, it is probably the students I miss most.

Now let me turn from the subject of customers to the subject of finance. Here we encounter some intriguing paradoxes. As we compare colleges to companies, companies are said to be "bottom line" oriented, while colleges are commonly characterized as "not-for-profit" institutions. Well, I'm here to tell you that, in my case, the financial side of the organization took up just as much time and was just as important at Babson as it has been at Barry Wright. Now, colleges might not have a bottom line called "profit", but if you are familiar with funds accounting, you are aware that there is an item at the bottom of the income statement called "transfers". And there is a final item called "net increase or decrease in fund balance". That's the one to look at to see whether it is an increase or decrease . . . and by how much. At Babson, we made sure there was always a yearly increase.

Kidding aside, the financial pressures faced by colleges are just as acute and worrisome as in any company. And the situation on the academic campuses is, in my view, likely to get worse. One reason is because of the prospect for falling enrollments. One doesn't have to be a genius to know that, because of birthrate trends, the number of 18-year-olds with high school diplomas will continue to decline steadily . . . thus diminishing the size of the traditional undergraduate market. In Massachusetts, for example, this decline is projected to be 30% between 1985 and 1995. Nationally, the decline will be almost as great. And, while colleges have been valiant in their efforts to try to tap new markets . . . such as adult learners and foreign students . . . eventually the falling enrollments are going to make themselves felt on campuses.

Moreover, this drop will be occurring at a time when educational institutions are going to be able to count on less federal support and perhaps less public support. The budget submitted by President Reagan two weeks ago, for example, calls for cutting expenditures on higher education from $9 billion in fiscal 1986 to $5.8 billion in fiscal 1988. And, unfortunately, most colleges have not yet received the word on inflation. They believe they can continue to raise their prices (i.e. tuitions) at twice or three times the rate of inflation, while the rest of the world is going along with price increases in . . . if they are lucky . . . the 2, 3, or 4 percent range. I believe this is going to catch up with the academic world in the not too far distant future.

Unfortunately, it is harder for colleges to try to improve their productivity than it is for most manufacturing companies. That is because education is a very labor-intensive service industry. Because of its very nature, it is far more difficult in education than in manufacturing to substitute capital and automation for people. Teaching, in the end, is still an art that involves a teacher and some students and a classroom. And while the computer can perhaps assist learning to a certain extent, in the end it is that basic equation of the teacher and the students that counts. There is a risk of trying to increase class sizes in order to cut expenses, because in the process you may sacrifice the quality of the education.

Colleges haven't been very successful in terms of controlling expenses or cutting costs while . . . at the same time . . . producing an education of excellence. One thing I think, however, that is clear about both colleges and companies is that in the next ten years improving productivity without sacrificing quality is going to be the name of the game. It is clearly the name of the game in the world of manufacturing, or at least in the "real" world I now live in. In the face of increasing worldwide competition, we must, as a nation, find a way to do better, smarter or easier all the things we are now doing. We must reduce total costs and control expenses better than we have been doing in the past, not only in our factories, but also among our white-collar workers, our professionals . . . such as accountants, lawyers, and doctors . . . and on our college campuses.

In the case of college campuses, one thing that strikes me as being absolutely intriguing is that most academics, unlike company presidents, still tend to have a nine-month mentality . . . again Babson excepted. They probably make worse use of their physical facilities than almost any other form of organization on the face of the earth. Can you imagine factories that are only being used from 9:00 a.m. in the morning until perhaps 1:00 p.m. or 2:00 p.m. in the afternoon . . . and essentially for only nine months of the year? Yet this is what happens in the case of most classrooms on most college campuses. All too often the lights are out in these classrooms during the late afternoons and evenings and in the summertime. In this regard, Babson and a few other academic institutions have been exceptions. Babson has done an excellent job of operating around-the-clock and around the calendar. A lot of other colleges are going to have to do more of the same in the future. They are also going to have to do some of the other kinds of imaginative things that I think Babson has done and is about to do with respect to making use of their real estate and their various intrinsic resources.

In the case of Babson, I think the creation of the North Hill Retirement Community, the Babson Recreation Center and, in the future, the creation of the Executive Education Center are going to help mightily in terms of the college's future vitality and vigor.

Let me turn now to another difference between colleges and companies. Colleges, unlike companies, do not have available to them an equity market. They have to go to alumni and to foundations for their equity. What I have found as a company president is that sessions with financial analysts in Boston and on Wall Street with the New York Society of Financial Analysts are remarkably similar to alumni meetings. Basically, the mission is the same. It is to try to tell the story of one's organization in such a way that will generate interest and involvement and equity support from either the financial community, on the one hand, or from the alumni community on the other.

In the end, the kind of support involved is equally important to the respective institutions, be it an investment in the stock of the company or in the form of checks written to the annual alumni fund or to the capital campaign of the college. So that is a standoff, I would say, in terms of the role played by the company president versus the college president.

But there is one form of financial tyranny that company presidents have to face that college presidents don't have to face. That is the tyranny of the quarterly report and the quarterly financial results. It is very clear to me, after nearly five years as a company president, that the orientation of the financial community and of most shareholders is far too short term. We weigh the baby not only once a day, but often several times a day to see what kind of health it is in. In the process, we have succeeded in creating a whole nation of managers who are so concerned about making their quarterly financial results look good that they often lose sight of the longer term.

I think that private sector managers in this country have to resist mightily this temptation to be too short term in their orientation. They should strive harder for balance between the concern for today as opposed to the wise and intelligent planning and investment for the future. In my view, the Japanese have learned that lesson better than we have. Have you ever looked at how the profit statements of the 50 largest Japanese companies compare with the 50 largest American companies? The profits of the

Japanese firms as a percentage of sales and return on investment are typically miniscule compared to their American counterparts. Japanese managers and investors tend to be less concerned with short-term profits and more concerned with healthy longer-term growth. The reasons for this are many and complex. But the bottom line for America is that if we are able to maintain a strong manufacturing capability and continue to be viable competitively in the world of tomorrow, we are going to have to tilt the balance in this country away from short term profits and more toward long term investments designed to improve productivity. So in terms of not have to worry about the quarterly financial tyranny, score one for the college president.

Let me talk, now, for a moment about another tyranny of the corporate world. This one is more or less also linked to the financial side of the business. It has to do with the ultimate financial play. I refer, of course, to the rage and scourge of the 1980's in the corporate world . . . the great unfriendly takeover game . . . with all its perverse excitement and its positively medieval lexicon of plays and players involving white knights, black knights, poison pills, shark repellants, LBO's, staggered boards, and on and on. Then, depending on one's point of view, there are all of its swashbuckling heroes or villains . . . such as T. Boone Pickens (even the names are wonderful) Ted Turner, Carl Icahn, Ivan Boesky, Irvin Jacobs, William Agee, Mary Cunningham, Jimmy Goldsmith . . . whose greed and need to be macho all too often drive them to irresponsible acts of corporate rape and pillage.

In this unfriendly takeover game, the only short-term winners, in my view, are typically the raiding pirates' pocketbooks, the arbitragers, the investment bankers, and the selling shareholders, most of whom are not people but are institutions whose managers are under pressure, again, to produce short term results. The losers are nearly everyone else: the employees of the companies being taken over and their families and communities, the customers of the companies being taken over, and the industries of which the companies being taken over are a part. As you see, I am not a big fan of hostile takeovers.

Lest, however, I be accused of being totally one-sided in my views, let me hasten to add that mergers and acquisition can make sense and can work, but they must be friendly. They must have a raison d'etre. The chemistry has to be right. The cultures have to be compatible. There has to be enthusiasm on the part of both partners. We all know in our personal lives that it is tough to make a marriage work without a willingness to give of oneself to the other partner and a willingness to stick it out through thick and thin. Shotgun weddings seldom work.

What goes on in the process of consummating an unfriendly takeover is not a healthy atmosphere in which to start off the marriage of two partners. The courting process is absolutely essential and has to be friendly. Much time needs to be spent talking about whether the cultures are compatible with one another, whether the managers are going to be compatible with one another, whether the people are going to have fun working together, and whether both sides can be winners in the game. Only after satisfying ourselves on these points do we talk about the dowry or actually walk down the aisle to say, "We Do".

Interestingly, the question of mergers also has relevance to the academic world. In my view, there are many colleges now in existence that should consider the possibility of attempting to consummate friendly mergers with other academic institutions. In light of all the pressures I was talking about earlier, it probably would make sense for a number of academic institutions to join forces and combine resources so as to be able to make better use of their campuses and their faculties. Unfortunately, colleges talking about mergers are like porcupines sniffing each other. So I wouldn't hold my breath too long waiting for the next merger around the Boston area. The last successful one was probably Newton College of the Sacred Heart that was absorbed by Boston College. That merger made great sense for all concerned.

Let me turn away from such subjects as customers and finances and mergers to the basic management process, as I see it, in companies compared to colleges. In this regard, it is my view that the corporate presidency is intrinsically a more powerful position than the college presidency. The buttons are typically a bit more responsive. Why is this?

First of all, for better or worse, companies are typically more hierarchical. Company CEO's tend to have a few more prerogatives, many of them related to having more latitude when it comes to hiring and firing and compensating managers, professionals, and employees. Colleges, on the other hand, tend to have flatter organizational structures and, as a result, college presidents often end up dealing personally with more constituencies than their corporate counterparts. They have to deal with students, faculty, administration, coaches, hourly employees, alumni, the corporate community, the parents of students, the government, foundations, local communities, trustees, corporation members, other colleges, academic associations, and so forth. Members of each of these constituencies are absolutely certain they know how best to run the college, and none of whom has the slightest hesitancy about telling the president personally just how it should be done.

Among these constituencies, it seems to me the faculty deserves special mention. In my view, more college and university presidencies have foundered on the shoals of the faculty than on any other single factor. In a sense, a college is organized more like a government than like a company. Operationally, the college president is analogous to the executive branch and the faculty is analogous to the legislature. One acts as a check and a balance on the other. For an academic institution to be successful, there has to be substantial agreement between the faculty and the president with respect to ends and means. Without such agreement, what occurs is at best stalemate and at worst, chaos. In practice, all too often presidents and faculties never get on the same wavelength. The nature of the beast is that the individual faculty member seldom agrees with other faculty members and almost never agrees with the president.

Overhanging the whole equation is the wonderfully mischievous and anachronistic institution of tenure. For, unlike senators and congressmen who can be voted out of office, most faculties today are heavily tenured and cannot be removed from their jobs no matter how much they suffer from a prima donna complex, and no matter how unsuccessful, illogical, incompetent, or unsupportive their behavior might be. Consequently, when push comes to shove over a major disagreement, on most college campuses it has been the president who has left . . . either as a result of being forced out or because of sheer exhaustion! Babson, of course, was a magnificent exception to the rule. All Babson faculty members were invariably paragons of logic and constructiveness. They were solid in their support of each other and of the college's goals and of the president. And if you believe that, wait until you hear about the beautiful bridge I am prepared to sell you. Kidding aside, Babson was a presidential paradise compared to most other educational institutions.

However, the generalized moral of the story is that even more than company presidents, and almost as much as U.S. presidents and governors, college presidents must learn to lead through logic, persuasion, great patience and interminable committees and faculty meetings. To survive, one must have the patience of Job.

By the way, if you have never sat through a faculty meeting, you have clearly missed one of the more zany experiences in life. Alice, as she walked through the looking glass into her topsy-turvy wonderland, never beheld any more delightfully offbeat or unusual forms of behavior than those that can be witnessed at any old run-of-the-mill faculty meeting or academic committee meeting. Of course, you all know what committees are. They are groups that keep minutes and lose hours!

Lest I sin by overdrawing the case, let me emphasize that I have discovered that logic and persuasion and patience and persistence are also absolutely essential in order to be a successful company president. A sense of humor doesn't hurt either. It is just that company presidents can, on rare occasions, when they are sure they have logic and the Almighty firmly on their side, indulge in the thoroughly satisfying and heady luxury of management by fiat. And what is more, management by fiat sometimes even works . . . at least in a corporate setting.

In spite of all the differences I have been reciting, let me end by saying that, deep down, I believe that the role of the college president and the company CEO are fundamentally very, very similar. Both must have a vision. Both must ensure there is a mechanism in place for developing strategic objectives and common-sense plans for achieving these objectives. Both must ensure that effective control systems are in place. Both must set values and establish the tone. Both must be exemplars and keepers of the culture. Both must be pickers and developers of good people. Both must be good coaches, good team builders, and good role models. They have to be the head cheerleaders, the chief encouragers, and the keepers of faith and courage in dark days. In short, both must be true leaders.

Being all these things, the wise leader, whether in a college or in a company, will then get out of the way and let others in the organization have the fun of actually managing the place!

APPENDIX H

25TH HBS REUNION REFLECTIONS

Ralph Sorenson, MBA Class of 1959
Harvard Business School Bulletin
October 1984: Pages 76 & 77

What I've learned from my work:

A sampling might include:

- Satisfaction comes from feeling that you've done a good job, that you have addressed an assignment with the utmost of your ability, that you've done the job better than it has ever been done before—and, in the process, made something beautiful out of the experience.

- If there isn't a substantial element of fun in what you are doing, you should stop doing it and find work that you do enjoy.

- There really is such a thing as synergy that comes from working together as a team. "One-person-shows" usually aren't successful and usually don't endure—unless one is an artist or a poet or a writer.

I still hope to achieve the following:

From a career point of view, my first priority is to do the best job I can in providing continuing leadership for the company I now head.

My long-term priorities include at least one more career change. The possibilities are still fairly broad, but they might encompass a return to teaching, public service, writing, or perhaps an entrepreneurial venture. Whatever the outcome, family considerations will figure heavily in any future career moves.

On a more personal basis, before I pass from the scene, I want to read more of the world's good literature, listen to more music, learn at least one more language, design and personally build at least one dwelling, explore some parts of the globe not already explored, and master the art of serenity to test whether it is really possible to shed a "Type A" approach to life. At the same time, I want to achieve more of the satisfaction that comes from nurturing friendships and contributing to the wellbeing of others.

If I had it to do all over again, I would . . .

Having serial careers as teacher, college president, and chief executive officer of a manufacturing company has given me more than my fair share of challenge, fulfillment, satisfaction, and enjoyment from the "work" part of my life. Having warm family relationships and a variety of outside interests, coupled with living for seven years outside the United States, have added both spice and deeper meaning to my life. For the moment, then, I have no retrospective revision to the script to suggest. I'd rather count my blessings than worry about what might have been.

I have changed in the following ways since 1959:

Over the last 25 years, I've gained a greater appreciation of how important family and friendships are in one's life. Also, I now have a better understanding of how little I know—and how much there is to learn—than I did when I was a freshly minted MBA graduate. And I like to think that I take myself a bit less seriously, have fewer anxieties, and am more accepting of life's absurdities.

However, one absurdity of which I find myself less accepting is the nuclear arms race. Devising a means for nations to remain strong, while simultaneously finding a workable way to reverse the arms race and insure that nuclear weapons are never used, will be the ultimate test of human ingenuity and common sense. Historical precedent notwithstanding, I remain optimistic that we humans will pass the test.

Turning from the absurd to the physical, the lines on the face are more deeply etched now and the grey is beginning to show . . . but I still weigh about the same amount and probably have a healthier cardiovascular system than I did in 1959, thanks to running four or five times a week for the past ten years.

Advice to the Class of 1984:

Realize that:

- What matters most in the majority of organizations is to have reasonably intelligent, hard-working managers who have a sense of pride and loyalty; who can get to the root of a problem and are inclined toward action; who are decent human beings with a natural sense of empathy and a concern for other people; who can deal effectively with change; and who are able to couple drive with stick-to-it-iveness and patience in the accomplishment of a goal.

- For career success, old-fashioned virtues such as those just described are at least as important as the functional knowledge, analytical skills, and decision-making abilities you have learned during your two years at the Harvard Business School.

AIN'T NO MOUNTAIN TOO HIGH: SUMMITING MOUNT KILIMANJARO

Excerpts From My African Journal
Ralph Sorenson

It is midnight, Friday, July 5, 1991 . . . but still July 4th in the United States. We are in the Kibo Hut at 15,000 feet on the slope of Mount Kilimanjaro in Tanzania, Africa.

I am already awake when the knock comes on our door to arise at midnight. It is cold and we shiver as we layer up our clothing for the summit ascent. I dress with two pairs of socks inside my boots and have polypropylene long underwear, a pair of pants and an outer pair of ski pants on my legs and about six different layers on the upper part of my body. I also have a woolen ski cap and a wind parka that covers my head. I have decided to put my down-filled ski parka in my pack and use it only once we get to the summit—if we get to the summit! I've also decided to start out with a pair of polypro gloves on my hands covered with a pair of leather gloves. I stick my heavy mittens in the pack. In the pouch of my wind jacket I put my camcorder to see if it will function if we make it to the top. I also take along two 1-liter containers of water, some trail food, and a chocolate bar. Finally, I take along my monopod for the camcorder that I hope can double as a walking stick should I need it.

There are five of us in our immediate climbing group: my daughter, Trina, my son, Eric, and two of Trina's friends, Nate and Susan, classmates of hers from Dartmouth's Tuck School. In addition, there are our local guides: Tomas, our head guide, and his two brothers, Tony and Moses. Nate has not slept well at all and has become violently ill from the altitude in the course of the evening.

He bounds out of the hut and barely makes it outside before he vomits. He feels awful. So does Susan. But they didn't come all this way to give up without even trying the final ascent. Trina, Eric, and I all feel okay.

We all start out together at about 1:15 am. After about half-an-hour, Nate is feeling sufficiently weak that he drops behind the main pack with Moses staying with him to guide him. Soon he has dropped far enough behind that we lose sight of him.

Although several of us have headlamps, we don't need them since the moon is out and is about half full. It illuminates our way sufficiently that we can see to climb. And climb we do . . . one step at a time . . . the ascent is much, much steeper than anything we have encountered so far. After about an hour we reach a scree field that is even steeper. We then begin a series of doglegs up the mountain. It is extraordinarily exhausting work. There is no way I could have imagined in advance how difficult it would be. Tomas, our guide, sets a slow, but steady pace. The watchword on this portion of the ascent is polé, polé, which means slowly, slowly. By this time, the air is so thin that, despite taking mighty deep breaths, my body is very conscious of oxygen deprivation and I feel myself beginning to tire.

We continue to proceed step-by-step upward in stretches of 30 to 45 minutes. At the end of each stretch, when I feel almost at the breaking point, we stop for an absolutely necessary rest. I take in huge gulps of air to revive my tired body. Susan, who has continued to have bouts of diarrhea and nausea, is a real trooper and just keeps on climbing right along with the rest of us. After about 2½ hours we reach the halfway mark to Gilman's Point, the mountain's false summit, which is our first goal. By this time, I am so tired I can barely speak. Remarkably, Trina and Eric seem to be in high spirits and even sing as they make their way step-by-step upward. They are great at buoying everybody else's spirits. There is a kind of gallows humor quality about the comments they make. At the same time there is a great deal of encouragement and mutual support given to all members of the group. "Come on, we can all make it—I know we can." We all feel that the real accomplishment will be if all of us can make it to the top. We are concerned about Nate, but we know how stubborn he is, and we know he will continue to try as long as he has an ounce of strength in his body.

By this time, it has become considerably colder and the wind has begun to blow. The wind-chill factor as we approach Gilman's Point is probably about zero degrees Fahrenheit. Nevertheless, because of my level of exertion, I don't feel very cold. Every time we stop to rest, though, I begin to shiver uncontrollably and my body tells me it's time to start climbing again.

Appendix I

At about 18,000 feet, we end our zigzag trail up the scree field and enter into the final leg of our climb to the false summit. This leg takes us up a rock field that is heavily covered by snow and crystalline ice. We pick our way very carefully, each step an agony. My spirits begin to lighten, however, because with each step I become more and more certain that we can make it—at least to Gilman's Point. My feeling is one of lightheadedness. I still have no headaches or nausea, but my vision does seem to have a psychedelic quality to it. The snow and ice seem to glow and when I look at various objects, some seem to have a kind of aura. It's hard to explain the exact feeling that I was experiencing. I look at my watch and see that it is 6:25 a.m. and that the sky is lightening in the east. Five minutes later at 6:30—Voila ! we have reached Gilman's Point. We congratulate ourselves all around and take shelter in the rocks surrounding the cairn marking the top of the false summit.

The moment we hit Gilman's we are blasted by an icy wind that is blowing at a tremendous rate of speed. Various members of the party estimate its force to be anywhere from 50 to 100 mph! It cuts right through all the layers of our clothing. My first thought is to take a couple of gulps of water and to take off my outer wind shell and put on my warm parka that has been in my pack. This I do with considerable difficulty. But once my parka is on, I feel fairly comfortable. Oddly, my hands with only a thin pair of inner gloves and thin leather outer gloves feel fine. So do my feet.

After a few minutes we are treated to one of the most spectacular sights I have ever seen. The rising sun makes its way above the horizon and is sandwiched under an overlaying layer of clouds. It is breathtaking in its beauty. At Gilman's Point, we can look over the backside of the mountain into the volcanic crater that is a hallmark characteristic of Mount Kilimanjaro. There are spectacular ice cliffs in the distance on the other side of the crater.

Meanwhile, we are all concerned about Nate. But after about 20 minutes of waiting, someone gives a shout and says, "I think I see him. He's still climbing." Sure enough, there's Nate. A few minutes later, he joins us. He looks awful and feels incredibly weak, but he also has a look of total determination on his face.

After giving Nate some time to rest, we start climbing onward toward Uhuru Point, the real summit of the mountain. It is about 500 feet of additional altitude and a kilometer of extra distance. While the trail is not so steep, I find this part of the climb to be, if anything, even more tiring than what we have done so far. This is largely because of the howling gale and wind-chill factor that we now estimate at minus 20 degrees Fahrenheit. It is grueling, exhausting work for me. First Trina and then Eric stay with me to give me encouragement. I am greatly touched by their thoughtfulness and moral support. It means a lot.

Never once, in my mind, does the thought occur to me that I won't make it. No matter what happens, I am absolutely determined to reach the true summit. Having left Gilman's Point at 7:15 a.m., we continue our slow pace for about an hour and a half.

And then, suddenly—almost miraculously—we are there. Uhuru Point! 19,340 feet!

VICTORY!

In Swahili, Uhuru means freedom and independence. With a little mental arithmetic, I calculate that with the time differential, it is still the Fourth of July in the western part of the United States. This somehow gives the climb a symbolic meaning. We have reached Independence Point on Independence Day in the United States, a universal symbol of freedom. Our feeling is one of total exhilaration. We congratulate ourselves. We break out our cameras and raise imaginary glasses to toast Charlotte and Kristin and tell them how much we miss them. We also tell them we suspect they are probably happy not to be with us at this moment, given the ordeal involved in getting here.

I have brought along a Harvard pennant along with an Overseas Adventure Travel flag and, given the fact that I had written an OAT case study for Harvard, I get one of the other members of our party to record on the camcorder and also on camera the fact that the Harvard pennant and the OAT flag made it to the top! A bit corny, but nevertheless, a touch of whimsy.

It is COLD on top! So we are not tempted to linger too long. Though there are clouds swirling around us, we can see far enough to sense the wonder of this spot—19,340 feet above sea level. It is certainly by far the highest I have ever been and perhaps the highest I will ever go using my own two legs for propulsion. I, along with all the others, feel an extraordinary sense of accomplishment. The greatest feeling of accomplishment is the fact that all of us have made it together. It is an incredibly bonding experience. Without the mutual support and encouragement and humor that characterized the entire adventure, I doubt that all of us would have made it to the summit. But that support and encouragement and humor was there in abundance and we *did* make it.

At this point, we all realize that while we had attained our goal, we still had to make our way safely down from the top. So we turned our backs on the summit and started retracing our steps. To say going down was a lot easier than going up would be an understatement. It is incredible how much gravity helps one's energy level. We got back to Gilman's Point in about half an hour and then made our way downward through the rock field in about 15 minutes. Then the fun began! We reach the scree field that we had so painstakingly crisscrossed on our way up. It was all loose granular rock and scree down to a depth of nine inches to a foot. It was also very steep. Each step we took we could slide double the distance in the scree. So we almost literally bounded down the scree field. We felt like Gulliver in his seven-league boots!

Eric and Trina were far in the lead. They got far enough ahead of us to be able to record each of our styles as we bounded downward. First Eric recorded Trina in her polished Telemark ski style. Then Trina, in turn, videoed Eric who looked like a real "hot dog" skier with incredibly graceful form. Then came Pop showing more élan than good form. As I approached Trina I realized I was rapidly running out of energy and started yelling, "Cut! Cut! Stop recording!" But Trina ignored me and recorded the whole inglorious caper with me passing her and finally just flopping down totally exhausted and feeling as though my heart was pumping 300 beats a minute. I had clearly exceeded the aerobic limits of my cardiovascular system. But it sure was fun.

Susan and Nate were also videoed as they made their way down.

We arrived back at the Kibo Hut at about 11:30 a.m. After a brief rest and a bit of sweet tea and biscuits there, we descended another 8 to 10 miles and 3,000 feet to the Harumbo Hut. Though we were all tired and aching, the trek down went fairly quickly and we made it to the hut in about 2½ hours. All of us were absolutely exhausted but in good spirits. After dinner at 5:30 p.m., I fell asleep in the hut at seven o'clock and slept straight through until 6:30 a.m. the following morning. It was the end of a day never to be forgotten.

CPSIA information can be obtained
at www.ICGtesting.com
Printed in the USA
BVHW052151120622
639526BV00002B/3/J